BEYOND THE GREAT STORY

BEYOND
— THE —
GREAT
STORY

*History as Text
and Discourse*

ROBERT F.

BERKHOFER, JR.

— THE BELKNAP PRESS OF —
HARVARD UNIVERSITY PRESS
Cambridge, Massachusetts
London, England
1995

Library of Congress Cataloging-in-Publication Data

Berkhofer, Robert F.
Beyond the great story : history as text and discourse /
Robert F. Berkhofer
p. cm.
Includes index.
ISBN 0-674-06907-2
1. History—Methodology. 2. History—Philosophy.
I. Title.
D16.B464 1995
901—dc20   95-2005
CIP

Designed by
Gwen Frankfeldt

For Robert F. Berkhofer III
and the next generation
of historians

Contents

Preface

THIS BOOK begins in the midst of scholarly conversations and disciplinary dialogues. In this sense at least, it is a product of its times, to use a favorite phrase of historians. First, as some scholars hail the end of theory or even of postmodernism itself, the time seems right for an assessment of the implications of postmodernism and poststructuralism for the practice of history. Second, because multiculturalism and feminist theory impugn the overall viewpoint traditionally used in synthesizing history, it is necessary to reconsider what constitutes an appropriate perspective from which to view and compose a history. Third, it seems important to explore the significant role claimed for historicization in both literary studies and the social sciences today. Poststructuralist and postmodernist theories question the possibility of writing history at the very time that such historicization has become a way of grounding literary studies and the social sciences. That historicization is considered so vital by some scholars just when its whole approach to representing the past is being challenged by others poses the paradox that inspires this book.

This paradox suggests that in view of the postmodernist and multiculturalist challenges both historians and scholars in other disciplines underestimate the difficulties of representing the past as history. Throughout these various disciplinary debates literary scholars and social scientists alike have too unproblematic a view of the nature of history when they theorize about historicization in their fields. Historians, on other hand, have too unproblematic a view of history as discourse and methodology when they defend their discipline against literary and rhetorical theorists.

To address these various concerns this book combines in its arguments insights and interests from several disciplines. It discusses history but is not the kind of work customarily called a history in the discipline, because it combines intellectual history, philosophy of history, literary and rhetorical theory, historiography and methodology, and metahistory, without claiming to be any one of these. Nothing less than a combination of all these genres is needed to explore the many facets of what a new historicization involves, and why. This book, then, aims to introduce the possibilities of new forms of historical representation rather than serve as a comprehensive guidebook on how to achieve them. The fulfillment of these possibilities lies in the hands of those who would historicize in new ways regardless of discipline. Although I may argue too much about what the implications are in theory and too little about what they are in practice, my book is nevertheless directed to those who would historicize today.

Because the arguments offered in the following chapters select from among contending ways of looking at matters, the proponents and opponents of those competing ways will classify this book variously as structuralist and poststructuralist, late modernist and postmodernist, deconstructionist and formalist, depending upon how they define or feel about these intellectual methodologies. To explicate these contending positions and their corresponding dilemmas, I have employed a kind of dialogic presentation of the tensions between modernist and postmodernist orientations and between textualist and contextualist methods. Such a dialogue attempts to translate across interpretive and discursive communities even if it cannot reconcile them. Because any such dialogue is itself contestable, I often phrase problems as questions. As part of that dialogue I frequently provide quotations to exemplify positions. Perhaps my most obvious rhetorical strategy is to discuss what I call normal history as a more unified practice than its textual exemplars might warrant. This simplification proceeds from my desire to present a vision of what new forms historical discourse might take. When pursuing such a goal, one falls all too easily into positing a dualism between what one warns against and what one suggests as desirable. In the end, my text frequently resembles a collage or pastiche as much as a dialogue, because I build my arguments from the conceptual bricks most readily at hand, often extricating them from their customary intellectual context for my purposes.

This volume exemplifies, like so many books that talk about theory today, the problems of language talking about language. The difficulty in using words stems from the assumption of universal linguistic categories in discourse but the practice of local language customs, especially academic ones. Although this book is addressed to all time rhetorically, it is of course addressed to fellow scholars mainly in the United States at this moment. As a result the terms "history," "historical practice," and "historical discourse" seem to refer to the doing of history everywhere but in context refer to the practices of various historians arranged according to an imaginary set of concentric circles. At the center is American history done in the United States. The next circle applies mainly to other national histories done in the United

States. Outside this circle is another one of English-speaking historians else-where and their practices. Larger but less clearly defined circles include historians in other nations and scholars in other fields, all of whom must decide how applicable the book is to their own disciplinary concerns. This volume also distinguishes between formal or professional history and what we might call lay or folk history. This avowal of my own parochial viewpoint parallels the essentially provincial context of every history and highlights the predicaments facing professional historians as they try to make their publications and teaching multicultural, self-reflective, and self-critical.

The subject matter of this book and its organization follow from my perception of the problems facing any historicization today, whether done by historians or by other scholars in the social sciences or the humanities. In the end, I believe that modernist and postmodernist outlooks ought to be in creative tension in historical practice and discourse today. Structuralist and formalist ways still have much to teach historians, as do poststructuralism and postmodernism at this conjunction of scholarly trends. Late modernism and postmodernism hold equally important consequences for changed ways of representation in historical discourse. That is why I have tried to construct a dialogue among changing intellectual influences.

What anglophone historical practice needs at this juncture is the opposite of literary studies. As literary theorists turn to historicization, historians should explore textualism to see what remains useful for historical practice. Given normal professional methodological concerns for deriving facts from evidence, I have stressed the problems and methodology of synthesis. Hence my use of the word "text" to designate usually what historians produce rather than what they use as sources—although the two are never unconnected in practice. "Textualization" and "historicization" refer to the processes of constructing a text or history. Both processes result in publications, films, classroom lessons, lectures, and museum exhibitions, among other forms.

In line with my impression of the challenges facing historians, the first half of the book (Chapters 1 through 5) treats some of the implications of the linguistic and rhetorical turns as incorporated in modern literary and rhetorical theory for the writing, reading, teaching, and reviewing of history—in short, it examines history and histories as forms of representation. My special concern in these chapters is that, in repudiating some of the implications of textualism, historians not deny those understandings pertinent and useful to their practice. Thus Chapter 1 surveys the challenges now gathered under the rubric of postmodernism and how historians have responded. Chapter 2 covers the diverse roles of narrative in the creation of historical facts and their synthesis into what is termed (a) history and the possibility of multiple stories. Chapter 3 examines the relationships among factual reference, the structure of interpretation, metahistory, and truth in historical texts and in history itself. Chapter 4 explores the distinctions offered by a new rhetoric and poetics of history for reading historical texts and history as a text, while Chapter 5 focuses on how time is historicized by patterning through emplotment.

The second half of the book examines contextualization of history in general—in histories as texts and of historians as a professional community—in light of a textualist approach. Chapter 6 makes the transition from rhetoric to politics through the roles of voice and viewpoint in history. Chapter 7 tackles the implications of multiculturalism for the selection of viewpoint as well as voices in a historical text by focusing on the problems involved in representing otherness. Chapter 8 moves from the politics of viewpoint, to the politics of historical practice and professional authority, to the self-reflective problems of the sociology and politics of historical knowledge, and ends with the relation between power and knowledge and the politics of competing disciplinary frameworks. In the concluding chapter I discuss some of the implications of the book for writing and teaching, reading and reviewing history today. I explore briefly what I term reflexive (con)textualization as an option open to historians for creating new histories in light of the challenges confronting them.

BEYOND THE GREAT STORY

CHAPTER ONE

The Postmodernist Challenge

As ANOTHER millennium approaches, even scholarly discourse seems to echo the apocalypticism expressed in popular culture. Certainly, the proliferation of "posts"—industrialism, colonialism, modernism, feminism, Marxism, and even history, theory, and postmodernism itself—betokens a sense of change with regard to the once secure intellectual foundations of modernist scholarship. Among professional historians these fears have focused upon the implications of postmodernism for the discipline. Both those who oppose and those who favor the implications of postmodernism for the writing of history agree upon its chief consequence. Postmodernist theory questions what history can be, both as a real past and as a discourse about it. Historians disagree about how best to meet the challenge.

Interdisciplinary Challenges

If Clio, the muse of history, had followed the intellectual trends of recent decades in the English-speaking world, she might have become quite dizzy as that amalgam of social, moral, and literary studies the French call the "human sciences" took first a "linguistic turn," then "interpretive" and "rhetorical" turns. Although the linguistic, interpretive, and rhetorical turns differed from one another, all questioned the received viewpoint grounding the social sciences: an ideal of scientific positivism and its corollary, the strict separation of objectivity and subjectivity, whether as fact versus value or as empiricism versus political and moral advocacy. Each of the three turns stressed language, meaning, and interpretation as central to human understanding and therefore to understanding humans. All asserted that the methodologies and knowledge embodied in scholarly disciplines were not universal and timeless but socially and culturally constituted and therefore historically specific like other realms in human affairs.[1] The stimuli for all these turns were the structuralist and poststructuralist movements on the European continent. Their perspectives and premises provided strong new foundations for understanding literature broadly conceived according to general theory and, in the process, impugned the very basis of traditional historical practice. Whether the theorizing emanated from the positivist search for formal systems of the structuralists or from the antipositivist antiformalism of the poststructuralists, it challenged history as traditionally conceived and practiced by raising doubts about the discovery of truth and the foundations of knowledge, the autonomy and unity of the "individual" as agent and subject, the basis of disciplinary boundaries and practices, and the stability of meaning in language.[2]

When French pundits announced the "death of the author" as they dissolved authorship into socially based discursive practices, the "end of man" as they reduced the ego-based autonomous subject to cultural codes, and the death of metaphysics as they deconstructed the "logocentrism" of Western thought, they also proclaimed the "death of history" as a teleological enterprise.[3] Although this dramatic declaration was directed at the grand narratives of progress and emancipation that sustained liberal and Marxist history alike, the implications for traditional historical practice of the collective postmodernist challenges went beyond teleology. In the end, postmodernist theorists questioned the very dichotomies that grounded the paradigm of traditional history: the supposedly inherent differences between literature and science, reality and its representation.

With the recent announcement of a "historic turn," have the human sciences come full circle to the traditional starting point of historians?[4] After their dizzying dance with the all-encompassing and universal theories of Talcott Parsons and others (now labeled the Structural-Functional school), sociologists and other social scientists repudiated such grand theorization in favor of the historicization of their subject matter.[5] Historical sociology now dominates its discipline, and a historical approach is now also considered fundamental to anthropology and political science.[6] Similarly, as continental grand theory has receded in the literary fields, scholars there too have sought a revival of historicization in their studies, with the "New Historicism" being the most obvious instance.[7]

To many anglophone historians the return of history in the other human science disciplines appears to authorize their traditional practices and focus of study. From their perspective, anglophone empiricism has survived a period of attack and vanquished francophone theorizing; the postmodernist challenge to traditional history has at least retreated from its own excesses. But this self-congratulatory verdict seems not only premature but also unfounded, for it fails to consider how the linguistic and other turns have reinterpreted what any historic (re)turn could mean as methodology or practice. If nothing else, late modernist and postmodernist challenges altered the terms and the grounds of the debate and created a new urgency and a more comprehensive challenge.[8]

What is now called the postmodernist challenge to traditional history began as the crisis of representation raised by late modernist and structuralist theorists. To what extent can historians combine the two meanings of history as actual past and modern representation when all we know of language seemingly subverts that very goal? What if a realist theory of the correspondence between history as written and the actual past is abandoned for a constructionist view of history as a form of representation? How can we judge the accuracy of the modern representation of the past against a postulated original when it is, by definition, past? How can we hope to re-present the past as it was when we must do so through present-day (re)creations? Ultimately, since both late modernism and postmodernism question how history is traditionally written, should this last question be answered by new kinds of histories more in keeping with late twentieth-century intellectual fashions, be they modeled after postmodernist novels or recent reflexive social scientific monographs?[9]

Poststructuralist and multiculturalist theorizing produced the second crisis of representation: Who can speak for whom in histories and history? By denying the universality of viewpoints and knowledge, multiculturalism and poststructuralism repudiated the unified and usually omniscient viewpoint of traditional history-telling in favor of diversity of gender, race, ethnicity, and other social distinctions. The representation of the "Other" through voice and viewpoint also posed problems for the representation of history as textual construction. Were new forms of history-telling needed to incorporate more representative views and voices from the past as they were constructed as a representation of that past? The more diverse the representation of voices and viewpoints, the more fragmented traditional historical representation as discursive construction became.

If the first crisis of representation questioned whether and how historical actuality could ever be re-presented, the second crisis of representation undermined both the authority and the objectivity of traditional history. The first crisis of representation is encapsulated in the slogan "Question Reality," the second in another, "Resist Authority." Thus the explicit general goals of the historical turn become both paradoxical and problematical as a result of the two crises of representation. The advice always to historicize—whether texts, persons, events, or even disciplines—subverts the former in achieving the latter, or vice versa. If texts, subjects, and events can be represented, then the disciplinary practices and written histories are not rendered problematic by and through their representation. If disciplines and written histories are socially and temporally located, then their ability to persuade others of their representations of texts, events, or subjects is severely constrained or eliminated.

Without tracing—some would say creating—the (a?) history of recent scholarship or disciplinary politics in the human sciences, I would argue that some of the major implications—others might argue achievements—of this scholarship not only undermine older ways of practicing history but also challenge much of the new cultural history said to embody the new theories of representation and social production they supposedly engendered. Likewise, the implications of so much of this once new and grand theory in literature and the human sciences subvert their own perspectives as modes of understanding just as they challenge history as a way of understanding, for the theorizing in the human sciences resulted in no consistent set of intellectual premises, no single paradigm or problematic.[10]

The implications of so-called grand theory in the human sciences centered on and culminated in recent tendencies to denaturalize, demystify, deconstruct, and, one might continue, dehierarchize and dereferentialize. While some of these trends focused on, and resulted from, contemporary concerns with race, ethnicity, class, and gender, the implications spread far beyond these categories to the foundations assumed to be fundamental to all fields of human study, including historical studies. Since these implications challenge our very ways of understanding, they question what we are about as scholars and persons and how we represent our understandings to ourselves and others. In the end, these trends deny any easy separation of texts from contexts and vice versa, any easy division of politics from methodology or vice versa.[11]

Denaturalization and Demystification

The clearest, and perhaps most widely accepted, trend is the denaturalizing of race, ethnicity, and sex. Much of what previous generations of scholars ascribed to the effects of biology in the understanding of racial and ethnic differences among peoples and the sexual differences between men and women, recent scholars attribute to social arrangements and cultural constructions. Thus so much of what was once explained by inevitable natural distinctions has come to be seen as socially constructed, hence as culturally persistent and therefore politically arbitrary. In this view, the biology of race, ethnicity, and sex becomes the culture or ideology of racism, ethnocentrism, and gender. Even the conception of human nature as a uniform biological grounding for all human behavior is denied in favor of a highly changeable, very plastic conception of human potential.[12] What distinguishes recent denaturalization from the antiracism and the rise of the concept of culture after the Second World War is how thorough the penetration of culture has been into areas hitherto considered natural. So complete has this penetration been that the priority given nature over culture in that dichotomy has been over-thrown in the human sciences, and culture has become the preeminent expla-nation of human behavior.[13] Whether or not racism, ethnocentrism, and patriarchy result from social structures or from cultural systems reveals conflicting foundational assumptions and explanations, but both sides of that issue can agree on the need to reconsider the specific social provenience of canonical texts and artifacts and who and what appear in the historical con-text.

Accompanying and reinforcing this trend to denaturalization and the study of the Other was one we might call demystification, which traced human behavior, texts, and artifacts to their social production or societal genesis. At its core such an approach postulates societal relationships as systems of structured inequality. Demystification as a methodology explores the connec-tions between the inequalities of social relationships and power in shaping human behavior, ideas, and artifacts. Presumption of such structured in-equalities in a society transforms strata or groups into classes, and, along with denaturalization, converts sexes into gender systems and peoples into racial systems. To tie literature, the arts, and ideation in general to social class and political power turns ideas into ideologies and texts into discourses. Scholars replace the search for a single, fixed, and unified meaning of a text with the exploration, in a text, of multiple, contested meanings that reproduce the class, gender, and other conflicts within a society. The revival of class and conflict analysis in literary, historical, and other scholarship has renewed the emphasis upon ideology and the prevalence of such terms as "hegemony" and "domination" in academic discourse. Even the conception of human nature as the universal biological foundation of all human behavior is portrayed as nothing more than a rationale for bourgeois hegemony and a liberal econ-omy. As Roland Barthes argued long ago: "The status of the bourgeoisie is particular, historical: man as represented by it is universal, eternal."[14]

If the terms "post-Marxian" and "neo-Marxian" indicate that orthodox Marxian analysis according to the base/superstructure model of simple eco-nomic determinism is out of intellectual favor, the phrase "social construc-tion of . . ." demonstrates the continuing popularity of the relativization of ideas and actions to society as a system of structured inequalities, hence a site of conflict. In fact the framework of so much of the cultural studies prominent in so many fields, especially in the form of popular culture, rests on just such a social interpretation of culture.[15] Although culture is not relegated to some simple superstructural level, its seeming autonomy as an independent variable in the explanation of social phenomena appears se-verely limited by the nature of the social matrix.[16] In the end, all categories of human knowledge, like cultural categories in general, are relativized to their overall societal genesis, be it class, gender, race, or other social origins. As Robert D'Amico concludes in *Historicism and Knowledge*, "Reasoning is always local and locatable."[17] Thus Elizabeth Deeds Ermarth points out, "A postmodernist would never speak of 'historical reality' not because 'reality' doesn't exist except as defined locally but also because 'history' doesn't exist either, except as defined locally."[18]

Demystification possesses consequences for the conceptions both of culture and of the individual. Culture, like history, is always a site of social struggle. Culture can never be represented as a unified system for a whole society, because the divisions within a society find one of their expressions in the conflicts within (a) culture. Moreover, because individuals are both created and circumscribed by their location in the social matrix, the seeming autonomy of the individual is a bourgeois humanistic myth to conceal the social origins of personal experience and the social constitution of the self.

Dehierarchization

Still another clear tendency in recent theory was one I shall label dehierarchization. Such a trend was most evident in the erosion, even dissolution, of the scholarly and aesthetic boundaries dividing elite from popular cultures. Although it may be difficult to pinpoint when the Beatles became as legitimate for academics to study (and appreciate) as Beethoven, or Superman as legitimate as Shakespeare, or everyday commercial objects as legitimate as high art ones, cultural studies as studies of popular culture blossomed first outside the academy, then within it.[19] Cultural studies undermined the criteria sustaining the canons in literature, art, and music. Just as Russian formalism made folktales a model for all narrative, so semiotic, structuralist, and poststructuralist methodologies provided models and methods that eliminated the distinction between elite and other forms of literature, art, and music. What popular and cultural studies started was subsequently reinforced by the New Historicism, which studies high cultural literary texts by juxtaposing them with ordinary historic documents to show that all were part of the social and cultural arrangements of a given period. Under the aegis of the New Historicism, a canonical literary work becomes just another document "circulating" within an overall cultural system. This conflation of the literary with the nonliterary undermined the previous scholarly hierarchy that distinguished literary icon from mundane documents and, in the process, fused text and context.

Culture with a C became just another part of culture with a *c,* but that "reduction"—earlier critics said "degradation"—rested upon certain ways of understanding texts as a context and contexts as texts and had political as well as cognitive and aesthetic implications. Repudiation of the criteria distinguishing elite from popular, folk, and other cultures rested upon a denial of transcendent or universal principles or values in the evaluation of literature, art, and music and the relativization of aesthetic standards in general. Thus "literature," as Terry Eagleton emphasizes, becomes nothing more than "a name which people give from time to time for different reasons to certain kinds of writing," just another one of many signifying practices.[20] When judgments of taste, form, and pleasure are demystified, they can be traced to the specific social location of an observer, to a specific interpretive community in a society.[21] Once again cultural and social arrangements circum(in)scribe what had been previously presumed transcultural.

Much of the new historicization in the humanities, and particularly as found in the new cultural studies, seems devoted to the demystification of abstract terms, subjects, or categories long considered basic to Western culture, hence projected as universal to Culture (and therefore fundamental to the humanities themselves). As Richard Johnson, former director of the Centre for Contemporary Culture Studies at the University of Birmingham in England, says:

> I would describe the evolving agenda [of cultural studies] as a series of critiques of innocent-sounding categories or innocent-sounding practices . . . obviously culture and art and literature, but also communication, and consumption, entertainment, education, leisure, style, the family, femininity and masculinity, and sexuality and pleasure, and, of course, the most objective-sounding categories of all, knowledge and science.[22]

Even while a study of how the concepts or categories came about reveals how they became reified as concepts and mystified as persistent essentialist and foundational universal categories, such a history can also expose the political uses of the naturalization, the mystification, and the essentializing of them in (a) society.[23] In the end, such demystification creates a story of how a presumably shared culture, but eclectic both in its contents and in the social divisions of its audiences, was transformed into categories of culture segregated by the social classes of its sponsors and recipients.[24]

The new cultural studies seek to fuse cultural and political critique in practice through contextualization.[25] The aim of combining cultural and political critique is not new, but its current vitality represents a new phase. If demystifying the class origins and uses of ideas transmutes them into ideologies, however, then do cultural and social arrangements also generate and circumscribe their own theorization? Such is the reflexive dilemma of the sociology of knowledge, as Karl Mannheim noted long ago.[26] Should the study of how the concepts or categories arose in the past also reveal the scholar's own political uses of denaturalization, demystification, and deessentializing in the present? Does—must—the reflexive critique of culture lead to the questioning of its own premises of contextualization as ideology and politics? Must—should—the social construction of cultural reality give way to the cultural or textual construction of social reality?

Under such conditions the very definition of history must take on a more reflexive meaning, one that shows its socially constructed nature, its self-consciousness of its own creation, and the social conditions that allow such a practice. Thus denaturalization, demystification, and dehierarchization when applied to history not only suggest new subject matter, additional actors, and in general a history more inclusive of multicultural viewpoints; they also spotlight the politics of historical methodology, the politics of the traditional viewpoint from which history is seen and told, and the politics of the discipline as a professional community. In short, they highlight the relationships among the nature of historical knowledge, the social bases of its production, and its implication in the power system in a society. They call attention to the very purpose of history as a discipline and the moral and political ends a history serves. Must a history ultimately support or oppose the existing social, economic, and political order?

From this point of view history as method and product is pervaded by values and should expose the wrongs of the past as it espouses the correct political orientation. Cathy Davidson points out the proper role of literary history as a part of the New Historicism:

> Oppositional or dialogical history challenges conventional . . . history by questioning both the relative value of what is examined and the implicit values of the examiner. It sees the very processes and ambitions of historiography as products of much larger forces and it seeks to understand the relationships between those present forces and the hierarchical imperative of the past . . . Dialogical history gives us a choice of pasts, too. But that very choice or pluralism is subversive since it implies that . . . [history] is not simply inherited but constructed, and constructed according to the . . . categories we devise.[27]

Although denaturalization, demystification, and dehierarchization have broadened who and what are to be included as part of history and the self-consciousness of the social production of a history, they have hardly transformed the basic assumptions about how such history is to be written. Just how much a dialogical or oppositional history challenges the presuppositional paradigm of traditional history is a question to be considered both through possible exemplars in current practice and through the theory of its future creation.

Perhaps the greatest hierarchization of all was the belief among Western scholars that their intellectual categories and their ways of thought were superior to those of other peoples. Part of that ethnocentric and dominating self-privileging and hierarchization entailed the very categorization of persons as Others on the basis of gender, class, age, race, ethnicity, culture, society, nationality, or other classification that presumed the superiority of the classifier over the others. Decolonization and civil rights movements since the Second World War have called this approach into question. By asking whose interests any set of ideas serves, multiculturalism combined with demystification extends canon-busting to all disciplines, all methodologies, all paradigmatic viewpoints grounding knowledge. As with other disciplines, multicul-turalism challenges the viewpoint basic to traditional history and in turn its authority to interpret the past. It raises questions about whose perspective is represented in traditional history and whose interests such perspectives serve. In the end it queries whether the non-Western or the nondominant Other can be represented fully in any form resembling traditional history.

Dereferentialism

Far more challenging to traditional historical understanding and therefore the guild's practices in writing and reading than denaturalization, demystifica-tion, and even some aspects of dehierarchization are deconstruction and dereferentialism. It is these last two sets of presuppositions that some scholars see as the ultimate grounding of the linguistic, interpretive, and rhetorical turns, and that others accuse of reducing all life to language, all scholarship to sound and fury ultimately signifying nothing.

Taken to its logical limit, conceptual dehierarchization challenges the whole idea of according some foundational assumptions ascendancy over others for the grounding of judgments, be they conceptual or aesthetic. In the realm of ideas, it is antiessentialism, hence antifoundationalism in its strong-est form.[28] Such a perspective impugns the capacity of theories to mediate as metalanguages between concepts and reality. Even scientific theory is denied status as a superior form of discourse. Science is reduced to the narrative it uses to announce its discoveries.[29] Dehierarchization in aesthetics opposes universalism, elitism, even in a sense aestheticism. In its strongest version it denies the traditional distinction between literary and other forms of lan-guage. Eagleton's claim that the relationship between "literature" and other discursive practices is arbitrary is supported by Vincent Leitch, who asserts: "'literature' is not an immutable ontological category nor an objective entity; rather it is a variable functional term and a sociohistorical formation."[30] Literature, like science and history, is demoted to just another text, like films, cartoons, and other cultural objects.

Theory is never accorded superiority over other language uses and never separated from its practice as a socially based discourse. The questioning of all essentialism as a form of unwarranted privileging implies that conceptual and aesthetic judgments are as much politics as philosophy, as much ideology as ideal. Accordingly, Barthes declared, "The disease of thinking in essences . . . is at the bottom of every bourgeois mythology of man."[31] In politics, dehierarchization once again implies antiprivilege and antielitism; to resist authority is to oppose the standard ways of looking at things as well as the standard ways of governing people.

The dehierarchization of language eventuates in dereferentialism and ulti-mately in deconstruction. Conceptually, dereferentialism questions the extralinguistic "reality," or transcendental signification, as well as persisting essentialism of abstract categories. That textual or other representations do not correspond to an extratextual, extralinguistic reality challenges referentialism in literature, the arts, and especially in history and the social sciences.[32] Not only are such categories as race, ethnicity, and gender thereby transformed into cultural constructions, but even such other conceptions as social class and the state are categorized as essentialist and foundational if they are not construed as culturally arbitrary in definition because they are historically and socially specific. To historicize such concepts undermines their traditional utility as historical explanation or as historical concepts.

In the end, transforming the social construction of concepts into culturally construed categories reduces all modes of human communication to their forms of signification or representation. When dereferentialism questions the real status of the subject or object, it also questions the nature of the entities that go into constructing a context. Such obscuring, if not denying, of the referentiality of the subject undermines the legitimacy and authority of all traditional representations by normal historical (re)construction.

Deconstruction

Deconstruction—no matter how many ways it is defined today—is the ultimate dehierarchization of language, for it treats texts and discourses as nondeterminative of their ostensible meaning.[33] The method denies the apparent unity of a text in favor of its heterogeneity and its internal tensions by revealing how a text subverts its own message through self-contradictions, ambiguities, and suppression of contraries. Deconstructionist critics expose authors' attempts to naturalize, essentialize, or universalize the categories they employ as foundational to their texts. Deconstruction aims at bottom to expose the nature of all representations for what they patently are: socially based discursive constructions. Many followers of Jacques Derrida, the founding father of deconstruction, have translated his now famous words "Il n'y a pas d'hors texte" as "there is nothing outside a [or the] text."[34] Therefore, everything ought to and can be interpreted textually. Although the focus of the method is on the tensions in a text, the method presumes that the conflicts within a text exemplify and exhibit the oppositional discourses within a society. As a result, deconstruction particularly challenges the implied primacy of the first term over the second in such classic Western dichotomies as male/female, nature/culture, real/artificial, reason/emotion, self/other, public/private, and even signifier/signified, theory/practice, cause/effect, and truth/fiction.

In line with the deconstruction of the last four oppositions, deconstructive critics offer their own texts not as new truths and authoritative works but only, presumably, as further moves in continuing conversations: today's contentions for today's debates. Whether defined as unraveling the hierarchical binary oppositions in a text to show how the text ultimately contradicts itself or as a more freewheeling interpretation in which the critic supplements the voids and pursues the duplicities of the text's language far beyond its apparent significations, the deconstructionist's suspicion of language as subversive of its own meaning allows the de(con)struction of a text by exposing its dilemmas and ultimate illogic. While deconstruction reveals what is suppressed in any apparently unified representation of matters, it also undermines efforts at mediation between representation and referentiality, between texts and "reality," even if that reality is presumed to be socially constructed. Men and women may make their worlds, their worldviews, and their words, but can they make the connections among them in ways that can be comprehended according to their own theories of language?[35]

With their deemphasis on, even denial of, extratextual referentiality and conceptual foundationalism or essentialism, the linguistic and rhetorical turns seemed to collapse all reality into its representation, all history into its text(ualization)s.[36] Many scholars see the New Criticism as having prepared the way for later textualist approaches in the United States. Thus they often accuse deconstructive criticism, like its predecessor, of focusing exclusively on the text to derive its meaning and of denying the value of context in interpreting a text.[37] Unlike the earlier New Critics, however, many deconstructionists viewed texts as products of socially based discursive practices. Extreme or pantextualists extended the premises of their approach to the very understanding of life itself as a text. From this viewpoint, not only do human behavior and social interaction produce texts, but humans and their societies understand themselves through and as interpretive textualizations. It is only through such textualizations that humans can reproduce their cultures and social institutions. All behavior can be interpreted like texts because it was produced in the first place through a process of textualization broadly conceived.[38]

Debating the Implications

Is the writing of history possible, or do the theoretical contradictions of its practice deny its empirical pretensions? Although the question had been posed before, the answers seemed to change as a result of poststructuralism and postmodernism. For most of the twentieth century, both the question and its answer were framed in terms of the modernist paradigm. Scholars who raised these issues wondered how historians could unite in their practice the dual but contrasting perspectives of art and science said to ground the discipline.[39] Historians sought in their writing and teaching to combine intuitive insights with rigorous empiricism, generalizations and abstractions with concrete and specific facts, argument and analysis with story-telling, interpretive understanding with logical explanation, creative organization with objective reporting, impartiality and detachment with moral judgment and advocacy. What historians strove to join together in their practice, scholars in other disciplines put asunder in their theorization. What historians tried to unify as a single way of understanding through their practice, other scholars criticized as ways of understanding as they separated the strands of that historical practice. While historians attempted the reconciliation of art and literature with science, all too many philosophers, literary theorists, and social scientists pointed out the dilemmas if not the confusion and impossibility of such an aim. Whether, let alone how well, historians could reconcile intuition and empiricism, generalization and specificity, analysis and narrative, interpretation and explanation, creativity and reporting, objectivity and advocacy depended as much on what other disciplines defined as the nature of these various practices as on how historians went about their business in these matters.

On the whole critics and advocates operated within the modernist paradigm. They assumed that the dichotomies reflected the inherent conflict between the positivist program of the sciences and the humanist foundations of the arts. Both programs were predicated on the separation of fact from value and the past from its representation. Commitment to a realist epistemology and ontology, however, allowed historical relativists and historical objectivists alike to assume that historians could know what the past had to have been even if they could not always represent it accurately or completely.

Although the question remains the same today, the answers seem increasingly different as scholars attack the premises of the modernist paradigm. The traditional dichotomies are denied as invalid, irrelevant, or improperly framed. The gaps between science and literature, fact and fiction, story and explanation, objectivity and advocacy narrowed or disappeared as the problems of representation increased under the aegis first of structuralism and then of poststructuralism. The implications of these theories can be seen not only in the repudiation of history as some grand teleological enterprise but also in the changed definitions of historical practice itself or in the panicky reactions of those opposing postmodernist trends.

The definition of history takes on quite a new meaning under the aegis of dereferentialism and textualism. Thus Hayden White defines a "historical work as what it manifestly is—that is to say, a verbal structure in the form of a narrative prose discourse that purports to be a model, or icon, of past structures and processes in the interest of *explaining what they were by representing* them."[40] The French linguistic scholars A. J. Greimas and J. Courtés take a similar view in their *Semiotics and Language: An Analytical Dictionary,* under "hi/story":

1. By hi/story (history) is understood a semantic universe considered as an object of knowledge, the intelligibility of which, postulated *a priori,* is based on a diachronic articulation of its elements. In this sense, "history" can be considered as a semiotic system as object (or as a set of semiotic systems taken prior to their analysis) the approach of which is determined beforehand by certain postulates.

2. Hi/story (as story) corresponds, on the other hand, to the narration or to the description of actions the veridictory of which status is not fixed (they can be past and "real," imaginary, or even undecidable). From this viewpoint, hi/story is to be considered as a narrative discourse.[41]

We can get a better idea of what is at issue in this latter definition by looking at how they define "truth": "Truth designates the complex term which subsumes the terms *being* and *seeming* . . . It might be helpful to point out that the 'true' is situated within the discourse, for it is the fruit of the veridiction operations: this thus excludes any relation (or any homologation) with an external referent."[42]

Such a definition of history questions the ability to recover the past as history, complicating, perhaps denying, the connection between history as a text and the past as what occurred. Sande Cohen makes this complication clear in the semiotic definition he offers as part of his political critique of narrative history:

History is a concept of last resort, a floating signifier, the alibi of an alignment with obligatory values. It pertains to no signified at all; depending upon how the past is positioned, it can preclude confusion of temporal coordinates, preserve the imaginary idea of collective relations, substitute when for where, or dismiss present intensities. "History" must be radically severed from "past": the former is always calibrated with cultural contradictions, whereas the latter is much more fluid a notion. "Past" is involved with both active and involuntary memory, but "history" can only project the simulation of the remembered.[43]

How far removed in conception as well as in phrasing these definitions are from what is usual in the historical profession may be seen in the definition of "history" provided by Harry Ritter in his *Dictionary of Concepts in History.*

1. In ordinary usage, the human past. 2. In professional usage, either the human past or (more significantly) inquiry into the nature of the human past, with the aim of preparing an authentic account of one or more of its facets. The term may also refer in both popular and professional usage to a written account of past events. From the *historical* viewpoint—that is, from the standpoint of the history of historical thinking itself—*history* may generally be defined as a tradition of learning and writing, dating from ancient times, based on rational inquiry into the factual nature of the human past.[44]

Aside from their contrasting rhetorical styles, the four definitions rest upon quite different approaches to language and its relation to the world it supposedly represents, and therefore to the linkage between history as actual past and history as present record.

As the most extreme challenge of all, the strongest versions of demystification and dereferentialism deny the primary premise of the historical profession: the separation of history as the past from history as writing about that past. Radical dereferentialism by reducing the past to its textualization denies the ability of historians to know the past as such. For all practical purposes, the past and written history are the same, for only as a present-day text is the past constituted. Radical demystification by reducing historians and their histories to their social location make their practice just another form of contemporary ideology. And histories as ideologies transform the past into its textualization just as surely as dereferentialism does. Both radical demystification and radical dereferentialism reinforce each other's tendencies to treat written history as a present-minded, ideological practice, although the basic reasons for this conclusion differ greatly between the two. Thus both tendencies contradict historians' belief in their ability to use the separate reality of the past to validate their interpretations of it. No wonder some historians have reacted with dismay to this double whammy.[45] Although those advocating radical demystification and radical dereferentialism did not always deduce the same lessons, they emphasized the same horn of the dilemma.

Gertrude Himmelfarb has pointed out the implications of such postmodernist premises for the traditional approach to texts, whether as documentary sources or as modern representations, in the historical profession. She objects to the extension of deconstruction from literature to history because it removes the authority that customarily grounded the discipline of history:

> In literary criticism, deconstruction means the liberation of the text from all constraints that have traditionally given it meaning, starting with the intentions of the author—the "authorial voice," as is said. The author, according to this view, speaks with no more authority than the reader or the critic. To the extent to which the author (putative author you might say) is presumed to exercise authority over the text, that authority is "authoritarian." (The play on words is deliberate, and deliberately pejorative; that illicit authority has been described as "tyrannical," "reactionary," "imperialistic," "fascistic.") The deconstructionist also liberates the text from the tyranny of what is called "context"—the context of events, ideas, conventions, which informed the text not only for the author but for contemporary readers. "Nothing outside the text," Jacques Derrida has proclaimed. And the text itself is said to be "indeterminate" because language does not reflect or correspond to reality; there is no correspondence between language and fact, between words and things. Indeed there are no facts apart from language—which is why "facts" in deconstructionist discourse normally appears in quotation marks. Moreover language itself is "duplicitous," "cryptic": it has to be "decoded" before it can convey any meaning. And since there is no single correct code, no reading of the text, no interpretation, has any more authority than any other. This interpretation is as "indeterminate" as the text itself.[46]

The collapse of text and context through such an approach to the past (and the present) indicate at least to Himmelfarb that those historians who would follow deconstructionist tactics would deconstruct themselves as well as misunderstand what peoples in the past meant and how they understood themselves. Himmelfarb resents that a deconstructive hermeneutics of suspicion has in effect discovered the word "lie" residing subversively in the word "belief," thus jeopardizing any practical historical exegesis, let alone authoritative narrative history.[47]

From the conceptual point of view, denial of referentiality and the collapse of history into its representation pose major problems for traditional historians' assumptions about the categorical differences between texts and contexts in the past and as subjects of their discourse, between textualism and contextualism as ways of understanding the past as the context of history, and between reading histories as texts and reading the past—that is, all of history—as a text. The implications of what we might call the strong program of the linguistic and rhetorical turns for traditional history (reinforced by radical demystification in the form of extreme historicization) are summarized by John Toews in a long essay review in 1987 on the ramifications of the linguistic turn for intellectual history:

> If we take them seriously, we must recognize that we have no access, even potentially, to an unmediated world of objective things and processes that might serve as the ground and limit of our claims to knowledge of nature or to any transhistorical or transcendent subjectivity that might ground our interpretation of meaning . . . This perspective . . . is radically historicist in the sense that all knowledge and meaning is perceived as time-bound and culture-bound, but it also undermines the traditional historian's quest for unity, continuity, and purpose by robbing them of any standpoint from which a relationship between past, present, and future could be objectively reconstructed.[48]

Emphasizing the same horn of the dilemma between radical dereferentialism and radical demystification but with quite another lesson are those who agree with Bryan Palmer about the consequences of "the descent into discourse," as he titled his polemical book on the implications of poststructuralist theory for the discipline. As a result of this "hedonistic descent into a plurality of discourses that decenter the world in a chaotic denial of any acknowledgment of tangible structures of power and comprehensions of meaning," such theory discounts or denies entirely the realities of class and economic systems in historical analysis.[49] Poststructuralist theory in stressing the power of language to shape reality discounts the power of social, economic, and political forces to shape language like all other social reality. This reduction of life into language destroys the conceptual foundations of political commitment in the contemporary world. Palmer accepts the validity of historical materialism in order to criticize contemporary society and condemns this latest version of historical idealism as empty both morally and conceptually. Although he sees some value in discourse theory for studying how a society conceptualizes gender, race, and colonialism, in his view the gains of poststructuralist theory have been more than offset by the political paralysis resulting from the reduction of lived experience to linguistic texts.

Those who choose radical demystification based upon the social realities of class, gender, and race face the same dilemmas confronting Toews in his effort to contextualize meaning in experience. In the end, radical social relativization and extreme social constructionism lead in the same direction as, and reinforce, radical textualization and dereferentialism. Radical demystification in the strongest version of social constructionism makes the texts that historians produce just another social practice grounded in the social system, hence just another ideology. In this sense, both radical demystification and radical dereferentialism reduce the past realities of historians to the texts describing those realities. Even a weaker version of the demystification and the social construction of historical practice historicizes historians and their practice, and in doing so transforms history into a historiography that studies changing ideologies as propaganda appropriate to their social contexts. That history may serve as ideological critique in political discourse contradicts the traditional ideal of objective reality that supposedly grounds the discipline and justifies the profession in the eyes of so many.

A Problematic Defense

As literary theorists turn to history in their criticism and explication of texts, should historians turn to literary theory in their description and explanation of contexts? If historians recognize that "Fable is always the double or other of History," the ultimate "revenge of literature," as Linda Orr argues,[50] must they adopt a broader view of their enterprise, whether as product or practice? Do literary and rhetorical theory offer what historians need at this time, or should they continue doing what they do because the very success of history as an enterprise depends upon its practitioners' not recognizing the impossible contradiction that lies at the bottom of their endeavor, as Orr also maintains?

Probably most anglophone historians hope that the historic turn has restored the profession to what they would regard as its traditional common sense. Until recently, if one is to measure such trends by articles in the major professional journals or by books written by those active in the field, these historians have denied the conceptual threats of the various intellectual turns in the human sciences by simply proceeding with business as usual.[51] The ideas advanced and developed by Michel Foucault in *The Order of Things* and by Hayden White in *Metahistory* have been pursued mainly in fields other than history.[52] Intellectual historians were the first to discuss these matters. While some explicated the importance of European theorists for written history, others warned against the danger of conceptual nihilism and the skeptical relativism inherent in the more radical claims of the linguistic and rhetorical turns.[53]

Thus in his review essay, "Intellectual History after the Linguistic Turn," John Toews argues that the issues center on the relationship between "the autonomy of meaning and the irreducibility of experience." The dilemma arises from two seemingly valid but ultimately irreconcilable propositions: (1) all experience is mediated by meaning, which is "constituted in and through language," but (2) experience constrains or determines the possible meanings. He admits that language is not a transparent medium and that therefore neither is written history. To the extent that language not only shapes experienced reality but in the process constitutes it, it also reduces experience to meaning. Such a view, however, affords no grounds for arbitrating between meanings and experiences, no last resort or objective Archimedean place for distinguishing between the interpretations of reality and reality itself. In the end, history, like other specialized assertions of knowledge, is constituted by its system of language, but Toews denies that all knowledge is therefore reducible to language constitution or ideology. Although the linguistic and rhetorical turns stress the structures of meaning apart from the users and uses of language, the historic turn need not go so far, he argues, for "within that perspective, historiography would be reduced to a subsystem of linguistic signs constituting its object, 'the past,' according to the rules pertaining in the 'prison house of language' inhabited by the historian." Thus he goes on to argue that a dialectical unity of and difference between meaning and experience exists. In the end, viewing (intellectual) history "as the investigation of the contextually situated production and transmission of meaning," he prefers experience to meaning as the ultimate explanation of ideation.[54]

Thus Toews concludes according to the ideology customary to anglophone history:

> Although expressions of apocalyptic fear of the end of history as we have known it or millenarian hopes for a totally new kind of history can occasionally be discerned in the current literature, the predominant tendency is to adapt traditional historical concerns for extralinguistic origins and reference to the semiological challenge, to reaffirm in new ways that, in spite of the relative autonomy of cultural meanings, human subjects still make and remake worlds of meaning in which they are suspended, and insist that these worlds are not creations *ex nihilo* but responses to, and shapings of, changing worlds of experience ultimately irreducible to the linguistic forms in which they appear.[55]

With this affirmation of traditional historical premises, Toews concludes that historians should and must find a path beyond the skepticism, relativism, and politicization of the linguistic and rhetorical turns in order to "connect memory with hope,"[56] but he does not suggest a way to find this path in the brave new world postulated by some literary and rhetorical theorists and a few intellectual historians.

For Toews and most other anglophone historians, the solution is to grant ascendancy to the Anglo-American empirical tradition over continental idealism or skepticism, to experience over meaning, to reality over its postulation.[57] Stressing as it does lived experience over its representation in others' texts, it possesses wide appeal for those who espouse traditional anglophone common-sense philosophy. According primacy to social reality, it also attracts those who favor a materialist over an idealist explanation of history. In many of these cases such a resolution supports the political goals of groups both in the "real world" and in academia. By reinforcing the intellectual authority claimed by the discipline, it provides a basis for both the political and conceptual ends of historians.

Only very recently have anglophone historians outside intellectual history begun to discuss the implications of the various turns in the human sciences. Social and political historians condemn their moral relativism and paralyzing political consequences. Bryan Palmer, for example, argues that the "reification of language" subverts the political realities of social class and class struggle. For him, "critical theory is no substitute for historical materialism; language is not life."[58] He warns that linguistic indeterminacy, if permitted to dominate the profession, will destroy political advocacy. Palmer and others fear that Clio will turn to the right rather than to the left if she follows intellectual fashions in literary circles.[59] Gertrude Himmelfarb, from the opposite political perspective, is equally worried by any prospect of a postmodernist history, which she sees as leading to "intellectual and moral suicide" in the name of "liberation and creativity." Because it denies traditional criteria of reason and a humanistic appreciation of the individual, postmodernism, in Himmelfarb's view, supports a new left agenda. As a result of its assumptions about linguistic indeterminacy in texts and the arbitrary relation of signifier and reality, postmodernist history, for Himmelfarb, is "a denial of the fixity of the past, of the reality of the past apart from what the historian chooses to make of it, and thus any objective truth about the past." It "recognizes no reality principle, only the pleasure principle—history at the pleasure of the historian."[60] Thus she assumes that pleasure and arbitrariness, in politics as in history, support radical causes.

The arguments of Palmer and Himmelfarb echo the political debate in literary and rhetorical studies about the intellectual implications and political challenges of poststructuralism and postmodernism for disciplinary findings and practices. Are these orientations or practices radical, in that they oppose and resist established outlooks and practices in academia and the larger society, or are they accepting of and complicit with dominant disciplinary, social, and political structures? Should literary studies aim to destabilize disciplinary, academic, and societal systems alike? This debate involves, among other matters, the nature of the individual as subject and the nature of power in our society. Is the notion of the freely acting, autonomous individual a liberal humanist delusion or a realistic basis for social and ethical theory and therefore also for political practice? On the one hand, the debate over the power of the individual versus the power of society focuses on the classic issues of what ought to be the nature of the good society and what sorts of theorization as well as practice produce that kind of society; on the other hand, it presumes knowledge of the actual nature of existing social and political arrangements. The politics of modern varieties of liberalism, like those of modern radicalism, claim sure knowledge as a basis for both what is and what ought to be in our society. Palmer's and Himmelfarb's positions represent only two in a wide array of stances regarding theory and politics now beginning to circulate in historians' debates. But there is no consistent clustering of opinion, along either political or theoretical lines, by either proponents or opponents of poststructuralism and postmodernism.[61]

Similarly, proponents and opponents alike take both sides on other conceptual issues, including the relationships between texts and contexts, authors and readers, theory and practice. Whether they address the nature of discourse, the connections between poetics and rhetoric, the role of social institutions in disciplinary methodologies, or the connection between literary theory and politics, these debates frequently try to reconcile the classic dualism between idealism and materialism.[62]

The debates concern the practice of history in at least two ways. First, to what extent must resolution of these political and theoretical problems— if the two can be separated analytically if not in practice—be found in the historicization of subject matter in all disciplines? If discussions of these problems like all other discourses are specific to their times as well as to their places, then some form of history must be created to describe and perhaps ground the resolution of poststructuralist and postmodernist concerns. Second, do poststructuralism and postmodernism deny the fundamental premises necessary to the practice of history as a discipline, as Himmelfarb and others charge? The two questions, of course, demand answers that are sometimes contradictory.[63] In the end, the theory and politics of poststructuralism and postmodernism demand the application of those theories and politics to themselves. Thus demystification, denaturalization, dehierarchization, deconstruction, and dereferentialism undermine the grounds of poststructuralist and postmodernist theories as much as they do late modernist and structuralist ones, because they contradict themselves in application.

Texts and Contexts

The dilemmas of the opposing positions in this debate and their underlying paradigms receive focus in differing definitions of that word so basic to the historian's lexicon and methodology: context. What is at stake can be seen in the different approaches to defining context according to traditional historical and strong contextualist and textualist premises (designated in the following paragraphs by H, C, and T, respectively).[64]

Historians ordinarily distinguish among three basic kinds of context, all tied to the relationship conventionally presumed to exist between past and present in historical methodology.

H1. The first kind of context is the network of relationships in the actual past itself and the experiences of the people in it. Since no historian can mediate or intervene in the past as such, this context exists independently of its study. This understanding of context grounds all forms of historical realism, from the most sophisticated to the most naive interpretations. Historical method is employed to reconstruct this actual past from the evidence remaining from that past. In the process historians hope to represent the actual context through their histories.

H2. The second kind of context consists of the documentary and other artifactual sources remaining from the past itself and, perhaps, those historical representations constructed close to the documentary or other artifactual sources themselves, such as edited letters and diaries or reproduced artifacts. From the texts of the past, historians hope to infer the contexts that make sense of those texts so they can present them as part of their histories.

H3. The third kind of context is the historian's construction or interpretation of the past as the larger framework of past beliefs and behaviors. This is the represented context synthesized from the evidential or documentary context that allowed the reconstruction of the context of the actual past.

Paralleling these definitions of context is a series of assumptions about their nature as social reality. Strong contextualist presuppositions about how people experience and know reality provide the starting point for defining context and therefore what grounds contextualizing as a method from this position.

C1. The strong contextualists' first context presumes the reality of the world and the experiences of the people in it. At its most extreme, such a position presumes that the results of the process of contextualizing are transparent to the reality past peoples experienced. Therefore, this first context is directly lived and felt; it is the unconstructed and uninterpreted—in short, prelinguistic—experience of past persons.

C2. The second context in a strong contextualist series presumes to understand how past reality, social and otherwise, is experienced and, possibly, interpreted by those living it. We might label this approach ethnocontext because the contextualizer seeks to place matters within the context and terms of those living and experiencing it. Frequently such an approach tries to reconstruct it through evocation or other methods of "recapturing" past peoples' experience of their times. The measure of successful ethnocontextualization is correspondence to the unreconstructed actual context (C1). To consider whether there is any difference between the living and experiencing of the actual context (C1) and of ethnocontext (C2) and the scholarly interpretation of those two contexts requires a third definition of context in this series.

C3. The third context refers to the interpretations or constructions of those studying and describing the previous two contexts. Hence we might call this the interpretive context. At their most extended, these interpretations lead to constructions of such contexts as (a) society, culture, polity, gender, or other system. For both those who live the actual context (C1) in this series and those who interpret it as (C3), the past as history or historicization is equally given and real. Thus, both past and present texts, according to contextualist premises, are the works or artifacts themselves, but their production is according to extratextual, socially specific discursive practices, and their interpretations are grounded in specific, extratextual interpretive communities or reading formations.[65]

Postmodernist theorizing challenges this scheme of classifying contexts through what is called textualism or textuality. Textualism as orientation and method begins with a new definition of text. Theorists of textuality do not accept a written, oral, or other communicative artifact as a concrete phenomenological object with a fixed meaning. Rather, they regard such artifacts as sites of intersecting meaning systems receiving diverse readings and various interpretations. Texts are "read" as systems or structures of meaning flowing from the semiotic, social, and cultural processes by which they are constructed or textualized. Such an approach to texts and their systems of textualization broadens the potential array of communicative artifacts. Paintings, films, television programs, clothing styles, sports spectacles, political rallies, and even societies and cultures come to be read as texts in addition to the books, letters, speeches, censuses, or other artifacts that historians customarily consider documents.[66]

Theorists and critics read these textualized meaning systems variously as formal structures of rules based on semiotics models, as "processes of signification" in Roland Barthes' phrase, as "discursive practices" in Michel Foucault's terminology, or other ways of showing how the process(es) that constituted the text also provide its meaning for its producers and perhaps for its various audiences. Whether explicated and interpreted as and through universalist formal structures (structuralist and semiotic models), as readings by interpretive communities and audiences (reception and reader-response models), as supplementation and criticism through deconstruction and ideological demystification (poststructuralist and post-Marxist models), or as products of anonymous but socially and historically specific sets of rules (Foucauldian models), all such readings of texts produce their own supple-

mentary or countertexts, which in turn can be read as further text(ualization)s. Whether textualists take as their topic explicit or implicit meaning
systems, they frequently reveal the subtext of what they explore as they
reconstitute it as a text(ualization).[67]

Textuality has important implications for traditional historical methodology and representation. It adds complexity to the reading of documentary
remains from the past by conflating what they signify with how they signify.
It supplements, when it does not dissolve, the notion of authorship and
intention into the social, cultural, or other textualizing practices that produced the document or remain, thereby repudiating the traditional notions of
intention and authorship that had supplied the premises necessary to interpret
documents as evidence for the reconstruction of the past as actual context. By
fusing past and present as textualization, textualism also unites history and
historiography, in contrast to usual disciplinary practice. How can historians
in the end distinguish between context and text when they appear to be the
same under textualist readings?[68]

Thus textualism challenges the traditional method of reconstruction and its
mode of representation, which was postulated as fundamental to historical
practice. Another series outlining the contrasting approach of the strong
textualist position highlights what is in contention. The staunch textualist
position starts and ends with the notion of text itself, even when it seems to
extend beyond it, and produces a quite different series with quite different
implications for historical discourse.

T1. The first textualist definition of context reduces it to the system or
structure of words or signs themselves in a text. Contextualization according
to this definition might be called autotextual or, better, intratextual because
the process of contextualization supposedly remains or occurs within the text
itself by comparing one part to another or a part to the whole. In normal
reading and reviewing such (con)textualism shows as the consistency of the
argument or story, especially through a comparison of annotation and the
generalizations it supports.

T2. In the second definition from a textualist perspective, the context of a
text comes from, or is constructed from, other texts. This approach may be
called intertextuality, in distinction to the intratextuality of the preceding
definition.[69] Intertextuality can refer to one text drawing upon one or more
other texts as pre-text(s), or it can show how one text is referred to by others
as their pre-text. Such pre-textual analysis is an important source of interpretation for intellectual historians as well as literary scholars. Annotation refers
to other works and thereby engages in the dialogism of intertextuality, as a
dialogue within either the profession or one of its specialties. This intertextuality serves as context. Interpretations and grand histories are necessarily
intertextual because they build upon other interpretations or monographs,
but all historians' texts depend for their form and, in many ways, their

content upon professional discursive practices. Historians begin with other historians' interpretations and address the past in terms of how the discipline defines it. Even what constitutes a source, how it should be read as evidence, and what facts it provides depend upon professional intertextual conversations. As these examples illustrate, intertextuality translates the intersubjectivity of the contextualists into its textualist analogue.

T3. In the third textualist definition, the context of a text is found outside texts and so might be called extratextual. Such an approach to context seems to be the same actual past customarily presumed by historians as foundational to both their methods and their representations, but both the antipositivist and antifoundationalist premises of this perspective lead elsewhere. In the strongest versions of textualism, not only do human behavior and social interaction produce texts, but humans and their societies can be understood only as textualizations they produce about themselves. A set of behaviors is constituted as a set through collective interpretation as a category. As a set of behaviors is defined through interpretation, its components are isolated from their general context as a sort of textualization. In historical practice, of course, all past behavior is interpreted like texts because it is only (re)constructed by means of textualized evidence. In all cases, the context of such textualization is also constructed through isolation, categorization, and interpretation, and never more so than through such abstractions as society, culture, and polity. Since the latter are obvious textual constructions, so contextualizations employing them are also textual constructions. In this series social construction therefore becomes sociality as text.[70]

Critics of strong textualism accuse all three definitions of being products of structuralist and poststructuralist emphases on language, because each of them derives from a linguistic and symbolic context. Opponents charge that such an approach is tautological because, in the end, the referent is reduced to the signified or, worse, to the signifier itself. As Art Berman expresses this critique: "The system of linguistic signs becomes a self-contained, endless, internal self-referential system of signifiers, whose meanings are generated by their own network."[71] Thus critics of textualism consider the intertextual context (T2) to be as self-referential and solipsistic as its intratextual context (T1), for the interpretation (constitution, derivation?) of the intertextual context (T2) is still within the closed conceptual realm postulated by the linguistic turn. Although the textualist's extratextual context (T3) appears to break out of this circularity of signifiers to provide a referent in the outside world, that social reality is both constituted and understood through textualization broadly conceived.

In the eyes of its critics, textualism's linguistic solipsism appears to lead only to a useless skepticism or an unacceptable idealism.[72] Its approach to context contradicts the traditional understanding of context in the historical guild because it depends upon evidence or analysis internal rather than external to the text or set of texts even when appearing otherwise; hence the complaint so often leveled against the New Historicism by historians. Opponents of this approach might label it "textual fundamentalism." Others have characterized this position as "vulgar linguicism" or "vulgar representationalism."[73]

Since the two versions of contextualization start from contrasting positions and problematics, they end up in different places. Although the contextualist third mode of interpretive contextualization (C3) relies upon the same kind of textualization and re-representation as the textualists' extratextual context (T3), its premise, like its method, is based upon the assumption that the extratextual world is both actual and knowable as such. As a result of this premise, most historians and other anglophone scholars would label only this approach truly or properly contextualist in problematic and methodology, and it is the usual definition of context employed in historicization, whether by scholars of literature, music, and art or by historians and social scientists. Textualist opponents of this whole approach ask how, in light of the challenges raised to all text(ualization)s by the linguistic and rhetorical turns, strong contextualists can describe the social reality they presume grounds their approach to context without employing textualization. Do not all the contexts of the contextualists reduce in actual practice as well as in theory to the contexts of the strong textualists?

This brief examination of the contending approaches to context and how it applies in historical practice reveals that the notion is as ambiguous and contestable as that of history. Similarly to history, contextualism as a methodology refers both to a social reality described as a context (usually in terms of a strong contextualist approach) and to its textualization as a description and interpretation of that context (increasingly understood according to textualist definitions of context). Thus the idea not only is basic to historicization but also shares its problems of conceptual ambiguity. Such an impression of context(ualism) as dual-sided both oversimplifies and clarifies some of the disagreements among historians about their practices and among other scholars in the human sciences who take a historic turn.

Thus the popular contemporary advice always to historicize only takes one back to the fundamental issue of how to construct a history. Describing contextualism in terms of contending positions points out what is at issue but not how to do it. Neither proponents nor opponents of textualism and contextualism specify what should be included in and as context. Each group offers clues in its own way about the framework of the story and the grounds of the explicit and subtextual argument. Each supplies the ends but not the means to determine what should be contained in any given example. Each offers generalizations as conclusions but no guidance on how to organize the facts that support them. For both contextualism and textualism, how to contextualize is ultimately an arbitrary matter.

Clio at the Crossroads

The crisis in the historical profession today is both conceptual and political, both methodological and practical. To the crises of the decline of great narrative history for the popular audience, the multiculturalist challenge to Eurocentric history, and the loss of faith in grand themes of progress and liberation that provided moral and political guidance through history's lessons must be added the crisis created by the implications of literary and rhetorical theory for the very practice of history itself.[74] The crisis posed by postmodernist theory makes problematic the appropriate subject matter of (a) history, the proper methods, the preferred philosophy of method, the appropriate role of politics in the profession, and even the best mode of representation. Plural presuppositions in the various paradigms or problematics result not only in competing histories of history but in conflicting approaches to the past. Contending rhetorics show opposing premises and competing positions, contradictory paradigms and divergent interpretive communities.

Despite the fears of Palmer, Himmelfarb, and others that the postmodernist infection has spread throughout the profession, few books or articles by anglophone historians have exemplified in practice the possibilities of the linguistic and other turns for writing histories. On the whole the few books and articles that have supposedly practiced deconstruction or followed the linguistic or rhetorical turns look more like the old history in how they approach their subject, present their findings, or represent the past than the challenges would seem to imply or demand.[75] In most cases the supposed adoption by historians of the interpretive, linguistic, or rhetorical turns has changed some vocabulary and introduced some new subjects and ways of handling that subject matter. Perhaps the nearest models for historians of any new approach to the writing of history might be those works labeled the New Historicism in literary studies, but historians are skeptical as to whether these works constitute proper history according to traditional criteria.[76]

Important as these possible models may be in relation to current ways of writing history, they pale beside the challenge to the fundamental presuppositions of traditional historical writing and practice posed by the various turns and contradictory problematics in the human sciences. While historicization supposedly solves problems of theory in other disciplines, these historicizations in turn do not solve the theoretical problems those disciplines pose for doing history in these postmodern, poststructuralist times. Just what forms any historicization can possibly take after the severe challenges literary and rhetorical theorists themselves issued to traditional ways of representing history is the question we need to consider at this moment in the practice of history. The challenges are clear enough; the proper responses are far less certain despite the enthusiasm for a new cultural history and new historicisms in general.

CHAPTER TWO

Narratives and Historicization

ONCE upon a time and until fifty years ago, according to the story of history-writing given by Lawrence Stone in his article "The Revival of Narrative," all histories were narrative histories.[1] Historians and their readers understood clearly what the relationships were among history, story, narrative, plot, voice, and viewpoint. A history was a true story about the past. Historians arranged their empirical evidence and facts into a story modeled upon the narrative conventions of nineteenth-century realistic novels. A plot was the author's arrangement of the actions in the story according to the chronological conventions of history-telling. Voice and viewpoint gave historians a synoptic, if not also an omniscient, outlook upon their subjects.

A good sense of what narrative once meant in the profession is conveyed in Savoie Lottinville's advice to the neophyte historian in *The Rhetoric of History:*

All successful historical construction of the narrative kind exhibits these characteristics:

It develops the required setting and the time of historical action . . .

It develops action swiftly and economically through conscious and unremitting attention to the actors in the historical action.

It utilizes such well-established narrative conventions as viewpoint, the plant, characterization, all the devices of continuity and the maintenance of the suspense implied in A. J. P. Taylor's dictum that historical characters do not know what fate has in store for them.

It treats chronology as unfolding rather than as past time.

It utilizes indirect discourse, when it may legitimately be drawn from documents, as an admissible convention in place of novelist's dialogue.

It intends to recreate what did in fact take place at the time of its occurrence. Its concern is the now of history, not the was.[2]

In recent decades, according to Stone's narrative, various historical schools had repudiated story-telling along with the subjects traditional to historical expositions. The *Annales* school of French historiography emphasized long-term trends and demographic and environmental factors at the expense of specific individuals and events. In the end, some theorists of the school even denied change and chronology as the main focus of historical studies in their pursuit of the *longue durée* as opposed to the history of mere events.[3] Social science history, particularly in the United States, sought nomological or generalized explanation through the explicit testing of social science theories and substituted a purportedly analytical model for the customary story. Its practitioners condemned narrative history for failing to explain through precise causal modeling the phenomena under investigation.[4] In opposition to this trend Stone believed he saw the beginnings of "the revival of narrative" as some of the most noted French historians moved away from describing climatic influences on social change and preindustrial cycles of life to emphasizing the *mentalités* of the peoples they studied. Although these historians concentrated upon the poor and obscure rather than upon the rich and famous, included analysis with narrative, stressed symbols as well as behavior, and told their stories in ways somewhat different from classic nineteenth-century models, they nevertheless employed narrative forms, he argued, to explicate their understandings of past societies.[5]

Stone's perspective on the history of history-writing shaped his definition of narrative in opposition to analytical approaches to the past:

> Narrative is taken to mean the organization of material into a chronologically sequential order and the focusing of the content into a single coherent story, albeit with subplots. The two essential ways in which narrative differs from structural history is that its arrangement is descriptive rather than analytical and that its central focus is on man not circumstances. It therefore deals with the particular and specific rather than the collective and statistical. Narrative is a mode of historical writing, but it is a mode which also affects and is affected by the content and the method.[6]

In addition to using a nineteenth-century rather than a twentieth-century model of narrative, Stone oversimplified the relationship between narratives and the structuring of the past as history with respect to four factors: (1) the role narratives play in general in historical practice and the resulting similarity as well as difference between narrative and nonnarrative histories; (2) the relation between history and fiction—or the connection between the structure of interpretation and the structure of factuality—in a specific text and in history in general; (3) the difference between argument and narrative in historical practice and their relationship to narrative and nonnarrative histories; and (4) the relationship between structures of expression and structures of content in patterning historical discourse.

The Paradigm of Normal History

Among the current challenges to professional historians, few seem more important—and less heeded—than those advanced by literary and rhetorical theorists. Why many historians find the implications of literary and rhetorical theory so devastating becomes clearer if we follow the process by which they presume to create written history from past evidence. What must historians predicate about the past in their methodology in order to conceive of it as history in general and to represent it in what we today call *a* history? How and what can they presume to know about the past if it no longer exists? Historians answer the how by reference to the idea of contextualism and the what by reference to the notion of plenitude. In this case, the how determines the what, for the assumption of the past's plenitudinous complexity requires contextualism as its chief methodology, if we are to make sense of the methods by which historians supposedly create written history. These methods and their philosophical justification are founded upon the paradigm of what might be called "normal history."[7]

Normal historical practice depends on the use of professionally accepted methods for obtaining facts about the past from surviving evidence, or sources. But combining those facts into a coherent narrative or other form of synthesis is even more important, if a history is to be more than a mere assemblage of facts. Thus from sources presumed to be about as well as from the past or history, the normal historian creates generalizations that are assembled into a synthesis that is once again in the present called (a) history. The ambiguity of the word "history" is deliberate, for the written history is supposed to reconstruct or portray past events, behaviors, thoughts, and institutions as they once existed. The presupposition grounding normal historical practice is, therefore, that historians' works are accurate representations of an actual past, ideally as photographs are popularly thought to be of their subjects or at least as maps are of their terrain, in a more frequently used analogy.

Thus written history acts as if it were a transparent medium between the past and the reader's mind. F. R. Ankersmit argues that the common assumption of transparency by historians presumes two postulates:

> In the first place the historical text is considered "transparent" with regard to the underlying historical reality, which the text reveals for the first time. Next the historical text is seen as transparent with regard to the historian's judgment of the relevant part of the past, or, in other words, with regard to the (historiographical) intentions with which the historian wrote the text. According to the first transparency postulate, the text offers a "view through the text" of a past reality; according to the second, the text is the completely adequate vehicle for the historiographical views or intentions of the historian.[8]

Although both historians and readers would deny these postulates if raised to their consciousnesses, the central presupposition of the idealized historical enterprise still premises a transparency of medium if the exposition is to convey, or at least parallel, past actuality. Otherwise, why assume that the truthfulness or validity of a history can be tested by reference to the actual past itself—although the past is presumed to embrace far more than the sources or the remains from which it is derived?

Figure 2.1 portrays the idealized process of normal historical practice. In this diagram and the next, the solid lines designate the linkages established in actual practice, and the dotted lines represent the inferences undergirding those practices according to the normal paradigm for constructing history.

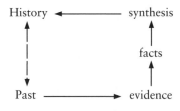

Figure 2.1

In normal historical practice, then, historical methods usually refer to the ways in which historians derive facts from sources rather than how those facts are combined into a larger expository synthesis. The standard handbooks discuss how to validate sources as evidence and how to derive reliable facts from such evidence, but they say little about how to connect those validated facts into a coherent narrative or other exposition.[9] Since historians believe that moral and political judgments shape both the selection of topics and the synthesis of facts and that historians' perspectives on basic human nature and social arrangements also influence these steps, the diagram above should be modified to reflect this two-way process. Figure 2.2 also indicates that I use the term "methodology" to mean the philosophy of methods rather than the methods themselves.

Professional historians' theorizing about the nature of their task usually ends at this point, because beyond this stage of practice understanding the past or its representation as history no longer seems very problematical. Yet this is the very point at which the philosophers and literary and rhetorical theorists begin their analyses of historical practice. Literary and rhetorical theory raises issues that force a reconsideration of the entire left side of the diagram in Figure 2.2.[10]

Such a conception of the historian's tasks still neglects the question posed earlier: what must normal historians presume about the past in order to conceive or represent it as (a) history? To consider historical sources as evidence of the past, historians predicate that they remain from past real events and behaviors and bear such a relationship to those past realities that

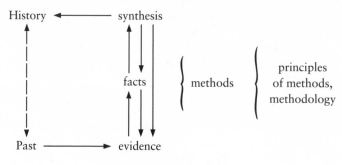

Figure 2.2

the historian can reconstruct those past events and behaviors from them. Whether documentary or other evidence stands in some sort of direct, symbolic, imitative, or other semiotic relationship to past thoughts and actions is less fundamentally important to working historians than the general proposition that surviving artifacts, no matter how numerous, are but a small part of what were once produced; they necessarily reveal only a minute portion of full living past reality.

Normal historians and scholars in other disciplines, often of quite different methodological persuasions, worry about "capturing" the plenitude of the past in its full complexity. As the American intellectual historian Thomas Haskell succinctly stated: "No paradigm can master the richness of reality."[11] Likewise, the historical sociologist Charles Tilly concedes that "it is not humanly possible to construct a coherent analysis of the history of all social relationships: the object of study is too complex, diverse, and broad."[12] Regardless of its difficulty, the French philosopher Henri-Irénée Marrou makes just this effort the chief goal of normal history: "explanation is the discovery, the comprehension, the analysis of a thousand ties which, in a possibly inextricable fashion, unite the many faces of human reality one to the other. These ties bind each phenomenon to neighboring phenomena, each state to previous ones, immediate or remote (and in like manner to their results)."[13] Each of these scholars in his own way conceives of past reality according to the postulate of plenitude.

To the extent that historians and other scholars presume the past as plenitude, they confront a paradox: how (what?) can they know of the larger past for which they have no evidence but which they nevertheless presume is basic to understanding part or all of the past as history? To the extent that they acknowledge the existence of the paradox, they must seek modes of interpretation or explanation to transcend it, whether in the writing of a monograph or a general history or in thinking about history in general. This is not the issue of selection that all historians stress so often in the choice of a topic, the way of interpretation, or even the modes of proof and the choice of evidence, important as these may be to working historians and their readers. Such selection is necessitated by the postulation of plenitude, but selectivity is not the mode of comprehending history as plenitude. Rather, the problem of reconstructing plenitude cuts to the core of how historians conceive of and interpret the past as history, because it connects how much they can know of the past to how they know of history in general.

Contextualism as a Methodology

For the historian the notion of context is a way of both comprehending past plenitude and portraying it through "thick description," to borrow a term from Clifford Geertz.[14] Contextualism is the primary mode of historical understanding, even for those who espouse other forms of exposition than narrative.[15]

So basic is the idea of context to historians' ways of looking at the past that it rarely receives explicit formulation except from philosophers and theorists. Yet historians constantly urge themselves and others to "put things into their context(s)." Classroom students and readers of histories, like neophyte historians, soon learn the meaning and wide applicability of the term. Words and sentences must be read in the context of the document, and the document as part of its community of discourse or of the ideological and belief system that gave it meaning at the time. Discourses and worldviews in turn demand the context of their cultures and times. Likewise, human activities and institutions are to be understood in relation to the larger network of behavior or social organization and structure of which they are said to be part. Social, political, religious, economic, family, philanthropic, and other institutional practices make sense only when placed in their proper social and cultural contexts. Although historians may differ among themselves about what constitutes a proper context in any given case, they do not question the basic desirability of finding one as the appropriate background for understanding past ideas, behaviors, and institutions. As we shall see, even quantitative and sociological historians see the past in essentially contextualist terms. Thus eras and nations, wars and social movements, individuals and events, and speeches and diaries must all be situated in their contexts.[16]

Historians share the notion of context with other disciplines. Like literary scholars, they seek the authorial, discursive, and cultural contexts of texts and documents. Like anthropologists, they develop the cultural and social contexts of the subjects they study. Like social scientists, they attempt to place social, economic, political, and other institutions in the network of relationships said to constitute a society or a nation. Historians cannot even claim that they alone seek to place things in the context of their times, although this claim is the supposed differentia of the discipline.[17] No greater historiographical sin exists than committing anachronism, by representing something outside the supposed context of its times.[18]

Important as the process is to them, however, historians rarely discuss what "putting things in their context(s)" involves as a practice or what the larger implications of such a practice are for the profession or its audience of students and other readers. Handbooks of historical practice presume the practice without discussing it as method. Usually only intellectual historians explicitly debate the role played by context in the interpretation of a book or document, but their arguments all too often center on issues of reductionism: How large a role did the social and cultural context play in generating a text? Should the author's invention as well as intention be explained mainly or solely by his or her social and cultural context? Does such a contextual explanation oversimplify the novelty of great ideas and prevent appreciation of a great work of literature or major feat of science for what it was?[19]

To discover the intellectual presuppositions of contextualism that are basic to historical practice one must turn to philosophers of history and other theorists. W. H. Walsh described the process of contextualization under the term "colligation":

> The historian and his reader initially confront what looks like a largely unconnected mass of material, and the historian then goes on to show that sense can be made of it by revealing certain pervasive themes or developments. In specifying what was going on at the time he both sums up individual events and tells us how to take them. Or again, he picks out what was significant in the events he relates, what is significant here being what points beyond itself and connects with other happenings as phases in a continuous process.[20]

As process, then, colligatory contextualism is always relational but need not be strongly integrative. In his book *Metahistory*, Hayden White described at some length how contextualism operates as a methodology:

> The Contextualist proceeds . . . by isolating some (indeed, any) element of the historical field as the subject of study, whether the element be as large as "the French Revolution" or as small as one day in the life of a specific person. He then proceeds to pick out the "threads" that link the event to be explained to different areas of context. The threads are identified and traced outward, into the circumambient natural and social space within which the event occurred, and both backward in time, in order to determine the "origins" of the event, and forward in time, in order to determine its "impact" and "influence" on subsequent events. This tracing operation ends at the point at which the "threads" either disappear into the context of some other "event" or "converge" to cause the occurrence of some new "event." The impulse is not to integrate all events and trends that might

be identified in the whole historical field [plenitude?], but rather to link them together in a chain of provisional and restricted characterizations of finite provinces of manifestly "significant" occurrence.[21]

Underlying this approach is the principle of historicism: what happened is described and thereby explained or interpreted in terms of when it happened and what happened around it at the same time or over time, depending upon whether synchrony or diachrony is emphasized.[22] Whether events are configured or clustered as coexisting at the same time or whether events are described as part of a process or development over time, their meaning derives from interrelationships embedded in some temporal framework. Hayden White explained well what such an approach entails:

> The informing presupposition of Contextualism is that events can be explained by being set within the "context" of their occurrence. Why they occurred as they did is to be explained by the revelation of the specific relationships they bore to other events occurring in their circumambient historical space . . . the Contextualist insists that "what happened" in the field can be accounted for by the specification of the functional interrelationships existing among the agents and agencies occupying the field at a given time.[23]

Whether or not contextualism achieves true explanation according to scientific standards, its exponents believe they establish a pattern that is more than mere temporal contiguity or randomness. Even though such loose contextualist patterns do not explain according to a strict determinist mode, they meet the explanatory criteria of normal historical practice, despite any assumption of contingency and free will. While social science historians and other advocates of a general scientific model of historical explanation may question whether contextualism explains anything well or at all, they themselves can present no better methodology for understanding the plenitude of the past that they too postulate.[24]

Once again this is not to argue whether historians do or do not abstract, generalize, select, and organize data as they contextualize, for they do. Rather, the question is how these methods and ways of understanding contribute to contextualism as the primary mode of comprehending the past as plenitude. Most historians and other scholars subscribe to contextualism as not only the basic way but the only way in the end to weave "all," or at least so many, of the facts of the past together. It is in this sense that Clifford Geertz's term "thick description" applies to normal historical practice.

Contextualism as a strategy of understanding is both relational and integrative. Through relating elements or parts to each other and thereby to some explicit or implied whole, it explains the parts and the whole simultaneously. Such explanation is presumed to be achieved when the unit of study and its context become the same or coincident. In this way contex-

tualism tries to bridge the dispersion inherent in the multiplicity of parti-
culars basic to the notion of plenitude with the coherence and integration
essential to the description and understanding of a past as a story about that
plenitude.

Thus the approach seeks, in essence, "unity in diversity" to describe and
thereby to explain and interpret the past as history.[25] Walsh presented it in
the following terms:

> The underlying assumption . . . is that different historical events can be regarded
> as going together to constitute a single process, a whole of which they are all parts
> and in which they belong together in a specially intimate way. And the first aim
> of the historian, when asked to explain some event or other, is to see it as part of
> such a process, to locate it in its context by mentioning other events with which
> it is bound up.[26]

Contextualism, then, as the preceding quotations show, postulates a holism
that is purposely left vague. Whether it employs functionalist, organicist,
systemic, or mechanistic models, whether it is called a system or merely an
assemblage of data, the method—is perspective the better word?—stresses the
interrelationships of parts and elements.

The methodological assumptions of contextualism tend to present a subject
or unit of study as unique, whether the subject is a set of events, an era, or
all of history. As the context—be it cultural, social, or other—of events,
behaviors, thoughts, and so on is enlarged, the overall pattern of meaning that
is discerned and elaborated emphasizes the nonrepetitive elements at the
expense of those that might be common. Contextualism thus stresses the
individuality of the overall network of relationships. In the end, the subject
of study and its context become the same or coincident under contextualization as both a method and a mode of understanding. The more fully coincident the network of relationships becomes with an entire culture or society,
the more peculiar or unique the overall pattern will be in relation to other
societies or cultures.[27]

Because contextualism renders the unit of study and its context unique, for
the historian using it as a method for either understanding the past as
plenitude or representing that past as history, comparative history practically
becomes an oxymoron. Most historians consider comparison and history to
be mutually exclusive. The French historian Paul Veyne, for instance, flatly
denies that history can ever be comparative, for it depends upon types, which
"are nothing but concepts."[28] The few historians who urge comparison upon
their colleagues see its usefulness as primarily heuristic in framing inquiries
and designing research. At most they support its use for testing theory, never
for generating theory. Raymond Grew, editor of the journal *Comparative
Studies in Society and History,* advocates what he calls comparisons in the
"middle range":

The term is imprecise, but obviously comparison is most enlightening when the choice of what to compare is made in terms of general and significant problems, the elements compared are clearly distinguished, and attention is paid to the intricate relationships between elements compared and particular societies in which they are located. These criteria are most likely to be met when there are models or theories that can be concretely applied, when the evidence is extensive and rooted in its historical *context* (which often means it has been generated with just these problems in view), and when the cases are delimited. Then one seeks explanations and generalizations but not universal laws.[29]

George Frederickson suggests that historians who do comparison are taking a holiday "from their normal role of historians of a single nation or cultural area."[30] Thus he distinguishes between historical sociologists and historians "squarely in the historical profession."[31] In Frederickson's view, "History . . . remains—or should remain—distinct from the more systematic social sciences in its feel for the special or unique in human experience. Producing a comparative historiography that does justice to diversity and pluralism without becoming so particularistic as to make cross-cultural reference impossible or irrelevant is a difficult task."[32] As Grew remarks,

> for many professional historians comparative study evokes the ambivalence of a good bourgeois toward the best wines: to appreciate them is a sign of good taste, but indulgence seems a little loose and wasteful. In part such hesitance reflects some of the admirable if modest qualities most widely respected and fully shared in the historical profession—caution, accuracy, unpretentiousness, and respect for the integrity of documents and for the particular.[33]

Those few historians who claim to practice comparative history often do no more than place a nation's events or period's ideas in a larger but still unique context, usually through some classificatory scheme.[34] Thus, in his well-known work *The Age of the Democratic Revolution,* Robert R. Palmer compared the various national revolutions in the latter part of the eighteenth century, but in the end, as his title in the singular indicates, he integrated them into one overall historical setting.[35]

Given that contextualism presumes and therefore produces uniqueness as its chief explanatory or interpretive mode, it also predicates that the past, or at least a part of it, when transformed into history can be comprehended as a singular, hence single, story. Although the "revival of narrative" discussion among historians oversimplifies current conceptions of narrative, Lawrence Stone correctly set forth the implications of narrativization for historical practice. To repeat the crucial sentence: "Narrative is taken to mean the organization of material into a chronologically sequential order and the focusing of the content into a single coherent story, albeit with subplots." Narratives embrace more forms and pervade more aspects of historical discourse than Stone allows, but his emphasis upon the singularity of the story holds important implications for conceiving of the past as history. As a consequence of contextualism's presuming and producing uniqueness as its chief explanatory or interpretive mode, normal historians tend to describe past ideas, activities, events, and institutions as more and more self-contained and distant from the present day as they are increasingly contextualized to their times. This distancing of the past as history through self-containment underlies the notion of anachronism. Such disjunction is especially apparent in synchronic treatments, in which the historian slices time horizontally, so to speak, in order to stress the interconnections and interdependencies existing at a certain time. Whether embracing a short span of time or a century or more, whether using the older notions of *zeitgeist* and the "climate of opinion" or the newer ones of "paradigm" or "episteme," the historian pictures a sharp break or "rupture" in continuity as the analysis freezes the action, as it were, at a moment in time.[36] Diachronic treatments, emphasizing change over time, can also make ideas and institutions more relative to our times, especially the longer ago they are said to have taken place. Dialectical analysis, for example, postulates transformative breaks between stages of society or social formations so that later or present stages are different from previous ones. Even events and activities as recent as a generation ago can be seen as quite different from those of the present if they are strongly enough contextualized to their times, as those who compare the radical 1960s to the conservative 1980s like to point out.[37]

Given this perspective, historians place things in their temporal context by presuming various degrees of historical relativism, which today depends on the allied notions of cultural and social relativism. Does historical relativism also imply moral relativism? Should the actions of the past, heinous or beneficial, be judged by the standards of their times or of all times (which must, in the end, mean our times)? Are the Holocaust under Hitler in the twentieth century and the enslavement of Africans in the eighteenth and nineteenth centuries better understood as part of their respective times? Or are some events and practices so terrible that they are wrong for any (and all) time?

The Multiple Roles of Narrativization

Contextualism and narrativization are two sides of the same historiographical coin. Normal history, as a consequence of its contextualist search for unity in diversity, presupposes narrative as its main way of describing the past. Conversely, in normal historical practice contextualism operationalizes the narrativization of the past as history. To context as plenitude and method we must therefore add the ideas of narrative as product and of narrativization as its process if we are to understand what historians must presuppose about the past in order to conceive of it as history.[38]

Although scholars postulate that narrative is cross-cultural and transhistorical, they disagree about the exact nature of narrative and narration.[39] At its heart is some sense of story.[40] A story presents a sequence of events or actions, but just as a chronology is not a history, so a story is not just one random thing after another but rather one thing because of another.[41] Either one thing follows after another in sequence because they in a sense cause each other, or several things work together to bring about a situation or condition without necessarily "causing" one another in a strict sense.[42] Whether or how historical narrative explains is a controversial topic,[43] but a one-thing-after-another sequence is customarily labeled an "annal" or a "chronicle," while a one-thing-because-of-another sequence is termed a proper "history."[44] The author or narrator connects the events and actions of the story through a plot, and the actions and events form a plot through a causal network of narration.[45] Narrative, in short, constructs a context by connecting what seems unrelated into a story.[46]

Just how narrative should be conceived as a form or logic in general or in historical discourse in particular is less important to my argument at the moment than considering in which phases of historical practice the normal historian utilizes narrative thinking. Historians apply plotting and narrative logic (no matter how defined) not only to their synthetic expository efforts but also, I would argue, following the reasoning of Louis Mink, to the past itself conceived as history.[47] Postulating the past as a complex but ultimately combined or unified flow of events organized narratively allows normal historians to presume that their sources—as created by a past so conceived—enable them to "reconstruct" the story of that past according to some narrative structure. Historical methods can operate only if historians conceive of contextual plenitude as a continuum of structured events organized according to the same narrative logic as they employ in their own synthetic expositions, which in turn supposedly represent the past as homologously structured. Hence the importance of the argument over whether or not people in the past conceived of their activities according to narrative forms and acted correspondingly.[48] Simon Schama, for one, sees the correlation between life as narrativized by those living it and history as narrativized by historians as fundamental to any historical practice.[49]

Modern historical practice makes sense only if historians predicate that the living past as contextual plenitude, or any part of it, can be comprehended as a unified—or at least a combined—flow of events that in turn can be organized into some kind of unified exposition or story. Once again, the exposition as story and the flow of actual past events are presumed to be maplike or at least homologous. Whether the past is actually structured as we conceive narrative or only our understanding is structured in this manner, we can see through a simple diagram (Figure 2.3) how such predication of narrative structure affects historical practice and methodology. (In this and succeeding diagrams, unlike in the previous two, the solid lines designate what I take to be empirically based in normal historical practice and the dotted lines represent connections made through presupposition.)

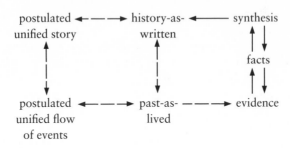

Figure 2.3

From the diagram we can see that normal historical practice uses narrative structuring in two ways to transform the past into history. First, the paradigm of normal history presumes that there existed a "whole" or "total" past that can be understood and constituted as history, even if only in the mind of a God or his secularized successor, an Omniscient Historian, according to narrative logic in some form. Second, each partial version of history can be organized according to the same logic both as a synthesis of factuality and as the actual past it supposedly resembles. If we recall Stone's definition of narrative and Walsh's description of colligation, we see that they apply to both the partial and "total" versions of history. Only by predicating that the plenitude and context of the past considered as history are comprehended from the viewpoint of a third person, an omniscient, or at least synoptic, narrator, can normal history practice be understood: first as the partial histories historians produce and, second, as the whole or total historical context of which they are said to be part.[50]

To suggest this multiple application of narrative organization to the postulated actual past as larger whole and smaller parts and to the representations of those pasts as histories, I would add the notions of the "Great Story" and the "Great Past." The Great Story, or what others might call the "metastory" or the "metatext," applies both to the larger context of the partial histories and to the whole past conceived as history that justifies the synthetic expositions of normal historians. The "Great Past" (or what others might term the "metapast," "Ur-text," or "metasource") narrativizes the source material as evidence for all of the past as history.[51] Figure 2.4 shows the relationship among these concepts.

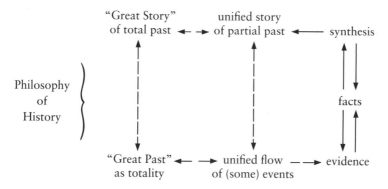

Figure 2.4

The left side of this diagram, designated the philosophy of history, indicates, first, that the Great Story was the province of classic, or older, philosophy of history and, second, that the presuppositions of historical practice are the subject of recent analytical philosophy of history in Anglo-American practice as well as in the metahistory of the poststructuralist enterprise.

As the diagram makes clear, the Great Story can mean either the larger (hi)story presumed in a partial history or the past itself conceived as (a) history. (The Great Past would also have two meanings correspondingly.) In terms of my argument about the role of narrative in traditional historical practice, the Great Story need not be any well-known "master interpretive code," "grand governing narrative," or metanarrative, because it can be organized according to a scheme different from any of the classic or more recent metanarratives. Hence I do not intend my term "Great Story" to be merely a translation of *meta-récit,* or "metanarrative," although it, too, is always constructed in some way to give meaning as well as context to a history.[52] Although the Great Story need not be equivalent to any one metanarrative, all metanarratives are Great Stories. As a consequence, one can speak of *a* Great Story in addition to *the* Great Story.

Thus the notion of the, or a, Great Story represents narrativization of both larger and smaller portions of the partial or greater pasts, because it designates the "larger context" of the partial and larger histories. Thus a, or the, Great Story can be the explicit or presumed larger contextual (hi)story behind the biography of a life, the history of a specific place or region, or the account of a year or a decade. On a broader scale a, or the, Great Story can depict the rise and spread of capitalism or nationalism or imperialism across continents and centuries. The notion of a or the Great Story also embraces the macro-processes and grand transformations that historical sociologists see as shaping the modern world.

The most thrilling Great Stories are those that seem to make sense of the grand sweep of history and illuminate human destiny itself. Such metanarratives as the Spenglerian decline of Western civilization or the stages of class struggle in history according to Marxian dialectics test the very limits of what is proper history according to normal historical practice, for these Great Stories seem to "fit" poorly the Great Past postulated by the normal historical paradigm.[53] Speculation about the ultimate meaning of History as a totality stands outside the pale of professional discourse. It is considered the subject matter of old-fashioned philosophy of history and is relegated in current historical practice to that hell enjoyed only by the likes of Hegel and Spengler. Although historians certainly point out the meaning of the events and actions they cover in their books and articles, they plead agnosticism and maybe atheism on the larger meaning of History itself considered as an entirety. At best such misbegotten philosophical musings are studied as intellectual history to exemplify the quaint worldviews of past persons and eras. Nevertheless, historians do convey the meaning of their specific histories explicitly through their contextualization or implicitly through a Great Story. Even a denial of meaning to the course of history is, of course, a philosophy about the meaning of history.[54]

Great Stories and the Search for a Larger Context

Great Stories function as the larger or largest context for a normal history in at least three ways. First, a Great Story provides a device for embedding partial (hi)stories in their larger context in order to show their significance or lessons or meaning. Second, a Great Story likewise offers a—really, *the*—larger context, and framing device, for an overall approach to a national history (so beloved of the profession that its academic organization is ordered accordingly). Third, the presumption of the singularity of a Great Story as context ultimately distinguishes the province of normal history proper from either comparative history or historical sociology. How a Great Story serves these functions can be shown best through examples.

That historians assume in practice a Great Story (and therefore a Great Past also) as the larger or largest context of their subject matter is poignantly demonstrated in the quest of American historians for a synthetic principle to tie the United States experience together. According to their story of their doing history, such a synthetic principle was once found in the conflict between haves and have-nots for control of the government and economy. When the have-nots won, democracy increased. When the haves prevailed, aristocracy flourished in the period before the Andrew Jackson presidency, and plutocracy overpowered the good and decent in the subsequent eras. The struggle for control provided the plot, the central subject, and the political meaning of the story. Such a progressive tale of middle-class morality found its supreme and exemplary expression in the two volumes of *The Rise of American Civilization*, by Charles and Mary Beard, published in 1927.[55] The so-called Consensus history after the Second World War, which emphasized the shared values throughout history of all groups in American society, repudiated the dramatic plot of conflict unifying the earlier so-called Progressive history by the Beards and others.[56] Social scientific and social history, which stressed the quantification of variables and the application of social science theories, fragmented the central subject by focusing on statistical groupings in U.S. society and presented at best a skewed sampling of past American experience.[57] Recent attention to race, gender, and ethnicity as the principle factors influencing American history only further fragmented the central subject and the unity of the narrative.[58]

In light of this pluralization of subject and loss of plot, Thomas Bender seeks a unified focus and perhaps a central subject in the competition and conflict of various groups in the creation of a public culture at a time and over time. He aims to use the scholarship of recent decades on the diversity and disunity of the American experience to reveal "a public realm that is not given but is, rather, a product of historical processes, one that is made and unmade in time. The process of making and unmaking supplies a focus for new historical synthesis."[59] For him, "The key to such a synthesis is an understanding of difference in America that is relational, that does not assume a discontinuity in social and individual experience."[60] Thus he hopes to make the best of the conflicts within contemporary scholarship by offering

a reconceptualization of our history that stresses the interplay of various groups, usually characterized as homogeneous, whether defined socially (for example, ethnic groups) or as private worlds (for example, the family), and the larger, heterogeneous, and contested political and cultural realm of the nation. How do the worlds of private life, the group meanings and interests of smaller social units, affect and effect the configuration of public life? How does the character and quality of relations with public life affect private life and the life of social groups? The present task is to begin establishing the relationship over time of the inter-class, multiethnic, and multicultural center, which I call public culture, and the smaller, more homogeneous *gemeinschaftlich* groups on the periphery . . . A focus on public culture and its changing connections with cultures smaller than the whole offers an image of society capacious enough to sustain a synthetic narrative.[61]

Accordingly he advises his colleagues in the profession:

Monographic studies of various groups need to be consciously oriented to the larger historical process of interaction in the formation of public culture. Rather than condemning, rejecting, or devaluing continued specialization, my aim is to suggest a reorientation in its conceptualization in the interest of a relational understanding of its parts. It is understanding parts in relation to other parts, as opposed to conferring upon them, whether by intention or through inadvertence, a false autonomy, that history becomes whole, a synthetic narrative.[62]

Despite Bender's efforts to use the current state of scholarship as the basis of his synthetic principle, scholars responding to his article rejected his vision of the contest over public culture either as too limited to capture the nature of American experience or as too unscholarly and premature.[63]

Likewise, the changing political fortunes of post-1920 Germany have elicited a succession of master narratives or Great Stories to provide the larger context needed to comprehend the continuity of that history or its rupture with the past. Although Michael Geyer and Konrad Jarausch point out the differences between German and American approaches to finding the meaning of Germany's history, they show how historians in both countries utilize a succession of Great German Stories in pursuit of the best overall interpretation of what happened. Historians in the 1980s, like those of earlier decades, continued to seek some Great Story as a single best interpretive framework.[64]

Albert Borgmann summarizes a thousand years of Western history in two paragraphs as prelude to his vision of what lies beyond the "postmodern divide." In his Great Story, colligatory terms and proper names provide shorthand clues to the substories encompassed by his master narrative.

> Schematically speaking, this essay begins by noting the three features that distinguish the Middle Ages from the modern era: local boundedness, cosmic centeredness, and divine constitution. The events we associate with Columbus, Copernicus, and Luther shattered the medieval edifice and opened up vast areas of exploration and construction. For heuristic purposes, we can think of Bacon, Descartes, and Locke as the founders of a new era, the designers of the modern project whose elements are domination of nature, the primacy of method, and the sovereignty of the individual. Technology and economy were the disciplines whereby the modern project was worked into a social era characterized by aggressive realism, methodical universalism, and an ambiguous individualism.
>
> Toward the end of this century, realism, universalism, and individualism have become the subjects of withering critiques. Although the modern project still drifts ahead as political and economic movement, it has lost its theoretical confidence and credibility. Yet the postmodern critique of modernism offers us no more than the weakest of constructive proposals: respect for nature, particularism, and communitarianism. One can detect a more concrete and consequential paradigm in the economy, a paradigm chracterized by information processing, flexible specialization, and informed cooperation.[65]

As this synopsis shows, a good Great Story not only orders the past and interprets the present but also predicts the future.

The singularity of the Great Story presumed by narrativization reinforces as it derives from the presumption of uniqueness in contextualism. Hence historians' wariness of comparative history, which seems to demand a violation of these basic premises. To the extent that comparativists share with normal historians a respect for the singularity of the Great Story, certain kinds of comparative studies seem congenial to normal historians. This is not so much a matter of whether the comparative histories employ primary or secondary sources, concrete or abstract units, or present their findings as analysis or narrative as of whether the comparative history presumes at bottom the contextual uniqueness and unified story framework that lies at the heart of normal history.[66] The more a comparative work predicates the basis of its overall synthesis in the contextual uniqueness of the partial and Great Stories, the more historians will find the study congenial (if not always useful). Thus those historical sociologists who argue for "world-time," "large-scale social processes," "great changes," "great transformation," or a similar conception essentially share with historians an ultimate commitment to plotting their history as a Great Story.[67] Perhaps one of the best-known examples of such an approach to historical sociology is Immanuel Wallerstein's notion of a "modern world-system" or "capitalist world-economy."[68] His approach to history as Great Story does not differ markedly from that of Palmer in *The Age of Democratic Revolution*, much as they might differ in political outlook and the lessons of the past for the present. Both scholars frame their studies according to a single historical setting with variations within it.

Those comparative historical sociological explorations labeled "individualizing," "universalizing," or "encompassing" under Charles Tilly's classification in his aptly titled *Big Structures, Large Processes, Huge Comparisons* or "general model builders" in Theda Skocpol's scheme in *Vision and Method in Historical Sociology* presume a unique Great Story, even if historians sometimes profess not to recognize the historical sociologists' Great Past as the same one they predicate.[69] On the other hand, those studies seeking, in Tilly's and Skocpol's terms, "variation-finding" or "causal regularity" pursue social scientific generalizations that are free of any specific historical context. Such historical sociologists as Tilly and Skocpol recognize the historicity of the social processes they expound. For them certain macroprocesses or major historical trends constrain and shape the subjects that sociologists too often try to make ahistorical and universal. For Tilly these macroprocesses include the great changes in the organization of capitalist economies and the increasing powers of the centralized state.[70] For Skocpol, they embrace "world-wide commercialization and industrialization, and the rise of national states and the expansion of European state systems to encompass the globe."[71] From this perspective of macroprocess, historians can espouse world or global history and still condemn comparative history as such through their allegiance to the singularity of the Great Story.

Today's historians and social scientists can agree on world history of the proper kind as desirable, because they cannot write and teach without some

Great Story either to understand their own times as a product of the past or to interpret the past through the lens of the present. To what extent, then, is the historic turn a (re)turn to new metanarratives about the heritage of the present? To what degree is the revival of narrative a revival of the use of Great Stories to frame the (hi)stories that contemporary historians want to tell? Although historians may be wary of Great Stories, given the profession's bias against such moral fables and their seemingly poor fit with the postulated big picture of the Great Past, it seems that they cannot do without them. Their histories need the larger or largest contexts that Great Stories provide, especially if the Great Past is conceived of as the Great(est) Context of all stories, small and Great. Great Stories give meaning to all kinds and levels of histories. Great Stories at bottom not only serve as the larger context for histories by colligating facts of (a) history but also provide the political and ethical grounding for history as text and as discursive practice. In this sense, Great Stories serve a symbolic or allegorical function in the narrativization of histories. Given the necessary function of Great Stories in historical narrativization, the postmodernist's slogan about the crisis of metanarratives resides in the dilemma between post-structuralist efforts to deconstruct all grand themes and revisionist desires to reconstruct allegorical Great Stories for ethical ends.

Recent Great Stories, like those of previous historians, contradict one another, and this incompatibility raises perplexing questions for the practice of history according to the normal paradigm. Can the plurality of Great Stories in actual practice be reconciled with the singularity of the Great Past presumed in theory? Does the notion of context, no matter how small or large, presume, even demand, one and only one Great Story in practice as well as in theory? Are the variant versions of the same subject or period equally valid, or must all variants be reconciled, that is, contextualized, by reference to a (the?) single Great Story? What criteria should historians and other scholars use to judge the value and merits of various works called history, or, more precisely, histories, if the premise of a single Great Past in its guise as *the* Great Story is challenged by postmodernist theory and multiculturalism?

CHAPTER THREE

Historical Representations and Truthfulness

GREAT Stories matter greatly to professional historians and the public alike, as conflicting approaches to the five hundredth anniversary of the historic events associated with the name of Christopher Columbus demonstrated. The debate about whether the story of what he did should be labeled a discovery, an invasion, a conquest, an encounter, an interaction, an intervention, or something else indicates the magnitude of the problem of finding the best Great Story for the history of this matter. The controversy over whether what followed in the history of the Americas should be depicted as the gift of one civilization to another or as the genocide of indigenous peoples and the enslavement of Africans signals the problem of constructing the larger context for that history. Scholars agreed no better than other persons on the difficult problems of larger context and Great Story in this matter. Facts alone did not settle the issues. Since perspectives and points of view seemed incommensurable among the proponents of various interpretations, no easy resolution or compromise existed for specifying a single Great Story portraying what Columbus did and what happened afterward.[1]

Despite—perhaps because of—the multiple interpretations so prevalent in the historical profession, its members seek principles to guide them beyond the relativism embodied in competing stories, Great and small. The question therefore remains for normal historical practice: are some interpretations better than most or all others? Although historians cannot agree on the single right or best interpretation of any given past any better than they can on the "whole" of the past they call history, they still seek criteria for limiting the profusion of narratives and arguments about any given past. What must historians postulate about the past to justify their approach to interpretation? What implications does such an approach have for the reading and writing of history today?

Interpretations and Historical Realism

Historians attempt to cope with the obvious difference between the numerous versions of the same or seemingly similar events and processes in their practice and their preference for a single (hi)story or Great Story by distinguishing between interpretations of history and History itself.[2] The distinction serves the same methodological purpose in historical practice as those between *parole* and *langue* in linguistics and between "discourse" and "story" in narratology: to divide the changing in practice (the first term) from the unchanging in theory (the second term) in order to render the complexity of each field comprehensible.[3] Historians recognize that interpretations arise in normal practice, but they attribute such differences to historical representation and not to history itself. Although there are multiple interpretations, there is only one (hi)story; although there are plural partial histories, there is only one Great Story as their larger context because there is only one Great Past.[4] Therefore, to write as if historical practice were naught but interpretations denies a fundamental postulate of the guild. As Jerald Combs, who devoted an entire book to two centuries of changing interpretations in American diplomatic history, warned his readers in the preface: "One further caution. A historiography such as this one inevitably will be somewhat misleading by emphasizing the theses of books rather than factual content. This may drive the neophyte to the conclusion that history is indeed only fiction temporarily agreed upon. Or it may inspire another round of the 'graduate school game'—since one can never know the truth about the past, memorize historical theses rather than historical data." The author goes on to advise his readers:

> It would be unfortunate if this book encouraged such aberrations. I believe that the information historians provide is more important than the theses they propound. There is much basic information that all historians agree upon. In addition, most historians have admitted the tentativeness of their interpretations and have sought to moderate the oversimplified assertions of the more popular accounts of politicians and journalists or those of their more polemical colleagues in the historical profession. If overall they have reinforced and legitimized their generation's perceptions of American diplomacy, they have also urged caution, emphasized complexities, and provided opposing views. Above all, in their extensive factual accounts they have presented material from which readers could draw their own inferences to refute the authors themselves. In the end, that is the historian's greatest contribution.[5]

Combs expresses the ambivalence that all normal historians feel about a word they use all the time: interpretation. All historians must interpret their materials in the quest for historical synthesis, yet all interpretations are secondary to the true end of history: factual knowledge. As Peter Novick summarizes some of the tenets of "objectivism" underlying the profession's approach to history:

> Historical facts are seen as prior to and independent of interpretation: the value of an interpretation is judged by how well it accounts for the facts; if contradicted by the facts, it must be abandoned. Truth is one, not perspectival. Whatever patterns exist in history are "found," not "made." Though successive generations of scholars might, as their perspectives shifted, attribute different significance to events in the past, the meaning of those events was unchanging.[6]

The Great Story, like the Great Past, is singular by methodological necessity. It is also timeless in the sense that its inscription as History does not alter once the Past is past, no matter what histories are written. Thus do historians exempt their paradigmatic assumptions from the working premise of change presumed so basic to their applied practice.[7]

As a direct corollary of this presumption that the singular Great Story follows from the unique Great Past, normal historians try to reconcile variant interpretations by *reference* to facts rather than by arguments over the nature of narratives as such. Dominick LaCapra calls this the "documentary model" of historical knowledge. He outlines its premises:

> In the documentary model, the basis of research is "hard" fact derived from the critical sifting of sources, and the purpose of historiography is either to furnish narrative accounts and "thick descriptions" of documented facts or to submit the historical record to analytic procedures of hypothesis-formation, testing, and explanation. The historical imagination is limited to plausibly filling gaps in the record, and "throwing new light" on a phenomenon requires the discovery of hitherto unknown information. It does not mean seeing the phenomenon differently or transforming our understanding of it through reinterpretation. Indeed all sources tend to be treated in narrowly documentary terms, that is, in terms of factual and referential propositions that may be derived from them to provide information about specific times and places.[8]

Historians must presume in practice that the factuality of a partial past and the Great Past possesses some sort of coercive reality in their synthetic expositions. Thus, when one young critic accused Natalie Zemon Davis of interpretive license in *The Return of Martin Guerre,* he appealed to the "sovereignty of the sources, the tribunal of the documents," to set her straight.[9]

As a grounding for these beliefs, normal historians subscribe to a philosophy of realism as fundamental to their practice. As Harry Ritter puts it, realism for the historian is "the belief that historical inquiry refers to a 'real' past that was once, but is no longer, present, and that written histories are valid to the extent that they accurately correspond to this real past."[10] Peter Novick believes that such realism is a basic tenet of the "objectivism" he sees underlying professional practice: "The assumptions on which it rests include a commitment to the reality of the past, and to truth as correspondence to that reality; a sharp separation between knower and known, between fact and value, and above all, between history and fiction."[11] And, he might add, between conceptual framework and finding. Peter Gay expressed this credo with great gusto:

> The objects of the historian's inquiry are precisely that, objects, out there in a real and single past. Historical controversy in no way compromises their ontological integrity. The tree in the woods of the past fell in only one way, no matter how fragmentary or contradictory the reports of its fall, no matter whether there are no historians, one historian, or several contentious historians in its future to record and debate it.[12]

In this view, actuality is the foundation of historical knowledge; factuality is the goal of historical practice. Both are the basis as well as the measure of historical synthesis, no matter what form that synthesis takes. Moreover, that reality is in the end a single Great Past. Although Gay maintains that interpretations can complement each other, in proper historical practice they can never contradict each other: "For the historian, an interpretation is a general explanation of events, nearly always providing a hierarchy of causes. To the extent that it is correct, any conflicting interpretation is false."[13] Thus he regrets subtitling his magisterial work, *The Enlightenment*, "An Interpretation" rather than "The Interpretation," as he first intended.[14]

Two politically and morally important examples show the hold the notion of a single right or best interpretation and its factual decidability has over the profession and its public. One example comes from U.S. legal history and its implications for interpreting the Constitution today and goes under the name "original intent." This debate is framed in terms of whether the authorial intent of the founding fathers represents the single best way of interpreting the U.S. Constitution. Not only do the supporters of this approach argue that such a construal of intention is the best way of interpreting the Constitution legally today as well as historically in the past, but also they presume that one can know the (collective) intentions of the founding fathers unambiguously. Thus what are legal and normative questions for lawyers present a major problem of interpretation for historians about the very construction of history itself. Both "originalists" and those who challenge them construct present-day interpretive texts as they discuss the relevant text or texts of the past. Although the two sides may differ in their interpretations, both argue that their own texts best represent what the founding fathers thought or what should be thought about the whole matter. They also point to the "facts" to support their contentions, even though they differ over what constitutes a fact according to their interpretation and its larger Great Story. Thus even those who admit that one cannot document with certainty what the founding fathers intended or even whether one should or can aggregate the differing opinions of those who left an evidential record assert the superiority of their interpretation as the single right one.[15]

Another important example of historians' commitment to the quest for a single best interpretation is the debate about how to textualize the enormity of the Holocaust perpetrated by the Nazis' "Final Solution." In some ways this quest for the definitive singularity of the Holocaust resembles the preceding debate over "original intent," for it too searches to comprehend the causes and the results of the Holocaust through an examination of the participants' intentions and attitudes as perpetrators and as victims. Still other quests for interpretive singularity center on finding the proper, that is, the best, Great Story as the context of the events. Was the Holocaust the inevitable result, that is the natural evolution of German history itself, and thus attributable to some special quality of being German? Or was it part of the development of European society or of capitalism? Was it the failure of the Enlightenment or even of civilization and humanity itself? As these searches for the best Great Story of the Holocaust—whether focused on intentions or on Germanness, Europeanness, and humanness—demonstrate, the acknowledged facts are not enough to guarantee a single best interpretation. To admit such interpretive diversity, however, is not to endorse the so-called revisionist denial of the acknowledged horrible facts. Rather, it shows that these facts can be admitted and still not provide a definitive (con)textualization of the set of events colligated by the term. The very colligatory term of "Holocaust" is already a complex interpretation itself and suggests a moral judgment as well as a Great Story. Since a Great Story is the context of ultimate resort in historicization, the very premise of its singularity, and thus its superiority, supposedly supports one interpretive version against all others in the professional disputes among historians.[16]

To normal historians, then, a plurality of interpretations in practice never implies a plurality of (hi)stories, let alone a plurality of pasts. Multiple Great Stories and Great Pasts are inconceivable according to normal methodological assumptions. Many historians therefore argue that the successive interpretations or versions of history in the profession approach truth about the past asymptotically.[17] But how can they know exactly what or where that truth is if the community of responsible scholars cannot agree? How do they recognize that truth in practice if multiple versions exist? Since the Great Story is nothing but a paradigmatic postulation of normal historical practice, what (or who) decides the validity of one version over another?[18] Other historians would use the analogy of the proverbial blind sages feeling an elephant to describe their approach to the past. Although the six blind sages mistook the various parts of the elephant for the whole elephant, at least they were all feeling the same elephant. Such a synecdochal maneuver, however, predicates what historians cannot know from their practice: that all historians study the same past.[19] Does the measurement against the Great Past or Ur-text decide between the variants or interpretations? But once again, the Great Past seems as much a paradigmatic presupposition as its synthetic equivalent, the Great Story. If past historical reality is reduced to the evidence persisting into the present about it, then what limits the interpretive stories and arguments that might be derived from these remains in the present?

The Fallacy of a Single Right or Best Interpretation

That two or more stories can be told about the same set of events deeply disturbs even sophisticated normal historians. William Cronon, for example, in a recent article on the role of narrative in historical writing expresses perplexity (and maybe some exasperation) that two books about the Dust Bowl in the 1930s United States with nearly identical titles "dealt with virtually the same subject, had researched many of the same documents, and agreed on most of their facts, and yet their conclusions could hardly be more different." Moreover, he notes, "Although both narrate the same broad series of events with an essentially similar cast of characters, they tell two entirely different stories." For Cronon such a postmodernist possibility, as he labels it, raises the question of whether "the past is infinitely malleable, thereby apparently undermining the entire historical project." His article describes his personal "struggle to accommodate the lessons of critical [narrative] theory without giving in to relativism."[20]

In an effort to sort out the practical from the theoretical problems, as Cronon categorizes this division, he offers a short chronological listing of the major events that any history of the Great Plains since the time of Columbus must include.[21] The prospect of multiple stories, Great and small in our terms, leaves Cronon quite dissatisfied. As he laments,

> This vision of history as an endless struggle among competing narratives and values may not seem very reassuring. How, for instance, are we to choose among the infinite stories that our different values seem capable of generating? . . . The uneasiness that many historians feel in confronting the postmodernist challenge comes down to this basic concern, which potentially seems to shake the very foundations of our enterprise. If our choice of narratives reflects only our power to impose a preferred vision of reality on a past that cannot resist us, then what is left of history?[22]

To overcome what they consider a fundamental challenge to the profession, historians seek criteria for distinguishing between better and poorer interpretations, better and poorer histories. Cronon lists such customary "rules of thumb" as greater depth ("the narrative that explains more, that is richer in its suggestions about past causes, meanings, and ambiguities, is the better history"), greater breadth ("preferring the historical narrative that accommodates the largest number of relevant details without contradicting any relevant facts"), elegance ("a simple story well told may reveal far more about a past world than a complicated text that never finds its own center"), inclusiveness ("a history is better, surely, when it incorporates many different voices and events to reflect the diversity of past human experiences"), and coherence (the components of a good history should "be tightly enough linked that it contains no unnecessary parts or extraneous details"). Moreover, good histories hold dialogue with the full historiographic tradition leading to them while simultaneously enlarging the boundaries of that tradition. They might even offer a subtle and original reading of primary sources and surprise their readers with new perspectives and interpretations. Good histories should even provide a good read.[23]

Excellent as these criteria may be, they are open, as Cronon recognizes, to the same sorts of value judgments (and I would add cognitive dilemmas) that generated the multiple narratives in the first place. Therefore, as he confesses, these criteria still leave one "rudderless in an endless sea of stories." Nevertheless, despite the difficulties he has experienced personally in locating a safe harbor (his metaphor) in this postmodern sea of narrative relativism, he states: "My goal throughout has been to acknowledge the immense power of narrative while still defending the past . . . as real . . . to which our storytelling must somehow conform lest it cease being history altogether."[24] In his yearning for the self-evident factual reality of the past to steer beyond the shoals of interpretive relativism, Cronon reveals that he shares basic assumptions with other normal historians.

In his own attempt to specify the criteria that would limit the proliferation of stories and establish one or some superior to others, Cronon first resorts to historians' customary obsession with "the facts." Thus he repeats the historian's first commandment: "Good history does not knowingly lie" by contravening accepted facts about the past. Likewise, good history must not contradict standard models of nature, human or physical, and behavior, social or individual, in ascribing cause, effect, or contingency.[25] In historical narratives witches can no more violate the laws of physics than abundant rainfall occurs in arid zones; gods can no more intervene in the outcome of wars than human beings can be assumed unequal by race according to standard scholarly models today. Last, and most important, the accuracy, the fairness, the truthfulness, the inclusiveness, and even the factuality of historical narratives are constrained by criticism from the community of historians and the public. Such public exposure limits the variety of acceptable narratives.[26]

Cronon's provocative and personal intellectual journey raises more questions than it answers. Will the criteria he adduces curtail the proliferation of narratives and interpretations any better than those he presents as common to the profession as historiographic rules of thumb? What of the traditional historians' resort to the facts? Although a single fact can "disprove" an interpretation, no number of facts can definitively "prove" one. As Cronon admits, narratives thus create their facts as much as facts create the narrative. What, then, is the relationship between facts, interpretations, and narratives in historical practice?

If public exposure limits the variety of stories historians tell, it also creates that variety. To the extent that perspectives and points of view appear incommensurable among (and to) communities of scholars, basic interpretations, as historians call multiple stories, Great or small, multiply to the chagrin of the historical profession. Can these be limited by the means traditional to history or suggested by Cronon? What criteria should historians use to judge the value and merits of any one history if the premise of a single Great Story is abandoned?

Even the criterion of standard models of nature and human nature fluctuates with the times, as any number of histories of the physical and social sciences will "prove," let alone those that chronicle morals and manners. In "fact," a good deal of such historical publication goes to show just how variable morals, models, and metastories have been over time. All these histories testify to relativism more than to explanatory and narrative security. Literary scholars face the same problems of pluralism and relativism in interpreting literary works. Paul Armstrong in his book *Conflicting Readings: Variety and Validity in Interpretation* argues that literary scholars follow rules or "tests" in practice for distinguishing among and limiting the proliferation of rival readings of a literary text. The first criterion is inclusiveness. The better reading embraces the most elements of the text without any obviously false assertions about what is there. "According to the test of inclusiveness, a hypothesis becomes more secure as it demonstrates its ability to account for parts without encountering anomaly and to undergo refinements and extensions without being abandoned." The second criterion stresses intersubjective agreement on the interpretation. Can it win the assent of others as to its claims? The third test asks if the interpretation has "the power to lead to new discoveries and continued comprehension."[27]

Once again, valuable as these are in perhaps limiting the number of rival interpretations, each one alone or even together, Armstrong argues, cannot produce only one correct interpretation from among others. Although the criterion of inclusiveness eliminates bad interpretations, it does not produce a conclusive resolution among the good ones: "Different interpretive methods based on different presuppositions can pass the test of inclusiveness with equal success."[28] Similarly, the test of intersubjective assent does not reckon with the power of rhetoric or social force to achieve disciplinary and cultural consensus.[29] Does democracy in the interpretive community(ies) lead to the proliferation of interpretations among people of goodwill? Ought, furthermore, a majority vote determine the best interpretation? Even what constitute new and interesting discoveries are prone to the same problems as the preceding criteria.[30]

In the end, the quest for a single best or right interpretation denies multiple voices and viewpoints. In the contention among these voices and viewpoints for primacy, facts are never enough, because they cannot be universally, that is univocally, interpreted and accepted by all in the same way for the same purposes. Facts, from this standpoint, become ploys in the political battles for scholarly supremacy through interpretive warfare.

The Insufficiency of Facts

Although facts are essential to historical interpretations, they are not enough to prove an interpretation. Surely wrong facts or a lack of facts can undermine the validity of an interpretation, but such refutation is more difficult to achieve than historians would like to admit. Just as the American public seems reluctant to accept the facts of the assassination of President John F. Kennedy and prefers a conspiratorial interpretation of his death, so many historians do not think that inaccurate transcriptions or mistranslations of documents or even errors of fact necessarily invalidate an interpretation of the collapse of the Weimar Republic as prelude to the rise of Adolf Hitler.[31]

It is a good thing that historians know a fact when they see one in practice, for their efforts to theorize about them would suggest otherwise. Even though methods books devote many pages to authenticating evidence from the past and deriving and validating facts from the evidence, the notion of fact remains slippery and vague in the theory of doing history. The problem with historical facts, as with histories themselves, is that they are constructions and interpretations of the past.[32] Evidence is not fact until given meaning in accordance with some framework or perspective. Likewise, events are not natural entities in histories, but constructions and syntheses that exist only under description.[33]

Even to look at a series of factual sentences shows the difficulty in separating facts as referring to a past reality from interpreting that reality and ultimately describing it in conformity to some conceptual framework. All of the following thirteen sentences except the last could be found in a purportedly factual discussion of George Washington in a history book:

1. George Washington was born on February 22, 1732, in Bridges Creek, Virginia.

2. George Washington was the first president of the United States of America.

The truth of these two seemingly factual sentences can be challenged. The date of birth as given accords with the new instead of the old calendar; the actual date at the time of his birth was February 11. Since Washington was inaugurated as president only on April 30, 1789, almost two months after the new federal Constitution had gone into effect, was the president of the old Confederation Congress the first actual president of the United States under the Constitution in the interim?

3. George Washington was (one of) America's greatest president(s).

4. George Washington was a founding father of the new nation.

5. George Washington was the most important founding father of the United States.

These three sentences can be construed as factual only if the reader subscribes to the interpretive framework of their author in each case—and to the metaphor in sentences 4 and 5.

6. George Washington was over six feet tall and held himself aloof from ordinary people.

7. Because he was so tall and aloof, George Washington was a charismatic leader.

8. Every new nation needs a charismatic leader until its leadership is routinized, and George Washington provided that leadership in the infancy of the United States.

Even if the reader agrees with the characterization of Washington in sentence 6, the other two sentences depend for their acceptance as fact upon a Weberian theory of leadership applied to a newly emerging nation.[34]

9. George Washington was a plantation owner and a successful businessman.

10. George Washington was a slave owner.

11. George Washington was therefore hypocritical about the human equality asserted in the Declaration of Independence.

12. George Washington did not sign the Declaration of Independence.

13. George Washington dreamed about Abraham Lincoln emancipating the slaves and thus fulfilling the clause in the Declaration of Independence about the equality of all men.

Sentences 9 through 11 combine fact and opinion. Moreover, to describe Washington only as a plantation owner without mentioning his exploitation of African Americans "whitewashes" the father of his country and from a multicultural viewpoint conceals by omitting some of the American experience. To say that plantation owning is a business implies that such an economy was based upon capitalism rather than upon precapitalist paternalism. Either assertion rests upon a lot of theory.[35] Last, although the statement that all *men* are created equal does appear in the Declaration of Independence, how should it be understood in light of women's history or the histories of peoples of color? Does the fact that George Washington did not sign the Declaration of Independence make him less of a hypocrite about race relations? Is the sentence about the ownership of slaves the most important of all these sentences, because of the Great Story summarized in the title of Michael Goldfield's article "The Color of Politics in the United States: White Supremacy as the Main Explanation for the Peculiarities of American Politics from Colonial Times to the Present"?[36]

At the least, these dozen sentences suggest differing degrees or orders of factuality, depending upon the proportion of empirical evidence and theory or ethics. Sentence 13 must be omitted from any professional history because no documentary evidence exists for such a dream. Finally, here, we encounter squarely the role of factuality and documentary evidence in historical practice. But even this sentence can be reworded so that its generalization is rendered factual in a historical account. Although no historian could include this dream as such (unless some new documentation is found), she or he could argue that the Civil War or Abraham Lincoln constituted the fulfillment of the American Revolution or the Declaration of Independence with regard to equal rights for all men. In this example the larger generalization or "truth" appears the same even if the modes of its presentation are quite different.[37]

Despite difficulties of interpretation, all except the last of these sentences could appear as "factual" in a history book. If a dozen of these sentences could be found in a factual history, then the truth of a history is more than just counting the proportion of factual propositions to the other meanings represented in the text. To reduce a history text to a number of factual propositions about a past reality overlooks the rest of the text as a multilayered form of representation. Thus the validity of an interpretation or a text cannot be a mere matter of calculating its proportion of factual propositions. It must also be based on the nature of the narrative organization or the rhetorical exposition. Hunting for factual propositions not only masks the larger truthfulness about the past that historians say they seek; it also reduces the text to a series of sentences while neglecting its cumulative effect. Such an approach fails to look at a text as a totality whose sum is greater than its "factual" parts.[38] Only such a conclusion would seem to make sense of the many contradictory histories proposed on a subject or for a period.

If the methodology of history is both factual and interpretive, can— should—the criteria for the truthfulness of history be unitary? If history is a hybrid of understanding, then the tough question is not so much what is wrong with any given history, but what is right and how to "prove" it, how to judge not what is false but what is "true" among the competing interpretations of facts, and why. Although historians reject some interpretations or explanations as manifestly wrong on the basis of factual inaccuracy or outdated worldviews, such as a providential interpretation, more often they differ on how to derive what they see as the larger meaning of the events they isolate for study or how to present the synthesis of the facts for the best understanding of them. Hence the conflict over interpretations cannot be resolved by facts alone, much as such an easy resolution appeals to those normal historians who swear by the notion of the Great Past as a single transparent Great Story.

Would not one need as many criteria as there are parts or layers to a history text? Such traditional criteria as accuracy and truth refer not so much to the larger interpretive framing of a text as they do to some of its aspects. Thus historians presume that other historians' transcriptions of the sources are accurate, that their translations are competent, and that they do not make up the evidence they purport to use. Even many facts are agreed upon by historians. No historian would argue that George Washington rather than Abraham Lincoln was the sixteenth president of the United States. On the other hand, the surplus of meaning supplied by historians in their texts through interpretation cannot be judged by the usual theories of truth. As F. R. Ankersmit argues in *Narrative Logic,* none of the normal theories of truth—correspondence, coherence, pragmatic, or performative—works for determining the "truth" of a historical *narratio,* as he calls it, given its nature as a re-presentation and its problematical relationship to the reality it is said to represent.[39] To speak of interpretations or Great Stories as "right" or "wrong" is a summary way of assessing those qualities of comprehensiveness, persuasiveness, suggestiveness, and other criteria usually used for discussing the larger implications of a historian's text. Some interpretations are considered interesting and important even when some of the "facts" are wrong. Other interpretations are deemed unimportant even though no one disputes their factual accuracy. Conversely, many genuine facts pertaining to a set of events or a period are not necessarily relevant to a given interpretation.

Historical facts have no one-to-one relationship to historical interpretations, and vice versa. The same basic set of facts can support several points of view. On the other hand, as Ankersmit argues, a point of view, by providing a perspective from which to view the evidence, not only influences the choice of facts but, more important, provides the basis for many of them.[40] Different facts derive from the same events depending upon the historical perspectives or political interests of the interpreters.[41] Finally, facts exist on different levels of the historical text depending upon the conceptual frameworks that provide their context. Although all normal histories pretend to operate predominantly with facts specific to particular events and persons or to particular societies and times, they also create facts that rely upon such middle-range or global theories as class conflict, long-range social or economic trends, and other macrohistorical developments.[42] For these many reasons, facts do not determine an interpretation; rather, all interpretations are underdetermined, as Michael Krausz puts it.[43] Facts are necessary but not sufficient to produce a proper history, just as a Great Story is necessary to supply context but not sufficient to comprise all of a proper history.

In the end viable and important interpretations of the same set of events or the same era must be considered incommensurable if they do not complement each other. To the extent that interpretations and Great Stories about the past are contested and contestable, they are living and relevant to the present. To the degree that they are living and relevant to the present, contests over them are as much political as they are epistemological. Thus whether or not the ultimate judgment about an overall historical text as interpretive structure or Great Story should be aesthetic, based on artistic coherence, or ontological, based on factual fit, is a matter of philosophical argument and political preference. Even if one criterion is preferred over another, judgment between them cannot be resolved by the simple "truth" and well-documented facts alone, for, as argued earlier, histories are complicated layers of textuality of which the factual aspect is only one (small?) part.

Thus interpretation plays a much larger role in normal history than the profession likes to admit in its texts, reviews, classrooms, or meetings. Historians' textual creations, especially those most prominent or popular in the profession, are more structures of interpretation than the structures of factuality they purport to be. In fact, I would argue, the more prominent the book or article, the more likely the structure of interpretation substitutes for factuality. Praise in the profession reflects the professional preference for metastories that are accepted as referential, but a close reading of any well-hailed text will show its major generalizations to be more metanarrative, hence metasource, than textual evidence from the actual documentary sources it cites.

The importance of metastory is most evident in the case of interpretations relegated to the scrap heap of past historiography. Thus, because of its racism, ethnocentrism, sexism, and imperialism, among other academically disfavored ideologies, it is difficult for anyone today to take seriously Frederick Jackson Turner's claim that the American frontier was the chief determinant of the nation's destiny and history. Because Turner's work relied so heavily upon certain mythopoeic stories beloved of once dominant white Americans, his facts no longer made "sense" once the intellectual climate that validated those ideologies as facts also passed. One can also accuse currently popular interpretations of being as much dependent upon ideology and metanarrative as they are derived from the cited evidential material. For example, in Sean Wilentz' effort to find continuity in movements in the history of the American working class in New York City, he entitles one chapter "Subterranean Radicals" while admitting that he is hard pressed to locate any authentic oppositional movements in the 1840s.[44] In Wilentz' case as in Turner's, the Great Story creates the major factual generalizations presented and therefore the reading of the evidence. Even in monographs and articles purporting to be almost solely factual, a check of footnotes against their supposed evidence will quickly show how easily sources become metasources according to some preconceived metastory. The more general and more inclusive the thesis is, the greater will be the proportion of the representational over the supposedly (f)actual.

Representation and Referentiality as Interpretive Structures

So far it appears that normal historians subscribe to at least four principles of historical realism as necessary to grounding their methodology: first, the reality of the past and the assumption of its actuality lie at the foundation of any practice; second, the establishment of facts rests on an evidentiary basis provided by remains from that past; third, the nature of the expository synthesis bears some sort of correspondence to the actual past; and, fourth, that correspondence can only issue forth in a singular account because the actual past itself was unique. Even historians who generally subscribe to all four parts of this credo need not—and probably do not—think that they reproduce in their books and articles past reality as it was. That is, they do not assert that loyalty to historical realism need issue forth in mimetic or literal realism in their actual works.

This mimetic "gap" suggests another definition of historical realism as a textual form that conveys the illusion of reality by its mode of representation. Realism as a mode of representation can take different forms, such as paintings, motion pictures, novels, and histories. In each case the supposed realism of the representation varies in accordance with the conventions of the form; the imitation of reality in a painting or a motion picture is quite different in form from the appearance of reality produced in a novel or history. The old expression "A picture is worth a thousand words" implies that showing establishes a more direct connection between the representation and its subject than does telling. Picturing, like writing, however, has only a cultural or conventional relation to its subject, as the variety of artistic styles shows. Even plays and so-called documentaries that imitate life through reenactment do so by means of conventions.[45] Narrative histories, like novels, convey realism by such means as constructing characters, setting scenes, and plotting events over time.[46] Nonnarrative histories impart realism by equally conventional devices, such as the models of factual presentation and objectivity provided by the literature of the sciences, mathematics, or philosophy.[47] Like all other forms of realistic representation, historical realism tries to bridge or conceal the gap between its form and its subject—to give the illusion of reality through its form. Hence the aptness of the title of one of Hayden White's articles: "The Fictions of Factual Presentation."[48]

As textual form, then, historical realism embraces and presumes its own set of principles or assumptions parallel or additional to those listed earlier as the basis of normal historical practice. Given their foundations in social and disciplinary conventions, these can be labeled discursive or cultural historical realism. First, the realism of what is represented in a text depends upon the generally accepted worldviews of (Western) society as to what is real and what is mythical. Thus what is conceived as the real world is the conventional postulation of the professional historians' society and their own subgroup. Such postulates limit the nature of what counts as explanation, what serves as subject, and what separates imagination from fact. Second, textual historical realism presumes the conventions of the genre with regard to what constitutes a realistic approach to the subject matter. Although the text cannot reproduce reality, it conveys the illusion of realism according to the "social contract" between historians and their readers. The basis of that contract is modeled on the realistic novels of earlier times or the scientific models of today. Third, textual realism objectifies the past so as to make readers believe that the text does not intrude between their apprehension of the past and the past itself. Although the readers of a history, especially as argument but also as story, are always aware of the text as the representational intermediary, even the most technical monograph presents its case as if its readers were considering the past for itself as opposed to reading a text for itself. Fourth, historical realism in a text represents the past as objectively understandable in the same way for all its readers regardless of their gender, class, ethnicity, generation, or other social location or cultural orientation. Hence, normal historical realism naturalizes the conventions of textual realism to present the past as an autonomous world that can be considered from the viewpoint of whoever creates it as history. In all these ways, discursive or textual historical realism presents what is abstract in practice as if it were concrete reality and out there rather than in the text.[49]

To the extent that a doctrine of realism presumes social convention, then mimesis is a discursive, or social, process. The Canadian historian Ruth Roach Pierson, summarizing the principles of realism in historical practice, frames the problem thus:

> Historians tend to operate on two such collective hunches, one ontological, that there is a reality out there in the past, and the second epistemological, that that reality is knowable, albeit imperfectly and incompletely. In other words, while few historians in the twentieth century would claim that it is possible to know precisely *"wie es eigentlich gewesen"* (how it really was), most would maintain we can establish *dass es gewesen ist* (that it really was). Historians on the whole are still "locked within" what [the French feminist theorist] Michèle Barrett would call a very traditional philosophical framework that "presupposes a somewhat optimistic confidence in empirical method and ontological reality."[50]

How many of the various postulates of historical realism are necessary to historical practice lies at the core of the dispute between literary and rhetorical theorists and normal historians. To explain how many of these working fictions generate the texts that normal historians produce is not the same as arguing how many of these postulates need to ground historical discursive practice.

The problems arising from what some scholars see as an overextended commitment to the many conflicting principles of objectivist realism in historical practice receive focus in the relationship between what we might call representation, defined as the (total) structure of interpretation as embodied in the synthesis itself, and reference, or referentiality, defined as the (total) structure of factuality presumed as the basis of that synthesis in a history. Structures of representation and referentiality encompass the many dichotomies that historians once supposed they bridged in their practice: abstraction versus concreteness, fictive invention versus factuality, art versus science, imagination versus reporting, narrative versus analysis, construction versus reconstruction.[51]

The literary job of normal historical realism is to make the structure of interpretation appear to be (the same as) the structure of factuality. The effect of such a representation is to impress the reader that the structure of interpretation is the structure of factuality, thereby reconciling and transcending the various supposed dichotomies endemic to the discipline. Rather than showing the reader how the (re)presentation is structured to *look like* total factuality, the normal historian's job is to make it appear *as though* the structure of factuality itself had determined the organizational structure of her or his account. Such a fusion of representation and referentiality is meant to convey the illusion of realism. We might christen this fusion the "referential illusion," after Roland Barthes' explanation of what he called the "reality effect."[52] Barthes quoted the program for writing history proposed by the French historian Louis-Adolphe Thiers as his example of the referential illusion: "To be simply true, to be as things themselves are, to be nothing more than by them, like them, as much as them." The rhetorical device of presenting an abundance of seemingly surplus facts with little apparent organization or relevance to the main exposition only enhances this realistic effect, making the description appear to be a transcription of what really was.

By supposedly separating representation from factuality in their syntheses, historians hope to gain the authority to reconcile variant interpretations of partial and Great Stories by reference to the past itself rather than by the nature of their representations. On the other hand, by presuming the separation of representation from referentiality, they can make factuality the seeming test of the validity as well as the basis of their singular syntheses. Thus the task of the historian is to make the structure of factuality appear to be its own organizational structure. Historians seek to conceal—or at least to suppress—how their representations are structured to look like total factuality as opposed to what they manifestly are: rhetorical representations. By supposedly substituting the structure of reference for that of representation, historians hope to make their text appear transparent to the reality they purport only to describe.

According to my argument so far, history is distinguished from the past in normal disciplinary practice inasmuch as historians divide representation from referentiality in order to make factuality the supposed test as well as the supposed basis of synthetic exposition. Figure 3.1 shows the implications of such a presupposition. The diagram indicates the general relationship between representation and referentiality, basic to normal historical practice, by showing their connection to narrative and factuality. In sum, it links methods and history-as-written with the postulated unified stories through synthesis as historical construction and as narrative. Representation, then, concerns both the mode of presentation as embraced in that linkage and the nature of what that mode of presentation covers in the whole process of doing normal history. Representation, as the upper half of Figure 3.1 indicates, embraces both the synthesis produced and the way it is understood as "history." The diagram also connects methods and pasts, partial and Great, as sources through evidence, as historical reconstruction, and as (f)actuality. Referentiality designates the mode of understanding presumed by the (supposed) recourse to (f)actuality and supposedly achieved through historical reconstruction. Referentiality, as the lower half of Figure 3.1 exhibits, encompasses both the process of creating facts from evidence and the methodological presuppositions about the past requisite to the process.

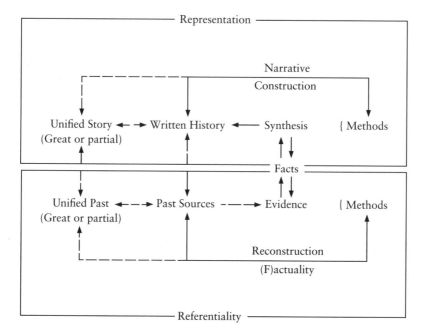

Figure 3.1

As Figure 3.1 shows, the normal historical paradigm connects representation and referentiality through the transition from the derivation or creation
of facts from evidence to the synthesis of those facts into an exposition. Hence
the statements so customary in the profession that history is both science and
art, both a reconstruction and a construction. The two realms are postulated
as connected but separated so that produced history can claim to be both
empirical and factual but also literary in its larger sense—factual because of
reference to (f)actuality, literary because of its synthetic (re)presentation of
the partial and Great Stories.

In the end, reference is only part of representation in a historian's text. To
judge a history solely, or even primarily, on the basis of its factuality is to
ignore the larger tasks of historical representation. Professional reviewing,
according to the normal history paradigm, usually neglects how a text goes
about masking the representational as referential.

The Role of Meta-Understanding

Contemporary literary and rhetorical theory questions specifically the strict
separation of representation and construction from referentiality and reconstruction and, in doing so, challenges the basic paradigm of normal historical
practice.[53] The core question that poses all the problems is quite simple: Just
what is the referent for the word "history"? It cannot be the past as such,
because that is absent by definition. If words, according to linguistic analysts,
are signs or signifiers that denote subjects in their stead, then "history"
designates a doubly absent subject. Normal history exists as a practice precisely because of the effort needed to imagine (predicate) in the present a past
presumed to have once existed. Because the past is gone, no one can point to
it in the same way that one can point to a horse and tree (or even a picture
of them) as the objects to which the words "horse" and "tree" refer.[54] As the
famed Dutch historian Johan Huizinga pointed out long ago, there is really
no *es*, "it," in Leopold von Ranke's famous formulation of the historian's
goal: *wie es eigentlich gewesen*, "as it really was."[55] Historians can point, at
best, to actual remains that supposedly come to us from the past as the
sources of the evidence they use for their historical reconstructions. Interpretation prefigures both remains and evidence and enables their use in historical
practice. Remains need to be interpreted in the present just as they were
themselves interpretations in the past. Moreover, according to the notion of
plenitude in the paradigm of normal history, these sources are used to create
pasts, whether partial or Great, that are larger than (what is inferred from)
the sources themselves. Those pasts, however, depend upon still another
predication or construction as observed by those interested in the poetics of
historical practice.[56]

The only referent that can be found for "history" in the eyes of such critics and theorists is the intertextuality that results from the reading of the sources combined with (and guided by) the readings of other historians of those same or other sources as synthesized in their expositions. "History," in the eyes of these critics, refers in actual practice only to other "histories." Thus they fail to see much, if anything, in the distinction drawn by normal historians between fact and fiction, for factual reconstruction is really nothing but construction according to the working "fictions" of normal historical practice, which in turn are the premises of historical realism and, far too often, even a naive objectivist realism that confuses the conventions of mimetic realistic representation with the knowing and telling of the past as it was.

As a result of such an approach to historical productions and practices, much, if not all, of what normal history presents as factuality becomes subsumed under the synthetic side of historical practice and therefore open to question as to just what it does represent. In terms of Figure 3.1, representation embraces almost the entire process of doing history, with referentiality referring to, at best, the actual documentary record or other remains in the present presumed to come from a past postulated as passed. In contrast to normal history, according to this view, most (all?) of what is presented as (f)actuality is a special coding of the historians' synthetic expository texts, designed to conceal their highly constructed basis. Regardless of how a historian might view the relationship between language and extralinguistic phenomena, the factuality of the overall synthesis is not of the same order as that of the individual facts constituting it. As a result, this argument about the constructed nature of the synthesis holds, I believe, independently of one's philosophy of language.[57]

That normal historical practice attempts to make its representation appear to present information as if it were a matter of simple referentiality indicates that some premises of realism as a literary form are basic to the paradigm. The illusion of realism enters historical practice to the extent that historians try to make their structure of factuality seem to be its own organizational structure and therefore conceal that it is structured by interpretation represented as (f)actuality. Once again, this is as true of analytic as of narrative expositions: in the former, art is presented as science quite literally, while in the latter supposed historical science is transformed into an art.[58]

Many contemporary scholars outside the profession who advocate such a revised theory of historical practice see history as just another mode of coding words and texts according to conventional presuppositions about representing the past as history. For many literary and other scholars today who regard realism as a cultural and not a natural category of representing things, that such coding is socially conventional also means that it is arbitrary. In the end, such beliefs about realism and the arbitrary coding of the past in the present collapse most if not all distinctions between the structures of representation and referentiality, for according to this view the latter can only be the former. The signified (the past) is naught but the signifier (history); no referent for the past itself exists outside the history texts themselves.[59] Ultimately, according to this view, the Great Past is the Great Story and nothing but the Great Story. Like the partial stories and pasts, the Great Past is coded according to the same paradigmatic presuppositions of realism. But the Great Story is no less a predication or presupposition of the normal history paradigm than the Great Past. Its referent can no more be pointed to than that of the Great Past. It exists in the mind of God or the Omniscient Historian to test and organize the variant versions of partial stories as (hi)stories. In practice, the Great Story is extrapolated from the many partial (hi)stories, and they must, in effect, be the referent for the Great Story, if it can even be said to have one apart from its own wishful predication according to the normal history paradigm.[60] In the end, the only referent for history in general is the paradigmatic presuppositions of the (a) Great Story extrapolated from the written, partial stories. Under this view of history as a mode of understanding or representation, the walls so jealously erected by historians between history as such and historiography, philosophy of history, and metahistory crack or tumble. Normal historical practice depends upon meta-understanding in all aspects of the basic process of creating a history—despite historians' rhetoric to the contrary.

Even if historians could by some means recreate the actual past in its totality, the result would not be history as we conceive it today. Historians would still need to select their themes and understandings of the past from the bewildering multiplicity of phenomena confronting them. Interpretation and representation would be as necessary if time machines existed as they are without them. As the *Harvard Guide to American History* advised decades ago: "If a time machine were available to carry the historian back through the past at will, he would confront, on stepping off the machine, the very problems of interpretation he thought he left behind."[61] Even if the total of past actuality were reconstructed for historians, it would still not be the Great Past, let alone the Great Story, without analysis and interpretation by professional historians, because the past as history cannot be predicated without interpretation according to some customary presuppositional framework, be it one Great Story or another.

Now it is possible to modify the previous diagrams to indicate the place of meta-understanding in historical practice from the viewpoint of a poetics of history. The presuppositions that ground the synthetic constructions of historical production or the coding of the past as a narrative in its most general meaning can be labeled "metastory," "metanarrative," or perhaps in some sense, "metatext." The terms "metasource" and "Ur-text" designate the presuppositions necessary to interpret sources as intertextual evidence of the

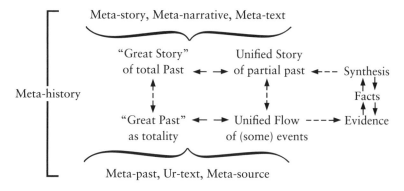

Figure 3.2

story of the past as history, and "metapast" to indicate the premises behind the narrativization of the Great as well as partial pasts. Metanarrative, in its most general sense, therefore pervades the paradigmatic presuppositions of normal history both through the connection of referentiality to representation and through the link between the partial and larger pasts. Because metahistory embraces the whole paradigm of presuppositions that create normal historical practice, it can replace the philosophy of history on the left of the diagram.

Metahistory equates metastory with metapast; that is, it collapses the presuppositional framework underlying representation with the one underlying referentiality, because the latter is considered primarily a postulation of the former in the paradigm of normal historical practice. Given this picture of the place of metahistorical premises in normal history, it is small wonder that some theorists of historical methodology see history, historiography, the philosophy of history, and metahistory as all quite interrelated, even coincident, to the chagrin of normal historians.[62]

One challenge of poetics and rhetorical analysis to history lies in the implications of this equation of representation and referentiality, of the collapse of history into metahistory. Normal history is shown to be a culturally conventional (hence politically arbitrary?) mode of coding communication as factuality by presenting the representation as if it were entirely referential and realistic. The transmutation of so much—some would charge all—of the referential side of history into the representational and narrative side of history destroys the overall factual authority claimed for historical texts.

Demystification of the historical enterprise, in this view, therefore delegitimates it as a discipline. To many normal historians such radical demystification appears to be the "end of [normal] history," because it implies that historical discourse refers to little or nothing beyond itself. After all, they would ask, of what use are maps or photographs if one cannot be sure what they represent according to the usual realistic or mimetic criteria or even if they represent anything beyond their own surface configurations? Thus by opening history construction to greater possibilities of story-telling and interpretive coding than normal history allows, metahistorians appear to have eliminated the legitimating authority of factuality for history itself according to traditional premises.[63]

History versus Fiction

To question or even to collapse the distinction between the structures of reference and representation in historical practice seems to gainsay the hallowed distinction between history and fiction. Of the traditional dichotomies said to characterize normal historical practice, none seems more vital to the truthfulness (and the true worth) of history than the distinction between fictive invention and factuality in historical practice (especially as a textualized production), hence to the legitimacy as well as the self-definition of the profession.[64] Literary and rhetorical theory does not deny the traditional difference assumed in normal historical practice between history and fiction; rather, it challenges the nature and force of that distinction in theory and in actual practice. Not all of the principles of cultural or discursive historical realism need be assumed an illusion, but the textualization of that realism is achieved mainly through mimetic illusion. The problem is not whether reality exists—let us admit it does—but rather the difficulty of knowing how a representation goes about its construction according to whose theoretical problematic.

The differences and similarities between history and fiction may be highlighted briefly through the example of historical fiction—a seeming oxymoron from the viewpoint of normal historical premises—versus a notion of fictional history.[65] The author of a fictional history could have a person of the American Revolutionary era, perhaps even George Washington or Thomas Jefferson, dream of the Civil War or Abraham Lincoln as the fulfillment of the human equality mentioned (promised?) by the Declaration of Independence. No historical novelist or historian could include such a dream unless some new documentation were found, but both could state on his or her own that the Civil War or Abraham Lincoln constituted the fulfillment of the American Revolution with regard to equal rights for (most adult white male) individuals. Supposedly no historical novelist would write that George Washington and Abraham Lincoln met and shook hands, but a fictional historical novel could. Thus traditional historical novelists, like historians, keep distinct the realms of fiction and fact in their books, even though the former might invent the chief characters of the novel but place them in as real a historical context as possible.

In recent decades many novelists have written books that cross the boundaries between history and fiction as traditionally conceived. Thus E. L. Doctorow's *Ragtime* (1976) presents both fictional characters, such as the black pianist Coalhouse Walker, and real historic persons of the era from 1906 to 1914, such as Emma Goldman and J. P. Morgan. The historical individuals meet and act together in the book even though no evidence exists that they ever did; moreover, fictional and historical persons interact with each other. Each case, from the normal historian's viewpoint, violates and distorts the historical record established by surviving sources. Doctorow and other recent novelists deliberately blur the distinction between historical fact and their imaginative invention in order to highlight both the fictionality of fact and the truthfulness of fictional representation. One traditional intellectual historian complains that *Ragtime* cannot be read "consistently either as playful fantasy or serious history. It is too historical for farce, too light-hearted for the rage of black humor, and too caricatured for history."[66] Whereas the notion of literary genre provides a clue, even a framework, for the reader on how to read and interpret a work, the blurring of genres confuses the reader about how to interpret not only the nature of the text but also its content and its import.[67]

As these examples suggest, history, historical fiction, fictional history, and fiction all exist along a spectrum ranging from supposedly pure factual representation of literal, historical truth to pure nonliteral, invented fictional representation of fantasy. No work of history conveys only literal truth through factuality, and few novels, even science fiction ones, depict only pure fantasy. Like histories, most historical novels have until recently tended toward invoking the authenticity of the time they describe, but both histories and historical novels employ devices of interpretation to flesh out the documentary and artifactual evidence. Similarly, novels, like historical novels, may evoke a time's reality to give context to their imaginary characters and plots. But even realistic novels, like fantasies, create the worlds their characters inhabit. Thus the issues of differences and similarities among these literary genres center upon both the actual existence of the characters and the reality of their larger contextual world, hence upon what readers expect from each genre.[68]

Perhaps it is the expectations of readers and their interpretive communities that are most important in assigning a text to a genre. A history is presented to its readers as a true story as opposed to, say, a novel because it alludes or refers to, and therefore implies, a world supposedly not of the author's imagining but of factual recreation. Historians refer to and try to (re)present actual events and persons in the past. They are not allowed to make up persons or events like novelists, who produce imagined or created worlds or persons and events. Realistic as a novelist's created world may seem to the reader, the novelist does not claim that these persons or events need actually have existed apart from the text in which they are found. A novel may be praised for its verisimilitude because of its simulation of reality even as its author makes up conversations, actions, places, characters, and plots.[69]

Historians, on the other hand, claim accuracy with regard to their subjects and fidelity to the past in their texts on the grounds that they do not create persons or actions as existing without some evidence from past sources, do not allude to acts or events for which they lack documentary information, and do not put words into their characters' mouths or minds without specific evidence of such (although they may imply that they know the entire climate of opinion of the times or the collective opinion of a group of people on the basis of documentation derived from only a few cases at best). When one of their guild makes up a document, as Simon Schama did in his narrative experiment, *Dead Certainties (Unwarranted Speculations),* his fellow historians castigate him severely for violating the historian's first commandment: Thou shalt not create documents and their evidence.[70]

In the end, novelists do not pretend that the worlds they depict actually existed, but historians assert that the world they recreate has happened in terms of its essential actions, persons, and so on. Thus many of the artifices of fiction, such as interior monologues and direct speech, do not seem available to historians even though, unlike most modern novelists, they seem to claim a godlike omniscience about the events and persons they describe. Whereas novelists create or construct the worlds their texts depict, historians (in their own opinion) recreate or reconstruct the worlds of the past in their texts.[71]

Literary theorists deny the grossly undifferentiated objectivist realism that historians so often use to justify their practice for a more "realistic" approach to their texts and presuppositional frameworks that give histories the normal or conventional forms they take. As Wallace Martin observes about "the most important convention of realism": "We assume that life has meaning, while admitting that meaning is produced from human points of view. The choice in life and literature is not between conventional practices and a truth and a reality lying outside them, but between different conventional practices that make meaning possible."[72] Hence the argument over the fictiveness of history must distinguish between factual references as such in histories versus the fictiveness of the total textual production through its conventions of representation. The difference between histories and novels, then, is not so much that the former deal with real things and the latter do not—novels often refer to real things and pertain to real life, as we have seen—but that history purports to tell only of real things and to refer only to a real, not imagined, world. As Martin goes on to argue about narrative fiction:

> Though the criteria used to distinguish fact from fiction have varied, the importance of the distinction has never been in doubt, and fiction has usually been the target of vituperation. But the question of whether or not an event took place can

be separated from that of narrativity as such—the ways in which events are causally and temporally connected. Is the structure of a narrative in any way dependent on the truth of the events it recounts?[73]

Although history and fiction may have different conventions of referring to the worlds they depict, they share narration and other modes of representation in doing so.[74]

The distinction must rest ultimately on the larger context given the story in each case and on the readers' expectation about the truth claims of that context.[75] Thus the difference between narrative histories and narrative fiction is not their structures of factuality as such but their overall interpretive structures and what those lead readers to presume about the narrated world represented. The difference between narrative histories and historical novels need not lie in the historical worlds they create but in the relationship between that world and the chief actors. Historical novels can be meticulous in depicting the larger context of an era while creating either the chief actors in that world or giving them undocumented thoughts and actions.[76] On the other hand, in creating a historical world historians make generalizations that go far beyond their documented evidence, whether they involve the general mental climate said to prevail, the supposedly typical behavior of the period, or the inferences drawn about the lessons of the history portrayed. Such a conclusion suggests that all the various definitions of realism need not—indeed, cannot—coexist in historical textualization, although some degree and form of realism always ground historical practice.[77]

An overextended commitment to realism by historians, however, conceals how sources become evidence in historical practice and how histories are put together as texts. Even truth claims advanced by historians demand the organization or configuration of the past as history through and by rhetorical and discursive conventions. Historians in narrative histories deploy the elements of their story just as novelists do. To that extent history and fiction share conventions of reference and representation and modes of narrativity and may be analyzed by the same methods.

In this sense, referentiality is but one mode of representation for coding the historian's communication among several other conventional approaches to claiming the reader's attention. If historians assumed with Roman Jakobson and Roland Barthes that referentiality is just one means of representation in putting together a text, just one part of a text's complex structure, then normal historical reviews, meetings, and books would take quite different forms from those they do now.[78] Thus we can talk about a historical text as a complex structure because its contents are layered and variously coded, and factuality of a positivist sort is but one layer or way of representing matters. Considering history as a complex textualization melds together the antinomies traditional to the discipline: abstraction versus concreteness, art versus science, interpretation versus empiricism, construction versus reconstruction, fiction versus factuality. But the criticism points in each dichotomous pair to quite a different emphasis from that usually assumed in the profession. Traditional historical practice insists that the second term in each pair governs the first as the basis of its textualizations, but the view of such textualization as a complex structure of layers shows that in actual practice the first creates and enables the second as the means of producing the complexity of representation that all historians would claim to be their goal.

To see the constructedness of history as a collapsing of representation and referentiality, as an integration of the structures of interpretation and fact, one has but to look at the elements of histories as textualizations. Only through the combination of interpretation with evidence can historical facts be adduced. Chronological numbers are transformed through interpretation into dates, the most "magic" of which signify their meaning in the very mention of their digits—for example, 1776, 1789, 1917, or 1968. An accumulation of incidents is converted into an event through interpretation, and events are summed through interpretation into renaissances, revolutions, and other shorthand terms for a complex of events or the christening of an era.[79] If facts are interpretive constructs, then so are the contexts of those facts in addition to the synthesis itself. Contextualization employs interpretation and rhetorical presentation to make its case or story. Even the mode of presentation, including its supposed realism, relies upon interpretive conventions. These elements all come together in the textual construction of a history and suggest that any overall view of the past as history should also be interpreted as a textual construction.

Contrasting Views of History as a Text

The differences between a normal and a metahistorical or rhetorical approach to history come down in practice to how a (the) text is viewed as the vehicle for representing the past as history. Historians and literary and rhetorical theorists alike agree that professional books and articles contain more than a series of sentences or propositions about humans and events in (purported) past reality, but just how much more is a matter of considerable dispute between the two camps. For historians and literary theorists alike, narrativity, representation, and referentiality all receive their embodiment in the text, but they approach the understanding of the text in opposite ways. Although both look at how the text constructs the world it purports to represent, historians and their readers deemphasize the actual text in favor of what it describes or talks about, that is, the world it purports to represent; rhetorical and literary theorists concentrate on how the text is constructed or how it goes about saying what it does. In essence they reverse the signifier and the signified; historians read their texts as history, literary theorists read history(ies) as text(s).

The chief way in which historians traditionally connect a text's contents to its represented world of the past, or the melding of representation and referentiality, is through the notion of an interpretation. Historians admit that interpretations shape their texts, but they do not see their texts' construction as primarily shaped by the interpretations. Thus they agree that interpretations are constructions but see them as not very arbitrary. For them, interpretations are always influenced, even demanded, by the facts themselves. Facts are presumed to be prior to interpretation. Interpretations refer to, or at least represent, not themselves but the actual past realities outside the text. Although there are plural interpretations that can be better or worse in historians' eyes, the structure of facts on which they are based is evaluated as right or wrong. Such an assumption or practice seems to reinforce the paradigmatic presupposition that representation is to be tested against some coercive, singular structure of facts.

But literary theorists and philosophers of history argue that no set of facts can go unstructured or unorganized according to some mode of representation, as historians would admit. Interpretations not only determine which facts they contain through selection and organization according to certain ways of coding or representation (which historians would also admit) but also constitute facts through collapsing a (the) structure of representation into seeming referentiality (to which historians would not agree so readily). For literary theorists, interpretations organize histories and therefore history; for historians, history ultimately organizes interpretations, because they supposedly follow how the past as history is organized.

Historians therefore see the melding of representation and referentiality as interpretations representing—designating, referring to—a real world outside the text. Whenever literary devices are used, they are incidental to the larger purposes of history as a true story. Whenever models or formal arguments are employed, they are germane to the understanding of the past as reality. On the other hand, literary and rhetorical theorists see historians as constructing that real world through the forms they use to give their texts the appearance of history. Moreover, to the extent that history is a story, ultimately it obeys the conventions of story-telling. In the eyes of literary theorists, historians' understanding of interpretation seems inadequate in two regards: it neglects the conventions governing its own construction, and it postulates an overly simple way of knowing the reality by which it purports to measure its own validity. To express this difference in terms simply of realism and factuality misrepresents by abridging the complicated process of transforming sources into facts, let alone the profound authorial intervention needed to combine those facts into a synthesis.

As a consequence historians and literary theorists view each other's understandings as not only wrong but also wrongheaded. Too many literary theorists in the eyes of normal historians seem to reverse the priority of experience to language. To historians the collapse of referentiality into representation appears to deny reality in favor of language games and halls of philosophical mirrors. By reducing all history to its vehicle, all histories to text(s), the reality of the past seems to be equated solely with the discourses that describe it. That linguistic conventions constitute a history and therefore the past looks like a form of latter-day idealism to most historians.[80] Even though normal historians accept that there are no histories without texts (or their contents), they also argue that history is more than the texts and their contents. They privilege, or give priority to, material over idealistic explanations of their practices as well as of the Great Past. They prefer what they phrase as reality over rhetoric,[81] and they eschew applying the word "fiction" to their actors' inventions whether as ideologies or as institutions.[82]

On the other hand, textualists would argue that texts contain far more than the bare facts that normal historians and their philosophical defenders assert constitute the truth of a history. Not only does any given text present less clearly factually-based sentences, but the text as a whole possesses many more meanings than the explicit factual message historians claim as the core of historical understanding.

Interpretation, Metahistory, and Truthfulness

Demystification of the role of story in normal history would seem to deny that any one single narrative or metastory need organize either the partial or Great Stories. Thus the story of the past should not be read simply as a history of progress or decline, as cycles or catastrophes, as class conflict or consensual pluralism, or even as change or continuity. No longer can any single master interpretive code be privileged over another as if one were somehow more correspondent to the (a?) "real" past than another. The denial of a single, metanarrative, Great or partial story to organize history challenges the omniscient viewpoint, probably the third-person voice, and maybe the ethnocentrism so evident for so long in history productions.[83] That the discipline is conceptualized basically by national histories and organized by national professional associations only demonstrates how deeply ethnocentrism pervades the profession and how natural it seems to the discipline as organized professionally.[84]

Demystification therefore frees the historian to tell many different kinds of stories from various viewpoints, with many voices, emplotted diversely, according to many principles of synthesis. By denying the standard presuppositions of normal history, the historian could liberate the ways of representing the past as history as well as how it is coded. For Hayden White, the demystification achieved through metahistory was intended to free historians to emplot their narratives according to choice—or will—and therefore to move beyond the modernist stance of irony.[85] If historical practice denied the premise of the single basic story as an ideal, would there be as many Great Pasts as there are Great Stories?

To many normal historians, however, such a radical demystification of the role of narrativity in historical practice appears to be the end of (normal) history. In their opinion a plurality of possible (hi)stories in theory as well as in practice certainly questions, if not eliminates, the legitimating authority of the discipline, which rested upon the search for the one and only Story as the single True account of the partial and Great Pasts. For normal historians, opening history as construction to the greater possibilities of story-telling and interpretive coding than they prefer appears to have abolished the factuality of history itself according to the traditional premise that the "best" representation of a set of facts comes in a single "right" version.

To measure truth in and of history would seem to demand an approach as flexible and diverse as history itself is said to be. If historians try to fuse or combine disparate ways of understanding into a unified mode of presentation, then should not the criteria of what is truthful vary by the mode of understanding? Thus judging the validity of (a) history as an artistic or literary production would be a different exercise from judging its validity as a scientific enterprise, but both activities would be appropriate to understanding historical discourse itself. To the extent that, say, story-telling or imaginative organization of the material produces a (specific or partial) history (rather than history as such), then aesthetic, stylistic, or other criteria might constitute the proper bases for determining the truthfulness of a history. To the extent that, say, analytical argument or social scientific explanation constitutes a history, then logical consistency and explanatory power might provide the grounds of judgment. To the extent that allegory or analogy is the lesson of a history, then the truth of a text lies not in the text but is the very text itself. Allegorical and analogical truthfulness is nothing more, and nothing less, than the text as a whole considered symbolically. Such truths must be judged by the moral, political, or other criteria appropriate to the higher hermeneutics that establish the greater or ultimate meanings of histories and history for readers.

If the practice of history is pluralistic, can the criteria for the validity or truthfulness of (a) history be unitary? If a historical synthesis is a multilayered text as presentation, then such truth criteria as coherence or correspondence (to use classic terminology), aesthetic wholeness or scientific verification (to use newer terminology), seem too dichotomous to be adequate to the task. If the criteria and therefore the nature of truthfulness multiply as Clio's tasks become more diverse, so too do the criteria and nature of what constitutes proper understanding in historical presentations as representations. In step with this diversity go varying tests of what constitutes the proper nature of categorizing what is at issue.

Thus the criteria of historical truthfulness are as varied as the nature of its textualization. Referential or empirical truth claims can be judged by correspondence to the evidence, but the degree of that correspondence is not self-evident to all alike. If the degree of correspondence can be debated, then other truth claims can also be argued in and outside the profession. Truthfulness can be measured by intertextual agreement, or how well any given history coincides with other histories. If historians usually read sources with other histories in mind, then their texts as fact and interpretation are intertextual from the beginning of their conception. The truthfulness of a history can also be judged by how well it accords with a reader's understanding and experience of how the world operates. Whose experience counts here and whence comes such experience offer grounds for argument among readers. A history's validity might be judged by how well its models of human behavior and societal workings correlate with its reader's models, but once again whose models count most? The overall validity of a history might be gauged by a reader's sense of aesthetic wholeness and order. Surely the verities of Great Stories are in the realm of allegory. Finally, the truth of (a) history will be held accountable to a reader's values and politics.[86]

In each instance, readers accept a truth claim or value in accordance with what they take the world to be like, but not all readers agree upon what the world is like. Readers' politics and ethics, like their disciplinary paradigms and belief systems, all operate as determinants of historical truthfulness, whether of a text, a Great Story, or history itself. In all cases, far more is at stake than the mere factuality of some propositions in the text. Only to the extent that documentary interpretation of the sources as evidence is at stake do the normal procedures of historical method seem to determine historical factuality, and even then their applicability is influenced by the other modes of evaluation. Disciplinary procedures always operate within a larger social context to measure the truthfulness of a history and of history itself. That truth claims operate both within a text and within the worlds of its readers provides grounds for both agreement and disagreement on the validity of histories.

Such a mixed-genre approach to the nature(s) of histories and the truths in and of them provokes uneasiness even in sophisticated practitioners of history who also theorize, as the reasoning of Lynn Hunt demonstrates. She begins by stating: "History is about telling stories. It is not a repository of facts or anecdotes because it has no ontological status whatsoever. No particular fact or anecdote that comes from the past can be presumed to have any particular truth status just because it comes from the past." On the other hand she argues: "History is 'out there' in some sense, but its thereness is not fixable . . . History is a search for truth that always eludes the historian but also informs her work, but this truth is not an objective one in the sense of a truth standing outside the practices and concerns of the historian." Hence, she goes on, "history is better defined as the ongoing tension between stories that have been told and stories that might be told. In this sense it is more useful to think of history as an ethical and political practice than as epistemology with a clear ontological status." Still, "on the other hand," she argues, "a concept of a history 'out there' does inform most historians' work and for good reason: it stands as a constant reminder that we cannot get at 'real' truth and yet that we must always try to do so." In her view, such an approach to history vindicates Nietzsche's admonition "that many eyes will tell us more than one" and that multiperspectivalism will result in a more "objective" historian and therefore a "more complete" (better?) history.[87]

Hunt concludes that histories do not have "an unproblematic ground of truth," because their stories are "a field of moral and political struggle in which we define ourselves in the present. The struggle will continue because power is control over the storytelling function." In the end, therefore, is the "truth" of (a) history or a Great Story only one according to the rules of its own interpretive community and therefore valid only as it is constituted by that subcommunity?

CHAPTER FOUR

The New Rhetoric, Poetics, and Criticism

BECAUSE of their preference for reference over representation, historians possess few and very limited ways of discussing the discursive aspects of the histories they produce. Thus the historical profession lacks any approach comparable to that of literary criticism in the evaluation and understanding of history as a text. For historians, "criticism" refers to ways of validating evidence as reliable or evaluating interpretations as factual, not to basic theories of a historian's text as a whole;[1] and a "text" is usually shorthand for a classroom textbook. Even long essay reviews in historical journals seldom analyze the nature of the text as representation as such but rather evaluate its argument or story for its factual content or interpretive implications for recasting the true story or best version of the past.[2] Analyzing histories as literary and rhetorical texts according to the ways of understanding embraced by literary and rhetorical theory, poetics, and discourse analysis today reorients historians' evaluations of one another's works, opens new areas of historical criticism, and ultimately points to the possibility of a new rhetoric and poetics of history. Indeed, a new poetics and rhetoric of history offer the opportunity for historical criticism to become an interest of everyone in the profession rather than a minor subspecialty.

From the perspective of a new historical criticism, historical truth is not so much a presentation of a text as it is the text itself in its entirety. If the truths of a history reside as much in its ways of representation as in the explicit statements contained in it, then the profession needs to revise its reading and reviewing of what it produces. If the truth of history as disciplinary practice results as much from its mode of textualization as from the nature of its professed method, then the guild needs to reorient its understanding of what it claims to demonstrate. Examining historical works as texts demands new forms of criticism in professional seminars, journals, and meetings. Criticizing history in terms of textuality requires a new appreciation of rhetoric that moves beyond simple matters of style to the very nature of textualization itself in historical discourse. Such rhetorical analysis presumes a poetics of historical discourse grounded in fundamental textual forms.

Toward Historical Criticism

Expression versus Content

Modes of historical representation, including referentiality, narrativity, and argument, find their embodiment—or concretization or objectification—in a (the) text. Thus the text is the actual vehicle of the forms that generate the content of (a) history. If (a) text designates the actual production or work of the historian, then the modes of representation, including referentiality, argument, and narrativity, are the forms of its content. The reader obtains knowledge of the author's argument or story from the actual words or structure of the text as a system of symbols or signs. Conversely, the modes of representation and the presumed story of the past are embodied in the text as forms of discourse. Story or argument and discourse exist only through the intermediary of the text, while the text exists only as the embodiment of the story or argument and discourse.

According to this view of the nature of textual construction, a critical analysis, be it rhetorical, narrative, discursive, or stylistic, usually separates expression from content—or the substance of the message from the nature of its presentation or the order of its appearance in the text. Thus what is represented is separated from how it is represented so that their relationship can be explored on the principle of signifier and signified by analogy to language systems. In this instance the text, viewed as the medium or structure of the sign system, is the signifier. The text is the signified, however, when it is considered the medium or structure of what is referred to.[3]

In all histories as productions we may separate the text as a form of discourse from the meaning or message of the discourse. For narrative histories we may borrow the customary narratological distinction between discourse and story to designate the separation of expression from content.[4] Whether or not such a distinction is justified in narrative theory, it is valuable when applied to historical narrative. For fictional narratives, the distinction presumes that authors of narratives supposedly had as their primary goal some sort of chronological story that existed prior to its narration as plot rather than the elaborated artistically integrated text they produced. For historical narratives, however, the distinction can be made between the chronology of the history that is the subject of the text and its sequence of presentation, that is, how it is arranged and plotted in the text.

A good example of this distinction is the use of flashback in narration, in which the author deliberately begins the history with a later, sometimes culminating, event or episode and then goes back in time to relate how things came to this pass. One of the great modern narrative histories begins with just such a discrepancy between chronological time and the sequence of its expository presentation. Garrett Mattingly opens *The Armada* with a spectacular event to catch the reader's interest. In the first chapter, fittingly titled "Curtain Raiser," Mattingly vividly details the execution of Mary, Queen of Scots, on February 19, 1587. In the next chapter, devoted ostensibly to the joys of the London populace the next day upon hearing of the execution, Mattingly ranges over events and ideas occurring anytime from that day to three decades previously in England and even back a century to the end of the Wars of the Roses and ascension of the Tudors to the throne. His third chapter, ostensibly limited to the following four days (February 19–22, 1587), not only speculates about how Queen Elizabeth felt in the ensuing days about the execution, but mostly examines the long-term factors that resulted in the rivalry between Catholic Spain and Protestant England. The fourth chapter purports to deal with "The End of the Gay Season, Paris, February 28–March 13, 1587," but once again ranges widely chronologically to argue the French court's interests in these English matters. Similarly the next four chapters extend chronologically far beyond the supposed successive days and weeks that serve as part of the chapter headings, describing the interests and outlooks of the Dutch, the Vatican, Spain, and Francis Drake. Only in the ninth chapter, a quarter of the way into the volume, does Mattingly restrict the events he describes to the relatively narrow time spans announced in each chapter title.[5]

Histories more ostensibly nonnarrative in their organization and presentation can also utilize a dramatic opening episode to which the rest of the book then serves as flashback. Thus *Salem Possessed: The Social Origins of Witchcraft,* by Paul Boyer and Stephen Nissenbaum, opens with "Prologue: What Happened in 1692," only the first half of which describes the events immediately before the trials, the trials themselves, and the executions that followed. Although the description of the events in Salem, Massachusetts, is not as vivid and dramatic as that in Mattingly's book, it serves the same function of catching the reader's interest. Only after a discussion of evidence in the remainder of the "Prologue," and then a chapter devoted to surveying previous perspectives and suggesting their own view, do Boyer and Nissenbaum go back chronologically to the founding of Salem. The remaining chapters range back and forth chronologically from the 1630s to near the end of the seventeenth century as they offer argument and narrative about the town's factionalism and personal disagreements that eventuated in the trials and deaths of fellow villagers.[6] Similarly, William Cronon opens his *Changes in the Land: Indians, Colonists, and the Ecology of New England* with a meditation upon Thoreau's lament for the lost wilderness and forests of an earlier New England before he himself turns to that previous time to contrast Native American and Puritan ecological practices in a series of quasi-topically organized chapters.[7]

Even these brief examples show that as in a novel or other fictional narrative, the actual sequence of events and actions as presented in a history need not follow strictly the chronology of their supposed occurrence in the past. And just as the relation between the sequence of content and that of expression in fictional texts is analyzed through the comparison of story and discourse respectively, so the analogous relationship in historical texts can be analyzed in the same way. Although drawing such a distinction between story and discourse seems particularly appropriate to narrative histories, it is also applicable to nonnarrative histories insofar as they presume both a chronology and a (hi)story of events, especially as Great Story, as context to their arguments and models.

In nonnarrative histories, the distinction between expression and content might also be designated the distinction between the rhetoric, style, or discourse of the argument and the logic or content of the argument. Many versions and aspects of historical textualization come under the general rubric of argument when they make a case in one way or another. Such a generalized use of argument thus covers a wide variety of professional histories: from the research monograph presenting new research results to the most speculative interpretive essay, from the social scientific history article or book applying quantification techniques and explicit models to its subject to the explicit or implicit argument contained in, that is, intertwined with, the story of a narrative history.

In their discussions and reviews historians customarily examine the explicit argument of a book or article under the notions of interpretation, thesis, or chief arguments. In considering the interpretation, thesis, or argument as explicit argument, however, historians are prone to neglect the expression of the argument for the content of it. Thus they stress more the explicit, formal content than the implicit assumptions that ground it, look more at the organization of the argument in terms of its formal logic than at its rhetorical devices in expressing that reasoning. Hence anglophone historians have an extensive guide to "a logic of historical thought," as David Hackett Fischer phrases it,[8] but nothing comparable to its rigor or magnitude entitled "The rhetoric of historical thought."[9]

A rhetorical approach to historical discourse as argument focuses both on the organization of a case as reasoning and proof and on the many means by which a case is presented as an argument to persuade its audience. Donald McCloskey applies a rhetorical analysis to one of the exemplars of the New Economic or Cliometric history, Robert Fogel's 1964 classic *Railroads and American Economic Growth in the Nineteenth Century: Essays in Econometric History,* which argued through counterfactual analysis that the extension of railroads across the North American continent in the nineteenth century had an insignificant impact upon U.S. economic growth (as opposed to other modes of transportation that might have been used).[10] McCloskey demonstrates through his rhetorical analysis that notwithstanding the explicit goal of econometric history to make it a science by writing according to the canons and rhetoric of science, much of that science was based upon tropes and metaphors, appeals to authority, and other devices of persuasion, even when cast as statistics, equations, and models. In what he regards as the "two most important pages" of the statement of the basic argument, he finds that Fogel used "nearly twenty classically recognized figures of speech."[11] For McCloskey, the success of this book in furthering, if not creating, a revolution in economic history depended upon Fogel's skillful uses of the standard rhetorical commonplaces or topoi in argument.

Thus modern rhetorical analysis, as it did classically, treats both the logic and the stylistics of argument as parts of a presentation meant to persuade its hearers or readers. Current rhetorical, like argumentative and discourse theory from a textualist perspective, stresses the stylistic side of a nonnarrative text by focusing on its modes of expression as ways of representing the content. Such an approach explores both the logic or path the argument takes as the content of the message and the means or forms in which that message is expressed, especially to achieve its persuasive purposes. Such a dual emphasis unites the logic and the style of a text as a whole or totality.[12] If the validity and credibility of a text reside in the fullness of its construction or its textualization, then the criticism of that validity and credibility resides in the fullness of its deconstruction as textualization.

Discourse, Story, Argument

Without trying to settle for the moment all the many perplexing problems of defining rhetoric, stylistics, or even discourse in argument and narrative, let us return to the rudimentary textualist distinction between the content and its expression in historical practice. "Discourse" refers to the actual or specific arrangement or expression of the content in narrative or nonnarrative histories; "story" and "argument" refer to the implicated message or substance of the discourse in narrative and nonnarrative histories respectively. Discourse conveys (and shapes) the information; story or argument is the information considered apart from the shaping and conveyance by the discourse. The distinctions can be set forth clearly in a table:[13]

	Narrative	Nonnarrative
Expression	discourse	discourse/rhetoric
Content	(hi)story	argument

Although text, discourse, and story and argument are integral in historical practice, historical criticism as a new rhetoric or poetics of history is grounded upon separate analysis of them:

1. The text is the structure that tells, or the structure of signs or words that presents the historian's synthesis, to use previous terminology. It is the author's vehicle for the representation of the discourse and the content of the story or argument. By analogy to language, the text is a system of signifiers in this case.

2. The discourse is the presentation of the argument or how the story is told—the ways in which it is presented sequentially as representation. Under this view the order of appearance of the arguments and the sequential presentation of the story are the focus of theory and analysis. Discourse is the vehicle of the argument or story just as the text is the vehicle of the discourse. For this reason, discourse is the signifier in the sense of vehicle and signified in the sense of its content.[14]

3. The argument or story is what is told or the logical or narrative contents of the discourse—or how the discourse (re)presents the world or what it talks about. In that sense it may be considered the signified or the referent depending upon one's theory of language. To the extent that one believes that complex texts can refer to a world outside their own linguistic system, then the argument or story is referential. To the extent that one believes that complex textual representations constitute the worlds to which they refer, story and argument are just another set of signifieds.[15]

Regardless of one's choice of linguistic theory, understanding histories as texts in terms of modes of representation and forms of story and argument diminishes the distinction not only between narrative and nonnarrative but also between fiction and history. One moves from seeing texts as history to seeing histories as texts and History as both (a) text and a textual invention. Such understanding is at once the fundamental premise and primary goal of any form of new historical criticism.

That historians of today, like those of yesterday, combine narrative and argument in the same work complicates the seemingly clear distinctions between them. There are usually argumentative elements even in manifestly narrative histories and often some narrative elements even in explicitly nonnarrative histories. Nonnarrative histories differ from narrative ones in the obvious level of presentation: some texts present their contents as a story; some offer arguments and the testing of models or logical propositions à la the social sciences or other disciplines. At the same time all histories presume the narrativity of the past as story. Although all histories suppose a story in the sense of the Great and partial stories, only some histories present their manifest content primarily as narrative. Others offer arguments, models, and the like as their explicit content, but even though they eschew a manifest story, they necessarily contain an implicit story referred to as the past.

Fundamental to all histories is the narrativity of all history based in the Great and partial story as opposed to the difference between nonnarrative and narrative histories as manifest content.[16]

Despite these mixed-genre problems, for critical purposes one can still separate both manifest and implicit contents from the expression and representation of them. The accompanying table sets forth the possibilities:

	Narrative	Nonnarrative
Expression as form	discourse	rhetoric
Expression as content	story	argument
Content as form	explicit story	explicit argument
Subtext as form	implicit argument	implicit story
Subtext as content	Great Story	Great Story

This schema affords a glimpse of the potential usefulness of some literary and rhetorical theorists to historians in examining the referential side of history as representation and in expanding the ways they might consider the nonreferential side of history.[17]

A brief critical analysis of two books on colonial American history reveals not only how the distinctions drawn in the chart may be applied but also how these elementary distinctions reveal that the basic truths of these histories lie in their rhetorical arrangements. Although Kenneth Lockridge's *A New England Town: The First Hundred Years* and William Cronon's *Changes in the Land: Indians, Colonists, and the Ecology of New England* were written an intellectual generation apart, both were hailed as exemplary ways of interpreting the early phase of American history at the time of their appearance.[18]

The explicit basic story and argument as content. A New England Town presents the (hi)story of Dedham, Massachusetts, from its founding in 1636 to its supposed transformation a century later plus some implications of its history for later American life. Lockridge argues that in its first half-century the town exemplified the harmony of its Puritan founders' ideals, but that during the second half-century conflict among its inhabitants increased as town lands became scarce through division as a consequence of population growth.

Cronon's book offers "an ecological history of colonial New England." *Changes in the Land,* as its subtitle states, compares the uses of the land by Native Americans with those of the English colonists who displaced them. His story traces a succession of ecological adaptations as the result of the change from native occupancy to English occupation.

The explicit organization of the discourse in relation to the content of the story and argument. Lockridge divides his text into three parts to tell his story and make his argument. Part One, "A Utopian Commune, 1636–1686," discusses how Dedham was established as a Christian utopian closed corporate community according to Puritan ideals. Four chapters cover the Puritan perfectionist ethic of peace and harmony along with social goals of unity, exclusiveness, order, and hierarchy as they were applied to the formation and subsequent organization of the town and the church and then manifested in politics, economy, and social class. A brief chapter titled "Decline" provides a transition to the second part by describing the disintegration of the common field system, the growth of subcorporate entities in the once unified community, and other evidences of the conflicts to come in the second half-century. Part Two, "A Provincial Town, 1686–1736," covers in three chapters the nature and sources of disharmony. The growth and dispersion of the population in the town and the consequent declining supply of land for family farms within the boundaries of Dedham caused and reinforced such changes as increased social inequality, reforms in the political system, and a rise in litigation. These changes all indicated the decline of the founding perfectionist ethic of social harmony and communal unity. A final part consisting of one chapter, both titled "Dedham and the American Experience," points out how the social division and conflict heralded the liberal individualism, the pluralism, and increased complexity of American society after the Revolution.[19]

Changes in the Land is also divided into three parts. Part One, "Looking Backward," consists of a single chapter, "The View from Walden," which begins with a meditation by and on Thoreau in 1855 considering the changes in the Concord landscape since 1633 and then discusses ecological theory and the kind of evidence needed for an ecological history of New England. Part Two, "The Ecological Transformation of Colonial New England," covers in six quasi-topical chapters the diversity of the physical environment of colonial New England; the indigenous peoples' use of, adaptation to, and transformation of their ecosystem; the differing Native American and English customs and practices of relating to the land through boundaries and ownership; and the rapid transformation of the environment through the commodification of animals in the fur trade, of trees in lumbering and ashes, and even of the land itself through exclusive property ownership and English farming practices. The third and final part, "Harvests of Change," consisting of a single chapter, locates the chief cause of the transformation from 1600 to 1800 in the English invasion of the area and the efforts to remake the New World into a familiar version of the Old in terms of political and social organization, systems of economic production, and intellectual and religious beliefs. Cronon concludes: "The economic transformation paralleled the ecological one, and so it is easy to assert that the one caused the other: New England ecology was transformed as the region became integrated into the emerging capitalist economy of the North Atlantic. Capitalism and environmental degradation went hand in hand."[20]

Although both books are divided into three parts, they differ in how they ultimately make their story and argument through their organization. The first two parts of Lockridge's book occupy an approximately equal number of chapters and pages: four chapters totaling seventy-nine pages (plus a transitional fifth chapter of another twelve pages that could have been included in the second part) describe the "utopian commune" that was the Puritan polity and church of Dedham; three chapters totaling seventy-four pages describe the decline of that Puritan utopia into a more pluralistic community. The final part, with its short (sixteen-page) single chapter, concludes both its argument and story about the connection between the first century of Dedham's history and that of the later United States.

In Cronon's book, the story of the ecological transformation of New England is sandwiched between two parts, each consisting of a short single chapter (about a dozen pages): Part One sets up the book's argument and story; Part Two's six chapters (totaling 140 pages) trace the changes between 1600 and 1800; Part Three, a single chapter of only a dozen pages, summarizes both the story and the argument.

The relationship between the explicit argument and the explicit story. In both texts the chapter titles and contents are topical or quasi-topical rather than chronological; the effect is to make the arguments more prominent. Thus Lockridge includes all stories and evidence of harmony, regardless of chronology, in his first part on the utopian commune, and all stories and evidences of decline and disharmony, regardless of when they occurred during the century, in his second part. In line with Lockridge's argument that Dedhamites lived their ideals in the first half century, the treatment in the first part is basically synchronic. In the second part, to reinforce the conflict theme of the latter half-century, the treatment is more diachronic. Similarly, although Cronon in his first chapter explicitly condemns the static analytical presumptions of functionalism in favor of the dynamics of a dialectical approach to culture and environment,[21] his analysis of the period from 1600 to 1800 is quasi-synchronic. He collapses the cultural diversity of New England's many Native American societies into two general approaches to the two major environments of northern and southern New England, and he subsumes the degree to which these societies changed their environment(s) within a larger synchronic "before" picture to heighten the contrast with the consequences of English settlement. He also aggregates English settlement into one more or less static collectivity in order to enhance the contrast before and after capitalism.

In Cronon's book the story of the transformation of the environment is told in the six middle chapters, which quasi-topically trace the historic (or prehistoric) environmental diversity, the Native Americans' adaptation to this environment, and then the English introduction of germs, plants, cattle, and hogs, their fencing and property laws, and ultimately the commodification of all nature that resulted in the first great stage of environmental destruction in the ecological history of New England. The specific changes are detailed with little mention of when they occurred. Cronon's book presents its argument as a before-and-after picture that seems to be given temporal progression through the sequence of its quasi-topical subject chapters.

Lockridge's book offers the same kind of before-and-after picture, but it employs a more dichotomous approach, devoting one part to harmony and the other to disharmony. If Lockridge had wanted to show the slow change or evolution of Dedham society and life, as he argues, should he not have employed the same organization as Cronon? He could have set forth the problems, theory, and basic argument in a single-chapter first part, then traced in five or six quasi-topical chapters the various transformations that he argues occurred in the church, the polity, the economy, and social system, and summarized his argument and pointed out its implications for the future United States in a final part and chapter. Of course, both authors could also have organized their stories in more traditional, chronological chapters and parts.

The organization of the content of the partial and Great Story. The organization, or the structure, of the story as opposed to the order of its discourse is the same in Lockridge's and Cronon's books. Both present, either explicitly or tacitly, a "before" picture as the beginning of their "real" story. The Native American societies of New England serve the same golden age function in Cronon as the early Puritan community does in Lockridge. Although neither author would explicitly accept these societies as golden age exemplars, Cronon's Native American societies operate textually as "utopian communes," for they serve the same narrative function as Lockridge's early Dedham. Then, in the second part of both stories, greedy capitalism destroys or degrades this paradise. In Lockridge's Dedham, population growth and dispersion and the resulting land scarcity brought the evils of conflict, pluralism, and eventually the individualism associated with the early nineteenth-century United States. In Cronon's New England, English possession of the land and commodification of nature resulted in environmental degradation by the early nineteenth century. Both authors therefore see as the third part of their story the same classic American individualism, although Lockridge associates it with the advent of social pluralism and Cronon with the rise of early industrialism. Both (hi)stories posit individualism as the final outcome of their (hi)stories, because both subscribe to the same larger Great Story of classic liberalism and capitalism as the ultimate context of their stories.

The implicit or subtextual argument. The implicit argument of both books is to be found mainly in the models of human behavior and society presumed by the authors. Why does Lockridge claim that the first part of Dedham's history is "utopian"? What image does he have of history and human behavior that makes such a characterization seem appropriate? Since Dedhamites, according to him, lived their ideals of perfectionist harmony during the first fifty years, they might be said to have created a utopia. Yet when one considers the book as whole, it is apparent that Lockridge uses basically a materialistic model of human behavior to explain why the Dedhamites engaged in conflicts over land allocation and other matters in the second fifty years. Only if the reader assumes a suppressed but presumed first part to Lockridge's book—one that assumes that the England from which the Dedhamites came was complex, in that the society was verging on pluralism there and that land was also scarce—is it possible to understand why he sees the first fifty years of Dedham history as idealistic, hence utopian and therefore necessarily brief and doomed. Utopia could exist in Dedham because there was ample land during the first fifty years to afford the luxury of living perfectionist ideals insofar as they were embodied in the Puritan values of harmony and order. Such a conjunction of material conditions and ideological goals was so rare, in Lockridge's opinion, that he could only describe it as utopian. When the historically customary conditions of land scarcity returned, materialism naturally overwhelmed idealism. Thus in Lockridge's textual model of human behavior the implicit story and argument presumes that economic scarcity and conflict are normal in human affairs, as was "proved" by both England and what he calls the later "Anglicized" New England. The brief utopian hiatus in that story was inevitably doomed as the economic conditions that sustained it disappeared. The explicit first part of his book thus presents an idealistic model of human behavior, that is of people living their idea(l)s, while the second and third parts, like the suppressed, subtextual first part, presume the more usual materialist interpretation of human behavior and history.[22]

Just as the term "utopian" leads us quickly to Lockridge's model of human behavior, so Cronon's treatment of Native Americans also illuminates his model. Why did he lump the many indigenous societies of New England into one overall group with two basic economies? If religious beliefs and ethical ideals are so important in distinguishing Native American from English uses of the landscape, why does he not at least detail the two overall groups' contrasting ideas about and orientations toward the physical environment? Both natives and New Englanders are described in terms of what the anthropologist Marshall Sahlins once called "practical reason."[23] Practical reason explains human behavior by projecting a bourgeois economic orientation onto all other cultures. As an explanation of human behavior, it denies the power of symbolic activity for the means/ends of utility theory and the material foundations of productive activity. Although Cronon argues that Native Americans and English possessed quite different attitudes and outlooks, he describes both of them only in their productive relations and neglects their religions almost entirely. A materialist model of human behavior fits an ecological interpretation particularly well because its basis is the interaction between "nature" and "man," as an epigraph from Karl Marx and Friedrich Engels argues at the beginning of the book. Thus Cronon assumes the eventual victory of capitalism, given his and its fundamental premises about the ultimate explanation of human behavior.

The explicit or implicit Great Story. Since Lockridge's and Cronon's books overlap greatly in terms of the period and place they cover, do they ultimately subscribe to the same Great Story to provide the larger context of their histories? Both accept the outlines of the same Great Story of the expansion of English capitalism. They probably agree on many of the same larger effects of it in history. They appear to disagree on the extent to which early Puritans were capitalistic, although this seeming difference may be more a matter of how large a picture they are delineating. Cronon portrays the Puritans as capitalist from the beginnings of English settlement, in contrast to the Native Americans. Since Lockridge treats the early Dedhamites in terms of later ones, he stresses the differences between early Puritan ideals and the later crass self-interest.[24]

That the books appeared more than an intellectual generation apart is evident in the presence or absence of Native Americans as part of their histories and, by extension, part of American history. Lockridge's story omits the native occupancy of Dedham lands before the English settlement of the chartered town. Cronon makes the native side of the story important not only as a foil for his argument but also, presumably, as an embodiment of the newer multiculturalist approach to the American past. Women are absent from both (hi)stories.[25]

Implicit or explicit moral judgments as subtext and Great Story. Cronon's book leaves the reader with the impression that environmental degradation only increased as industrialism replaced agriculture in New England, just as a slightly transformed but still "healthy" environmental balance between humans and nature under native occupancy gave way to destruction and drastic change under the colonial English. The only good environmentalists were the natives, who did few things to harm the ecological balance of their landscape; all the bad things were done by the New England colonists and their white successors. Yet Native American critics have expressed doubt that in fact Cronon in his text cares about indigenous peoples, since they serve mainly as pawns in his story and foils in his argument. He does not distinguish them as diverse societies any more than he differentiates among his English colonists. His image of the "Indian" fits into the standard modern iconography of the Indian as ecologist.

Although it is clear that for Cronon the changes he traces brought only worse results, it is less clear how Lockridge feels about the changes he describes and the eventuality he foresees. Although for Cronon industrialism results in even worse environmental degradation than colonial agriculture, Lockridge seems ambivalent about the change from Puritan communalism to American individualism. Whereas he seems attracted to some of the communalism of early Dedham history, he appears repelled by the religious and social bigotry that went with it. Likewise, the advent of individualism seems to have both good and bad implications. Democracy, though not an ideal of the Puritans, possesses important, if indefinite, value for him.

Although Lockridge writes to expose the myth of New England village democracy, he does not seem to desire his readers to change their world. Cronon's message, however, is coded to make his readers dissatisfied with the environment they have inherited. They should undo the havoc initiated by their ancestors. That even native peoples changed their world but conserved it is an indication that peoples today can also change their world to achieve a better ecological balance.

Expression as form. Lockridge and Cronon employ both argument and narrative to construct their texts. Since Lockridge is ambivalent about the outcome of his history and its associated Great Story, irony serves as his major trope. The unanticipated consequences of the Puritan utopia are no less ironic than the myth that American democracy began in the closed, narrow-minded communities of early New England. Cronon, who is certain of the baneful results of capitalism and industrialism, casts his story as tragedy, but his hope for the future is romantic collective action. A more complete rhetorical analysis of the two texts would examine use of figures of speech, stylistic devices, narrative devices, motifs and themes, and other poetic and rhetorical elements.

Brief as this example of distinguishing story and argument as form and content is, its outline suggests possible uses for a textualist approach to the critical reading and reviewing of historical books and articles. Historical criticism proceeds from this rudimentary set of distinctions to fuller rhetorical and poetical analysis of the textualization.

A Formal Taxonomy of Textual Analysis

The more the referentiality of history is diminished in relation to representation, the more applicable and useful rhetorical, narrative, stylistics, and discourse theories are to historians' understanding of what their trade entails. Often such analyses seek to go beyond the explicit or surface argument and story. Some formalists and structuralists explore what they see as the deeper as opposed to the more surface features of these categories as topics. Another table, modified from the previous one, shows some of these additional considerations:

	Narrative	*Nonnarrative*
Expression as form	discourse (surface; deep)	rhetoric (surface; deep)
Expression as content	story (surface; deep)	argument (surface; deep)
Content as form	explicit story (surface; deep)	explicit argument (surface; deep)
Subtext as form	implicit argument (surface; deep)	implicit story (surface; deep)
Subtext as content	Great Story (surface; deep)	Great Story (surface; deep)

Presumably a major aim of metahistory as advocated by Hayden White is to probe the deeper aspects of these categories. At the least, this chart serves as a basic taxonomic guide to where metahistorical as well as literary and rhetorical theories fit into the understanding of histories as textual structures.

Valuable as this table is to the theoreticization of histories as texts, its categories can be simplified for further discussion. Some of the categories, especially as surface and deep analyses, overlap in their conceptual goals. For example, the surface analysis of explicit story in narrative history rests on the same principles as the deeper analysis of the implicit story in nonnarrative histories and of the Great Story as subtext of all history. What appears subordinated or implicit in one form often becomes featured or explicit in the other. Given that both narrative and nonnarrative histories contain argument, both will benefit from rhetorical and other forms of argument analysis. To indicate some of this crossover, we can redo the earlier table to emphasize its basic orientations:

	Narrative	*Nonnarrative*
Expression as form	story	rhetoric
Expression as content	story	argument
Content as form	story/argument	argument
Subtext as form	story/argument	story
Subtext as content	story	story

This chart translates the dual allegiance of Clio to art and science into methodologies revolving about the poles of narrative and argument analysis.

Although story and argument are reciprocally implicated, always implicitly as subtext and usually explicitly as well, no standard proportion exists for what is explicit or implicit, surface or deep, or even what is the nature of the content versus its means of expression in any given textual example of history. Nevertheless, to look for story and argument in each example of history text in terms of these categories offers a more comprehensive approach to historical representation than is usual in professional meetings or journals. Thus the chief ways of examining historical representation as a whole seem to center on analyses of argument and narrative. These analyses separately call attention to the basic arrangement of the discourse both as content and as expression whether phrased as argument or as narrative. In combination argumentive and narrative analyses explore the textual and subtextual aspects of any given textual example of history.[26]

To the extent that all histories presume partial and Great Stories, one can explore the subtext of nonnarrative histories through analyses of narrativity. Although all historical texts presume narrative as subtext, not all aim to represent the past mainly or entirely through the medium of a story. On the other hand, since all histories implicitly, if not explicitly, imply that history is comprehended as partial and Great Stories, narrative theory has implications for all of normal history-doing in addition to just those works designated as narrative.[27]

The combined analysis of texts through comprehensive approaches to argument and narrative may be labeled either poetics or rhetoric in their (post?)modern guises or discourse analysis as it has developed recently. Modern rhetoric emphasizes the arrangement of a discourse as a whole. As argumentive analysis it comprehends both the logic of the argument and the nature, means, and effects (psycho-logic) of its expression. Contemporary narratology embraces both the logic or emplotment of the story and its stylistic devices or its reception by readers. For historians to appreciate such an enlarged approach to historical representation invites a reconsideration and a broadening of their use of the phrase "the rhetoric of history" in line with what Hayden White, Hans Kellner, and Dominick LaCapra, among others, advocate. Or they can adopt terminology new to the profession: "the poetics of history," as exemplified in Philippe Carrard's recent book on French historical discourse; or "historical discourse analysis," as advocated by Nancy Struever. Each embraces in its own way both the forms of contents and the contents of forms in a text or set of texts.[28]

Beyond Style

Extended, explicit analysis of expression as opposed to content seems superfluous to historians because of the decline of rhetorical and similar kinds of argumentative or stylistics analysis. When science as the preferred foundation for truthfulness became the model of scholarly discourse, knowledge of rhetoric diminished, even disappeared, as a tool of the well-educated scholar. In fact, rhetoric came to seem a mere embellishment, something that concealed as much as it revealed the truth of a scholarly text. As a consequence the word "rhetoric" took on its modern meaning of superfluous or meretricious verbiage. What scholars sought was a plain style that presented the truth of the text as its solely ostensible content, thus persuading the reader that it was transparent to reality. The referential side of Clio's craft as scientist concealed the representational side of Clio's charm as artist. Even those modern historical handbooks that stress the stylistic side pay scant attention to the nature of persuasion and argument in historical writing except for a few suggestions, often platitudes, on "plain words" and "clear sentences."[29]

In his now classic *Style in History*, Peter Gay analyzed style through its exemplification in the histories of Gibbon, Ranke, Macaulay, and Burckhardt. Like so many historians Gay maintained that "style" is a good thing in a historian's text, while "rhetoric" is a bad thing. As the first few sentences of his volume assert: "Style is a centaur joining what nature, it would seem, has decreed must be kept apart. It is form and content, woven into the texture of every art and craft—including history. Apart from a few mechanical *tricks of rhetoric,* manner is indissolubly linked to matter; style shapes, and in turn, is shaped by substance."[30] Because Gay subscribes to the traditional dichotomy historians make between reference and representation, he sees "the very idea of style infected with a central ambiguity: it must give information as well as pleasure. It opens windows on both truth and beauty— a bewildering double vista."[31] As a result of this dichotomy, Gay feels obligated to tackle his topic as a contribution to the history of history, or historiography, rather than as a straightforward presentation of the problems of stylistics in the textualization of history today. Only in this oblique manner can he offer guidance to historians on their own problems in this area.

Between Gay's volume and similar ventures by new literary and rhetorical critics, there is a notable difference in the focus of the analysis and what is at issue in understanding the expressive side of history texts. The new way of understanding history as literature is strikingly exemplified in Hayden White's *Metahistory: The Historical Imagination in Nineteenth-Century Europe,* the book that started the most recent phase of the rhetorical critique of historical practice.[32] White, like Gay, uses the works of great nineteenth-century historians to demonstrate his generalizations about deep structure in history texts, but there the similarity ends. Gay focuses on word usage, figures of speech, stylistic cadence, and the tenor of his exemplary historians' ideas and sympathies. White, in contrast, provides a formal "theory of the historical work" as prelude to his explication of the exemplary writings of four historians and four historical theorists or philosophers of history. His conception of the historical work, as outlined in his first chapter, unites its textual content and discursive expression through a series of interconnected levels: (1) the chronological chronicle; (2) the transformation of chronicle into a story through inaugural, transitional, and terminating motifs; (3) the meaning given to the story through emplotment (romance, tragedy, comedy, and satire, following Northrop Frye); (4) the explanation provided through formal argument (formist, mechanistic, organicist, and contextualist, following Stephen Pepper's theory of world hypotheses); and (5) the provision of prescriptions and morals through ideological implications (anarchism, conservatism, radicalism, and liberalism, following Karl Mannheim). Last, he argues, following Kenneth Burke, that these elements of the historical work are organized into a deeper structure through (6) prefiguration by the tropes of metaphor, metonymy, synecdoche, and irony. Other titles of White's books show his concerns quite well: *Tropics of Discourse: Essays in Cultural Criticism* and *The Content of the Form: Narrative Discourse and Historical Representation.*[33]

The difference between new and old ways of looking at historical discourse also becomes readily apparent from a comparison of J. H. Hexter's essay "The Rhetoric of History" (1971) or Savoie Lottinville's *The Rhetoric of History* (1976) with Hans Kellner's *Language and Historical Representation: Getting the Story Crooked* (1989).[34] Kellner explores tropology, narrativity, and allegory in historical texts in addition to word usage and the nature of historians' biases. Usually historiography is supposed to take care of this aspect, but relatively recent handbooks of trends in history remain silent on these matters.[35] How many historians read, let alone try to understand, the implications for their practice of the articles in *History and Theory?*[36]

At best those reviewers in historical journals who briefly mention the style of a book appear not to know what such a discussion demands today in the way of theory or principles. "Style" in normal history circles amounts to little more than graceful expression and clear writing. Lucidity of style seems equated with transparency of medium. "Style" in literary and rhetorical criticism leads to analyses based on such theoretical disciplines as rhetoric, poetics, stylistics, discourse analysis, or other approaches to textual form. For these disciplines to be useful to modern textual analysis, the meanings of style, rhetoric, discourse, and even poetics had to be retrieved from their trivialization in recent centuries.[37]

That trivialization was achieved through relegating style, rhetoric, and discourse to the literary, poetic, or oratorical uses of language as opposed to the logical, scientific, and supposedly literal or truth-telling uses of language. Whereas logic and scientific method dealt with truth and the universal in knowledge, at best poetics and rhetoric treated the emotive and particular in communication. At worst, poetics studied the language of the fictional and the fabulous, while rhetoric designated the propagandistic and the ornamen-

tal. Under this impression stylistics, rhetoric, and poetics all too often categorized figures of speech and devices of style, classified methods and forms of
argument, or concentrated on the arts of discourse rather than the supposedly
deeper and meatier content. In short, they studied the modes of the medium
as opposed to the meaning of the message. Hence historians, following the
intellectual trends of their times, considered style and rhetoric as extraneous
to the main goal of historical discourse.[38]

In recent decades what was once rent asunder in rhetoric, poetics, and
discourse analysis has, according to their practitioners, been reunified. Today
definitions of rhetoric, poetics, stylistics, and discourse analysis differ widely
according to philosophical or ideological ends, but all stress a broader, more
inclusive approach to their subject matter. Rhetoric embraces the logic of the
argument, or the content of the message; the grammar of the argument, or its
expression; as well as the psycho-logic of the argument, or its persuasive
effects on the audience. Poetics includes study not only of the rules and
procedures that operate in a given set of texts but also of their rhetorical
strategies through discursive practices and narratological conventions.[39] Likewise, discourse analysis has moved from grammatical and other classification
of linguistic elements to a more inclusive consideration of texts as a whole
both in themselves and in their larger social context.[40]

As a result of this broadening of definition and of intellectual turf, proponents of the varying definitions frequently absorb all of what competing
approaches study into their own favorite field. Thus whether rhetoric, poetics,
or discourse analysis is the most comprehensive field with the others subordinate is a matter of professional preference, but all such imperialistic definitions are meant to convey the idea that the verbal structure of a text can be
studied systematically as a comprehensive whole and in its contextual setting
as well as through a formal analysis of the text as text. Just as historians
possess plural interpretations and approaches to the past, so theorists of
rhetoric, poetics, and discourse analysis hold plural theories and approaches
to the text depending upon the methodological, philosophical, and political
orientations of the user. Often these theoretical approaches embrace or cut
across such contemporary literary theories as formalism, semiotics, structuralism, poststructuralism, reader-response or reception theory, neo-Marxism,
ideological critique, feminism, and hermeneutics.[41] Some of these textual
theories are compatible with each other; many are not reconcilable in terms
of premises or results. All assert that they are the single best approach to text.

In the hands of those most positivistically inclined, such study aims at nothing less than the systematic study of argument, prose, literature, and indeed all
forms of communication as the science of their subjects. Poetics, for example,
would be a science of literature, aimed to produce a theory of literary works. At
its most ambitious such analysis would derive the principles and theories of
various kinds of literature as forms of expression or communication, their cate-

gories and patterns of compositional structure, and the classification and connections among each form's subunits or elements. Such "formalistic" analysis takes linguistics as its model and stresses structures in and of the texts over more processual and contextual analyses of readership and interpretive communities.[42] Recent trends in literary theory question or repudiate the extreme positivistic formalism of the earlier structuralist phase. Scholars still seek to understand the constitution of meaning in a text and how it works as medium, but they also try to establish reader reception or audience response and the social and cultural processes that produce and consume texts of various kinds.

One major difference among these theories is the extent to which they postulate that a text can be understood as a text apart from its context at the time it is produced or the time it is consumed. The former approach leads to textualist analyses, often on formalist principles. The latter approach leads to contextualist approaches, placing a text in relation to reader formations or interpretive communities and to the presumedly larger society, culture, and politics that give both text and community meaning. As a result of this difference in theoretical perspective, the words "rhetoric" and "discourse" can possess quite different meanings depending upon whether they are used according to textualist or contextualist premises.[43] Whether displayed as formal structures of rules according to linguistic and semiotic models, analyzed as a "process of signification" (Roland Barthes's term), or traced as "discursive practices" (as Michel Foucault called them) and therefore exposited as either supposedly universal formalist structures, as the supplementary interpretations of readers, as common understandings of interpretive communities, or as anonymous but socially and historically specific bodies of rules, each method seeks to show what and how each process enables as it constitutes, that is textualizes, the (social) subject or the (cultural) object.[44]

The New Rhetoric of History

Textualist Approaches

How the various recent approaches to rhetorical and literary analyses affected those historians and scholars interested in their implications for historical practice can be seen through examination of some programmatic statements. Arbitrary as the following choices may be, they suggest the topics that any new rhetoric, poetics, or discourse analysis of history must include. Both in what they agree on and what they differ over (and how) these programs catalogue the general categories of historical criticism as an enterprise in the profession. Collectively, they provide some notion of the agenda needed for such a project.

What rhetoric classically entailed can be found in Richard Vann's use of the customary categories of elocution, disposition, and invention to expound the rhetoric of social history.[45] In his capable hands this ancient rhetorical trinity receives new application as well as new definitions as he moves from the stylistic expression of social histories to their disposition or arrangement of evidence and argument and on to their invention or selection of characteristic emplotments. Under style he discusses the connotative language of the *Annalistes* and the use of technical language and statistics in social histories. Under disposition of evidence and arrangement of the case, he writes about the difficulties of incorporating tables of statistics, the division of evidence and argument between text and annotation, and the dense narrative instance as thick description.[46] Under emplotment he discusses the differing narrative tempos of social and political histories.[47]

Donald McCloskey, who is both an economist and an economic historian, offers two general schemes for the narratives and rhetoric found in economics texts that seem useful in analyzing discourse in economic history texts as well. In his witty *If You're So Smart,* he asserts that the "whole rhetorical tetrad" is composed of "fact, logic, metaphor, and story." Facts and logic, for him, though rhetorically presented according to scientist criteria, often exhibit metaphorical and narrative characteristics. Economics and economic history alike use story and argument to advance their cases, although these must embrace both fact and logic. Argument, like story, is plotted and ideological. Metaphors in economics are models or analogies in addition to figures of speech, but the former are true in much the same way as the latter. He expands on this tetrad throughout the book, but especially in the fourth chapter, where he discusses how such classic rhetorical terms as "ethos," "pathos," and "inventio(n)" are combined with style and poetics into the ways economists "aid . . . the story line," as the chapter title has it.[48]

Priority of place as well as of publication should be given to Hayden White's "theory of the historical work," which started so much of this discussion. His model moves from what he calls the surface features of a historical discourse to a formalist analysis of the deep structure of the historical text.[49] Although he argues that all the interconnected levels of chronicle, story, emplotment, explanation through formal argument, and ideological implications are surface characteristics of the historical text as opposed to the tropological prefiguration of these elements, narratological and rhetorical theory suggest otherwise. Even White's own categorization of emplotment, following Northrop Frye, as romance, tragedy, comedy, and satire, or of formal argument, following Stephen Pepper's theory of world hypotheses, as formist, mechanistic, organicist, and contextualist, indicates that he seeks deeper structures of these categories than their ostensible surface manifestations. Likewise, narratologists explore both deep and surface elements of story. Furthermore, the ideological component of historical discourse rests upon implicit as well as explicit models of society, polity, and human behavior that ground the categories of anarchism, conservatism, radicalism, and liberalism, borrowed from Mannheim.[50]

Underlying what White calls the surface manifestations of the historical work are the four tropes—metaphor, metonymy, synecdoche, and irony—that configure (he says prefigure) the very poetic act of uniting expression and content in historical representation. Whether his standard tetrad of tropes is too few or too many or too inflexibly applied in their rigid, Vico-like succession, White's basic challenge to modern historical textualization has been to argue that the deepest structuring of language (and perhaps of human consciousness) is the key to the writing (and reading) of history.[51] Historical content as Great Story and even as partial story is a function of rhetorical devices. Thus the how and the what of historical expression produce both a history as a text and its imaged or projected history as a representation of the past.

Although White originally elaborated his scheme as part of his analysis of eight nineteenth-century historians and philosophers of history in *Metahistory*, he suggests its relevance in reading contemporary historical texts by briefly sketching a tropological analysis of E. P. Thompson's *The Making of the English Working Class*. What Thompson depicts metaphorically as a "biography of the English working class from its adolescence until its early manhood," White explains as normal progression in a "tropological theory of consciousness."[52] According to White, Thompson divides his discourse into four parts to explicate the four stages in the evolution of English working-class consciousness, from a vague sense of class awareness and a desire for liberty in the late eighteenth century, through the experience of class antagonism as a result of changing work discipline and other experiences under early industrialism, to a full-fledged and conscious understanding of the oppression of the class system for workers and their interests as a class in that system at the Peterloo "massacre" and beyond, and finally to the divergent intellectual comprehensions of class remedies and the schism in the working class movement.[53] White analyzes these four stages as proceeding from, first, a metaphorical (class) consciousness, "in which working people apprehend their differences from the wealthy and sense their similarity to one another, but are unable to organize themselves except in terms of the general desire for an elusive 'liberty'"; to a second, metonymic (class) consciousness, "in which the different forms of working-class existence, determined by the variety of kinds of work in the industrial landscape, crystallize into distinctive kinds, the whole having nothing more than the elements of series." During the synecdochal (class) consciousness of the third stage the "workers achieve a new sense of unity or identity of the parts with the whole." The fourth stage consists in the irony of "the ascent of class consciousness to self-consciousness but also and at the same time the fatal fracturing of the working class movement itself . . . through the simultaneous emergence and debilitation of the two ideals which might have given the working class movement a radical future."[54]

Whether or not one is persuaded that White's translation of Thompson's voluminous work is adequate or accurate, its goal is as suggestive as it is provocative. Some opposition to White's troplogical approach comes from those who question the value of such rhetorical theory to historical practice in general, because such "intellectual gamesmanship" substitutes the analysis of past or, worse, present language for the experience of past and present life.[55] Other opposition questions the primacy that White accords tropology in any rhetorical analysis but defends the larger aims of rhetorical theory applied to history.[56] Still others challenge White's specific use of tropology as such but provide alternative ways of applying such analysis.[57] All these critics, however, admit that "all kinds of historical discourse are structured by the conventions of form."[58] As a result, they accede to the significance of the text, regardless of their philosophies of context and the relevance of rhetorical theory to critical analysis of historical texts.

If nothing else, White's formalist scheme calls attention to the roles played by rhetorical, discourse, and poetic analyses in a comprehensive approach to historical criticism. Regardless of disciplinary domains, White's scheme suggests the importance of motif and of argument, tropological, narratological, and ideological analyses to the study of historical discourse as content as well as its expression. Motifs in stories and kinds of emplotment constitute part of the larger project of recent poetics or rhetoric as narratology, as does the tetrad of tropes. Argument theory is part of the larger enterprise of rhetoric, as are the types of ideologies and tropes.[59]

White's approach seems most interesting when applied to recent historical texts that appear to violate normal historical practice. White himself "decoded" Foucault's *The Order of Things* by pointing out how his sequence of epistemes of successive historical epochs from the Renaissance through the classical to the modern and beyond follows his theory of tropology. According to White, Foucault was unaware that his scheme of changing epistemic foundations of the human sciences from the late Middle Ages to the twentieth century rested upon a model of predominant (pre)figurative linguistic bases constituting the human sciences over time. Such transformation moved from metaphor to metonymy, synecdoche, and irony.[60] James Mellard elaborates White's tropological scheme in *Doing Tropology: Analysis of Narrative Discourse,* but he applies it to three twentieth-century novels and *The Education of Henry Adams.* In his chapter on *The Education,* Mellard borrows White's troplogical analysis of Foucault's succession of epistemes to argue that Adams' ironically self-subversive and seemingly disjointed text relied upon the same kinds of historical frameworks to depict the metonymy of his grandfather's eighteenth century, the synecdoche of the nineteenth century, and the metaphorical consciousness of the dawning, post-modern twentieth century.[61] Although many historians have found the organization of Fernand Braudel's *The Mediterranean and the Mediterranean World in the Age of Philip II* perplexing, Hans Kellner explains its peculiarity as an example of Menippean satire.[62] He explores the work as self-conscious aesthetic modernism that probes the limits of linguistic representation in historical discourse through the disorderly encyclopedic rhetorical ploy common to that genre.[63]

One of the few efforts I have come across to apply the entirety of White's typology to recent historical texts is Donald Ostrowski's article on four Russian narrative histories.[64] He investigates each of the histories for the four elements composing each of the four categories of emplotment, modes of argument, ideological implications, and tropes. He finds the same correlations among certain elements across categories as did White. As a result he calls for the further exploration of White's scheme in all its permutations in order to determine whether certain affinities predominate and whether some permutations do not—cannot—exist. Such an investigation ought to be an important priority on any agenda of a new rhetoric or poetics of history.

In what appears at first glance to be an extended application of Vann's classic approach, literary critic Philippe Carrard in *Poetics of the New History: French Historical Discourse from Braudel to Chartier* offers a book-length rhetorical analysis of recent generations of the *Annales* school.[65] He too divides his analysis into three parts, labeled "dispositions," "situations," and "figures." Under these rubrics he tries to extend poetics beyond formalist textualist practices. He defends his brand of poetics as consistent with poststructuralist criticisms of earlier narratology and poetics because he combines the supposedly deep structures of modes of emplotment and tropes with such surface features as enunciation and stylistics. He investigates epistemological and political premises of the "New Historians" in addition to their "machinery" of representation, their conflicts and heterogeneity as well as the common elements in their credos and practices. He combines narratology, rhetoric, and poetics to investigate such broad matters as methods of plotting, modes of voicing and viewpoint, and the construction of the reader in the text and such seemingly small matters as the nature of titles and footnotes, the use of personal pronouns, habits of punctuation, and figures of speech. Given his rhetorical approach, however, broader and smaller matters are intimately connected, and often the smaller are as revelatory as the larger in exhibiting the premises and ploys of historians in constructing texts and what they hope they achieve. In spite of the broadened approach of Carrard's poetics, his chief orientation and practices lie within the textualist tradition. In defense of this practice, he argues, such an approach is highly illuminating, and even a necessary preliminary, to any contextualist ways of exploring how historians go about their textualization.

Contextualist Approaches

What divides textualist and contextualist approaches to histories and history from a contextualist viewpoint is illustrated by a critic of White's use of tropology. Peter De Bolla in a review of White's *Metahistory* argues that the sequence of tropes should be applied to history itself rather than to historians' use of them to explicate that history.[66] Each of the tropes, according to him, dominated the others successively through the past centuries. Thus the sequence provides a genealogy of actual intellectual history as opposed to a way of analyzing intellectually the historians who write about it. De Bolla seeks to create a Great Story of tropology to serve as the larger context for that history. In that way, he would transform White's rhetoric of history into "historical rhetorics." Although he admits the figurative power of rhetoric to constitute its subject, he prefers to apply that insight to the past itself rather than to the textualization of that past as historical discourse. Proponents of White's approach would inquire whether the two are so easily separated in any textualization.[67]

The term "historical discourse analysis" is ambiguous because it refers not only to a critical analysis of historical documents as sources but also to the texts historians themselves produce and to past discourses in general. As Nancy Struever explicates this approach to historical texts, all three uses might combine for the purposes of historical criticism. She distinguishes the use of discourse analysis in the archives to read sources from the use of it in the study of written histories. Under the latter rubric, she lists three models of historical discourse: narrative, rhetorical style, and argument. Her brief exposition of narrative and argument advocates the newer, broader definition of those fields. Under "rhetorical style" she mainly criticizes Hayden White's rhetorical model of the historical text as being too general on one hand and too narrow on the other. She accuses him of reducing all historical understanding to a special version of rhetorical analysis rather than opening it up through a broader approach to rhetoric. At the same time, she argues, he expands the realm of the rhetoric of history to the "problem of poeticity and the production of stylistics" in literature in general rather than in historical practice specifically. She also complains of his neglect of the historical text's reception and manipulation by its audience.[68]

Such caveats seem grounded in the usual differences between textualist and contextualist perspectives on the text. In the end, she offers an "agenda of analytic tasks" that combine the two perspectives: intratextual analysis through narratology and argument, and intertextual analysis of such discursive practices as ideology and disciplinary customs. Her mention of the "discursive structures of diffusion and exchange" suggests both disciplinary practices in what she assumes is the larger world of academia and real-life politics as well as the social, cultural, and institutional contexts of the textualist analysis, as advanced by Michel Foucault and others.[69]

Such an approach to historical discourse as disciplinary matrix suggests that historical practice should be approached as a sociology of historical knowledge, or what Michel de Certeau calls a "sociology of historiography" in "The Historiographical Operation."[70] In that essay he explicates historicization as a combination of "place," "procedures," and product. Inspired by Foucault on discursive formations and French theoreticization of historical practices, he emphasizes the institutional aspects of all three aspects. Writing as product, or the ultimate textualization, depends as much upon the collective expectations of readers about what a history does as it does upon how historians collectively define what they produce. What does a society allow and want as a history? Who decides what is a history and whether it is a popular or a learned one? Under the rubric of "practice" de Certeau discusses how historians as a professional collectivity classify certain objects as "documents" and evidence, how libraries create archives through isolating and denaturing and thus creating those documents, how historians separate those procedures central to history proper from those procedures comprehended under studies designated auxiliary to them, how texts broadly conceived are divided and therefore constituted as primary and secondary sources, and how in recent times historians as a profession have broadened what they allow as sources of documentation. Archives, from this perspective, have their own histories as "collections," created by a group of persons who have achieved recognition as a branch of the historical profession. Archivists save some documents as sources (and in the process destroy others) and work in formally organized social institutions with professionally approved practices for storing such materials. These institutions, supported by public or private money, determine who has access to the collections. In the end, "practice" covers all the social and cultural processes of transforming or converting social and cultural institutions for doing history into symbolic products called histories.[71]

De Certeau applies his sociology of historiographic operations most broadly under the rubric of "a social place," a term that embraces the recruitment of the profession's members, the social milieu that allows them to practice their operations as a profession, and the institutional sites of their production. Contrary to the professional credo of historians that they exist as an autonomous professional body, he points out, they are the creation of their society, which allows (and supports) them to operate as they do. Within the historical profession itself, social and cultural practices determine the recruitment of who will be certified as a professional historian, what constitutes the proper training of a historian, what exists as exemplary symbolic products, what schools of interpretation exist, what constitutes proper documentation, who gets ahead in the profession, and how the hierarchy of prestige is allocated. Fellowships, chairs, prizes, and official positions in learned societies all reinforce as they reproduce these social practices. Universities where historians practice are, according to de Certeau, colonies of their societies that allow and prohibit what those societies want. Historical methods are the means of power by which historians as academicians and a profession defend their intellectual turf against other scholars. Seminars are the artisanal workshops for the advanced production of specialists by specialists. Historical books and articles are "akin to a car produced in a factory" because their origin, form, content, and reception are all a "collective fabrication."[72] Even what the past is and how it is properly interpreted as other to the present are socially determined, as the correlations between historiographical fashions and changing society demonstrate. For de Certeau, the contextualizations historians produce as texts must be viewed as products contextualized to their place(s) in their societies and their times.

In our last example, the political scientist John Nelson outlines a scheme as ambitious and comprehensive in its way as that of Hayden White. "Seven Rhetorics of Inquiry: A Provocation," the final chapter of *The Rhetoric of the Human Sciences: Language and Argument in Scholarship and Public Affairs,* is his attempt to summarize what is common to the diverse approaches of the twenty-one contributors to the volume.[73] Whereas White's scheme and terminology betray the bias of a scholar in the humanities, Nelson's categories and definitions embody the perspective of a scholar in the social sciences. As he defines and argues the various areas of rhetorical study, one leads to the other in an overlapping series from logics and poetics to ethics and politics. For Nelson, rhetoric begins and ends with persuasion and politics, and so his series comes full circle in the end. As a result, texts, for him, are best studied intertextually and contextually. In Nelson's own rhetoric, each category's name embraces both the discursive practice itself in texts and the study of it as a practice. Moreover, he extends the meaning of many rhetorical terms to enlarge their textual and social applications.

Professing a postmodern perspective, Nelson declares that the positivist, objectivist abstractionism that so many of the social sciences make the basis for their disciplinary linguistic paradigm is just another aspect of rhetoric in its guise as persuasion. Thus Nelson argues that rhetoric holds a place equal epistemically as well as practically to logic in the ways scholars of the human sciences communicate among themselves and with the public. Logics are "artifacts of rhetorics" in the larger context of disciplinary practice.[74] At best logic, as Nelson defines this term in his scheme, studies the various structures of argumentation in a discipline's texts. In line with these assumptions, he outlines the basic categories of rhetoric that ground general scholarly inquiry in the human sciences.

Nelson defines poetics as the covert constraints and implicit foundational conventions that shape the rhetoric of scholarly inquiry in a discipline. The study of poetics explicates the deep structures of disciplinary discursive practice, whether defined intertextually or contextually. Deep structure consists of the "*pre*suppositions and *pre*figurations of language or thought" in a field.[75] So fundamental is poetics to rhetoric as defined broadly today that he points out the difficulty in distinguishing between the two.

> If a poetic produces and comprehends presuppositions and prefigurations, a rhetoric could be said to select and develop them for the purposes of action. Then poetic is the domain of expression and communication, whereas rhetoric is the

realm of persuasion and motivation. Yet the two interact so much . . . that each usually calls forth or even becomes the other. Swayed by [Kenneth] Burke, in fact, many theorists of literature and communication long ago assimilated poetic to rhetoric, and vice versa.[76]

According to Nelson, whereas poetics constitute and study pre- or implicit figuration in texts, tropics constitute and study explicit figuration of textual language. Tropes are usually taken to mean such major figures of speech as metaphor, simile, metonymy, hyperbole, irony, and synecdoche;[77] but Nelson adds to the list explicit standard figures of social scientific language used in descriptions, explanations, and theories. Thus fabrications such as economic man, images such as equilibria, models such as free markets, and statistical procedures such as significance tests become examples of tropes in social science literature. Accordingly, Nelson argues that such standard social scientific practices as "turning information into statistical data, translating explanations into formal languages, representing relationships as models, transforming assumptions into ideal types, conducting experiments through intellection, selecting evidence through sampling principles, [and] defining variables by anecdotes" are rhetorical devices adopted as methodological procedures.[78]

Topics, or topoi, are the common strategies and accepted lines of argument. Whether this term should embrace not only the standard forms of argument but also their arrangement in an argumentative case and the tactics of their presentation in traditional rhetoric, in Nelson's scheme it encompasses "how (or how not) to deploy tropes" in argumentation. The strategies and tactics of argumentation include "defining terms, analyzing opposites, creating correlations, building part by part to whole, noting possible motives, citing consequences, [and] developing contradictions."[79] In the end, these are not just abstract logical techniques but methods of persuasion directed by scholars at others in an academic community or the larger society. Although Nelson denies epistemically favoring logic over rhetoric, he points out the possibilities of fallacy in the use and arrangement of topoi.[80]

In Nelson's scheme, dialectics are the "tools for criticism" of rhetoric as argument: justification, comparison, and reflection. He succinctly summarizes their relationship: "Justification involves reasons and warrants. Reasons justify claims or judgments, and warrants justify reasons."[81] Once again he is quick to point out that justification and reason rest upon rhetorical, hence communal, definition and not upon any transcendental epistemic grounds.

Hermeneutics is usually defined as the study of meaning in, or the interpretation of, texts. Nelson defines hermeneutics more broadly, as the rhetorical study of conventions. True, conventions are employed to study and interpret texts by translating a strange language into a more familiar one, "but the central categories of texts, contexts, and pretexts may cover vast sets of human objects and activities—encompassing anything conventional." He goes on to argue: "More generally, hermeneutics can explain how to learn and create conventions, how to choose and use them, how to conserve and replace them, how to assess them from within or without, and how to suit them to diverse circumstances or changing occasions."[82] Thus he wants to move hermeneutics from interpreting texts communally to interpreting the community as a text.

> As studies of interpretation, hermeneutics can come to terms with the ways in which successful foundations generate activities, conventions, and institutions stable and resourceful enough to earn notice as practices. Foundations are the favored pretexts that lead us to produce the texts of our lives in the contexts of our times. Practices that endure and expand within slowly changing limits become traditions that conserve themselves through the continual criticism that we call interpretation.[83]

Under this agenda hermeneutics would not only study the interpretive and communal basis for the dialectics of justification, comparison, and reflection in scholarly argument but also investigate the ethics and politics in and of scholarship in general.[84]

Whereas Nelson construes hermeneutics more broadly than the conventional definitions do, he restricts ethics to judging the morality and goodness of scholarly research procedures and the communities that establish and enforce them. Even so, ethics comprehends everything from fraud in research results and their publication to the moral implications of arguments, the proper uses of scholarship, the procedures and standards of disciplinary practice, and the policing of those standards by a disciplinary community.

For Nelson, ethics shades into politics, and rhetoric becomes political when considered in the broader framework of institutional foundations and the social context of disciplines. The politics of scholarship must "address the actions and organizations involved in founding disciplines, instituting their daily standards and procedures, maintaining their boundaries, regulating their relations with one another and with other kinds of communities, initiating their members, establishing their priorities, and deciding how to manage their concerns."[85] Just as there is a rhetoric (in the broad sense) of politics, so there is a politics of the whole rhetorical enterprise; just as there is a rhetorical side to ethics, so there is a political and institutional side to ethics. In line with such intellectual and moral reciprocity, Nelson preaches both a morality and a rhetoric of scholarship and its application as criticism of the larger society.

A New Poetics of Historical Criticism

These few schemes of approaching the historical text comprehensively afford a general idea of what a new rhetoric or poetics of history might encompass as historical criticism. At a minimum, historical criticism must embrace the textual, intertextual, and contextual aspects of historical practice. Historical texts chiefly take the forms of narratives and arguments and can be analyzed through logic and such rhetorical categories as invention, disposition, and style or through narratology and the poetics of emplotment, stylistics, and viewpoint. Both forms of representation employ models, metaphors, tropes, and other figuration explicitly and implicitly to structure the text. Textual explication may proceed through hermeneutics or ideological analysis, through theory or practice, through attention to author or to reader. Intertextual analysis can examine discursive practices, disciplinary conventions, and institutional politics as found in a series of texts. Contextual analysis is concerned with the role of the supposedly larger disciplinary, social, cultural, and political institutions operating at the time in shaping both the production and the consumption of the texts. Whether contextualist analysis can escape the epistemic and ontological limitations of textualist construction divides theorists but not necessarily the utility of their theories for historical criticism. To the extent that contextual analysis is another form of textualist construction, it is merely intertextualism by another name—that is, (con)textual—and therefore subject to rhetorical and poetic analysis itself.

At this point in the development of historical criticism, all schemes together, and perhaps more, ought to constitute what historians mean by the new rhetoric and poetics of history. Just as history texts embody techniques from both literature and social science, so any rhetoric or poetics of historical practice must employ premises and theories from both fields. Finally, a new rhetoric and poetics should employ both formalist and poststructuralist approaches to language and its relation to social reality.[86] Even if the supposed power of the hypothesized larger social context in shaping texts remains an important issue separating textualism and contextualism, the nature of historical representation and discursive practice, like the nature of the Great Stories, depends as much upon allegory and figuration as upon empirical knowledge. According to some of these theorists, in fact, only through allegory and figuration is empirical knowledge constituted as a historical text in the first place.

An ecumenical ideal of historical criticism would combine textualist- and contextualist-based poetics. Such eclecticism is not so easy, because the two approaches remain incommensurable in some important ways. Although the various schemes outlined above are implicated in each other and even complement each other, they rest upon ultimately conflicting definitions of discourse. While recent literary theory seems to repudiate the naive formalism of earlier theorists of narratology and poetics in favor of what appears to be a more contextualist approach, these textualist concerns still seem quite useful in looking at history texts, since the historical profession is contextualist by preference and by nature of its vested interest in realism. Textualist approaches to historical criticism call attention to the very silences of historical discourse as contextualization. If nothing else, attention to narratological concerns points out the problematic nature of history as text and discourse.

No matter how rhetoric and poetics or even discourse analysis is defined, the arrangement within the forms historical representations take is central to all of them. For the historian and teacher, historical representation is an art of arrangement, whether as narrative or argument. For the reader and critic, historical representation is the arrangement of that art, whether as narrative or argument. Both creator and consumer, then, regard the logic of the argument or narrative as the arrangement of content, and the psycho-logic of narrative and argument as the arrangement of expression.

Any new rhetoric or poetics of history must therefore explore the nature of the arrangement in the various layers of a text. Whether considering the implicit argument of a nonnarrative or narrative history or the explicit argument embodied in either type of history, the basic question from this standpoint centers on how the argumentive case is organized. Whether considering the explicit story of the narrative or nonnarrative history or the implicit story in either type of history, the central question centers on how the narrativity is organized. Poetics and rhetorical and discourse analysis provide the tools to achieve the historical criticism demanded by the nature of historical texts and the textualization of history as such.

CHAPTER FIVE

Emplotment:
Historicizing Time

SINCE the ways of representing time and the ways of representing history overlap in historical practice, the rhetoric and poetics of narrative and argument should be supplemented by a rhetoric of temporal arrangement and a poetics of temporal ordering in historical representations. To the logic (content) and psycho-logic (expression) of historical representations must be added the chrono-logic of those representations—the patterning of time in that content and the timing, as it were, of its expression. Just as narratives and arguments must be arranged, so the representation of time in them must be ordered and apportioned. Such patterning takes the form of emplotment broadly conceived.

The Time of Normal History

Time is basic to history both with regard to what historians purport to represent about the past and with regard to how they go about representing it. Although history is a genre of time par excellence, historians rarely discuss its nature or how it is textualized. They presuppose time and employ temporal ordering in three different but related ways.[1] The three ways exist in tension, and their synthesis poses problems for the textualization of a history as a text even while each way provides resources and opportunities for the textualization of history in general.

First, and most obviously, historians make events and persons in past time the subject matter of their texts and professional discourse. Most important, historians assume the otherness of past times: the longer ago they are, the more the then and there differ from the here and now. They talk about events and actions that occurred in previous times; they discuss persons and institutions that existed in the past. Historians represent past time(s) as real, hence as the referent of their discourse. Histories therefore describe the past and its ordering as what really happened. This first principle of historical realism is construed according to calendar time and aided by the grammatical construction of verbal tenses. Physical time is domesticated into human time through the socially invented calendar. The calendar both measures and expresses history in terms of events. The past as historical time is described from the moment in the present of the speaker or writer as enunciative narrator. Verb tenses designate what once took place narratively as really happening and is vital to the narrator's linguistic construction of a text as a history.[2]

Second, historians represent time through their textualization of it. Their discourses not only refer to the past but embody the representation of it through both argument and narrative textualization of those prior times. The historicization of time is achieved only through such textualized representation. Conversely, historians textualize time as story through what happens in it as if it were an empty vessel to be filled. According to the normal paradigm, time itself has no content; only through being given content can it be historicized. The idea of time as an empty vessel to be filled with history is another way of interpreting Paul Veyne's dramatic pronouncement that "time is not essential to history."[3] As Savoie Lottinville advises the beginning historian:

> The narrative management of time is best when it is unobtrusive although fully present. This kind of management is successful, usually, when the writer is busy advancing the topical significance of his account so that days or months or seasons emerge naturally from the story. Thus the emphasis is upon something other than time itself, which, while important sequentially, must always be secondary to action and significance in historical contexts.[4]

Arrangement is central to time as something to be filled: both to what fills it as content and to how it is filled through expression. Thus emplotment is fundamental to history both as referent and as representation, as explicit and implicit narrative or as the subtext of an argument.

Third, historians produce arguments and narratives that take time to read or tell. They use time in the present to describe time in the past. The ordering of past time as the content of history demands present time for explicating or narrating that history as expression. Representations of past times, as a result of the sequential arrangement of the text, require their own time to be heard or read. Even so, the sequence of past time as represented in that text is understood, paradoxically, all at one time at the end of its hearing or reading. Historical patterning, whether representing time as sequence or as setting, that is, as diachronic or as synchronic, dialectical or functional, is ultimately synchronic in its understanding by historian and reader alike, no matter how dynamic its content as story or argument.[5] The difference between synchrony and diachrony, between dialectical and functionalist analysis, lies in the referential story or argument and not necessarily in the sequential arrangement of the discourse itself or in the duration of its consumption. Although the representation of synchronic and diachronic time may be textually the same as discursive arrangement or in consumption time, there is a world of difference between the two kinds of emplotment from the standpoint of what they claim to do and how they go about it conceptually.

The goal of normal history is to synthesize the discrepancies among these uses of time. Historians assume that they unite the time of the real world of the past (RWP) and the time of that world as referred to in the text (TWT) through chronology. They seek to reconcile the time of that referred-to world in the text (TWT) with the timing of its textual ordering as the content of the representation (CR) through emplotment. That the sequential ordering of the discourse in the text (DT) need not follow the order of time in its referred-to representation (CR) let alone in the referred-to real world (TWT) complicates the plotting of history.

What normal historians seek to unite textually through chronology and emplotment, rhetoricians of history attempt to separate analytically through story or argument and discourse. Rhetorical and literary theorists explore the relationship between time in the referred-to real world (TWT), the time of that world as represented in the text (CR), and the timing or order of its textual presentation (DT) as part of their notion of the textual content as story or argument as opposed to its textual expression as discourse. The distinction between story and discourse in narrative history specifically and between expression and content in historical representation generally also rests upon certain assumptions about the nature of time as chronology. In turn, a conception of time as chronology creates problems for emplotment in historical representation even while it enables normal historical methodology.[6]

For the reader and critic, therefore, the rhetoric or poetics of temporal order in historical representations examines timing, or its patterning, in at least three ways as central to its analysis of histories as texts. First, how is the timing of the world of the past patterned or plotted by the historian? Time in the past is the world represented as the subject of historical texts, so what do the texts say explicitly about the arrangement of time and timing on various levels of the content? Second, what kind of patterning or plotting during representation does the patterning and plotting of the past receive in the text itself? How, in other words, is the expression patterned and plotted to convey its message about the patterned past? The first set of questions centers on the pattern of history itself as represented; the second set focuses on the pattern of the representation itself as presented in the text. A third set of questions concentrates on the timing of the textual presentation, on how the text goes about organizing the content and expression of the argument or narrative during the time of its consumption. Since the presentation of what is talked about as history in the text takes its own time to consume in the present, how do historians time their own sequential presentation of historical patterning? How long or short a time do histories devote to a topic through the allocation of textual space?

In one way, then, time is both trope and topic to historians and readers alike. Time as chronology both prefigures and figures historical representation. Time as timing or sequence constitutes both the subject of historical representation and its means of doing so. Historians take time as the topic of their presentation as they periodize or pattern the past to describe or explain what happened in history as the past. They arrange their argument and narration about time by how they emplot each to represent what happened in the past as history. In all these senses, then, the conception of timing as patterned for representing the past in the present leads to the multiple significance of what we can call plotting or emplotment in general historical practice. Emplotment in its broadest sense operates throughout the layers of a text, whether displayed as narrative or as argument, whether manifested in surface or in subtext, whether presented as referential fact or as interpretive structure.

Textual or Discourse Time versus Chronological Time

Historians and readers, metahistorians and critics alike presume time to be of a certain nature in order to serve as the framework of chronology. Although the times of histories are obvious social constructions, historians treat chronological time as if it were natural, physical time itself. Thus chronological time combines the human-invented calendar time of events with the naturalized time of a Newtonian universe. Historical time as chronology is treated as exterior to the events said to occur in it but which also mark its passage. Hence historians assume chronological time to be as universal, directional, and measurable as physical time. Measurement and direction allow assumptions about chronology and its implications for historical method. Universality permits all events and times to be embraced by a single overall chronology. Direction along with chronology enables assumptions about causality, contingency, contiguity, and nonconnection among events. Chronological time is homogeneous and unique in historical discourse. Such socially naturalized time exempts its own social construction from history; it is timeless in practice despite what historians know about its history.[7]

Historians postulate the existence of a time that is sequential, external, universal, and yet specific to the events that take place in it. Such a notion of temporal succession as real is fundamental to the ordering of their data in partial histories and Great Stories alike. What makes chronology work in historical practice is the assumption of the order or sequence of time that measures both succession and duration. Thus a historic event embraces a specific span of time while simultaneously being before, during, or after other events at the same or different times. Historic time is both singular for the moment of dating and continuous for measuring duration. The irreversibility of historic time allows assumptions about causality, contingency, irrelevance, and anachronism.

For the purposes of historical method and dating, time is presumed to move in one direction only and to be homogeneous in its measurement and uniformly present throughout the universe. Seconds, hours, weeks, months, years, and even decades and centuries are the same no matter when or where, for time is standardized as well as universal. Histories may be plotted as discontinuity and rupture, but ultimately even these disjunctions are measured according to the same kind of temporal units as those representing continuity. Systems of dating may vary by culture, but the professional method of historicizing time through dating is the same for all times and peoples by paradigmatic premise. Thus temporal measurements hold true wherever and whenever history is said to occur. Historians measure the past like the present and future, whether conceived as process or passage, stages or succession, according to a universal, unilinear time that provides the chronological basis of the partial and Great Pasts, and thus of the partial and Great Stories.

If some scholars question whether the distinction between story and discourse ought to be made in fiction, can—should—the distinction be maintained in examining history texts, given that chronological order seems to preempt the whole issue by ordering histories as discourse or plot time as well as story and argument? But many narrative histories violate the strict chronology of the sequence of historical events through rearranging the order of their presentation in the discourse. Even those histories that attempt to recapture past reality through recapitulating past events according to their dated sequence of occurrence must depart from a rigid chronological recounting to incorporate simultaneous happenings, to comment on sources, or to connect causes and effects to certain events and persons.[8]

Perhaps the most obvious example, discussed in the previous chapter, is the use of flashback from a dramatic event presented at the opening of a book or article. Flashback as a narrative technique depends upon an understanding, shared by the historian and the reader, of chronological time as a sequence or succession of events independent of their order of presentation in the text; the historian depicts a dramatic event before tracing the history or presenting the story that supposedly led to it, but the reader understands them in proper chronological sequence despite the order of presentation. Like flashback or retrospection, flashforward or anticipation or foreshadowing violates the chronology of the represented world to indicate in the narrative that some events in the historical present will affect those of the future. Both retrospection and foreshadowing introduce anachronism into the present or enunciative time of the narration. Although historians forswear committing anachronism in their explicit representation of the past as history, they frequently employ these literary devices of anachronism to establish the importance of their subject matter, to discuss the historical significance of events and persons in relation to past or future, and to show cause and effects in their narrations.[9]

Discrepancy between the presentational sequence of the discourse and the chronological sequence of the story also takes other forms in history texts. A topical as opposed to a chronological presentation of a period is grounded upon just such a discrepancy. Rather than tracing events and institutions as some configured whole over the years, a topical arrangement breaks up the configured whole to present its subject matter and discourse according to a set of themes each of which takes place over the same time span. Divisions into diplomatic, political, economic, social, religious, and intellectual topics are standard in such an approach. In contrast (and in theory), the representation of a period or era as such connects the various topics into some sort of overall configuration during its time span, thereby representing that configuration as its own kind of entity in relation to the periods that precede and follow it.[10]

To treat a period as a totally configured whole is to downplay chronology almost altogether in favor of a topical arrangement. Such a synchronic approach stresses time as a setting over time as duration. Synchrony multiplies the filiations among persons, events, and institutions at the same moment in time as opposed to tracing their causes and effects or contiguity over or through time developmentally. Synchronic analysis offers a cross-section of time to reveal the relationships among its subjects as morphological structure, while diachronic analysis follows its subjects through the stream of time and presents them as process. Both ways contextualize their subject matter, but synchrony elaborates a pattern that displays the effects of its topics on each other at one point in time, whereas diachrony exhibits that pattern as process through time.[11]

Synchrony is frequently used to portray what was once called the climate of opinion of an era or its "mind" or "spirit." In the classic synchronic history, *The Civilization of the Renaissance in Italy,* Jacob Burckhardt more or less "froze" the two centuries from 1350 to 1550 in order to present a "period of civilization which forms a complete and consistent whole."[12] His book offers a series of essays on "the state as a work of art," "the development of the individual," "society and festivals," and "morality and religion." In another classic of the genre, *The New England Mind: The Seventeenth Century,* Perry Miller covered Puritanism as "one of the major expressions of the Western intellect." To show that Puritan thinkers had "achieved an organized synthesis of concepts which are fundamental to our culture," he presented sixteen chapters about the various aspects of Puritan thought under four main rubrics: religion and learning, cosmology, and the modern-sounding anthropology and sociology.[13] More recently, Emmanuel Le Roy Ladurie's portrait of the early fourteenth-century French village of Montaillou seemed to many reviewers to reveal the very lives and thoughts of the inhabitants. Based upon the details recorded in an Inquisitorial register, his many chapters describe among other things the lives of shepherds, the nature of housing, sexual norms and practices, gestures and gossip, attitudes toward the past, magic, death and the hereafter, and other seemingly intimate details of the villagers' culture. His book was hailed as both anthropology and history and as a premier contribution to the history of *mentalités,* or the life of the mind of common people.[14] Even though his ethnohistorical account spanned at least a quarter-century, Le Roy Ladurie subordinated process to long-term structures in the first part of the book to describe what he called the "ecology" of Montaillou; and diachrony to synchrony to present the villagers' culture as a culture in the second part, on the "archaeology" of the town.[15]

Synchrony is also the basis of the notions of paradigm as advanced by Thomas Kuhn in his history of science and of episteme as advanced by Michel Foucault in his history of Western culture. Kuhn in *The Structure of Scientific Revolutions* appropriated the term "paradigm" to designate the set of fundamental assumptions and questions shared by a group of scientists during periods of what he termed "normal science."[16] Foucault applied "episteme" in *The Order of Things: An Archaeology of the Human Sciences* to the field of epistemological premises that gave coherence to diverse disciplines during a period in European history.[17] In *The Archaeology of Knowledge,* Foucault explained an episteme as "something like a world-view, a slice of history common to all branches of knowledge, which imposes on each one the same norms and postulates, a general stage of reason, a certain structure of thought that men of a particular period cannot escape—a great body of legislation written for once and for all by some anonymous hand."[18] To the extent that New Historicist work in literary studies depends upon Foucauldian premises, it too is usually synchronic in representation. Because its practitioners dissolve the difference between literary texts and other texts through intertextuality, their profound interest in diachronic explanation is subverted by their synchronic strategy of textualization. Since all texts circulate freely in a period, context becomes synchronic as it is dissolved into intertext even though many New Historicists claim allegiance to cultural materialist premises. As a result of these assumptions, Stephen Greenblatt prefers the term "cultural poetics" to "New Historicism," which he popularized in the first place.[19]

In all these cases, opponents condemned the notions as ahistorical because they could not account for change through such a static representation of a set of ideas. To the extent that these and other examples of synchrony represent the historical world explicitly as atemporal in their discursive form, they presume specifically or tacitly other periods before and after organized conceptually and discursively in the same way. Explicit synchronic modeling of successive eras or cultures in a historical discourse demands emplotment as rupture or discontinuity between paradigms and epistemes, as Foucault's explicit metaphorical reference to archaeological strata in the title of his methodological treatise indicates. The benefits and disadvantages of paradigms and epistemes in historical discourse are also those of synchronic analysis in general.

Sometimes the discrepancy between chronology and a historical discourse or representation seems to be used to clarify the narrative and make the argument stronger. Thus in *A New England Town* Kenneth Lockridge, as discussed in the previous chapter, places all instances of harmony, regardless of when they occurred during the first century of Dedham's history, in the first part of the book, which claims to portray the first fifty years of the town's existence; and all evidence of conflict, no matter when it took place during the century, in the second part, which is allegedly devoted to reporting the decline of community in the town during the second fifty years. In both parts the chapter titles are seemingly topical, but the chapters in the first part tend to be synchronic, whereas those in the second part are diachronic.

Paul Johnson in *A Shopkeeper's Millennium: Society and Revivals in Rochester, New York, 1815–1837,* used seemingly topical chapter titles—"Economy," "Society," "Politics," "Impasse," "Pentecost," "Christian Soldiers"— to explain through their very sequence the economic and social changes in the canal town that toppled an earlier elite's social leadership and subsequent elite efforts to control the new working class first through politics and then through religion. As in the second part of Lockridge's book, the simultaneous or overlapping events described in the various topical chapters are made to appear as sequential and thus as historically causative of each successive phase.[20] Similarly, the central chapters of William Cronon's *Changes in the Land* presented more or less topical chapters in such an order as to suggest the sequence of the process whereby Native American societies were supplanted by English ones on the land.

Presentation of simultaneity or overlap as sequence and change, if not as causation, seems endemic to immigration history. Oscar Handlin used such a form of temporal manipulation both in his scholarly monograph *Boston's Immigrants: A Study in Acculturation* and in his interpretive synthesis *The Uprooted: The Epic Story of the Great Migrations That Made the American People.*[21] In the former book, two chapters portraying equilibrium before and after the migrations bracket topical chapters on "The Process of Arrival," "The Economic Adjustment," "The Physical Adjustment," "Conflict of Ideas," "The Development of Group Consciousness," and "Group Conflict," which appear to present through their succession the process of acculturation.

Although these chapters are arranged in such a way as to seem to convey events in temporal order, in fact the events described occurred almost simultaneously or overlapped greatly. Similarly, *The Uprooted* follows the immigrants as they leave their old homes and cross the ocean, first settling into their new surroundings, then engaging (seemingly successively) in economic, social, cultural, and political activities in the new homeland, and, finally, reestablishing roots. In both books Handlin expands the historical simultaneity of many of these events into the sequential narrative of an odyssey.[22] That both Irving Howe in his popular *World of Our Fathers: The Journey of East European Jews to America and the Life They Found and Made* and social historian John Bodnar in his scholarly synthesis *The Transplanted: A History of Immigrants in Urban America* likewise present their histories as odysseys indicates that this is a standard way of plotting immigration history.[23] Howe's narrative follows his Jewish migrants from the eastern European *shtetl* to the East Side of New York City (with a generous treatment of economics, politics, and culture there) and then to a final redispersion throughout the United States (and American culture); Bodnar's story follows nineteenth-century migrants from their European homes through their arrival in America, discussing work and unionization, the rise of an immigrant middle class, the roles of church and club, and their ultimate relationship to the larger American society and culture.[24]

Another manipulation of temporal order in historical discourse as text involves the discrepancy between the duration of referred-to time and the duration of its representation in textual or discursive time.[25] In crudest form this discrepancy can be measured by the difference between the number of years elapsed in historical time and the number of pages devoted to those years in the text. A good example of this discrepancy in the duration of historical as opposed to textual time can be found in any textbook surveying what is taught as American history in high school or college. The number of pages devoted to the period from Columbus' landfall in the New World in 1492 or even from the beginnings of English settlement in 1588 to the American Revolution or the adoption of the U.S. Constitution are far fewer than the subsequent number of pages treating the remainder of U.S. history although the two periods are in fact of nearly equal duration.[26]

In all the examples discussed above, the discrepancy is between the sequence of how—when—time is (re)presented in the text and a presentation following an absolute chronological sequence. The discrepancy results from how time is inscribed in the discourse versus how it is described, or more frequently presumed, in that same discourse as referential content. Whether considering these problems under normal historians' assumptions about the coincidence between the real past and its textual representation or the metahistorians' collapsing of referentiality into representation, both groups can subscribe to the distinction between timing in and of the representation.

Such a variety of manipulations of chronological time in historians' presentational sequences reinforces as it exemplifies the desirability of distinguishing between expression and content in historical works. This division results from the discrepancy between history's being about time and history-telling's taking place in time. History as representation of the past describes time through a sequence of events taking place over time, that is, through time. As a representation, however, the actual written history is sequential in its presentation by the historian and in its reading by its audience. Its reading, like its presentation, takes place over time, that is, through time as well. It is this difference in chronological settings and durations that allows—indeed, makes for—the divergence of expression and content in histories, whether they be predominantly narrative or nonnarrative. Thus the arrangement of the story or argument in its presentation need not—cannot—be consonant with the past chronology to which it refers and which it seeks to represent. Since the subtext, on the other hand, is always implicit by definition, its organization as narrative could in theory always be chronological. Once made explicit, however, the subtextual story would encounter the same problems of representation and textualization as other narratives in combining chronological and discourse times. These problems demonstrate why a rhetoric of temporal ordering with regard to arrangements of narrative and argument is basic to historical criticism.

History versus Chronology: The Problem of Patterning

To what extent must historians pattern the events in the past in order to fill the presumably empty vessel of physical time to give message and meaning to the (hi)story? That the arrangement or sequence of events as presented in the text or discourse usually varies from their strict arrangement or sequence in chronological or referential time (that is, time in the actual past as represented in the text) poses the challenge of emplotment. Emplotment embraces both kinds of timing. How should the historian arrange the sequence of temporal elements in a historical text as opposed to the actual order in chronological time? Discourse time gives meaning to the chronological story. If meaning is given to histories through their temporal ordering, then how does emplotment serve this end?

According to the philosopher Karl Popper, "History has no meaning," if by meaning one intends some grand philosophy of history, or what we today call a metanarrative for all of the past: historians cannot "find the Path on which mankind is destined to walk . . . discover the Clue to History . . . or the Meaning of History." On the other hand, he argues, "Although history has no ends, we can impose these ends of ours upon it; and *although history has no meaning, we can give it a meaning.*"[27] Most working historians would subscribe to Popper's condemnation of any grand patterning of the past as history. At the same time they would also agree that "proper" histories must provide some patterning or meaning in their discourse. How historians draw the distinction between too much and too little patterning or meaning in history is the issue. That issue centers upon the nature and degree of plot(ting) in history.

W. H. Walsh, following Popper, clarified the distinction between finding "meaning in history" and trying to uncover the "meaning of history." Because all historians believe that history can be made "intelligible in principle in the light of such explanatory procedures as we can bring to bear on it," they can make sense of a set of historical events in order to create the causally plotted and implicated "unity in diversity" that constitutes a "significant narrative."[28] To that extent partial histories, in our previous terms, can be written.

But those seeking meaning in history lay claim to a much stronger sense of "meaning," according to Walsh, in that they pose the alternatives more starkly: "Either (it is said) we must admit that history has a meaning, that there is point, significance, intelligibility in the historical process as a whole, or we must accept the view that history is a chaotic aggregate of unconnected events and processes, lacking all rhyme or reason."[29] But here the historian's task ends, and the job of the historical sociologist and the speculative theorist of history begins.

> As a matter of fact, those who have asked the question "Does history make sense?" have been concerned with two distinct enquiries. One group of them has sought to discover certain constant factors governing all historical change; they have found the clue to history in race or climate or the development of the forces of production. History on this view would become intelligible if we could show why it took the course that it did; the "why" here involved is a causal "why." But other speculative theorists of history have not been content with this modestly comparative programme. They have wanted to find, not merely the factors governing historical change, but rather a single plot or pattern in the whole course of historical development. For them history makes sense only if it can be shown to be going somewhere, and only if the goal in question is something of which we can morally approve.[30]

How can the philosopher who argued that historians seek unity in diversity in their discourses also assert that some historians might go too far in their search for meaning? His answer seems to depend upon some quantitative theory of the relation between his idea of proper history and his conception of historical reality. Proper historians bring understanding through ordering a part of history, while historical sociologists or other social science generalists seek causal sequences in and across such portions of history. Both in our previous terminology produce partial histories, but to different ends and with supposedly different methods. Speculators about the grand meaning of history take as their domain longer spans of time or "all" of history. Such a differentiation between historians and social scientists and metahistorians speaks from the viewpoint of normal history (and to its own vested interest).

Even while normal historians carefully separate "proper history" from mere speculation, they are equally finicky about distinguishing "proper history" from mere chronology. Chronology may supply order in the temporal arrangement of events, but it does not supply explicit patterning, and that is what separates proper history from chronicles and annals.[31] The explicit plotting of time describes, organizes, and explains events, persons, and actions in the past all at one and the same time. Chronicles offer their readers "one thing after the other"; proper histories provide their readers with "one thing because of the other."[32] Proper histories thus contain self-conscious organization of arguments, interpretations, or narratives that offer the reader explicit closure through their arrangement in the text as opposed to their actual occurrence as "mere" succession or random conjunction in chronological time.

Whereas philosophers of history and historical sociologists seek (and find) too much pattern and meaning in representing the past, chronicles and annals seek (and find) too little. What does such a distinction presume about the nature of time and the plotting of history as temporal order? With what criteria are the distinctions made between finding too much or too little patterning in a small part of history, a larger part of history, and all of history? What is intrinsically different about putting some meaning or some pattern into partial histories but not into all of history, especially from a textualist perspective?

The Nature and Uses of Emplotment

Historicized time is given pattern and meaning through plotting, or emplotment.[33] At a minimum, plot can be defined, as it is in *A Dictionary of Narratology,* as "the main incidents of a narrative; the outline of situations and events (thought of as distinct from the characters involved in them or the themes illustrated by them)."[34] In previous terminology, plot arranges both the content of the story and its expression as discourse in a narrative. In a broader definition from the same dictionary, plot is "the global dynamic (goal-oriented and forward-moving) organization of narrative constituents which is responsible for the thematic interest (indeed, the very intelligibility) of a narrative and for its emotional effect."[35] In a still more general definition by another theorist, "Plot . . . is not a matter of typology or of fixed structures, but rather a structuring operation peculiar to those messages that are developed through temporal succession, the instrumental logic of a specific mode of human understanding. Plot, let us say in preliminary definition, is the logic and dynamic of narrative, and narrative itself a form of under-standing and explanation."[36]

In their most general meanings, plot, narrative, and life all intersect, or interact, through the experience of human time, its understanding, and its representation. As Peter Brooks writes:

> Plot . . . is the design and intention of narrative, what shapes a story and gives it a certain direction or intent of meaning. We might think of plot as the logic or perhaps the syntax of a certain kind of discourse, one that develops the proposi-tions only through a temporal sequence and progression. Narrative is one of the large categories or systems of understanding that we use in our negotiations with reality, specifically in the case of narrative, with the problem of temporality; man's timeboundedness, his consciousness of existence within the limits of mor-tality. And plot is the principal ordering force of those meanings that we try to wrest from human temporality. Plot is . . . basic to our experience of reading, and indeed to our very articulation of experience in general.[37]

As can be seen from this range of definitions, plot, time, story, and narra-tivity all have close connections in narrative practice and narratological theory. Emplotment transforms or configures a multiplicity of events, charac-ters, and conditions into a narrative, and narrativity constitutes its form of understanding chiefly through emplotment broadly conceived. Whether de-fined narrowly as a story (out)line or broadly as a configuration of all story elements, whether defined statically as formalist elements or dynamically as structuring operations, emplotment is what makes a narrative a narrative.[38]

Although emplotment is essential to understanding a narrative as a whole, it is not the same as the whole narrative. Nevertheless emplotment is the "anatomy," "armature," or other similar metaphor for the underpinning of the narrative and therefore of its theorization as narrativity. Whether con-ceived as a formalistic, even static, grammar or more dynamically as a structuring or organizing operation, emplotment performs the same function in organizing the temporal aspects of the narrative. Emplotment injects as it constitutes the continuity, coherence, and causality or contingency of the events in time that make a temporal miscellany (chronicle, chronology?) into a story or narrative. Plot, like context, turns an aggregation of materials into a significant narrative structure. In all cases, emplotment of a narrative encompasses subplots and themes subordinate to the main plot as it develops the story through turning points, crises, resolutions, and other well-recog-nized narrative devices.[39]

Some historians and philosophers debate whether present and past events possess emplotment and narrativity in their own right or merely receive emplotment and narrativity through their constitution as story. Interesting, even important, as this debate is in some ways to historians, its resolution is not necessary to an appreciation of the significant role emplotment plays in the construction of historical representations. We can study the function of emplotment in narratives without having definitive answers to the relation between life and its narrativization and whether or not narration is universal to humans, no matter how relevant, even vital, these questions are in other intellectual contexts.[40]

What emplotment entails as a general operation in both fiction and history is basic to Paul Ricoeur's three-volume *Time and Narrative*. In an effort to be inclusive Ricoeur offers a model of emplotment as mediation:

> First, it is a mediation between individual events or incidents and a story taken as a whole. In this respect, we may say equivalently that it draws a meaningful story from a diversity of events or incidents . . . or that it transforms the events or incidents into a story. The two reciprocal relations expressed by *from* and *into* characterize the plot as mediating between events and a narrated story. As a consequence, an event must be more than just a singular occurrence. It gets its definition from its contribution to the development of the plot. A story, too, must be more than just an enumeration of events in serial order; it must organize them into an intelligible whole, of a sort such that we can always ask what is the "thought" [point or theme] of this story. In short, emplotment is the operation that draws a configuration out of a simple succession . . . [It] brings together factors as heterogeneous as agents, goals, means, interaction, circumstances, [and] unexpected results.[41]

Emplotment transforms events into episodes and chronicles into stories.

To create narrative unity from chronological diversity demands nothing less, in Ricoeur's opinion, than the resolution of the paradox of time. "By mediating between the two poles of event and story, emplotment brings to the paradox a solution that is the poetic act itself" as it "extracts a figure from a succession" of events and enables the story to be followed.

> It reflects the paradox [of time] inasmuch as the act of emplotment combines in variable proportions two temporal dimensions, one chronological and the other not. The former constitutes the episodic dimension of narrative. It characterizes the story insofar as it is made up of events. The second is the configurational dimension properly speaking, thanks to which the plot transforms the events into a story. This configurational act consists in "grasping together" the detailed actions or what I have called the story's incidents. It draws from this manifold of events the unity of one temporal whole.[42]

If emplotment is the operation that derives narrative unity from the diversity of chronological incidents in a historical world, then it is the heart of what in Chapter 2 was termed colligation or contextualism. To the extent that all histories presume story as subtext and many present an explicit narrative, the notion of emplotment is basic to historical discourse as a whole, for it is the process by which history itself is created from a mere compilation of dates, names, and events.

To historicize time, therefore, is to emplot it as (a) (hi)story. In the best of all possible historicizing worlds, emplotment would be a simple congruence among the basic chronology, the (hi)story, and its discourse. The representation of past change and continuity would not need emplotment, because it would result seemingly naturally from its own constituent parts. Happy indeed would be those historians who discovered a conspiracy by past actors to bring about the resulting action. In that case the plots of the past, the story, and its discourse as history would all be the same.[43] Such a Panglossian view is not held by even the most positivistic and traditional historian today. Normal historians seek plottings of their materials that extend beyond their presumed empirical and referential bases. From where do these plottings come? Are there certain modes of emplotment that historians share with the other members of their culture? Are there only a limited number of these plottings? To what extent does the nature of narrative as discourse limit or determine the emplotment of history?

These questions raise the most interesting implication of rhetorical and narratological analysis for the textualization of histories. The fundamental question becomes: to what extent do structures of expression constrain or create the structures of histories and perhaps all history? This question presumes other ones. Are there certain structures of narrative and argument that pattern expression as historical discourse? If so, how do they operate in normal historical practice? More important, to what extent do they determine historical representations and, ultimately, history? In the end, can representations of the past be given only certain patterns and plots if they are to be shaped as "proper histories" and not as chronicles or annals? Does the same hold true of long spans or all of history when conceived of as the Great Story? Too little thinking has been done on these questions to do more than suggest their implications. They presume answers that are controversial in literary and rhetorical theory as well as in the historical profession. One argument challenges whether textual representations can or should be reduced to formal rules and grammars. Another debates the relationship between structural analysis and voluntarism or agency in human affairs as applied to the interpretive and creative acts themselves in literary and historical practices.

Beginnings, Middles, and Endings

The quest for pattern and meaning as well as plot in histories is both encouraged and aided by the professional presupposition that time is directional. That things and events occur in linear chronology fosters before-and-after pictures in and of history. Although historians are handicapped by their inability to examine the past as such, they have the advantage of knowing how things turned out—at least in their opinion(s). Thus they know in theory the conclusions of their arguments and the endings of their stories from the beginning. Their endings in turn point to their beginnings. All they have to do narratively is to fill in the in-between. Significant and difficult as that filling-in operation may be, its subsequent textualization is determined conceptually by the beginning and end points. Grand-scale teleology may be dead in professional historical practice, but narrative teleology remains alive and well in historical texts.

A minimal structure of historical representation, like a minimal structure of narrative, must embrace at least two events or conditions and the change between them.[44] Such historical notions—one might say metaphors or even clichés—as crisis, watershed, and transition have become colligatory terms for how historians synthesize minimal narratives of beginnings, middles, and ends.[45] Perhaps this minimal triad of narrative representation accounts for the magic of the tripartite divisions in historical discourse: the classic first, second, and third generations of immigrant history, for example, or even the triple stages of the dialectic.

At the least, then, all historians face the classic Aristotelian problem of providing beginnings, middles, and endings for, first, their stories as plots and, second, their arguments as cases, whether the discourse is presented primarily as narrative or argument. Why do historians choose the particular chronological and discourse times they do for beginning and ending an article or book? How do beginnings and endings constrain interpretation even while they prove the story or case of a historian? This is a question not of the relation of teleology to plotting and narrative structure but rather of how a narrative or argument is constructed in textual practice. Endings give coherence to the overall story, just as beginnings are selected to make sense of that coherence.[46]

Historians must find starting points for both their chronological (hi)stories and their textual discourses. This problem of dual beginnings arises from the discrepancy customary between time as textualized in the narrative or argument and the actual beginning chosen for the discourse of that story or argument. Thus Garrett Mattingly began his exposition of *The Armada* with the beheading of Mary on February 19, 1587, but his actual chronological history began centuries earlier with the Wars of the Roses and the long-standing rivalries among England, Spain, and France. Likewise, Paul Boyer and Stephen Nissenbaum began their text with the Salem witchcraft trials of 1692, but their chronological story actually commenced with the founding of Salem in 1626 or, implicitly, with its inhabitants' English heritage. Kenneth Lockridge, on the other hand, started right off, after a preface, with the founding of Dedham in 1635 and 1636, so that the beginning of his exposition coincides with the chronological beginning of his story. But the implicit beginning of his Great Story is early seventeenth-century English society, which not only produced the first Dedhamites but also served as a tacit basis of comparison throughout the book.

As with beginnings, so with endings: historians are faced with the dual problem of ending the textual discourse and the chronological (hi)story. In the original edition of *A New England Town* (1970) Lockridge ended his century of Dedham history not in 1736 with the reemergence of complexity that the Puritans had tried to escape through migration to the New World, but almost a century later with the classic individualism and economic liberalism of the nineteenth-century United States. In this way he sought to connect his local history to the larger Great Story of American pluralism and individualism. In any case, Lockridge ended his discourse time at the same time as his chronological history time, late as that date is in his argument and narrative. In contrast, Cronon ended *Changes in the Land* with a brief essay summarizing the changes that occurred in the New England landscape as result of the Puritan commodification of that region's resources, but his latest chronological time appears at the beginning of his text, where he discussed Thoreau's *Walden* and the implications of early industrialism for ecology. In both Lockridge and Cronon, the implicit end time of their argument and narrative is the present day of their readers, for their histories are forms of the same Great Story of the rise of capitalism in American history. Thus their allegiance to a Great Story determines variously the beginning and end points in their represented chronological story, their implicit subtext, and in their explicit discourse times.

What can be asked of the beginnings and endings of partial histories can be asked also of a larger history, such as that of the United States. When, for instance, does that history begin, and why? Should it commence with the migrations of the Asian ancestors of Native Americans 12,000 or more years ago, with Columbus' expeditions, with the establishment of Spanish or English settlements in the area that is now the United States, or only with the Declaration of Independence and the winning of the American Revolution? This question about the beginning of U.S. history is not about ultimate origins as such, but about the problem of plotting and patterning American history as an overall story. The choice of beginnings depends on which of the various Great Stories an author or teacher decides constitutes American history. Ultimate origins as metahistorical beginnings probably coincide with the chronological beginnings of a discourse only in Great Stories as metanarratives, for the function of a metanarrative is to explain through some sort of fundamental characterization how the present got to be what it is from how it all "started" in the past.[47]

Likewise, how and when should U.S. history end? According to Frederick Jackson Turner, one phase of that history concluded with the closing of the American frontier at the end of the nineteenth century. If white expansion upon "free" land produced all those characteristics Turner believed to be uniquely American, how could democracy and individualism be preserved in a United States without a frontier? Has another phase of American history concluded again with the end of the so-called American century? As the United States increasingly shares economic and political power with other nations and faces a united European community and an increasingly stronger East Asia in the last decade of the twentieth century, will—must—American historians relinquish the exceptionalism that lies at the bottom of so much of their interpretation of their national experience? Is increasing attention to placing the history of the United States in a comparative context a sign of the end of the Americanness of American history? Is this the significance of debate about the decline of the United States initiated by Paul Kennedy's book *The Rise and Fall of the Great Powers?*[48] As in both of these *fin-de-siècle* jeremiads about the ending of American democracy or power, all historians subscribe to their own Great Stories, with their own beginnings and endings.

Middles do not normally possess the same explicit textual significance in themselves as beginnings and ends, although they provide the expository and explicatory functions between the other two. Vital as those functions are to the text as a whole as both argument and narrative, such middleness is rarely the focus of the text itself. However, Richard White in his aptly titled *The Middle Ground: Indians, Empires, and Republics in the Great Lakes Region, 1650–1815,* uses what one could call an extended middle as the narrative and analytic focus of his text. In seeking a narrative site "with no sharp distinctions between Indian and white worlds," he settles upon the region that neither European imperial powers nor Indian tribal societies could dominate sufficiently to establish a single hegemonic style of life.[49] Instead the style that evolved, according to White, was a transacculturative combination of Native American and European practices of diplomacy, economics, religion, marriage, and war created by the diverse peoples of the region. Instead of the traditional discrete white and Native American social entities, White depicts a world of multiethnic villages composed of tribal remnants and factions and European and American traders and other agents; international and intertribal alliances for military and economic purposes; and multiple meanings attached to gifts, sexual unions, murders, alcohol, religious visions and conversion, and leadership. Thus the metaphor of his title serves also as his thesis, as a symbolic and moral as well as a physical and temporal space.

For White's narrative and argument to hold, he has to begin and end his book abruptly. "The Middle Ground" remains a narrative medial site between Native American and white worlds only to the degree that the author downplays both its origins and termination in the sustained imperial power relationships of France, England, their colonies, and later the United States in the Great Lakes region. Hence White devotes very little space to the background or even the description of the mid-seventeenth-century Iroquois wars that supposedly created the physical conditions that allowed the multiethnic middle ground to evolve. Likewise, his book closes abruptly at the conclusion of the War of 1812. Since the victory of the United States ended the balance of power and the opportunities for Indian participation produced by the century and a half of conflict among the international imperial powers, the author treats this culminating set of events as briefly as possible. Thus extending the middle ground as argumentive case and narrative to support symbolic and moral goals demanded the near elimination of a beginning and an end to the textual discourse.

Whether an event or series of events (as a colligatory term) is depicted as a beginning, an end, or even a middle depends on the needs of the argument. With this idea in mind, Judith Walkowitz offers two beginnings and four endings for one chapter in her *City of Dreadful Delight: Narratives of Sexual Danger in Late-Victorian London.*[50] In plotting her chapter on the "Men and Women's Club," she traces its "Beginnings" to the same date in July 1885 but to two different origins. One origin was private and lay in the personal and political agenda of its founder, Karl Pearson. The other was a newspaper exposé of child prostitution in London (W. T. Stead's "The Maiden Tribute of Modern Babylon"), which provided public impetus to middle-class "radical-liberals," socialists, and feminists to join. In four separate sections, each labeled "Ending," Walkowitz provides four explanations for why the club disbanded in 1889: because men were dissatisfied with the women members' performance in studying sexuality scientifically, because the marriage of one of the women members to the founder cut short her scholarship, because the founder became increasingly absorbed by the scientific professionalism of biometrics and eugenics as the solution to the sexual question, and because the focus of public attention changed as popular newspapers switched to debating whether the institution of marriage was a failure and to covering the sensational murders attributed to Jack the Ripper. The book as a whole has multiple beginnings and endings because Walkowitz accepts that the same documentary artifacts have multiple readings in the present since they had multiple readers in the past. Conversely, similar readings can be given to different events. Thus the book concludes with a chapter discussing multiple interpretations of Jack the Ripper, but the epilogue provides a second ending with the seemingly copycat murders of the Yorkshire Ripper from 1975 to 1981.

Different beginnings and endings, whether of partial or Great (Hi)Stories, produce varying histories of what seems like the same basic subject, topic, or time in order to present different moral and political lessons, as Margaret Somers argues in her narrative analysis of the classic master narrative of English working-class history. That master narrative, according to her, posits a beginning in traditional society, a middle in the crisis of the Industrial Revolution, and as an end "resolution into modernity" plus "leading protagonists in action (classes in struggle) and causal emplotment (the engine of industrialization, proletarianization)." Although such a narrative appears to offer a concrete version of events, Somers argues that it reified English history through a self-conscious effort to dehistoricize and denarrativize its concreteness in favor of its abstraction as an analytical social science quasi-narrative, which universalized its schema through the omission of specific spaces and times. In short, it denied historicity in the name of history. As a result of this reification and denarrativization, historians and social scientists alike ponder whether the English working class during the Industrial Revolution was reformist in its practices, "revolutionary in the 1830s but suppressed by the 1850s," or "backwardlooking" artisans rather than factory workers who were "reactionary radicals." The problem with these three approaches, Somers argues, lies in their addressing the same question—"why did the workers not act in 'classlike' ways?" Why "did the class in itself for itself prediction" fail? Those questions make sense only in light of the presumed, reified master narrative. In conclusion, she argues that the similarity of the three answers depends upon a question derived from the same basic story. They are merely three different endings for the same beginning and middle.[51]

Emplotment as Meaning and Lesson

That historical time is conceived as having direction encourages historians to draw lessons "from" history in the discourses they construct. That the textualization of (a) history is always after the fact means that historians always know how (in their opinion) things might have turned out as well as how they did turn out. That such hindsight is always considered accurate grounds the very construction of histories and the practice of history in general. Reinforcing these foundational prejudices are certain long-standard ways of plotting histories in our society that give meaning to time as history and offer a message to the present. Such master narratives as progress and degeneration once patterned all of history as moral lesson in addition to providing an emplotment of that story.

Although historians today condemn the use of grand metanarratives as organizational frameworks for their discourses, master narratives all too often still provide both teleology and political lesson. Thus although William Cronon admits that "the repertoire of historical plots" that might apply to his chronicle of Great Plains events "is endless," he divides all these many possible plots into two "large groups." One group narrates Plains history "as a story of improvement, in which the plot line gradually ascends toward an ending that is somewhat more positive—happier, richer, freer, better—than the beginning." In the other group the "plot line eventually falls toward an ending that is more negative—sadder, poorer, less free, worse—than the place where the story began."[52]

Progress as a way of interpreting and emplotting history is both a method-ology and a moral outlook. Such an interpretation presumes not only that the past leads to the present but also that the present is superior to the past. Progress presumes a moral standard by which to judge the events and peoples of the past in relation to those of the present and thereby provides a guide for the selection of events, peoples, and institutions to be included in a historical discourse. In that dual sense, such an approach to progress shapes what Herbert Butterfield called *The Whig Interpretation of History*.[53] He named such an interpretation after those optimistic nineteenth-century English gen-tlemen who believed that the history of the world was providentially intended to culminate in their times, which translated meant their England, their way of life, and ultimately their class. Such Whiggism also gave meaning to the so-called modernization or developmental theory so popular among social scientists after the Second World War and became inscribed in the terms First and Third Worlds.[54] Whiggish approaches to history still ground accounts of the "progress" of science, medicine, technology, or even democracy, philoso-phy, and the writing of history.[55] Even historians usually emplot the story of their profession as moving from poorer past histories to better present ones.[56]

Whereas the theme of the decline of community and other typological categories contrasting the past with the present once illustrated progress, this theme as often now argues, either explicitly or implicitly, degeneration. Nineteenth-century and later scholars developed the typological categories of community to aggregative association, status to contract, traditional to mod-ern, sacred to secular, and rural to urban to show how different modern times were from earlier eras, just as anthropologists and other scholars employed, sometimes even developed, these same typologies to rank "primitive" socie-ties against contemporary European nations on the scale of social and cultural evolution.[57] By the twentieth century, the loss of an earlier, less complex society and culture was mourned by cultural critics reacting to industrialism, militarism, imperialism, liberalism, or other "ism." As a result of this history of its conceptualization, the loss-of-community theme seldom avoids some kind of moral judgment, even if only implicit in the contrast between then and now, through its representation in historical discourse.[58]

Jeremiads about the "decline" of morals, manners, and the quality of life postulate an explicit or implicit richer, better past. Degeneration as a theme in history is as old as the expulsion of Adam and Eve from the Garden of Eden and the golden ages mythologized by the ancient Greeks and Romans. Modern historians postulate their own golden ages, before community de-clined, capitalism prevailed, Western imperialism spread, industrialism tri-umphed, or patriarchy predominated. William Cronon depicts Native Ameri-can tribal life as communal utopias to heighten the contrast with the subsequent ecological degradation wrought by the extension of European capitalism to New England. The Great Story in working-class history begins with the paradise of a harmonious artisanal workshop before the specialization and degradation of labor resulted in class struggle under industrial capitalism.[59] Women's history likewise once supposed an earlier better time for women when they shared economic responsibilities for the family with men before capitalism removed the workplace from the home and separate spheres segregated men's and women's work.[60] In a more perverse view from today's middle-class values, the progressive rise of democracy can be seen as the decline of aristocracy and gentility just as the emergence of the bourgeoisie can be viewed as the demise of knighthood and chivalry.[61] With the resurgence of fundamentalism around the world, should the emergence of secularism in the modern world be depicted as the loss of religiosity rather than the rise of science?

Historians give cycles meaning by representing them as ups and downs rather than as mere phases. Should the story and its discourse begin and end with a trough or with an apex, with a moral low or a moral high? If the story goes from a trough to an apex, does it represent progress, while a movement from apex to trough shows the opposite? Should the story go from trough to trough or from apex to apex? The latter story might move from one stable equilibrium state to another stable equilibrium state, although apex-to-apex might be seen as progress to decline and back again, while the trough-to-trough story might be pictured as decline to progress and back again. Moral and political messages usually lie at the heart of those many histories based on cycles of religious enthusiasm and revivals, demographic changes (especially generational ones), and alternations in politics and world affairs. Choosing beginning and ending points to suit moral and political cases occurs even in the histories of economic cycles.

Trends in history as Great Story can be interpreted as either progress or decline. Progress as the Great Story of Western civilization configured the Whig interpretation of history. Although it is the fashion for historians to repudiate such (hi)stories as grandly ethnocentric and chronocentric, their discourses nevertheless carry on the tradition of giving meaning and lesson to history through such standard forms as progress and decline. In fact, a favorite version combines decline from the past with hope for future progress as the result of "learning" the truth about what happened in the American and European pasts. The Great Story of modern European history still offers lessons for today's students of wars, nationalism, racism, ethnicity, and gender. Even the Great Story of Western intellectual currents carries its lessons for how people today should understand their conceptual problems. Perhaps the grandest scheme is that enunciated by Michel Foucault in *The Order of Things,* but the story and the lessons are also provided by Jacques Derrida as part of his deconstruction of Western logocentrism.[62]

Even an almost parenthetical paragraph can encapsulate both Great Story and lesson. Giles Gunn, for example, prefaces his argument for the revival of pragmatism as a useful counterpoint to poststructuralist cultural criticism by suggesting the "remarkably parallel genealogy" of pragmatism and psycho-analysis.

> Each is the product of a process of spiritual disinheritance from the common "cultures" of Judaism and Christianity—a process that began as early as the age of exploration and discovery in the early modern period; that was furthered by the development of physical science in the seventeenth century and the new spirit of enlightenment and philosophical criticism in the eighteenth century; that was propelled forward even more rapidly by the social, political, and economic revolutions of the nineteenth century; and that in the deep inward turn of the twentieth has now seemingly found its culmination in what Philip Rieff calls the "triumph of the therapeutic."[63]

Just as Gunn employs a Great Story of the rise of secularism as the basis of his intellectual history, so other scholars derive lessons from the emergence and development of capitalism and a market economy (the rise of the middle class) or the expansion of a world capitalist system and European imperialism (the rise of the West) as Great Stories. As part of Margaret Somers' argument about the nature and three endings of European working-class history, she presents as condensed a version of this Great Story and its supposed larger context as can be found:

> Simply, it is the story of the Industrial Revolution—the emergence of an industrial capitalist society from a preindustrial past. It is, of course, a story told in many idioms—the transition from feudalism to capitalism, the emergence of the market society, the emancipation of civil society from the state, the increasing division of labor, and the rationalization of the modern world. For each, the societal trans-formation—whether it is called industrialization, proletarianization or the divi-sion of labor—ushers in "the birth of class society." It is a story that has economic, political, and cultural components. In the economic realm it is a process by which commercialization, an increasing division of labor, and techno-logical development gradually break the bonds of relatively static preindustrial economies into industrial and capitalist growth. Politically, it is the story of the emergence of the liberal state that provides the framework and/or actively sup-ports the new laissez-faire economy and its subsequent class relations. And it is a process by which "traditional" relations are transformed into class relations, and communitarian artisanal cultures organized by moral economies are supplanted by the force of new class alignments—from the "bread" nexus to the wage nexus.[64]

Even if scholars can agree on the outlines of their Great Stories, they can differ over the lessons, and hence over their emplotments as history. Somers' own lesson is that as long as historians do not disaggregate this master narrative into its component parts through a more detailed and specific approach to narratives and histories, they will continue to be fooled into asking unhistorical questions of their facts and drawing incorrect lessons for their own political ends.[65] Modernists, postmodernists, and antimodernists all draw their lessons to construct their histories as they argue over what the lessons of the Great Story are.[66] In the ultimate inference of a moral from history, Immanuel Kant concluded, according to Hayden White, that the study of history taught three major lessons: that the human race was progressing continually, degenerating continually, or "remaining at the same general level of development continually."[67] White then draws his own conclusion: these three lessons when cast as plot forms represent respectively comedy, tragedy, and irony. When considered as worldviews, they reflect respectively idealism, cynicism, and skepticism. Thus the lessons of history in order to authorize certain moral and political judgments must emplot the past according to certain standard forms. Perhaps the greatest lesson for historical practice is to suspect any history teaching lessons. Master plots provide Great Stories, which in turn serve as context for their "proof" through "facts."

Toward a Poetics of Emplotment

Narrative and rhetorical analyses imply, as all our examples suggest, that histories cannot just describe change without emplotting such change, or continuity, as explicit or implicit story. Now is the time to ask the converse of this point: to what extent does the very nature of emplotment itself, in its imposition of temporal ordering in and on a discourse, determine the content of that discourse as history? Are there, in short, certain (master) plottings of history that result from the forms that narrative emplotment itself must take? Do the plottings in historical texts, like those in other forms of literature, especially popular formulaic works, follow from certain standard conventions—even structures—of story-telling and emplotment? To what extent, in the broadest sense, do the structures of expression in historical discourse shape the nature of its content as history?

Without a great deal more scholarship on the possibilities of a poetics of emplotment, no satisfactory answer to these questions can be offered. Two different aspects of the emplotment of temporal order in historical texts, however, suggest some possibilities of how structures of expression shape historical discourse as content. One possibility centers upon what we might call broadly periodization in and of a history as text. The other possibility is inspired by the efforts of narratology to categorize and classify the basic forms and components of narrativity.

Time, to be narrated, must be filled; and to be measured it must be partitioned. Historians divide historic time both in their texts and in their practice by such conventions as years, decades, centuries, eras, and even phases and stages. In use each represents some sort of organized emplotment of that piece of time or method of timing. Thus years, decades, and centuries, like eras, phases, and stages, represent more to historians than just their temporal duration or chronological location. Hence the year 1776 or 1789, the 1930s or the 1960s, or the twelfth or the eighteenth century calls up immediate images and stories of the European and American past to historians and their readers just as surely as does the mention of the baroque and jazz eras or the stages of capitalism.

Such devices of timing come under the rubric of periodization in historical practice. Periodization as a textual practice involves at least two complementary, overlapping operations. First, it designates the division of referred-to time in discourse by the various conventions. Second, it covers the ways of representing those periods in a discourse through their patterning, especially in the form of emplotment. In both cases, the rhetoric of temporal ordering overlaps with the rhetoric and poetics of narrative. As a result, we may get some notion of how standard modes of expression shape the content of histories—and history—by examining how the number of acts, stages, and eras or periods used in the plotting of a (hi)story as textual representation also divides time in those texts. In cleverly constructed texts, the organization of chapters and sections embodies as well as presents the periodization. Their sequence, like their division, represents as well as follows their emplotment as narrative and as argument. Their logic, expression, and temporal ordering all reinforce one another.

No better example of this correlative reinforcement in argument and story exists than Richard Hofstadter's chapters on the Populists in *The Age of Reform: From Bryan to F. D. R.* Even the chapter titles reinforce the disparity he constructs between what the Populists believed about their world and what he contends was its actuality. The first chapter, "The Agrarian Myth and Commercial Realities," contrasts the agrarian myth of the yeoman farmer and frontier independence with the international market in which the Populists as commercial farmers participated. The second chapter, "The Folklore of Populism," further transmutes the oppressive forces the Populists claimed to see into an ideological mixture of bigotry, conspiracy, and oversimplicity. The third chapter, "From Pathos to Parity," argues that only as agriculturalists stopped confronting the inevitable advance of an industrialized and economically integrated United States through such means as third parties and instead lobbied to gain a bigger piece of the pie within the system through legislative remedies did they become realistic and therefore gain their ultimate goals. The sequence of chapters and sections and the sequence of the argument tell the story that Hofstadter wants his readers to accept as the truth about the Populists' ideas and their world.[68]

In some histories the formal divisions of the text into, say, chapters and parts may or may not coincide with the temporal divisions represented as being in the past, but in many texts the formal divisions follow from even as they also constitute the narrative and argument. Many a (hi)story organizes its narrative, like its argument and discourse, as a trinity of stages, eras, or acts. This practice probably stems more from the perceived requirement of providing a clearly delineated beginning, middle, and end in the narrative than from any demands of the documentary evidence. The period after the American Civil War traditionally called Reconstruction provides a good example of the use of a tripartite temporal ordering and presentation as argument and story in historical discourse. Even though the moral judgments on and even the supposed facts of that era have changed greatly over the past century, the basic structure of the period remains represented in three acts: the time before, which embraces Abraham Lincoln's and Andrew Johnson's plans for the defeated Southern states; the in-between time, that is, Reconstruction itself; and the time after, once known as "Redemption."[69] Likewise E. P. Thompson divides *The Making of the English Working Class* into three unequal parts. In his own summary:

> In Part One I consider the continuing popular traditions in the 18th century which influenced the crucial Jacobin agitation of the 1790s. In Part Two I move from subjective to objective influences—the experiences of groups of workers during the Industrial Revolution which seem to me of especial significance. I also attempt an estimate of the character of the new industrial work discipline, and the bearing upon this of the Methodist Church. In Part Three I pick up the story of plebeian Radicalism, and carry it through Luddism to the heroic age at the end of the Napoleonic Wars. Finally, I discuss some aspects of political theory and of consciousness of class in the 1820s and 1830s.[70]

Whether or not Thompson's own summary does justice to his very long, multisectioned book,[71] it does suggest the power of the dialectical trinity of stages as an organizing principle in historical textualization. As Somers points out, Thompson was but one in a long line who accepted as they contributed to the master narrative of English working-class history with its tripartite organizational framework.[72]

As the examples drawn earlier from New England community studies show, the decline or loss of community as model is analytically dichotomous as an argument, but frequently trichotomous in its representation through emplotment of that story. Whether the historian is treating a Puritan community, a nineteenth-century factory town, or all of the United States at a certain period, the story is the same transition from *gemeinschaft* to *gesellschaft* as the original typology had it. The story portrays its subject as moving from a simpler community whose inhabitants shared meaning to an aggregation of people without those seemingly primordial bonds. Thus the beginning of such a (hi)story as discourse usually starts with a picture of the original stable community, moves through some sort of transition process, and ends with a new kind of society. The end point of what must be yet another Great Story form is as determined as the presumed community at the beginning.[73]

Whether conceived as a two-stage before-and-after model or as a three-stage model of beginning state to transition to new state, the loss-of-community archetype posits a rigid narrative model of what I call the community-go-smash plot, no matter how skillfully it is concealed in its exposition or its moral lessons. Even historians who try to sidestep the traditional Great Story of community from *gemeinschaft* to *gesellschaft* organize their texts according to its model, so powerful is its blandishment conceptually. For example, David Grayson Allen, whose long subtitle describes his subject, "The Movement of Societies and the Transferral of English Local Law and Custom to Massachusetts Bay in the Seventeenth Century," offers the diversity of five colonial New England towns' legal and social institutional forms to prove the variety of communities existing there. Even though his book's chapters explicitly focus on societal diversity among the towns, he arranges those diverse forms along a spectrum from most to least communitylike.[74]

All the classic typological models of sacred to secular, rural to urban, traditional to modern society follow the same basic story line as loss of community, hence posit the same kind of plot and beginning and end points. The original purpose of these typologies was to show movement from an older, usually static model of earlier era or society to a newer or present-day, usually dynamic society or era. Progress was both plot and lesson. In European history the standard starting point for such emplotment was a stereotypic image of the Middle Ages, standing in contrast to the end point of an industrialized nineteenth or twentieth century. Radicals and other dissenters criticizing what Europe had achieved often used the same beginning and end points to impart their story of degeneration and their lesson of needed change through reformation or revolution. The Whiggish reification of this Great Story of Euro-American history from the Middle Ages to the Second World War also became the conceptual and political foundation of modernization theory in the postwar period as applied by First World scholars to Third World societies.

This typological mythologization of a starting point in a static past and an end point in a dynamic present was applied in a variety of ways to American history. First, the history of the United States long stood as an exception to this story: European and American scholars alike maintained that this new kind of nation lacked a feudal past, and so was "modern" from its founding.[75] Second, the original Native Americans lost not only their cultures in the past but also their histories in the present. Such an approach to the narrativization of their history presented as inevitable their supersession as "static" cultures and societies by a dynamic "America." Thus their inclusion was always presented in terms of conflict, defeat, and eventual disappearance.[76] Third, American immigration history pictured European immigrants as leaving a passive peasant society to be transformed by the vigorous American one.[77] Fourth, traditional or preindustrial society was opposed to modern or industrial society on the same terms.[78]

So far these examples emplot their (hi)stories and frequently their discourses as two or three stages or phases of periodization. Such emplotment appears to follow the minimal narrative sequence of beginning, middle, and ending.[79] These different modes of periodization raise the question of how many stages or phases might be usefully employed in any one history. Are there upper limits on the number of stages or phases that can make sense in and of a historical discourse? Although the number of periods into which the past can be partitioned appears unlimited, the number generally employed as the focus of argument and narration in a specific discourse may be limited. Almost no research has been done on how this aspect of expression influences the content of a history, but Philippe Carrard raises the issue in his analysis of *Annaliste* poetics.[80] Although he finds that three stages are common in *Annaliste* literature, he also offers examples of four stages (for example, Philippe Ariès' representation of death in Western history) and even one of seven stages (Michel Vovelle, *La mort et l'Occident*). He suggests that seven may constitute the upper rhetorical limit of periodization, given the nature of human cognition. In textual explication, he goes on to argue, stages observe criteria of proportion and size just like chapters and parts of a book. Stages as discursive devices for narrative and argument must be roughly equal in length of exposition. His hunch about the upper rhetorical limit on the number of stages or periods a text can embrace challenges scholars of historiography to explore his hypothesis in other areas of historical literature.[81]

If scholars of fictional narratives may legitimately search for the minimum number of basic plots and their elements across types of stories and across media, ought not historical critics also to investigate in how many—or how few—ways histories can be emplotted? Are there only so many narrative plots? If so, how many are there, and what do such limits mean for textualizing history? Are only certain plottings available for use in history as Great Story as well as in partial histories?

Just how far we can carry this line of thought is tested by the recent efforts of Hayden White and a few others to discover what might be termed deep structure in historical narratives. This approach is inspired by formalist and other structuralist efforts to uncover a grammar or morphology underlying the narrativity of narratives. White acknowledges as inspiration the literary theorists Northrop Frye and Kenneth Burke, but most narratologists usually trace the history of their approach to Vladimir Propp's formalist analysis of Russian folktales.[82] All such efforts search for the structural models uniting characters, events, plots, and even time across their specific narrative discourses. They seek a morphology of actions in terms of their narrative functions and a logic of actors in terms of the roles they serve in the story.[83] Scholars dispute the value and applicability of such formalist approaches in narratology and poetics, but the increasing number of computer programs designed to aid writers are based upon much the same idea of generating plots, characters, and situations.[84] Such stock approaches to the basic idea of what emplotment entails suggest that they are also useful for historical practice and criticism.

One suggestion along these lines about the limited number of emplotments in historical discourse comes from a study of the stories underlying four centuries of (white) American understanding of the alien Other through ethnicity. In *Beyond Ethnicity: Consent and Descent in American Culture,* a provocatively organized book with an equally provocative thesis, Werner Sollors provides clues to what we might call a poetics of ethnic narratives.[85] Such standard narratives as Adamic newness and innocence, Mosaic exodus and chosen peoplehood, Christ-like rebirth, melting-pot regeneration, the dire outcome of intermarriage, and the metaphor of generations reappear in literature through the centuries. More importantly from the viewpoint of this chapter, Sollors argues that these stories also provide the conceptual foundations for recent historical and social scientific monographs. Thus, for example, the saga form not only shapes many novels about immigrants but also grounds the histories of Oscar Handlin, Irving Howe, and John Bodnar.

What Sollors suggests about the limited number of stories that underlie the understanding of ethnicity in (white) American history (and fiction and social science), Dale Porter in *The Emergence of the Past: A Theory of Historical Explanation* formalizes for the plottings of all histories. Borrowing from R. S. Crane's notion that in any narrative synthesis of action, character, and thought one of these will predominate over the others, he postulates that there are in historical narrative three basic categories of plotting: plots of fortune, which stress change of circumstance over change in character or perspective; plots of character, which emphasize the agent's choice; and plots of thought or perspective, which look more to internal or more abstract change in the evaluation of the actor(s) or situation. Under each of these major categories he describes four or five varieties to offer a total of fourteen plot forms. Combining these fourteen plot forms with his seven levels of abstraction (ranging from specific events, individuals, groups, and institutions and ideas or doctrines as concepts to larger historical forces or factors and what he calls "universals") produces a maximum of ninety-eight "categories of development, to which any event or narrative account can be assigned."[86] He applies the scheme to clarifying the point of view and the varying levels of abstraction embodied in the three customary plot forms narrativizing the abolition of the British slave trade from 1784 to 1807.[87]

Hayden White's tropological scheme for providing the deep structure of historical narrative not only suggests the most thoroughgoing critique of traditional conceptions of the relation between rhetorical expression and historical content; it also raises as a result the most serious questions about the entire role of structures of expression in determining the very nature of textualizing the past as history. His tetrad of tropes works in two ways to organize history as history as a result of their sequential ordering from metaphor through metonymy, synecdoche, and irony. If this sequence prefigures all the interconnected levels of chronicle, story, emplotment, explanation by formal argument, and ideological implications, then the content of a history as well as its representation is a poetic act largely independent of the supposed data and chronology. The tropological sequence orders the textual content as conceptual arrangement, as the application of his scheme to E. P. Thompson in the previous chapter was meant to demonstrate. To the extent that the tetrad as sequence also operates to characterize the succession of eras in European intellectual history, it configures the very conception of the subject in the discipline. Thus, for White, the succession of Foucault's epistemes from the Renaissance to the classical, the modern, and the contemporary can be translated as successive dominant verbal styles and modes of understanding according to the sequence of tropes.[88]

Whether or not one is persuaded of the adequacy or accuracy of White's theory of historical tropes, its goal is as suggestive as it is provocative. White's formalist theory, more than any other one based on rhetorical and literary theory, keeps pointing to the obvious problem: how many conventions of form shape historical discourse and therefore the number of ways in which history can be represented? From the standpoint of the discussion here the question can be worded broadly: how many and what kinds of structures of expression constrain as they constitute historical discourse and therefore histories? Although White's and Porter's schemes may not answer these questions for many (most) scholars, their attempts offer a starting point for such explorations. The important lesson of their efforts is that scholars, but especially historians, need to investigate not only how literary and rhetorical conventions and forms shape historical discourse but also how those conventions and forms constrain the representation of history and thereby the patterning of the past itself as history.

Narrativity and the Great Past

Such narrative and rhetorical analysis ultimately raises questions about the nature of historians' conceptions of the past itself. Do rhetorical and narrative analyses suggest that there only so many ways of conceiving of the past as history, or as the Great Past? Does the past conceived and represented as history in general have any plot, or is it mere chronology and chronicle? How many Great Stories of the past are there: one, several, many? Are the arguments over the number as well as the nature of master interpretive codes or metanarratives pertinent to answering these questions? Whether or not history possesses any ultimate meaning as philosophy of history or whether history is merely the presupposition of the Great Story, the conceptual problem is the same with regard to plotting or how to conceive of "all" of history. If the subtext of both narrative and nonnarrative histories is the past conceived of as a story, then how should the resulting Great Past be represented or told as a Great Story?

Do all the analyses of narrative histories apply equally to history conceived as the Great Story? Can, for example, all partial pasts and the Great Past be divided in terms of surface and deep structures like explicit stories? Should historians see Great and partial pasts as only so many stories? Should historians accept plural pasts if the number of plots is several or more? Further inquiry into the number and nature of grand governing narratives, metanarratives, and master interpretive codes would aid historians in approaching these questions.

One of the popular lessons of history according to professional and lay persons alike is summarized in the aphorism that there is nothing new under the sun except the history you don't know. Such a slogan implies either that past episodes recur or that their organization duplicates standard plots. Such a lesson presumes its own emplotment. Not only does history repeat itself; even the history of thinking about and textualizing history recurs. But all such lessons seem as much the consequence of narrative plots serving ideological needs and cultural practices as empirical methods proving foregone conclusions.

To argue that all history must be emplotted does not mean that all history need have only one plot or deterministic sequence. To maintain that the emplotment of history follows standard patterns does not imply that the actual past possesses a pattern as such. The rhetoric of temporal ordering only suggests that the emplotment of history through discursive representation must follow certain forms; it does not assert that the Great Past must be emplotted in any one way. All histories have patterns; all Great Stories have patterns. The Great Past when represented as a Great Story must have a pattern. Although the Great Past can be represented only through emplotment, the actual past need not be presumed to be patterned. Historians need not subscribe to any metaphysical or other metameaningful pattern of the past to believe that its representation will always occur through some form of patterning, even through only so many plottings of that patterning. The historicization of time through emplotment therefore does not imply any rigid, deterministic pattern of history of the sort Karl Popper feared under his definition of historicism.[89]

In the end, metahistorical analysis challenges whether the normal professional assumptions about time in historical narrative and argument limit current historical practice too much in the very act of constituting history as a genre today. To what extent do normal historians' notions of time circumscribe, first, their conception of what constitutes history and, second, the nature of their representations of it? Must, for example, the ordering of history as textualized presume the customary uses of time? What if assumptions about time as singular, uniform, irreversible, and so forth as the basis of chronology and emplotment are abandoned for several or more time scales and time spans? To what extent can the historian abandon the continuity of representation or the unity of the subject for disjunction and diversity? Would other conceptions of time produce other kinds of histories?[90]

CHAPTER SIX

Partiality as Voice
and Viewpoint

To move from considering a work of history as a text to examining the relationships among a text, its author, and the social context of each is to ask how and by what means (and by what authority) the historian acts as mediator between a postulated past and an experienced present through the medium of the text. If we examine the text side of the relationship, then we construct the author and point of view and perspectives from the standpoint of their embodiment in the discourse or their appearance in the text. If we explore the author's side of this relationship, then we enter the realm of the author's social context and the scholarly authority claimed by the discipline. To look at the historian as a mediator between the past and present through the medium of the text is to begin to explore the professional and societal context of the practice of history as embodied in its customs as well as in its productions.

Two perspectives suggest themselves for the reading of histories in this latter way: what are the politics of interpretations, and how are politics embodied in interpretations? What are the politics of the discipline itself as incorporated into normal historical practices, and what politics are argued in the discipline as part of the larger society? Only such a double perspective offers interesting answers to a series of questions about histories, historians, and history: who speaks, and for whom? from what and whose viewpoint? for what and whose purposes? To pose these questions is to move from a textualist analysis of historical practice to a contextualist perspective on the historical profession. In the process the definition of discourse shifts from a textualist mode of representation to a social practice and contextual or interpretive communities.[1]

The Problems of Partiality

Bias and Objectivity

Given the professional ideal of the Great Past and yet the practice of plural interpretations, historians confront what we might call the problems of partiality in all phases of their practice, whether validating evidence, deriving facts, or producing a synthesis. These problems derive variously from the incompleteness of the sources from and about the past, from the partialness of histories as represented by the multiple interpretations supposedly about the same past period, and from the gap postulated between the totality of the past presumed in the Great Past's plenitude and the inadequacy of any Great Story. All these problems of partiality are the consequences of methodological assumptions.

Both more obvious and more subtle (and, in the opinion of many, more bedeviling) are the problems of partiality stemming from political partisanship and moral judgment. That historians, like those they study and discuss, are members of social systems produces political partiality and advocacy in histories. That historians are participants in their social and political environments undermines the validity of their practice and their products in terms of the professional ideal of objectivity. To consider histories and historians as part of their social contexts and times subverts the seeming authority of the profession claimed through the ideal of objectivity. To historicize historical practice is to relativize its presuppositions to an interpretive community or a cultural system. To historicize historians is to relativize them to their social locations and their social systems. Thus political and moral partiality plagues both the products of historical practice and its presuppositional foundations.

According to the normal historical paradigm the various kinds of partiality are related but separable in theory. Historians usually discuss the moral and political problems of historical practice in terms of "objectivity" and "bias." The traditional professional ideal is objectivity and balance and, for some historians, neutrality and detachment also. Although the very subject matter of history is value loaded, historians try to construct their histories to be independent of their own most cherished values or those of their value-loaded sources and subject matter. Biased histories are condemned as propaganda because they support or advocate an ideological position or are "present-minded" in their interpretations of the past. Some historians view any framework or perspective or even hypothesis as conducive to bias rather than to objectivity.

Peter Novick insists that the ideal of political impartiality is fundamental to normal historical practice. As prelude to his history of the "objectivity question" in the American historical profession during the past century, he summarizes the tenets of this goal of impartiality:

The objective historian's role is that of a neutral, or disinterested, judge; it must never degenerate into that of advocate or, even worse, propagandist. The historian's conclusions are expected to display the standard judicial qualities of balance and evenhandedness. As with the judiciary, these qualities are guarded by the insulation of the historical profession from social pressure or political influence, and by the individual historian avoiding partisanship or bias—not having any investment in arriving at one conclusion rather than another. Objectivity is held to be at grave risk when history is written for utilitarian purposes. One corollary of all this is that historians, as historians, must purge themselves of external loyalties: the historian's primary allegiance is to "the objective historical truth," and to professional colleagues who share a commitment to cooperative, cumulative efforts to advance toward that goal.[2]

Many historians believe that only through such impartiality can history really prove useful. In this view the ultimate usefulness of history lies paradoxically in its lack of immediate or obvious utility.

On the opposite side, historians believe they should render judgment upon the actors, events, and implications of their subject matter, even if that judgment has political consequences. After all, according to some, the role of Clio, the muse of history, was to inspire and exhort her listeners to great feats as well as to record the great deeds and personages of the past. At the same time, they admit that political and moral biases are inherent in choice of subject, viewpoint, frame of reference, and perhaps even selection of evidence. As Henry Steele Commager once lectured schoolteachers:

> Let us admit at once that history is neither scientific nor mechanical, that the historian is human and therefore fallible, and that the ideal history, completely objective and dispassionate, is an illusion. There is bias in the choice of subject, bias in the selection of material, bias in its organization and presentation, and, inevitably, bias in its interpretation. Consciously, or unconsciously, all historians are biased: they are creatures of their time, their race, their class, their country—creatures, and even prisoners.[3]

In this view of the matter, one person's truth seems, and must be, another person's propaganda. This is bias stemming from the partiality of authorial subjectivity and social context combined with the limits of the historical method itself.

For some historians the problems of partiality are solved through distinguishing simply between proper and improper judgments in professional histories. Proper judgments are part of factuality and reconstruction according to the authority of the historical profession itself. Improper judgments arise from flagrant moral and political advocacy. If interpretation is inevitable in histories, bias need not be its accomplice. In the end, difficult as objectivity may be to achieve in the face of pervasive bias, most normal historians expect to have their historical pudding and eat it too if they merely profess their moral and political advocacy so that the reader can compensate for the inherent biases. This solution to the deep and perplexing problems of partiality would seem to many historians to require nothing more than the self-conscious and self-announced statement of biases—all too often placed in the preface. We might call this approach the "full disclosure" or the "truth in historicizing" doctrine.[4] Such a recommendation assumes that a warning to the reader of the presumed biases would seem to overcome them, or at least balance them, in the reader's mind. The advice also assumes that authors would or could know of all their biases so as to expose them fully to their readers.

Full Disclosure

Full disclosure would seem to work best when the goal of a historical text is to draw explicit political and moral lessons from the past or to advocate a definite political position. National school systems use history to teach patriotism to their pupils. Readers expect histories to bear witness to the evils or goodness of past peoples and events. Professional historians often feel that their works should provide their readers with moral and political guidance in the present through the lessons they draw about the past.[5]

Sometimes the lessons historians draw have quite obvious political or moral purposes. The plots of progress, decline, and cycle discussed in the last chapter all made political points. Even a 200-year cycle as projected by Joyce Appleby in her *Capitalism and the New Social Order: The Republican Vision of the 1790s* can offer hope to the present.[6] Just as the Jeffersonians inaugurated a new liberal society some two centuries ago at a turning point in the history of the United States, so today's citizens, according to her interpretation, are confronted with a momentous choice (and opportunity in her opinion) in that the United States once again confronts a major turning point in its history as that liberal society wanes. The new era will repudiate the Enlightenment view of human nature as selfish and acquisitive that originated in that period to justify the economic and political liberalism associated with the expansion of capitalism and the spreading market nexus. Thus a kinder, gentler political system could arise in the United States if Appleby's readers only grasped the lesson of her book and applied it in their electoral choices. To argue that one phase of American history is coming to an end with the potential for the beginning of a new era depends upon Appleby's not only subscribing to a standard Great Story of the development of capitalism in Western civilization but also giving it meaning through her political hopes.

For historians to provide perspective on history is often to judge the past events or people's actions in terms of praise or blame. On the whole such judgments make tacit but obvious comparisons on such topics as slavery, the Holocaust, atomic warfare, genocide, or capitalism—with the judgments depending upon the readers' shared standards of ethics and justice and

consequent revulsion or approbation.[7] In the heat of polemical debate, however, such standards might be spelled out, as David Brion Davis does for the
nineteenth-century antislavery debate:

> Few historians would maintain today that abolitionists were hypocrites who
> consciously exploited humanitarian sentiments for ulterior aims. Few historians
> would argue that abolitionism was simply a spontaneous eruption of virtue,
> wholly unrelated to the rise of modern capitalism and the concomitant redefini-
> tion of property, labor, and contractual responsibilities. The abolitionists were
> neither otherworldly saints nor the agents of a capitalist conspiracy. Whatever
> their virtues or shortcomings, they have been vindicated by history: morally, they
> were right.[8]

More likely, such ethical lessons are confined to adverbial praise and blame
through words like "rightfully" or "wrongfully." More often, moral lessons
are taught through paradoxes, contradictions, or ironies presented by the gulf
between a society's ideals and practices. Many books on slavery in the United
States, for example, point out the incongruity arising from white Americans'
subscribing to an ideal of human equality as embodied in the Declaration of
Independence and yet owning so many slaves in the eighteenth and nineteenth
centuries (especially, of course, Thomas Jefferson himself).[9]

At other times historians seek to correct what they consider misunderstood
lessons from the past. Foreign policy history abounds in such didactic use of
the recoded past. Thus the Versailles Treaty and the end of the First World
War, appeasement at Munich and the beginnings of the Second World War,
the dropping of the atomic bomb at the end of that war, the origins and
continuation of the Cold War, French and American involvement in Vietnam,
and the end of the Cold War and the breakup of the Soviet Union all are
continually reinterpreted to provide new lessons through setting the record
"straight" and therefore reeducating the people and their leaders as to the
correct action in similar circumstances in the future.[10] Such lesson-making is
one object of history as a public policy science, be it about economic cycles,
urban blight, demographic developments, or voting patterns. Such a use of
history not only provides obvious lessons but also supports an obvious
politics. So-called radical history professes openly such a political approach
to the past to raise the consciousness of its readers in the present to do
something about the future.[11] Politics and morals shape the choice of topics
and subject matter of histories, but such selection is not supposed to bias the
findings. Thus no one is surprised to find historians of the working class
concentrating on labor strikes and unions or historians of business focusing
on corporations and entrepreneurship. Likewise, historians of religion and
historians of science might differ on their topics in the same way that economic and diplomatic historians might. In all these cases, the historians of
each kind of subject matter might diverge in their politics and the lessons they

draw from their histories but still agree on their commitment to standard historical practices. What happens, however, when they treat the same topics but diverge in their conclusions and therefore their lessons? What if they disagree on the partial and Great Stories?

In these examples the partisan purposes are fairly explicit and often deliberately aimed for in the text, but they raise the question of whether the findings followed as much from the political preferences of the historian as from the nature of historical practice itself. How politics and moral choices framed research designs has surfaced in such well-known controversies in the American historical profession as those over the nature of the U.S. Constitution and the economic self-interests of the founding fathers as advanced by Charles Beard in *An Economic Interpretation of the Constitution of the United States* (1913); the profitability of antebellum Southern plantations and the welfare of slaves as argued by Robert Fogel and Stanley Engerman in *Time on the Cross* (1974); and the role of German businessmen in the breakdown of German democracy and the rise of Hitler as maintained by David Abraham in *The Collapse of the Weimar Republic* (1981).[12]

If the writer and the reader of histories had to guard against only the obvious political partiality of explicit partisanship and moralities, then full disclosure would work well. Moral judgments and political biases pervade the history productions in subtle as well as obvious ways, however. Full disclosure works best when the implications of the moral and political outlook embraced in a text are part of the argument or story. At other times, though, the political and moral purposes or uses of a history are entwined with the very methods of historical practice and textualization. Supposedly, the more historians realize that the whole of historical practice is potentially tainted by bias, the more they can guard against it in their teaching and writing.

Partiality exists in the political bias of sources as well as in the incompleteness of those sources. Historians assume that documentary evidence comes more often than not from past elites and therefore that archives reproduce their political and cultural biases. Even a survey of all pertinent evidence therefore does not compensate for the initial biases and incompleteness of the sources. This twofold partiality of sources is only compounded by the moral and political partiality of historians themselves.

The derivation of facts from evidence can be also corrupted by the bias of the hypotheses used to question the evidence. Thus not only the selection of the problems for investigation but the criteria for what counts as a solution all can be skewed by the biases of the historian. Historians' political and moral outlooks shape the contours of the research design, the choice of evidence, and the conduct of the research as well as the uses of story and argument. The uses of the past for present political lessons shaped several cycles of research and publication on whether the American Dream was realized in the nineteenth century. The original set of publications transmuted the supposed reality of upward social mobility into a complex of myths and symbols.[13] By suggesting that what previous Americans considered the reality of the American Dream was naught but wishful thinking at best and an ideology justifying corporate America at worst, these historians sought to undermine the beliefs of present-day Americans in the established system, or at least to question their optimistic assumptions about past social mobility and the opportunity to climb the social ladder. Their methods were those standard to intellectual history at the time: the reading and interpretation of selected various written texts. Their results were what they sought to prove: the transformation of lay people's reality into false consciousness (not their term). Thus political and moral commitments determined their methods as well as their results.

With the reality of past American social mobility questioned, another set of historians tried to quantify the amount of past social mobility in order to establish what, in their opinion, had really happened in the past. Among the first of these studies was Stephan Thernstrom's *Poverty and Progress: Social Mobility in a Nineteenth-Century City.*[14] To get at social reality, he analyzed the 1850-to-1880 census schedules for Newburyport, Massachusetts, as his test case. To measure mobility he divided that town's class structure into four categories: nonmanual, skilled, semiskilled, and unskilled labor. In order to make upward social mobility difficult and therefore to prove his thesis about the failure of the American Dream, he defined the American Dream as valid only if an unskilled (male) laborer (his bottom stratum) rose into the non-manual class (his top stratum). By concentrating only on the bottom stratum rising to the very top stratum, Thernstrom showed what he sought to prove: widespread opportunity to rise socially did not exist in Newburyport and therefore by implication in the United States.

By providing only figures on what happened to this lowest stratum Thernstrom skewed the representation of the town's (male) social structure and overall social mobility in that system. Since the unskilled constituted only 8 percent of the town's (male) population, perhaps Newburyport was an American success story, given his own figures. Fully two-thirds of Newburyport's males were in the top two categories of nonmanual or skilled laborers, and another quarter of the male population was semiskilled. Through manipulation of the definitional framework of his quantitative analysis, Thernstrom assured his political ends.[15] Later analysts challenged his reading of inter- and intragenerational mobility by asking whether immigrant ownership of houses in Newburyport showed that workers bought into the capitalist ethos and the ideology of the American Dream or whether they only continued the supposed European pattern of seeking property to foster economic security and perpetuate the family line.[16]

In these and other ways ideology enters even the framework of such supposedly neutral modes of analysis as quantification. In the end, for example, the degree of social mobility is as much a function of the number of classes used in the analysis as the nature of the social site being studied. The more class divisions in a system, the more lines possible for crossing on the paths up and down. Likewise, whether a town or city is pluralist or elitist in distribution of political power may be as much a function of the mode of analysis used as of its size, economic base, or history. Researching who knows whom and who marries whom supports power elite models just as investigating who spoke to whom and who saw the mayor proves pluralist models.[17] In fact the number of class divisions—whether one, two, three, or more—used to model a social system proves as much about the researcher's politics as it does about the society under investigation. To apply statistical analysis to social class may be a political decision that proves as it reinforces a certain approach to the social and political system.[18] Even to choose between the terms "stratification" or "classes" indicates political preference as much as method.[19]

In the textual synthesis partiality enters not only from adopting avowed political positions but also from taking sides in historiographical controversies. How should the role of third parties in U.S. political history be converted into a lesson? Did the People's Party or the so-called Populists of the 1890s espouse a realistic forward-looking program for opposing the corporate transformation of America, as Lawrence Goodwyn argues in his aptly titled *Democratic Promise: The Populist Moment in America,* or did they misunderstand the changes that surrounded them and advocate a backward-looking, impractical program for the realities confronting agrarian and other interests at the time, as Richard Hofstadter maintained earlier in *The Age of Reform: From Bryan to F. D. R.?*[20] Hofstadter portrayed Populist thinking as folklore concealing the inevitable transformation wrought by industrial integration and an international market. Lawrence Goodwyn a generation later saw the Populists as seizing the moment to choose a cooperative commonwealth over the corporate state then emerging. According to Hofstadter, the Populists chose wrong because they misunderstood their times and their country; according to Goodwyn, they sought the right remedy but were unfortunately defeated by those who misunderstood or were bamboozled by the emerging hegemony. Goodwyn favored the Populists because he too believed in participatory democracy and opposed a bureaucratic state. Hofstadter capitulated to modern American society and believed interest group politics to be the only way to cope in such a situation. Hofstadter espoused the common political wisdom of the 1950s, while Goodwyn favored the movement culture of the 1960s.[21]

Should the historian support conservative thinkers or radical doers, utopian political aspirations or regular parties—or do the very terms bias the answers to the questions, hence the framework as well? Even the language of description can incorporate bias through its efforts at vividness and stylistic variation, for so many terms carry political and moral baggage from the past. No anglophone scholar has explored the political presumptions of terminology more than Raymond Williams, most notably in his dictionarylike *Keywords: A Vocabulary of Culture and Society*.[22] Even dates show the political premises of understanding history as nationalism. Thus books with only a year as a title—such as *1776* and *1789*—convey their meaning with perfect clarity.

The organization of the story or argument contains the bias of emplotment, in the forms of beginnings and endings, progress and decline, cycle and stage. Even the overall story may be shaped by partisan considerations. Thus, according to the progressive or economic interpretation school of American history, the history of the United States consisted of conflict between haves and have-nots as they struggled for and against the advance of democracy.[23] As so-called consensus or counterprogressive historians showed how the American people shared ambivalences and dilemmas throughout their history, they also revealed, according to their critics, a conservative bias toward contemporary political problems by deemphasizing or even concealing the conflicts of the past.[24] After the 1960s new concerns about the oppression of minorities and women and the updating of old concerns about the conflict over the ends of the state became the focus of American history according to what was originally called New Left history or history seen from the bottom up.[25] Since this approach to U.S. history today posits constant contestation between hegemonic groups and the others they repress or oppress according to their sex, race, ethnicity, or social class, it might better be christened neoprogressive history.[26]

For most historians these biases result naturally from historians' loyalties in their social context. Historians embrace explicitly or reflect implicitly their nationality, ethnicity, region, religion, class, gender, generation, or cultural outlook and values. Even historians in opposition to their own apparent social and political contexts only adopt other biases in the process.[27] To personal biases and group prejudice must be added, according to William Walsh, theories of human nature and behavior, theories of causation, and metaphysical beliefs. For him histories incorporate the politics and morality stemming from ultimate judgments of value and propriety in human affairs (the worth of freedom over slavery, for example) and theoretical conceptions of human beings (economic self-interest versus altruism, for example) as well as allegiance to conflicting schools of interpretation (pluralist versus Marxist, for example) and theories of causation in human affairs (great man versus the masses, for example).[28] To this list we might add presuppositions about normal causation in the world (divine providence versus secular causation), theories of the state (pluralist versus class), and modes of explanation (human agency versus social structural).[29]

In light of the pervasiveness of partiality in normal historical practice, full disclosure and truth-in-historicizing seem both obvious and unachievable remedies in histories. Full disclosure in the end oversimplifies the connection between the role of morals and politics in historical practice and the presuppositional foundations of historical methodology. If all historians had to do to achieve objectivity was to expose their own (unconscious as well as conscious) biases, then why is the whole question of objectivity and bias so vexing in the profession? What must historians know of the presuppositional framework of (normal) historical (re)construction in addition to their own (unconscious) predispositions if readers are to be alerted adequately to how authors' biases pervade texts? To what extent do the very presuppositions of normal history conceal some of the basic problems?[30]

The Historian in the Text

The pervasiveness of bias in historical discourse suggests that the very construction of texts entails partiality as part of the operation. That historians seek to mediate between the past they posit and the present they presume of themselves and their readers through the medium of their texts produces the very problems of partiality their professional code and methods seek to eliminate. In producing a text that attempts to bridge the gulf between the ideal of the Great Past and the goal of professional history, the historian faces the problem of telling rather than showing from a literary point of view.

Showing and telling in literary productions go under the names of mimesis and diegesis, scene and summary, enacting and recounting, simulation and reportage, among the more popular designations.[31] Today the distinction between Aristotle's terms *mimesis* and *diegesis* centers on contrasting modes of representing actors and actions in various media. As "enacting" and "showing" suggest, mimetic representation is direct reproduction of words, actions, and scenes through the medium. Such direct imitation is denied novelists and historians. They are limited to summarizing or recounting what happened. Thus histories, like novels, are mimetic only in the sense that they sometimes use the words of the actors—and even then they are written, not spoken, words. They cannot be mimetic in the classic sense because they cannot replicate words and actions as in a film or play or duplicate the scene or the action as in a painting or photograph. Their mode must therefore be primarily diegetic. Similarly, their "realism" derives not from a seemingly direct reproduction but from representation through other, indirect means conventional to the medium.[32]

With this elementary distinction we can examine better the degree of invention and interpretation in historical texts that produces the problems of partiality historians see. If the historian acts as mediator between the postulated past and the presumed present through the medium of the text, then in what ways? What forms does that role take in creating the text? To what degree must historians intervene in any textualization claiming to be history as the mediator they seek to be?[33] To aid us in this endeavor we can construct a scale of intervention ranging from showing to telling to lecturing or moralizing. Such a scale, idealized though it may be, also suggests the degree of factuality as opposed to interpretation and fictional invention from the viewpoint of normal historical practice.[34]

Degrees of Intervention

The basis for this scale cannot be the reproduction of the past itself, since the past has by definition disappeared. Rather the basis for the scale—and for the first degree—begins with the reproduction of remains from the past. From the viewpoint of historical practice, remains become evidence through interpretation. Within the framework of this scale, however, only the reproduction of the remains themselves, unmediated as possible in their reproduction, provides the foundation for the scale. If the remains themselves are as close to the past as the present comes, then only the reproduction of these remains can simulate what was the past itself.[35]

First degree: reproduction of the documents or artifacts. The more nearly the artifact or text is reproduced as a whole, the less chance there is that the editor's or other intervener's selection and interpretation will enter the mimetic process. Thus all of a set of letters or an entire diary is better than abridged sections from them or selected quotations scattered in some historian's text. Translation, editorial apparatus, footnotes, documentation, even the nature of printing or other reproduction all distance the final representation of remains from the remains themselves. In this sense, source books, editions, microfilms, photocopies, and other means of documentary and artifactual reproduction all exhibit some degree of intervention by the historian just through the reproduction process, let alone the editorial apparatus. Hence even this degree shows the historian's mediation. What does not remain from the past in the present is as important as what does. Its very absence demands the historian's intervention through imagination (hence fictional invention and bias?).[36]

Second degree: reproduction of part of a set of remains through quotation in a text. Such quotation is mimetic of the absent past through that portion of the remains, but the historian now employs what pieces she chooses to make her case or story. The historian's discourse contains the actual words of the documentary evidence, whether of expressed thoughts and feelings, descriptions of actions and scenes, or narrative, commentary, and argument, but the context of these quoted words is established by the interpretation of the historian rather than by the whole of the document or artifact system. As a consequence, quotations can be biased through their very selection to support the historian's story or argument. Although historians may employ quotations as indications of what past persons thought, such evidence represents only what past persons themselves wrote or what others wrote about them. Even here the structure of expression may influence importantly the content of the source. A diary, for example, may contain formulaic statements of standard emotions and outlooks common in the society rather than unique to the writer. Such firsthand accounts thus manifest intertextual and contextual as much as individual significance, but the document itself does not show such alone or uninterpreted.[37]

Third degree: description with a minimum of authorial voice or interpretation. This degree is achieved mainly through paraphrasing past descriptions and other parts of the documents. Such scholarly plagiarism through paraphrase fuses the author's words with words from past remains in present narrative and argument. The ability to paraphrase or to summarize is also the power to reconstrue and to misrepresent what was given in the sources.

Fourth degree: description beyond paraphrase. The historian describes through her own words situations, events, and ideas contained in a document or series of documents so as to convey them as "factually" as possible. The more the historian employs her own words, the greater the chance there is that interpretation and therefore partiality will enter into her discourse. Yet nothing less is demanded by and from the synthetic function of historical practice. Does fictive invention balance documentary factuality at this degree?

Fifth degree: extrapolation by pointing out implications and meaning in terms of what happened later. The distance from a period in the past comes from knowing the (f)actuality of later times. Yet knowing the future of a past time reduces the mimesis of the historian's report of that time through the documentary record, even though that future is also created from another documentary record from the later past. No matter how mimetic the construction of that future of a past in the historian's synthesis is to those future remains, the very introduction of a future to a given past violates the integrity of that past by providing knowledge of what those who lived then could not know or, more precisely, what their documents could never show. Thus the historian's overall text, no matter how factual in its various mimetic uses of various documents from different times in the past, contains a fictive or inventive, even anachronistic, element with its knowledge of the future of a given past. It is only at this degree that proper history as defined by normal historical practice enters the scale. Even at this degree the discourse could be more exposition than commentary, but only such a minimum level of interpretation would be considered a proper history text by the profession.

Sixth degree: extrapolation of conclusions and lessons. In pointing out the meaning of a past for the present, the historian allows interpretation and judgment to supersede the evidence she either reproduces or interprets. Such didacticism is an extrapolation from the evidence the historian possesses about both the given past and her living present. Intervention through commentary thus outweighs the exposition of the evidence in the production of this judgmental layer in the discourse. As a result this degree is far less mimetic of any reproduced remains than the preceding degrees, even though such interpretive extrapolation is frequently considered the very essence of a good history.

Seventh degree: representation of the past in a text. At this degree attention moves from how the parts of a text represent the past to how the text as a whole presents that past in the entirety of its discourse. It emphasizes the overall structure of interpretation as embodied in the text and how the structure of factuality is transformed into a proper historical synthesis.

Eighth degree: interpretation as a school. No one historian's interpretive discourse need be the referent for what an interpretation designates in the profession. Although one or several texts may be the exemplars of an interpretation, the meaning of an interpretation in historical practice is usually larger than the exemplars. Thus the frontier interpretation of American history or the economic interpretation of the American Revolution embraces many books and articles, even though these interpretive syntheses are associated with certain prominent historians' names and their works. It is at this degree that interpretations and Great Stories merge. Both are highly removed from any reproduction of the remains as such; both are greatly dependent upon the inventive function of rhetoric and allegory in historical discourse.

Ninth degree: postulation of the Great Past. At the most remote degree or level from reproduced remains is the comprehensive synthetic interpretation of the past itself as (a) history. At this level the Great Past legitimates the authenticity of historians' representations.

Whether or not this scheme contains too few or too many degrees or levels, it is designed to suggest how often and how much historians must intervene as mediators between the past they postulate and its representation in their texts. Even editions of seemingly first-degree sources combine several degrees of intervention when the editor acts as historian in the overall text. The early volumes of *The Papers of Thomas Jefferson,* edited under the direction of Julian P. Boyd, are usually hailed as the first modern critical scholarly editions of historic personages' papers in the United States. In addition to the editorial and typographical interventions used in transforming hand-written documents into printed texts or the combining of similar versions of a document into one printed one that never existed as such, Boyd included elaborate annotations through introductions and footnotes that presented a consistently one-sided interpretation of Jefferson as a democrat as opposed to a conservative, in accordance with historiographical debate at the time of editing. In at least one instance that I found, this interpretive editorial intervention went so far as to invent a reason utterly without any evidential basis for a vote by Jefferson on the 1784 Ordinance that created what would become eventually the territorial system for governing emerging trans-Appalachian American settlements.[38]

Even those texts that depend for their effect on evoking the past through reproducing chunks of documentary evidence reveal great amounts of intervention. Laurel Thatcher Ulrich, for example, in *A Midwife's Tale: The Life of Martha Ballard, Based on Her Diary, 1785–1812*, transcribes some entries from the diary of a Hallowell, Maine, woman but essentially constructs a biography around these documentary excerpts, using quotations liberally from other parts of the diary supplemented greatly by thorough research into contemporary community records to flesh out the medical practices and the life of this woman.[39] In many ways, Ulrich constructs a modern equivalent of the diary-based life-and-times biographies traditional to the nineteenth century but incorporating current approaches from women's, family, and community history. In the process, her text ranges through second through fifth degrees at a minimum.

If even the very reproduction of past remains affords ample opportunity for intervention, then how omnipresent must intervention be in any text considered a proper history. Still further removed from the smallest degrees of intervention are such classics as Carlo Ginzburg's *The Cheese and the Worms: The Cosmos of a Sixteenth-Century Miller* and Emmanuel Le Roy Ladurie's *Montaillou: The Promised Land of Error*.[40] Both books purport to reproduce the popular culture of the common people, one through the worldview of Menocchio, a sixteenth-century Italian village's miller and sometime mayor, and one through the emotions and attitudes of French villagers in the early 1300s. As words from these people both books quote confessional statements that appear at times in the third person in Inquisitorial registers. Both authors appear to accept these words as if they were transparent to what they refer and not framed to appeal to their interrogators or reshaped by the clerks taking the supposedly verbatim testimony. Both texts, after acknowledging the source of their evidence, suppress the Inquisitorial power structure that produced and preserved the words in the first place. In the end both texts, according to their critics, synthesize their versions of popular culture as much from their presuppositions about the relations between hegemonic and popular cultures as from their research in the documents. Critics also accuse both authors of romanticizing the common people's culture as oppositional to formal, high, hegemonic culture at times when that very power was in question, as the very source of their documentary evidence would seem to indicate.[41]

Regardless of who is correct about the nature of popular culture in these matters, both authors' texts as a whole are far removed from the smaller degrees of intervention as they contextualize the villagers' worldviews by extrapolating and synthesizing their worlds. Ginzburg's Friuli miller and Le Roy Ladurie's Montaillou villagers, like Ulrich's Hallowell midwife, derive their reader impact and acclaim from their seemingly minimal, second-degree intervention between historian and the past that comes from the shorter and longer quotations from the sources. Unlike the diary of Martha Ballard, which was written by the subject herself, however, the words of the miller and the Montaillou townsfolk are derived from formal testimony taken by others and often further edited by still others. In all three cases, however, the overall impact of the books derives from the fifth- and sixth-degree and beyond interventions that shape and give meaning to the texts and thereby transform the lower-level interventions into "proper" histories.

A Story Scale

Just as there are degrees of intervention ranging from quotation to interpretation, lesson, and beyond in the writing of a history, so too there are degrees of mediation in the story already told in a source. What Natalie Zemon Davis starts in *The Return of Martin Guerre,* she elaborates as method in *Fiction in the Archives: Pardon Tales and Their Tellers in Sixteenth-Century France.*[42] The first book (and the motion picture of the same title) tells the story of a well-to-do fifteenth-century Languedoc peasant who suddenly leaves his wife, child, and property and then as suddenly returns during the trial of a man who had turned up and impersonated him for several years. The basic story in both the book and the film follows the narratives of the two books describing the case, one by a judge of the court, that appeared soon after the trial. In this instance, the narrative of the sources and that of the history book and film are basically the same.[43] In *The Return of Martin Guerre* Davis subordinates the nature of how the story was told, or its structure of expression, to the historical grounds for its representation, or its structure of referentiality. She takes as her topic in the second book the "rhetorical craft" and fictive invention that went into the narratives contained in letters of remission, petitions attempting to persuade kings and courts to pardon the supplicants for their crimes. According to her introduction:

> I am after how sixteenth-century people told stories . . . what they thought a good story was, how they accounted for motive, and how through narrative they made sense of the unexpected and built coherence into immediate experience. I want to see how their stories varied according to teller and listener and how the rules for plot in these judicial tales of violence and grace interacted with wider contemporary habits of explanation, description, and evaluation.[44]

Here Davis admits to being influenced by recent narrative theory in addition to the traditional historian's concern for the documented social and cultural context. Throughout the book are transcriptions of such documents so that the reader can see a sample of the sources, their narrative conventions and construction, and their interpretation by Davis.

As Davis' exploration of the narrative nature of her sources demonstrates, the story told by a historian can be quite similar to that found in a source. Consequently Martin Jay distinguishes between a first level of narration, the one found in the sources, and a second level of narration, the one produced by historians in their own texts.[45] Margaret Somers sorts out four kinds of narratives in historical practice: "ontological" ones that individuals as social actors use to orient themselves to and act in their worlds; public, cultural, or institutional narratives about interpersonal experiences of time as history, whether in families, institutions, or the nation; conceptual, analytic, or socio- logical narratives that social scientists and historians construct to explain social forces as structures or constraints upon the actors; and master narra- tives that give organization to the historians' and social scientists' own narratives as social persons and scholars.[46] These and other scholars suggest that a scale of levels or degrees of mediation or intervention for the story can be constructed just as it can with regard to sources. This spectrum or scale can vary from repeating a story found as such in a source to constructing a story nowhere told as such in the sources.

First degree: the story presented is the story found in a source itself. The historian's text is a reproduction or transcription of the source itself, as Davis does at times in her book on the pardon tales. Similarly, Michel Foucault presented the reader with the numerous narratives constituting the (hi)story of Pierre Rivière's violent murders of his mother, his eighteen-year-old sister, and his seven-year-old brother on June 3, 1835.[47] The book's first part presents the various sources: testimony of witnesses, interrogations of Rivière by officials, court documents, newspaper accounts, medical opinions, the judge's opinion, and, most remarkable of all, Rivière's own long memoir. The second part of the book offers seven commentaries on the documents by Foucault and other scholars. Thus the reader is faced with many narratives already constructed—those of the sources and those given or presumed in the commentaries—as well as those to be constructed by the reader from those given in the book.

Second degree: the story presented derives from a sequential series of sources. Should the basic story of Martin Guerre, especially as presented in the film, be placed at this level of intervention?[48] And Laurel Thatcher Ulrich's basic story comes from Martha Ballard's diary, but she provides both elements and context from many sources. As both Davis' and Ulrich's works show, to provide contextualization of one sort or another necessarily forces even those historians highly dependent upon the stories in a major or a few sources to intervene beyond them in the final creation of the text's story.

Third degree: the story presented is partly found in the documents and partly inferred from the documents. This degree begins to approach proper history in normal practice. Both Ginzburg's *The Cheese and the Worms* and Le Roy Ladurie's *Montaillou* probably fit here. Similarly, Charles Rosenberg's *The Trial of the Assassin Guiteau: Psychiatry and Law in the Gilded Age* treats a violent murder and the intersection of medical and legal norms and their history quite differently from Foucault's book on the parricide. Rosenberg constructs his history of the trial of the assassin of President James A. Garfield as an overall story for the reader. Although he states that the chief source for his book was the three-volume trial transcript, he reproduces it only in brief quotations or through paraphrase. His note on sources cites many other documents and books used to provide the biographical, legal, and psychiatric context of his history, but he provides no notes to guide the reader to his sources or any explanation of how he used them other than their mention in the text itself.[49]

Fourth degree: the story presented is not found in any of the documents as such but is a historian's interpretation. Not only would the retrospective creation of statistics and their interpretation in economic histories come under this rubric, but so would histories that present a story of common beliefs as false consciousness. Economic and social science historians construct employment, demographic, and other kinds of statistics that pertain to past populations but were not available to the actors at the time. To argue that the best interests of an individual or a group are contrary to what they write or claim through the documents is to substitute the historian's ideas, often ideals, for the actors' documented understanding.

Fifth degree: a Great Story.

Sixth degree: the Great Past as a Great Story.

This scale, like the preceding one, calls attention to the role of the historian in a discourse. Fewer or more degrees or levels might be employed to get at how much and where the historian intervenes in the creation of present from past stories.

Both scales or spectrums make sense only in terms of a presumption of realism in normal historical practice. Thus the lowest degree of intervention is between the explicit sources and the historian's scholarly and social context by way of the paradigm of normal history. Mimesis in this case presumes only that there is some story given in the source(s) to imitate. At the greatest degree of intervention the historian speaks as historian no matter what her text pretends (and sometimes the documents state). Mimesis at this level presumes the ideal of the Great Past as the model to be imitated. At this level, realism in history, as in the novel, is realistic by illusion and not by imitation, by convention and invention rather than by firsthand (re)experience.[50]

Given their ideals, any degree of mediation looks like partiality to normal historians. The greater the degree of intervention, the more obvious the mediation appears to readers, but does a higher degree of intervention guarantee a fuller disclosure statement? However, since no historical text can be constructed without some—indeed much—intervention, historians' very presuppositions about the nature of the Great Past mask most of their interventions; hence their inability to disclose all their biases according to the classic ideal of objectivity in the profession.

Voice and Viewpoint

Much of what historians practice as intervention and discuss under the rubrics of objectivity, perspective, partisanship, and bias in historical productions resembles what literary theorists examine as point of view and voice. Historians confront obvious problems of voice and viewpoint each time they try to represent viewpoints and even voices of peoples they ascribe to the past. What is the relationship between the historian in the present and the postulated historical actors of the past as mediated through the historian's text? Must a historian adopt the outlook as well as the words of past actors in order to explain them and then present them fairly in their own terms? To what degree must historians be sympathetic to those they write about in their texts—no matter how repugnant their worldviews, behavior, or morals—in order to produce a valid history?

These problems of voice and viewpoint in historians' works have surfaced most visibly in the recent debates over who can understand whom in terms of gender, race, ethnicity, class, and otherness in general. Can a white male even understand, let alone represent in a text, persons of color or women? Or can only a person of color or a woman understand such persons through supposedly shared experience and therefore give the past actors present-day voice? And if so, does that mean that African-American historians cannot truly understand or write about Southern white plantation owners? Or does present as well as past oppression of African Americans lend an objectivity and perspective to African-American historians that historians from hegemonic groups can never appreciate or depict? In the end, to what extent must presumably shared experience between present-day historians and past persons warrant the validity of a historical text? Can such a bond between the past and present be known apart from its presumption in the master text of a Great Story?

Voice and viewpoint are united in a literary text, but they can be separated analytically. In the most elementary sense, voice tells us who speaks in the text, while viewpoint tells us from what perspective a voice speaks. Literary theorists go on, however, to distinguish between who sees and how in point of view and who speaks and how in voice. These distinctions in each case depend upon the usual textualist differentiation between content and expression. Point of view therefore embraces both narrating or arguing from a point of view and arguing for a point of view in a narration or argument. Likewise, textualists investigate not only who speaks but how and explore who is represented by what is said. Whether who sees is also who speaks or whether what is spoken or what is seen is from the same viewpoint are questions that hint at the perplexities of voice and viewpoint in literary productions. Only such double perspectives, however, offer interesting answers to the questions posed at the beginning of this chapter about histories, historians, and history: who speaks and for whom? from what and whose viewpoint? for what and whose purposes? Literary theory about voice and viewpoint suggests answers to these questions not so much in terms of categories of biases in historical practice as in terms of where and how biases necessarily infiltrate historical discourses.[51]

Voice

Literary theorists discuss voice in texts in two complementary ways: in terms of who speaks for whom, and in terms of who speaks to whom. Although the author speaks through the totality of the text (her creation), not all of the text necessarily speaks for the author. In what person(a) does the author insert herself into the text? How obtrusive is the author's personal presence in the text in relation to that of the subjects themselves? These questions about the relationship between the author and the text ask not so much what or who is an author but where and in what ways an author speaks through the parts or layers of a text. Their answers treat not the author's actual professional and social context but how that context is represented in the discourse.[52]

In a narrative text the author's voice can be found in any of several places or layers. Do the voices vary by degree of intervention? Just as authors envisage the ideal readers of their texts as they write for (that is, inscribe) them, so readers return the favor by inferring images of the authors from their texts. But is the author that a reader can construe (invent?) from the text like the author who wrote it? Who speaks in or through the text might be a convenient fiction of exposition or what we might call the inferred or imputed author, more commonly called the implied author or the textual author.[53] Moreover, in a novel what is the connection between the implied author and that of the world (re)presented in text, or between her voice and those of the actors (re)presented in the text? Does the author speak from within or outside of the narrated world? Does the author seem to speak through one or more of the characters or to remain aloof from them? Thus literary theorists commonly distinguish between the inferred or imputed author of the text as narrator and what she talks about, and thus what the characters can say and do, and what the inferred or imputed author says and does in the text for herself. In this case the text must be considered a combination of author's discourse and characters' discourse. But what if one of the actors or characters in the novel is the supposed narrator of the story? This role could range from mere eyewitness to minor participant to protagonist. The result is to add still another category of voice or speaker to those of the implied author and the narrator: the actor as narrator.

All these potential voices in the text—actual author, implied author, narrator, narrator as actor, actor(s)—except that of the actual author are found only in the text. Any or all or almost none of these voices in the text might speak for the actual author.[54] Who speaks for the author in the text might vary by whether the reader or the author attributes the voice. One need only read several book reviews of the same book to see diverse readers' responses to who speaks for the author. One need only read authors' replies to their book reviews to discover the difference between authors' intentions or images of what was supposedly said and meant and what their readers construe they said and meant.[55]

Since the author and the reader construct each other through a series of similar categories, it is possible to construct for the reader a scheme parallel to that outlined above for the author: actual reader, implied reader, model reader, narratee as actor, actor. In this instance, the narrator as actor hypothesizes a narratee or hearer-actor of the narration at the same time as the author constructs the implied reader as the ideal reader of the text. The theorist can construct through the text itself a model or superinformed reader of the text who understands the text as "perfectly" as the theorist. In no case need any of these hypotheses about each other's roles in relation to the text coincide with the actual persons writing and reading or their extensions through hypothesis. The author could mistake the competence or understanding of the reader as implied reader, just as the reader could confuse the voices and viewpoints of the actors and implied author for those of the actual author.

How the reader understands, that is, imputes, the various voices and viewpoints of the author is part of the subject of reception theory and reader-response theory in literary criticism.[56] Try as they might, authors cannot control the context in which their texts will be read and interpreted even at the time of writing, let alone in the future. That readers' responses to the same text can be diverse obliges scholars to look beyond any simple theory of authorial intentions to interpret discourses and their intellectual and social contexts. As such multiple readings indicate, readers have considerable power in constructing a text as they construe it. To the reader inscribed in a text as a model or implied reader therefore must be added the reader's interaction with a text or even the reader's dominance over a text. Some theorists construct the reader as implied through his inscription in the text according to textualist conventions. In stronger versions of reader-response theory, the reader constructs the text as part of a socially based discursive practice (which is why genre conventions are so important). From the viewpoint of the strongest version of reader-response theory, no text exists unless it is read, and no reader exists outside an interpretive community or reading formation.[57] A text as a result of the diversity of its readership possesses many meanings and therefore is better defined as a process of multiple significations according to diverse interpretive communities. Regardless of the specific theory of reading or of its context, let us call this theorized person the active reader, because she coinvents the text with the author as she interprets it.

The previous schemes can now be combined into a single series of voices stretching between the actual author and reader through the intermediary of the text: actual author, implied author, narrator as actor, actor(s), narratee as actor, implied reader, model reader, active reader, actual reader. All but the actual author and actual reader (and perhaps the active reader) are found in the text. Equipped with these simple but basic categories we can now distinguish among the voices in a historical text in terms of (1) those of or representing the author, (2) those of the historical actors, and (3) the relations between the voices of the author and the actors. Likewise, we can distinguish among the relations between author and characters on one hand and the (4) implied reader and the (5) model reader on the other hand as well as all of the previous with the (6) actual reader actively interpreting.

Historians can construct their discourses for fellow professionals, for the general public, for a student audience, or for any combination of these. Seldom, though, does a text attract all three, if sales figures are any indication. Even the category of fellow professionals is not a homogeneous group of readers. Is the text addressed to a specialist in a very specific area or to scholars in the general field of national or topical history? Or is the text meant to appeal to all historians and even to scholars in the social sciences and literary studies? These various scholarly audiences have differing interests and standards of judging a work, as reviews in the many different kinds of scholarly journals attest.[58]

Historians in the United States, England, and France debate whether they should write for a popular audience. To do so, they assume, requires a more exciting narrative or more interesting topics than are current in professional discourse, for the terms "popularization" and "scholarly" are considered antonyms in the profession. Nevertheless, some historians worry that their authority and reputation will decline if a large readership for histories is not recreated much as it existed in the nineteenth century.[59] Whether such assumptions about the need today for story-telling and "sexier" subjects (often literally so) are warranted is unclear, for what sells well and therefore presumably gratifies popular tastes does not always fulfill the standard hypotheses about what attracts a large readership (or television audience). What students read, of course, is as much a matter of what the teacher wants the students to learn as it is a matter of what the teacher thinks the students would like to read.

In terms of the historical or textual discourse, we can distinguish between the implied or inscribed reader as we construe that from the discourse itself and the model reader the theorist posits as the ideal reader. Presumably model readers are like the reviewers in professional journals, but even they argue over how a specific discourse should be read. Most historical texts posit the implied or inscribed reader as a fellow professional, if footnotes, bibliography, preface, and scholarly vocabulary are any indication.[60]

When we turn to the historian's voice in the text or who is speaking, we can ask not only about the form of that voice, whether as author itself or as narrator, but also how obtrusive the author's voice or its surrogate is. Narratologists discuss both these matters in terms of a scale ranging from explicit and intrusive to implicit and unintrusive. Does the voice speaking in the text for the author designate itself as "I" or "we," and how often does the author in the text speak as and for herself?

At one end of the range of possibilities, the author speaks directly to the reader as and for herself. Most intrusive, most obvious would be the use of "I" addressed to the reader directly. Direct address, including the use of "I," is most common in the preface or in the footnotes. Prefaces by convention are considered outside the historical text proper and so can address the reader directly. Their paratextual nature offers a less formal opportunity for authorial self-reference. Annotation, in the form of either footnotes or endnotes, likewise affords the author an opportunity to address the reader directly over such matters as the nature and quality of the evidence or the defects of rival interpretations.[61] Sometimes authors interject such commentary and themselves into the text itself. At other times the historian appears in the main text as a persona to lend authenticity to her observations as having witnessed the scene or observed the locale and thus lend the same kind of authority to her text as an anthropologist.[62] This tradition extends from before Edward Gibbon surveyed Rome through Samuel Eliot Morison's retracing of Columbus' voyage to the present day.[63] Finally, historians can appear in the discourse as themselves to draw a lesson or offer a conclusion, but according to normal historical presuppositions about historical reality this practice is also paratextual in a sense.

Can historians ever be the heroes of their own stories, outside their own autobiographies? Such seems doubtful in normal practice, for historians adhere to a professional creed that appears to demand a more neutral or seemingly objective voice. Historians can borrow a page from anthropologists and appear as coauthors in a combined oral and professional history, as in Timothy Breen's narrative synthesis of some of his Easthampton, Long Island, histories. As a result of his innovative format, he frequently enters the text as "I."[64] More often historians enter the text as "I" to justify an experience in the archives or to objectify the observer-actor relationship. Still others employ the first person singular to signify identification with their subject.[65] Whether or not the personal engagement of the historian in the textualization process itself demands acknowledgment through use of the first person singular in exposition is highly questioned in the profession. Is the use of the first person a more honest approach to the personal production of a historical text than the customary use of the third person?[66] Will postmodernist historical practice increase the use of the personal pronoun in historical textualization to demystify historical authority and to show its reflexive nature?[67]

Martin Duberman, in his effort to discover the nature of community during the Black Mountain experiment in North Carolina from 1933 to 1956, interjects himself into his account in many ways.[68] Although such persons as composer John Cage, artists Josef Albers and Willem de Kooning, and dancer Merce Cunningham made the experimental community famous at the time or in retrospect, Duberman sought to find how the many others less well known as well as the famous experienced their lives as they tried to unite ideals and practice in the three-plus decades of the community's existence. In the introduction he confesses his personal identification with what the community attempted to achieve. He hopes to put his personality as well as his research skills into the book and produce a different kind of history. Throughout the book he discusses his feelings toward the community's goals, achievements, and personalities. He reproduces in the text his first-person questions and the personal give-and-take of the oral interviews he conducted. He includes passages from his own journal describing his interventions during the oral history interviews and conveying his emotional reactions to those he interviewed. He compares the aims and problems of his own teaching to those of persons who taught at Black Mountain. Throughout the book he gives the reader his personal opinions on what happened at the community without hiding behind the third-person facade of neutrality. The reader finishes the book with as vivid an impression of Duberman as of Black Mountain. That Duberman is a playwright as well as a prize-winning historian enables him to pull off this personal approach to historical narration.

At the other end of the authorial voice spectrum lies the author inferred, the implied historian who speaks only in the third person. This is the textual norm for professional history. Hence the advice of Savoie Lottinville to the neophyte historian: "he never—or almost never—intrudes the personal pronoun 'I' into his account."[69] In historical texts personal production is suppressed in favor of seemingly neutral and distanced description; the use of impersonal linguistic conventions promotes a seeming transparency to the past.

As a consequence of this professional practice, historians' voices and who speaks for them more often than not must be inferred by the reader.[70] To what extent can this imputed author be distinguished from the narrator in a historical text? Unlike the case of novels, in the case of historical discourse one assumes they are always the same.[71] Moreover, the identity presumed between implied author and the narrator is customarily extended in historical criticism to collapse the distinction between the implied author and actual author. Not all of an author appears in a text, but frequently an attentive reader can discern more than the author wishes to present. Although historians try to repress contradictions and, normally, inconsistencies in their discourses, the critic's job is to deconstruct the text's tensions in order to reconstruct the author's contradictions.[72] Even then, the critique establishes only the contradictions of the discourse and the imputed historian constructed by the critic.

What of the use of "we" as opposed to "I" in historical discourse? Use of the first person plural implies three different but interrelated things. First, using "we" might imply the author's attempt to coopt the reader to her views through verbal association. This "we" is an attempt at author-reader complicity through the linguistic construction of the text, an acknowledgment of the social contract underlying the genre. Second, "we" could indicate some link between the implied historian or narrator and the historical actors in the discourse in order to establish the author's right to narrate their history. Third, the "we" could be the imperial "we" of the community of professional historians who self-authorize their practices as a guild. In each instance, the "we" is a social practice policing the representation of the past as history. This "we" is ultimately the one of credentialed professionals asserting their superior right over present others to interpret past others as historic Others.[73]

Patricia Nelson Limerick provides an interesting example of the use of first person singular and plural in her interpretive synthesis, *The Legacy of Conquest: The Unbroken Past of the American West*. In arguing against traditional images of the American West as a refuge for those trying to escape the complexities of eastern American society, she writes:

> When the weight of Southern civilization fell too heavily on Huckleberry Finn, Mark Twain offered the preferred American alternative: "I reckon I got to light out for the Territory ahead of the rest, because Aunt Sally she's going to adopt me and sivilize me, and I can't stand it. I been there before." The West, the theory had gone, was the place where one escaped the trials and burdens of American civilization, especially in its Southern version. Those "trials and burdens" often came in human form. Repeatedly, Americans had used the West as a mechanism for evading these "problems." Much of what went under the rubric "Western optimism" was in fact this faith in postponement, in the deferring of problems to the distant future. Whether in Indian removal or Mormon migration, the theory was the same: the West is remote and vast; its isolation and distance will release us from conflict: this is where we get away from each other. But the workings of history carried an opposite lesson. The West was not where we escaped each other, but where we all met.[74]

In arguing for the West as a meeting ground of European, Asian, Latin, and Native American societies with all the resulting problems, Limerick represents a multitude of voices. The use of "I" is the voice of Huck Finn in Twain's novel of the same name. Thus Limerick employs a fictional character's voice, speaking in the first person, as representative of both those real Americans in the past who saw the West as refuge from complexity and also those historians who accepted this "American" myth as the true image of the real Western past. The middle of the paragraph discusses the problems of such a view in the third person, but Limerick puts the terms "trials and burdens," "problems," and "Western optimism" in quotation marks to distinguish her voice from the voices of those about whom she writes. At the end of the paragraph, in order to draw the lesson she intends for the reader, she moves to the first person plural. To enhance her moral she fuses the "us" and "we" of past people's difficulties with the "we" of her and the reader's times and problems to bolster her argument that the problems of the West have been continuous from the so-called frontier period into the present.

As this quotation suggests and the minimal degrees of intervention in a historian's text imply, historical actors can be given their own voices in historical discourses. By having (being given?) voice the historical actors move from being the objects in and of the discourse to being subjects with their own views. As with the author, the actors' voices can range from explicit and personal to implicit and impersonal. The most explicit voice comes when past actors speak directly for themselves. Like authors, historical actors can use the "I" and "we" of first person or speak in the third person in quotation. Likewise, the actors can address one another in the past as part of their world, but can they speak to the future? More frequently the historian speaks for past actors through indirect discourse—"he/she/they said/thought."[75] The most remote method of giving actors their voices is through summary of their views or as part of a commentary on their ideas and outlooks.

All these many forms of voicing receive an interesting combination in Carlo Ginzburg's *The Cheese and the Worms* as he interweaves the Inquisitorial sources with his own commentary on those sources in telling the story of the Friuli miller and contextualizing his world. Menocchio speaks directly through quotation, sometimes even using "I," and indirectly through Ginzburg's paraphrasing as "he." In addition to using the normal third person historian's voice, Ginzburg speaks both as "I" and "we" throughout the book as he weighs evidence or infers and construes the intellectual, religious, and political context of Menocchio's times and place. Likewise, other persons from the sixteenth century, famous or ordinary, receive voice through quotation and paraphrase. About the only people relevant to this book who do not receive direct mention let alone quotation in the text proper are Ginzburg's fellow professional historians, but their names and opinions receive notice in the preface and notes. Although the very nature of Ginzburg's project may make it such an excellent example of the multiple forms of voicing in a history text, his text, like other, more traditional ones, supplies the voicing through his purposes, his selection of quotations, his paraphrases, and his commentary and interpretation.

To what extent does one or more of the historical actors speak for the author in a text? Is this connection acknowledged by the author or only imputed by the reader? These questions raise the whole issue of the historian's relationship to the historical actors in a text. Historians' discourses can suggest degrees of equivalence with or separation from the actors' voices and views. Historians through their discourses manifest sympathy or empathy for the(ir) subjects and their views or display distaste or hatred for them and what they stand for in the past (and thus in the present?). Conventional wisdom in the profession counsels that better biographies come from biographers who like their subjects.

To give voice to past actors, must historians accept their words and views at face value? To what degree must their discourses adopt the language and views of past actors to represent them in the present?[76] Should historians write like radicals or conservatives if they are to write about their politics? Must an author be radical if he writes about a radical or even adopt the rhetoric of a radical to write a "good" history about radical activities and polemics in the past? Similarly for conservatives. Likewise, in regard to religion, should the author write like a Catholic, Protestant, Jew, Muslim, Buddhist, or atheist to convey such views and voices when they constitute the subjects of the discourse? These questions also apply to gender, generation, race, region, ethnicity, and class when they are the subjects of discourse. Finally, can only direct, extensive quotation from the sources convey adequately the voices and viewpoints of postulated past persons and groups?

Historians can adopt an ironic, ambivalent, or playful tone toward their subjects. Ambivalence and playfulness, like irony, subverts the voice and view of past characters and substitutes those of the author.[77] No more common device exists for differentiating the author's voice from those of historical actors (or even from other historians' voices and views) than quotation marks to suggest the problematic—or polemical—status of an otherwise common word or phrase.[78] The use of quotation marks around words to give new meaning and context to them was well illustrated in the brief passage above from Patricia Limerick.

The relationships between authors, whether implied or otherwise, point to the nature and problem of multiple voices in historical texts. Do historical actors speak for themselves in the end, or do authors always ultimately speak for them in historical discourses? Can the reader discern the various voices and their associated viewpoints in text through the tensions and contradictions embodied in the discourse itself?[79]

To ask who is the Great Story-Teller and who speaks for the Great Past raises the ultimate problem of voice in historical practice. In the end, the job of a normal history is to suppress or conceal the personal intrusive voice so that the facts seem to speak for themselves. Although not many historians today would assert with the nineteenth-century French historian Fustel de

Coulanges that it is "not I who speak, but history which speaks through me,"[80] they in effect follow this advice in presenting the partial story as if it were the partial past in terms of voice. The Great Story, let alone the Great Past, speaks for itself in normal historical practice; hence Lottinville's advice to suppress the use of "I" in favor of third-person narration.

Viewpoint

If we can ask who speaks for (or as) the Great Story-Teller, we can also inquire from what (or whose) viewpoint the Great Story is told. Historians, like novelists, must adopt a point of view along with a voice.[81] To the extent that the novelist speaks through his characters, they not only represent his view but also limit his perceptions and understanding of the imagined world he creates. Even though the novelist creates the minds that the narrator can know as well as the narrator's mind itself, the novelist frequently confines his overall perspective and therefore the reader's to a less than omniscient position when representing the narrated world through the consciousness of his characters. The historian, in contrast, who knows far less of the actual consciousnesses of historical actors than the novelist does of the characters he creates, presents or pretends to greater omniscience about the world she creates in her history. The historian as the Great Story-Teller follows as an ideal the role of the author as set forth by Gustave Flaubert: "like God in creation: invisible but all-powerful, everywhere felt but nowhere seen."[82]

In accord with such thinking, Savoie Lottinville in his primer for the fledgling narrative historian distinguishes two kinds of viewpoint. "Author viewpoint," which predominates in historical practice, lies "somewhere between heaven and earth, high enough so that individual actions and the unified whole can be seen clearly . . . We can call it 'omnipresent' viewpoint, principally because a historian is not permitted to do what a novelist is fully entitled to do, that is, make himself, as narrator, part of the action."[83] "Character viewpoint," on the other hand, presents a perspective contemporary with that of the historical actors. According to Lottinville, such a viewpoint is particularly appropriate for biography but can be used in other kinds of histories.[84] These two kinds of viewpoint raise as many questions as they answer: Must our consciousness of the world represented in a historical text come from either within or outside that world? Or can we see from one or more consciousnesses both within and outside it? If our consciousness comes from outside, then does the reader see one or few or all consciousnesses and their viewpoints? Is the overall viewpoint godlike or more limited? At its most comprehensive, a godlike view entails perspectives from and in all places plus knowing all consciousnesses and what really happened and caused everything.[85]

Questions about viewpoint in novelistic practices suggest similar ones for historical practice. Does viewpoint vary with the number of voices in a historical text? Does the historian's effort to separate past from present in the text necessarily presume a separation of present viewpoint from the voices and viewpoints of the past?[86] Must this separation result in a multitude of viewpoints in every historical text? Do viewpoints vary by the type of history? Does an economic history display a different viewpoint from a religious or political history? Can the Great Story-Teller be without viewpoint, or must the Great Past be viewed from partial perspectives like all other histories? Answers to these questions proliferate as examples expand, and they suggest the perplexities of viewpoint in historical practice just as in novelistic practice.

There is a difference between arguing for a point of view as opposed to arguing from a point of view. In the latter sense point of view refers to the prism, angle of vision, perspective, lens, or focalization through which the narrative (and one might add argument in history) is presented. Although point of view is usually presented in ocular terms, it is a conceptual as well as perceptual position in terms of which the narrated situation and events are presented. At the literal level, point of view sees the represented world in the text through someone's eyes in terms of its physical aspects, as the quotation above from Lottinville on author viewpoint shows. This is the perceptual plane of viewpoint. At a more figurative or conceptual level, point of view understands the world from someone's worldview, ideology, or conceptual system. At an evaluative level, point of view assesses the represented world from the vantage point of interest, well-being, profit, or value-system. At the psychological or emotive level, point of view feels the represented world according to someone's psyche: how does the implied author or narrator feel toward the actors, events, and institutions in the discourse?[87]

Juxtaposing the kinds of voices with the kinds of viewpoints in a literary text yields some sense of what topics concern theorists of narrative:

Voice	Viewpoint
(Real vs.) implied author	perceptual
Implied author vs. narrator	ideological
Characters vs. authors	evaluative
Implied (vs. real reader)	emotional

The table facilitates as it clarifies questions about the relationship between voice and viewpoint. From whose viewpoints and from what kinds of viewpoint is the represented world presented? Is the viewpoint of the text from within or outside the represented world, from the characters', narrator's, or author's viewpoint? Does the narrator speak from a viewpoint within or outside the represented world? Whose viewpoint is presented as the objective one, by which the reader is supposed to judge the validity of the others? Do multiple voices foster multiple viewpoints?[88] To illustrate what various kinds of viewpoints can be represented by and through the various voices, without discussing all the possible combinations in the table, we can divide voices into whether they represent viewpoints from within or outside the represented historical world.[89]

From a perceptual plane, must knowledge of a represented world be seen from a viewpoint from within and from outside that world? In historical discourse, are not the two viewpoints combined more often than separated? Both space and time are customarily seen from within and outside the represented world. Ecological history, for example, highlights the relation between how historical actors supposedly viewed and used the land and how present-day historians describe the implications of those views and uses for a balanced ecology. Likewise, historians contrast explicitly or implicitly past actors' views of their times with what they as historians know of the past's outcome. To what extent must the results and consequences of past actions always be seen from outside the represented world? Such an approach to the perceptual plane raises the whole issue of omnipresence and omniscience in historical discourse. What spatial and temporal perspective must the historian adopt to produce the represented world of the discourse? In the end does the text offer a bird's-eye view of the represented world, a synoptic or a panoramic perspective?[90]

The synoptic perspective in historical interpretation thus means that colligation and contextualism depend upon the very concrete act of adopting perceptual and other viewpoints on the historical subject of a discourse. Perceptual viewpoints constitute objects as being, that is, seeming, natural through ideology. A perceptual viewpoint may accordingly be hegemonic or oppositional from a social and cultural viewpoint—or rather from the viewpoint of a discursive practice and interpretive community. Such perceptual ideology can be as basic as geography. Should, for example, the area inside the present United States but once part of Mexico be referred to as the American Southwest, the Mexican Northwest, Aztlán, or a Lost Land?[91] Are its Spanish-speaking inhabitants Latinos, Chicanos, Mexican Americans, or Aztecan? Or should the hemispheres be designated as East and West (from whose perspective and direction?) or, worse from a multicultural viewpoint, Old and New? To what extent does a perceptual ideology ground the nature of the system of chronology used in history? Such perceptual ideology can be as fundamental as the framing of a photograph or a film, as in the notorious "male gaze."[92]

On a conceptual plane, must the represented world be viewed from the perspective of a belief system or ideology, and does that belief system or ideology come from within or outside that world? Often the ideologies and belief systems from inside and outside the represented world are more fused than historians admit, as liberal, conservative, and radical histories demonstrate in terms of both issues and polemics. How often and how far can authors' ideologies and belief systems depart from those about whom they write when their subjects live in or near their times and come from their own cultures? Thus debates over how radical or conservative the 1930s New Deal was reveal how often those who argue for its radical consequences use the same judgmental criteria as those who enacted the New Deal.[93] In the end, must not the very foundations of explanation in history and the social sciences be considered ideological from the plane of conceptual viewpoint? Social and methodological individualism or collectivism correlate all too frequently with political individualism and collectivism in historical and social scientific explanation. Adherence to and advocacy of structuralist, textualist, symbolic, sociological, and other approaches to human behavior and thought all represent ideological as well as conceptual ways of understanding societies and cultures. Do epistemology and ontology ultimately serve ideological ends in historical and social scientific explanations? In response to these questions, many argue that the social sciences are nothing but moral sciences, like the rest of the human sciences.[94]

On the evaluative plane of viewpoint, are interests in a situation, or profits from a system, or the well-being of humans in a society measured according to the standards and value systems of those from within or outside the represented historical world? Once again, historians usually employ evaluations from both within and outside the worlds represented in their texts. That one task of the historian is to point out (and judge) unanticipated as well as aimed-for consequences and implications of past human behavior fosters such a dual evaluative perspective. Time's consequences flow from time's passage, and the passing of time necessitates post hoc evaluations. Thus it is difficult for historians to avoid, either explicitly or implicitly, appraising the past according to present-day viewpoints. Seemingly neutral judgments are normally viewpoints favoring one or another of the participants.

On the emotional plane, what are the feelings conveyed by the historian toward the past as opposed to the present world? How detached or involved is the historian in relation to a past represented world? Must the historian be empathic or sympathetic to past worlds we have lost in order to evoke their inhabitants' activities and worldviews as "good" history? Some histories favor as well as evoke a golden age. Others present a past hateful for its sins and crimes in contrast to the present or the future. Still others condemn the chaos or disorder of the past or lament that of the present. The big question from a multiculturalist viewpoint is who can share emotional viewpoints of and on race, gender, and class. Must those who speak for also speak from the experience of a group?

Any historian's text incorporates diverse viewpoints into its discourse, and how they are combined inevitably shapes the viewpoint of the entire book. Thus Lawrence Goodwyn divided the Populists into what he called a "shadow movement" in opposition to the presumably legitimate movement. The very term implies that those Populists in the shadow movement were not only less moral, hence less authentic, than those whose goals and methods he favored but also less astute than the "real" Populists in understanding the "true" nature of the capitalist world they inhabited.[95] His advocacy of a certain kind of populist democracy today caused him to make that the very perspective from which the reader should also view the past. In the process of naming a division from a present perspective he constitutes it in the past.

From this brief exposition of viewpoint in historical discourses, we can suggest answers to the questions posed at the beginning of this section. Does viewpoint vary with the number of voices in a historical text? Not necessarily, for the historian can, knowingly or unknowingly, present all the viewpoints in terms of one viewpoint, especially her own. Does the historian's effort to separate past from present in the text force a separation of present viewpoint from the voices and viewpoints of the past? Again, not necessarily, for the historian can as easily present all viewpoints from outside the represented world as from inside it.[96] Must this separation result in a multitude of viewpoints in every historical text? Once more, no. Do viewpoints vary by the type of history? Does an economic history display a different viewpoint from a religious or political history? Not necessarily. Can the Great Story-Teller be without viewpoint, or must the Great Past be viewed from partial perspectives, like all other histories? The Great Story must be represented according to some viewpoint. Omniscience is no more vouchsafed to the historian than to the novelist or any person on the street, even though the ideals of the Great Story and the Great Past demand nothing less.

Given the various kinds of viewpoint and the many places they enter a historical discourse, we must accede to the argument of F. R. Ankersmit that it is only by taking a point of view that historians create in the first place historical narrative or interpretation as such. Taking a viewpoint provides the very way of "seeing" the past as history.[97] A viewpoint enables selection of facts and gives coherence to the narrative. It excludes as it includes. A viewpoint offers the unity in diversity that overcomes what Ricoeur designated the paradox of time traditional to historical discourse.

It is the vital role of author viewpoint in every aspect of historical textualization, of course, that creates the biases that confound historical practice. No mediation between past and present on any level can occur without the aid of viewpoint in its many guises. The more the historian intervenes in a text, the more aspects of viewpoint become incorporated into a historical discourse. The more aspects of viewpoint embraced in a discourse, the more biases create that history—and the more historians ought to confess in their full-disclosure statements.

Ultimately, the normal historical text is meant to be read from the same viewpoint that constructed it in the first place. In each instance viewpoint constructs the object as ideologically natural; hence the complaint about the very bias inherent in the conception of viewpoint as ocular, even if taken only metaphorically. Traditional use of viewpoint stresses that the proper view is from only one point, hence that only one viewpoint is best or right no matter how diverse the subjects' voices in the represented world of the text. An omniscient viewpoint presumes that a single viewpoint can exist independent of any of past participants' or present readers' various viewpoints. The supposed omniscient narrator who is present everywhere is situated nowhere in particular in relation to the social locations and contexts of the past and present alike. Increasingly, scholars consider such an unsituated viewpoint impossible. As a result they repudiate the whole "visualist ideology" grounding the idea of a single best or right viewpoint, for it stresses the singularity of point from which to view matters over the diversity of views on the matters and their multiple social locations. It subordinates subjects' viewpoints (as inferior) to the author's viewpoint (as superior).[98] Since causation and connections in traditional narratives and arguments are always also construed from a single viewpoint, their use in the construction of historical narrative or argument, according to those scholars who repudiate a monological or univocal viewpoint, rests upon an ideologically suspect foundation. Challenges to the notion of a single best or correct viewpoint thus impugn the whole traditional historical enterprise of postulating and creating partial and Great Stories, partial and Great Pasts.

CHAPTER SEVEN

Representing Multiple Viewpoints
and Voices

HISTORIANS have authority over the past in the sense that they determine which voices of the past are heard through their expositions and thus which viewpoints are represented in their discourses. To what degree do present texts reiterate past voices or, more precisely, continue past discourses? Or do historians' texts project present viewpoints on the past? Who speaks for the so-called inarticulate, the undocumented, in history? To what extent do historians use traditional notions of otherness to promote dominant stereotypes of self and to conceal the voices and thus the viewpoints of others within a society or across societies? Does the distinction between professional and folk history, documentary and oral histories, and learning over memory repress the diversity of past voices in favor of those of historians today? Can any one history embrace a variety of voices and various viewpoints? Does attention to gender, ethnicity, and class change the nature of story-telling or only the content of the story? Does a commitment to multiculturalism also require a commitment to multiple voices and viewpoints? Need multiculturalism therefore lead to the proliferation of Great Stories and therefore to plural pasts?

According to its advocates, a multicultural approach to scholarship and the educational curriculum challenges as hegemonic the traditional viewpoint that lies at the base of so many disciplines. No one has stated the implications of multiculturalism for traditional viewpoints in the human sciences more succinctly or more baldly than Paula Rothenberg:

> The traditional curriculum teaches all of us to see the world through the eyes of privileged, white, European males and to adopt their interests and perspectives as our own. It calls books by middle-class, white, male writers "literature" and honors them as timeless and universal, while treating the literature produced by everyone else as idiosyncratic and transitory. The traditional curriculum intro-

duces the (mythical) white middle-class, patriarchal, heterosexual family and its values and calls it "Introduction to Psychology." It teaches the values of white men of property and position and calls it "Introduction to Ethics." It reduces the true majority of people in this society to "women and minorities," and calls it "political science." It teaches the art produced by privileged white men in the West and calls it "art history."

The curriculum effectively defines this point of view as "reality" rather than a point of view itself, and then assures us that it and it alone is "neutral" and "objective." It teaches all of us to use white male values and culture as the standard by which everyone and everything else is to be measured and found wanting. It defines "difference" as "deficiency" (deviance, pathology). By building racism, sexism, heterosexism, and class privilege into its very definition of "reality," it implies the current distribution of wealth and power in society, as well as the current distribution of time and space in the traditional curriculum, reflects the natural order of things.

As a result of the hegemonic viewpoint grounding so many disciplines in the human sciences, she argues,

women of all colors, men of color, and working people are rarely if ever subjects or agents. They appear throughout history at worst as objects, at best as victims. According to this curriculum, only people of color have race and only women have gender, only lesbians and gays have sexual orientation—everyone else is a human being. This curriculum values the work of killing and conquest over production and reproduction of life. It offers abstract, oppositional thinking as the paradigm for intellectual rigor.[1]

These paragraphs advocate a drastic reorientation of viewpoint in constructing history, and yet Rothenberg's own remedy for all these problems of misconception is to let students "read our Constitution, Supreme Court decisions, and other public documents so that the 'founding fathers' and their descendants can speak for themselves."[2] Such a solution does not say who provides the viewpoint(s) from which these voices from the past are contextualized and interpreted. Who becomes the Great Teacher in the multicultural classroom? Who gets to be the Great Contextualizer in the Great Story that interprets how these documents relate to one another, to their times, and to the present?

Multiculturalism challenges both the viewpoint basic to normal history and in turn its authority. Multiculturalism highlights, first, the whole question of the relation between the author's voice and viewpoint and those supposedly represented in any given text. For whom in the end does this text speak, and from what viewpoint and by what authority? Second, multiculturalism challenges the whole idea of a single best or right Great Story, especially if told from an omniscient viewpoint. In questioning a single viewpoint as best for the Great Story and Great Past, multiculturalism undermines the foundation of historical authority used traditionally to justify the discipline. In line with this challenge to traditional authority, multiculturalism poses fundamental questions about how politics are embodied in the paradigm of normal historical practice itself through voice and viewpoint. Last, it poses the challenge of how to incorporate multiple viewpoints into historical texts, be they partial histories or Great Stories, or especially the Great Past.

New Viewpoints on History

Great Stories matter greatly because they establish the context of the historical context. Thus they have become the explicit focus of multiculturalist revisions of history as the Great Past. Who gets to be the Great Story-Teller and from whose viewpoint the Great Story is told are the questions on which the debates center. From the standpoint of this book, however, the questions become rather what can be remedied from within the paradigm of normal history and what must be done outside that paradigm in order to convey the complexity of multiple viewpoints. The difficulties of representing multiple viewpoints and voices in a single discourse apply also to a Great Story and the Great Past when considered as a text.

A comparison of old and new approaches to the history of the American West illustrates changing perspectives of historians on viewpoint and provides an extended example of the various kinds of viewpoints mentioned in the previous chapter. The understanding of space and time and the perspective from which they are viewed embody the author's perceptual viewpoint, while the political and ethical judgments convey the ideological viewpoint. Present judgments of past persons and actions reveal the evaluative viewpoint, and the degree of feeling for and identity with the place and the persons who lived there evince the emotive viewpoint.

One of the Great Stories—if not the greatest—of the Great American Past has been (is?) the frontier interpretation of American history as expounded by Frederick Jackson Turner, beginning with his classic 1893 essay, "The Significance of the Frontier in American History." From the vantage of our own time and place, the viewpoint underlying Turner's history is painfully ethnocentric and chauvinistic, repressing the many voices and viewpoints of those peoples who lived in and contended for what he called the American West. Even though he made class conflict and sectional difference fundamental to his interpretation, his history and Great Story seem univocal and single viewpointed from a multiculturalist perspective.

Assuming that there was a difference between Americans' ideals and institutions and those of Europeans, Turner attributed the cause of America's unique social and political development to "the existence of an area of free land, its continuous recession, and the advance of American settlement westward."[3] He elaborated his reasoning in a 1903 essay extolling the "Contributions of the West to American Democracy": "These free lands promoted individualism, economic equality, freedom to rise, democracy . . . Never before in the history of the world has democracy existed on so vast an area and handled things in the gross with such success, with such largeness of design, and such grasp upon the means of execution." Thus, Turner concluded, from within the "American" viewpoint: "American democracy is fundamentally the outcome of the experiences of the American people in dealing with the West. Western democracy through the whole of its earlier period tended to the production of a society of which the most distinctive fact was the freedom of the individual to rise under conditions of social mobility, and whose ambition was the liberty and well-being of the masses."[4]

In first propounding his theory Turner proposed a social evolutionary model of societal stages to explain how frontier settlement transformed Europeans and Easterners into the Americans he favored and represented in voice and viewpoint:

> The United States lies like a huge page in the history of society. Line by line as we read this continual page from West to East we find the record of social evolution. It begins with the Indian and the hunter; it goes on to tell of the disintegration of savagery by the entrance of the trader, the pathfinder of civilization; we read the annals of the pastoral stage in ranch life; the exploitation of the soil by the raising of unrotated crops of corn and wheat in sparsely settled farming communities; the intensive culture of the denser farm settlement; and finally the manufacturing organization with city and factory system.[5]

Reversion to the primitive conditions and institutions of an earlier stage of society each time a new frontier was settled reinvigorated American practices of democracy and self-reliance: "This perennial rebirth, this fluidity of American life, this expansion westward with its new opportunities, its continuous touch with the simplicity of primitive society, furnish the forces dominating American character." In line with this spatial perspective on America's past, he declared, "The true point of view in the history of this nation is not the Atlantic coast, it is the Great West," and when the 1890 census announced that the frontier had ended for all practical purposes, Turner also proclaimed that "the first period of American history" had ended at the same time.[6]

Turner's ideology of Americanism was typical of his time. Democracy promoted, nay demanded, free institutions and free enterprise according to the American model. Natural resources existed to be exploited by classic capitalist methods. Though siding with debtors against their creditors and with small farmers against large landowners and speculators in the past, he nevertheless avowed the economic and political liberalism of his time. Turner hailed individualism and social mobility as the birthright of all Americans and argued that the frontier had offered all Americans the opportunity to achieve the American Dream despite the role class conflict played in his history. His values, in short, were those of dominant white Americans, and they in turn hailed his history as the true point of view on the American past.[7]

Turner's evaluations of past peoples also reflected the racism typical of elite white Americans of the day. Thus his preferred frontiers*men* were of English, Scotch-Irish, and German descent. French Huguenots were approved, but not French Catholics. People lower in the era's racialist hierarchy—Latin Americans, Asians, and Africans—were either excluded from his history or relegated to its periphery. "Indians," like mountains and wild animals, appeared only as "obstacles" to white frontier settlement, fated to disappear from the American Great Story. Accepting contemporary stereotypes of the inconsequential nature of native tenure, he stated that "Indian" lands were "free" for the taking by white Americans. Correspondingly, Turner asserted that, in contrast to the history of European imperialism in the Western Hemisphere, there was no American conquest of the territories in what became the United States. His viewpoint on Native Americans was epitomized in his definition of the frontier as "the meeting point between savagery and civilization."[8]

Not only did Turner silence the voices of many participants in the Great Story of the frontier; he also denied or peripheralized their viewpoints. Almost a century after Turner's first essay, Patricia Limerick, in *The Legacy of Conquest: The Unbroken Past of the American West,* points out its limitations and attempts to incorporate the voices and viewpoints that he repressed or marginalized. As Limerick observes, "Turner's frontier rested on a single point of view": "English-speaking white men were the stars of his story; Indians, Hispanics, French Canadians, and Asians were at best supporting actors and at worst invisible. Nearly as invisible were women of all ethnicities." Limerick also points out Turner's preoccupation "with agrarian settlements and folk democracy in the comparatively well watered Midwest. Deserts, mountains, mines, towns, cities, railroads, territorial government, and the institutions of commerce and finance never found much of a home in his model."[9] In the end, she sees Turner's division of the nation's history into a pre-1890 frontier and a post-1890 West as an expression of nostalgia for small-town America, a nostalgia that repressed consideration of economic and social problems persisting through both "periods."

In prose as vigorous in its own way as Turner's, Limerick presents the West instead as a place "undergoing conquest and never fully escaping its consequences," because it was "an important meeting ground, the point where Indian America, Latin America, Anglo-America, Afro-America, and Asia intersected." Competition to occupy the same territory joined these diverse groups together into the "same story," and "conquest basically involved the drawing of lines on a map, the definition and allocation of ownership (personal, tribal, corporate, state, federal, and international), and the evolution of land from matter to property." Accompanying this economic competition and physical conquest was "a contest for cultural dominance," which "involved a struggle over languages, cultures, and religions; the pursuit of legitimacy in property overlapped with the pursuit of legitimacy in way of life and point of view." Although Limerick denies the social evolutionism and the racialist hierarchy underlying Turner's conception of the frontier, she too espouses both a recurring process and a social conflict model of society in her history of the West.

> The process had two stages: the initial drawing of lines (which we have usually called the frontier stage) and the subsequent giving of meaning and power to those lines, which is still under way. Race relations parallel the distribution of property, the application of labor and capital to make the property productive, and the allocation of profit. Western history has been an on-going competition for legitimacy—for the right to claim for oneself and sometimes for one's group the status of legitimate beneficiaries of Western resources. This intersection of ethnic diversity with property allocation unifies Western history.[10]

Unlike in Turner's interpretation, Limerick's West becomes part of American history rather than its determinant. As she so often states, the American West is a case study of common forces in U.S. and even world history. In the process of arguing the point, she summarizes many of the chief themes of her book.

> Conquest forms the historical bedrock of the whole nation, and the American West is a preeminent case study in conquest and its consequences . . . Cultural pluralism and responses to race form primary issues in American social relations, and the American West—with its diversity of Indian tribes, Hispanics, Euro-Americans of every variety, and blacks—was a crucial case study in American race relations. The involvement of the federal government in the economy and the resulting dependence, resentment, and deficit have become major issues in American history and in contemporary politics, and the American West was the arena in which the expanded role for the federal government first took hold. Cycles of prosperity and recession have long characterized the American economy, and in that long-running game of crack-the-whip, the West has been at the far end of the whip, providing the prime example of the boom/bust stability of capitalism. The encounter of innocence with complexity is a recurrent theme in American culture, and Western history may well be the most dramatic and sustained case of high expectations and naiveté meeting a frustrating and intractable reality. Many American people have held to strong faith that humans can master the world—of nature and of humans—around them, and Western America put that faith to one of its most revealing tests. A belief in progress has been a driving force in the modern world; as a depository of enormous hopes for progress, the American West may well be the best place in which to observe the complex and contradictory outcome of that faith.[11]

Although Limerick accuses Turner of telling the Great Story of the American frontier from a single point of view, her own interpretation of the American West seems susceptible to some of the same problems of viewpoint that she has set out to correct. Although she broadens the arena of competition, adding industrial class conflict, racial, religious, and other ethnic cleavages to Turner's agrarian conflicts, she subscribes at bottom to the same basic materialist version of social conflict. Although she disagrees with Turner's concentration on the white conquest of the West to the exclusion of other peoples, she devotes the whole first half of her own book to those same persons. Only in the second half of the book do "The Conquerors Meet Their Match." Although in opposition to Turner she stresses the persistence of Western problems into the twentieth century and accords ethnic priority of place to Native Americans in her (hi)story, her text implicitly agrees with Turner's starting point: white settlements in the West. Although the duties of patriotism and the demands of progress are far more ambiguous in Limerick's West than in Turner's frontier, her attachment to her image of the West as a physical place is clearly as great as Turner's was to the frontier as ideological terrain. She reflects the concerns of her time about race, class, gender, and ethnicity as he did those about class conflict, individualism, and democracy. Limerick also seems as dedicated to her ideal of what American democracy ought to be as Turner was to his. Her stance on the results of economic and political liberalism for all peoples in American history is far more ambivalent than Turner's as she explicates the persisting problems resulting from economic competition, social and cultural conflict, and racial inequality. Both subscribe to their visions of the American Dream in their versions of the Great Story of the history of the American West. Both share an emotional bond with the Western part of the United States, although they may locate the West somewhat differently.[12]

For bringing the story up to date ideologically, Limerick's account was hailed as the New Western History.[13] Do both old and new historians in the end share so much because of the limits imposed upon any Great Story, and therefore upon the understanding of the Great Past, by the paradigmatic presuppositions of normal history? Although, as we shall see, Limerick struggles mightily to escape Turner's ethnocentrism and monologic voice and viewpoint, she too surveys the Western landscape from an integrative viewpoint. Thus multiculturalism in the hands of many historians does not transform the presuppositions of the normal history paradigm so much as it expands their application to untraditional subject matter. Pluralism in, even of, interpretations need not result in plural pasts, because new and old historians alike insist that in the text their own voices and viewpoints must serve as the ultimate mediator between the past and the present. In the end, the historian's authority depends upon this practice.

Changing the Representation of Otherness

How do we as scholars understand and, more important, represent those who differ from us? How does "our" society mark the boundary lines both within and outside it and define otherness? Should scholars oppose or support their society's dominant viewpoint? If the other is as different as the notion of otherness claims, how is the other to be represented, and by whom?[14]

Both extreme ethnocentrism and extreme relativism make otherness unknowable. The first postulates that everyone else thinks and acts like those doing the observing or defining. What is general (that is, peculiar) to the defining group or society is considered universal to all societies. Under such a perspective history easily serves as a source of lessons for the present, because all humans act and react the same way when faced by the same problems. Extreme relativism, in contrast, presumes what it argues it cannot know: others are by definition completely different, and so nothing can be shared between observer and the defined other. With the beliefs and behaviors of others considered unknowable, the defining group encloses itself in a hermetic realm rendered solipsistic by the presumption of incommensurable worlds.[15]

Any study of otherness must assume degrees of difference and sameness: enough difference to warrant a description of otherness and enough sameness to permit knowledge and empathy. Who establishes these degrees and how they do it are the issues in representing others. If the Other is a construction by the self of another, how can a self get outside the Self to know the Other as another? Who in the end speaks for the other in the self's representation of the other? When the other becomes the self in its own representations, does it face these same problems?[16]

Originally, the very notion of the Other meant that the insiders spoke for the outsiders by representing them as the Other. How should historians respond to the demands today of others' posterity to reclaim their history according to their own insights? After all, those persons and societies considered as Others in the past had representations of themselves as selves. How are these self-representations (for example, "oral" histories by and about African Americans and Native Americans) to be presented and interpreted in the historical representation of their otherness today?[17] This dialogue in the present has reinvigorated construction of "selves" and "others" in the past through history. That both selves and others, like both the present and the past, are also social and political constructions feeds the controversy and simultaneously exacerbates the perplexities.

Under alien representation the diversity of actual others became categorized collectively as "the Other" on the basis of their imputed, often stereotyped, "otherness." Fundamentally such a collective representation requires a contrastive linguistic or rhetorical strategy for persons, societies, or cultures. Thus in sociological or anthropological usage otherness separated "us" from "them," either in terms of a societal center and its margins or in terms of an observer culture and a subject or observed culture; in historical usage otherness divided "us" and "them" in terms of "then" and "now." In each instance, to aggregate others as the Other required the selves to employ a single viewpoint in describing others as collective entities.[18]

Historically—that is, both in the actual past and in its historicization through textualization—the notion of otherness had entailed the construction of dichotomous categories and then the essentialization, usually accompanied by hierarchization, of the mutually exclusive groups posited. The presumption of differences between the observer self and the other has a long history. From at least as early as the Greeks of the fifth century B.C., other peoples have been designated as alien on the basis of language ("barbarian"), religion ("infidel," "heathen"), social organization ("native," "tribal"), culture ("primitive," "oriental"), nationality (various ethnic slurs), race ("Jew," "Negro," American "Indian"), or some other self-sanctioning criterion by the self-designating group.[19] In past centuries the poor, the criminal, the old, the young, the ethnic or racial group, the female, and the homosexual, among many others, have been declared marginal and usually inferior by and to those institutions, classes, and persons deemed central by those performing the categorization.

Nineteenth- and early twentieth-century social scientists historicized similar distinctions to create social typologies based on social evolutionary assumptions—primitive or traditional versus modern, sacred versus secular, rural versus urban, *gemeinschaft* versus *gesellschaft,* community versus association—with certain self-favored Western societies or groups at the top of the social ladder and others on lower rungs. Social biology as racism only reinforced the social evolutionism of the societal typologies to subordinate the "primitive" or "traditional" to the "modern" for those peoples who presumably preferred the sacred over the secular, the communal over the associative and the urban.[20] In their own societies social scientists applied the essentialized otherness of biology to subordinate women to their "sphere," the poor to the "dangerous classes," and ethnics to their "race."[21]

According to this Great (Hi)Story of Otherness, historians, like other Western scholars, served both imperial flag and scholarly canon by adopting the conventional viewpoint that race and nature explained cultures, the sexes, and the lower social classes. A direct result of this viewpoint was that supposedly inferior groups—native peoples, women, the poor, immigrants, and at times minority religionists remained "hidden from history."[22] Presumed to be captives of unchanging cultures and therefore outside history, they were "without history."[23] Even those peoples designated "oriental" (as opposed to "occidental"), who were presumed to have long histories of their own, were described only from Western, frequently imperialist, viewpoints.[24]

In the decades following the Second World War, as decolonization and civil rights movements came into being and burgeoned, those previously designated as others demanded not only more and better representation in their societies or the world of nations but also better, more "authentic" representations of themselves in scholarly texts. In the earlier phases of this movement, historical discourse all too often met such demands by merely adding new names and events as subjects to supplement traditional approaches. Thus in U.S. history the names of women, African Americans, Native Americans, and others who had "contributed" to that history were added to the pantheon of Great Persons. At first the criteria for a "contribution" remained those of the hegemonic culture, but later those who resisted the dominant elite and mainstream trends in American society were added. The outline and basic overall viewpoint of American history, though supplemented and apparently broadened, remained basically unchanged. Even Eric Wolf's important pioneering attempt to incorporate all the world's peoples into one story, *Europe and the People without History,* centered on Western expansion in the Americas, Asia, and Africa to give coherence to the narrative of the native societies of those continents.[25] As one criticism put it: "the book's rock-steady, univocal narrative voice elides the strangeness and polyphony of colonial encounters, and presents them as leading inexorably to a monolithic late-capitalism. In Wolf's text, cultures do not cross, they fall in line."[26]

At its best, such supplemented history tried to portray peoples hitherto subordinated in history and in histories as active determiners and coshapers of their destinies, transforming them from minor characters at best to protagonists. But as scholars revised North American history to produce texts centered on the pasts of women, Native Americans, African Americans, and Chicanos, they often created or found themselves in new intellectual ghettoes. While U.S. history as a whole became more inclusive, it also became more fragmented as a Great Story or still relegated the new revisionist histories to the periphery. Women and peoples of color, though more active in the texts concerned exclusively with them, remained passive and subordinate in discourses purporting to represent the "overall" course of history. Thomas Bender, having observed that history from the bottom up did not complement history from the top down so much as fragment any effort at synthesis, tried to overcome this shortcoming in his proposed new synthetic principle of contestation over and in the public arena.[27]

To overcome the increasingly apparent difficulties of representing those previously designated as Others, some scholars have turned to the idea that only those so designated could represent themselves accurately. Only through such self-representation, they argue, can groups previously hidden or treated as objects become subjects or actors in their own histories. Only they can know and represent their experience under the domination of those at the "center" of their societies, be the domination domestic or imperialist. Under this approach, experience becomes the crucial concept, for it is often presumed that only those who have shared the experience of those for whom they speak should voice any views on the topic. Accordingly, what Gregory

Ulmer christened "mystory" arose to challenge the voice and viewpoint traditional to history. The most famous conceptual and terminological challenges went under the name "herstory." In all mystories, the voice and viewpoint of the narrator is local, particular, and embedded clearly in the narrative.[28] If self-representation solves the problem of voice and viewpoint in others' texts, does it also solve that problem in historians' more general texts? What relation, in short, do self-representations bear to historians' representations of them?

The Question of Representativeness

Textual Sources and Translations

Deconstruction of the invidious hierarchical distinctions inscribed in the Self/Other dichotomy produced its own problems for representing others. When scholars forswore the concept of the Other they lost the unity provided by that dichotomous mode of understanding: what had previously been described as a single monolithic Other according to a single viewpoint fragmented into a diversity of others, often characterized according to a multiplicity of interacting social roles. Even a single other is not just one other but many others on the social axes of, for example, race, sex, age, ethnicity, class, or religion. The greater the number of axes is, the less possible it becomes to employ a unified or totalizing viewpoint in the narrative. How, then, is the historian as writer or teacher to represent this multitude of othernesses in any single textualization?

The Golden Rule of representing others as they would themselves all too often led scholars to unite the various viewpoints into a single text by means of nothing more than the book's binding. Such a solution does not solve the basic problems of including multiple viewpoints in an individual historian's text or classroom. The fundamental issue, from the standpoint of this chapter, is not whether others can (self-)represent themselves in a text (they can of course) so much as how are they to be represented by a historian in a text or in a classroom.

Various others' voices and viewpoints enter historical practice and its discourse in at least five ways: (1) scattered throughout the sources as evidence for a textualization of the past; (2) textualizations in the sources, especially as narratives, by past others about their present(s) and past(s) as they conceived them; (3) textualizations by present-day others, including scholars, about the past or present of themselves as others; (4) present-day textualizations by scholars and historians about past others; and (5) present-day textualization by a historian (or teacher) of multiple voices and viewpoints in a history. Of each aspect, one can ask the questions posed by the dual meanings of representation. On one hand, representation means speaking or standing for someone else. How representative is the voice and viewpoint of the other claiming to speak for those others? On the other hand, representation also means the re-presentation, that is, the reimaging of the absent events, behaviors, and values. When the two meanings of representation are combined and applied to the five aspects of historical practice and discourse, they raise a series of questions and problems for synthesizing otherness in an individual historian's text.[29]

First, if multiple viewpoints and voices are scattered throughout the sources, the problem becomes one of ascertaining or imagining whether enough past persons' voices and viewpoints are adequately represented in the evidence to depict that society. Are the archives biased in favor of or silent on one or more sectors of a society? Second, if past others have represented, that is, textualized, their experiences as a narrative, then to what degree should multiculturalist historians reproduce that narrative in its entirety in their own texts? Archival narratives can supply voice and viewpoint for historians through reproduction or quotation according to the degrees of story in the sources mentioned in Chapter 6. But the issue of representativeness or typicality poses the same basic problem here as for the third aspect of historical practice and discourse.

If present-day others textualize their pasts and in the process claim to represent a past other's voices and viewpoints more authentically than those who are not of their otherness, what is a historian to make of this claim? What relationship do these differing forms of self-representation have to a historian's own textualization of another's story and experiences? Even if one accepts the voice of the self-represented textual representations as typical of those it purports to represent, should one also accept automatically its viewpoint, or interpretation, of the persons, events, and results of its history? Should the self-representation of another be accepted as not only the voice but also the single best or right viewpoint or interpretation of a group's history because it claims to be part of that supposed voice and viewpoint? To what extent do the conflicts in a society and the differentials in power among its members shape the experience of those people, hence their viewpoints as individuals and as members of groups? What if others as individuals appear unaware of the consequences of their actions as groups or of their own larger social context? What if the personal experience of one member differs from that of another member of the same group?

If one person's truth is another person's myth, or culture, then what of conflicting truth-claims about nature, societies, or the universe itself held by others as opposed to the historian? Since, for example, Native American peoples believe that their tribes originated in the Western Hemisphere, why should one begin their histories with some migration story or myth about peoples crossing from Asia via the Bering Strait?[30] Are all ontologies equal in historical representation, or do historians judge other ontologies by their own? If they judge the truthfulness of an other's worldview, have they violated their goal of representing another's viewpoint?[31]

How can historians reconcile their own and others' worldviews and viewpoints? Historians cannot simply exchange frameworks by "going native," for they must translate back out again for their readers. In the end, translation is the name of the game in representing otherness.[32] The representation of another in someone else's text is a delicate and paradoxical task, for the process involves switching from the representation of another's representation according to one's own world to the representation of another's representation according to his or her own world. As Clifford Geertz phrases the task, it is to represent "one sort of life in the categories of another."[33] To know another in terms of that other's outlook and viewpoint necessitates transcending one's own categories and perceptions. What is so clear in the actual translation of concepts and meanings from one language to another becomes less certain but no less important in translating from other to self in terms of societies and cultures or as groups and subcultures. Whether the historian's imagined alterity corresponds to the other's self-knowing depends more upon subsequent political contestation than upon the degree of a historian's presumed empathy or assumed oppositeness. Ultimately the historian's text upon othernesses is tested less by standard historical criteria and more by how it is read and critiqued by its subjects as politics. Even so, the subjects form their critique and interpret their experience according to the very views that result in as well as from their experiences in the first place.

What applies to the representativeness of self-interpretations also applies to those offered by others as scholars and historians of their own pasts. Why should a historian accept those versions of others' past experience as both representative and the best representation? In that sense, other scholars' and historians' interpretations or representations of their own past are just another source for the historian's textualization of the (hi)story of those others.

Any multiculturalist goal of incorporating voice and viewpoint in historical discourse must therefore acknowledge not only the diversity of voices and viewpoints in the past but also the diversity of present-day voices and viewpoints about how to make history more inclusive of past experiences and present ideals. Such a view of the dialogue about multiculturalism within the present requires distinguishing between polyvocality and multiple viewpoints in professional and political debates over the focus and nature of historical discourse today as opposed to what is aimed for and achieved in any one discourse as a text as a result of this debate. Should commitment to multiculturalist ideals therefore require that any discourse as text exemplify in explicit practice what the tensions in the present make implicit in professional discourse? Should not the diversity of views about achieving multiculturalism in historical discourse be part of the polyvocal dialogue represented in the main body of textual discourses themselves (as opposed to the notes or other paratext)? The great challenge today of such a view of multicultural dialogue and the multiculturalist ideal is to combine within any given text, whether conceived as a partial history, a Great Story, or the Great Past itself, multiple viewpoints as well as different voices (1) from within the represented world of the past, (2) from outside the represented world of the past in light of subsequent events and ideas, and (3) from the conflicting or at least diverse viewpoints existing in the present. In each case we must ask who is represented, and how.

Experience and Self-Representation

The issues of self-representation and the representation of multiple viewpoints have been explored particularly in women's history as the result of the challenge from women of color to the initial voicing and viewpoint of women's history. Feminist women's history was grounded from the outset on the principle that the experience of women differs fundamentally from that of men. That different experience required the revision of all history to show the differences between female and male experience in (and of) the past. What was claimed initially as that female version of history was in turn challenged as representative of only white, heterosexual, middle-class women by women of different color, sexual orientation, class, or disability on the grounds of their quite different experiences. The latter claimed that white, heterosexual, middle-class women stood in the same relationship to them as men and therefore could not represent their experiences and therefore their histories.

Feminist women of color in the United States therefore broadened the meaning of the word "colonization" from the economic exploitation of subordinated peoples by imperialist powers to include "the appropriation of their experiences and struggles by hegemonic white women's movements." That usage was in turn broadened further to other discourses about the Other, especially as (that is, in) the so-called Third World. As Chandra Talpade Mohanty summarizes this semantic ploy, "However sophisticated or problematical its use as an explanatory construct, colonization almost invariably implies a relation of structural domination, and a suppression—often violent—of the heterogeneity of the subject(s) in question."[34] Thus a new principle of representing the variety of women as others was asserted, according to Ruth Roach Pierson:

> In the triangle of experience, difference and dominance and its relation to voice, it is not inexperience or difference in experience alone but different experience combined with "power over" that disqualifies: the dominant group's power systemically and systematically to negate or disfigure the experience of others separates it from the oppressed group's lived experience of that negation or disfigurement. What [the oppressed] is asking for is recognition of the "epistemic privilege of the oppressed." There does seem to be a compelling reason to accept

as "true" an oppressed person's account of the lived experience of the oppression. There seems to be an equally compelling moral argument against the right of a member of the dominant group to appropriate the oppressed person's story.[35]

As she concludes, "Dominance needs to be seen, in other words, as integral to the experience of difference and as capable of rendering the dominant insensible to the 'lived experience' of the oppressed."[36] In the more graphic words of Bell Hooks about such appropriation of another's experience:

No need to hear your voice when I can talk about you better than you can speak about yourself. No need to hear your voice. Only tell me about your pain. I want to know your story. And then I will tell it back to you in a new way. Tell it back to you in such a way that it has become my own. Re-writing you I rewrite myself anew. I am still author, authority. I am still colonizer, the speaking subject and you are now at the center of my talk.[37]

Alert to this abuse of cross-otherness, Pierson warns that those who would write about the experience of others must proceed with both "epistemic humility" and "methodological caution."[38] Does such epistemic humility demand any less than full quotation of the other's experiences in order to avoid the intellectual imperialism grounding normal historical practice on viewpoint? Is paraphrase in this instance just another discursive aggression colonizing the other in the name of multicultural representation?

At the same time that Pierson warns about the expropriation and colonization of others' experiences, she also points out that autobiography and oral history cannot be accepted solely as the other's history, for the job of the historian is not only "to reclaim voices" but also to "contextualize" them, "to reconstitute the 'discursive' world which the subjects inhabited and were shaped by."[39] To what extent does this second conclusion about the historian's standard task of contextualization undermine that of reclamation when considering, and representing, voices and viewpoints in a history?

Joan Wallach Scott expands upon what the contextualization of experience involves in her oft-reprinted article "The Evidence of Experience."[40] She pursues a poststructuralist strategy of denying individual experience for the socially based discursive practices that produce the sources: to accept experience as transparent to its own viewpoint and to judge its validity by that viewpoint is to fall prone to the liberal humanist delusion of the individual as autonomous subject. To credit experience as "uncontestable evidence and as an originary point of explanation—as a foundation upon which analysis is based," she argues, is to essentialize an individual's identity as if it were timeless rather than created through historical forces like all other subjects. "Making visible the experience of a different group exposes the existence of repressive mechanisms, but not their inner workings or logics; we know that difference exists, but we don't understand it as relationally constituted. For that we need to attend to the historical processes that, through discourse, position subjects and produce their experiences." As a result, the acceptance of others' experiences as history reproduces the categories and ideological systems that formed and informed those experiences in the first place rather than showing how the interplay of the actors' voices resulted from their social location(s) as subjects. Thus, she argues, "It is not individuals who have experience, but subjects who are constituted through experience. Experience in this definition then becomes not the origin of our explanation, not the authoritative (because seen or felt) evidence that grounds what is known, but rather that which we seek to explain, that about which knowledge is produced." To locate experiences in their specific social contexts becomes the historian's job. "To think about experience in this way is to historicize it as well as to historicize the identities it produces. This kind of historicizing represents a reply to the many contemporary historians who have argued that unproblematized 'experience' is the foundation of their practice; it is historicizing that implies critical scrutiny of all explanatory categories usually taken for granted, including the category of 'experience.'"[41]

For Scott, "experience is at once already an interpretation *and* something that needs to be interpreted. What counts as experience is neither self-evident nor straightforward; it is always contested, and therefore political." Thus she argues for a new history of concept and category formation as clues to the history that produces experience and the historical sediment that is said to be experience. "Subjects are constituted discursively and experience is a linguistic event . . . Experience is a subject's history. Language is the site of history's enactment. Historical explanation cannot, therefore, separate the two."[42] As these quotations suggest, Scott resolves the conceptualization of another's experience into the subject's discursive practices, which in turn presume a society of structured differences, always(?) embodied in inequalities of power, that the historian can employ in the representation of the voices and viewpoints. In Scott's appropriation of poststructuralist theory, the notion of a socially based discursive practice solves the problems of multiple viewpoints in historical practice by connecting the various viewpoints of evidentiary sources, others' stories, other scholars' texts, and the historian's own text into one interpretive system.[43]

Does this poststructuralist strategy solve the problem of representing multiple viewpoints in a historian's text? Although the strategy constructs the interplay of voices and viewpoints so as to offer the reader a dialogue that is polyvocal in one sense of that term, in another sense that polyvocality is still ultimately constructed according to a single best viewpoint. So long as the historian contextualizes the social formations that produced the categories of others' experiences, then so long does the historian's viewpoint ground that contextualization as in traditional history. Thus, from the ideal of a truly multiviewpointed multiculturalism, what many multiculturalists kick so ostentatiously out the front door Scott allows to sneak in through the back door. Her historicization merely shifts the univocal single best viewpoint from much or total repression of others' viewpoints to their textual incorporation through a single best approach to their interplay as a social system—or at least their location in an implied social system. In Scott's theorization, every experience is historicized, but her theory presumes that all is historicized according to a single best or right model. Although she may not stipulate the exact nature of a society and the relationships among its individuals, she does assume that there is a best viewpoint from which to describe them as a collectivity.[44]

Multiculturalism and Normal History

That multicultural, polyvocal history is more easily preached than achieved indicates that conceptual as well as ethical and political problems plague the enterprise. How much of this problem stems from the nature of the normal history paradigm as opposed to political or other societal inertia? Must the efforts of historians to reclaim the story of history in the name of gender, race, ethnicity, or class also lead to plural viewpoints in history-telling? Or will such efforts merely produce a history that is counterhegemonic in story and argument but still based ultimately on a single viewpoint? To what extent is the proliferation of voices and viewpoints in a history limited to—as well as by—the normal paradigm of historical discourse?

An example of an explicit attempt to represent multiple viewpoints within a single text offers lessons on both its potential and its limits for normal historical practice. Patricia Limerick in *The Legacy of Conquest: The Unbroken Past of the American West* defines the United States West as the meeting ground for several societies and their contest for political, economic, and cultural control of the land and one another; so she tries to be especially sensitive to the multiple viewpoints represented in the many conflicts. One of her favorite methods of representing different viewpoints is through quotation and summary of opposing positions, as in the following discussion of the Texas Rangers from Anglo and Hispanic American perspectives:

> In Hispanic history, as in every Western history, one never has the luxury of taking point of view for granted. Hispanics—like Indians, Anglos, and every other group—could be victims as well as victimizers, and the meanings of the past could seem, at times, to be riding a seesaw. Consider, for instance, the dramatically different images of the Texas Rangers. Early in the Anglo colonization of Texas, the Rangers began "as something of a paramilitary force" for fighting Indians. As the threat from the Indians diminished, the Rangers became a force for protecting the property of Anglo-Texans and for keeping Mexicans and Mexican-Americans subordinated. Surviving into the twentieth century as a kind of state police, the Texas Ranger had acquired a strong and positive standing in myth, "eulogized, idolized, and elevated to the status of one of the truly heroic figures in American history." In

1935, the historian Walter Prescott Webb published an influential study that reinforced the image of the Texas Ranger as "a man standing alone between society and its enemies," a law officer who was also "a very quiet, deliberate, gentle person who could gaze calmly into the eye of a murderer, divine his thoughts, and anticipate his actions, a man who could ride straight up to death."[45]

In opposition to this view, she quotes scholars of borderland folklore and history to establish the quite different Hispanic perspective on the Rangers:

> "The word *rinche* from 'ranger' is an important one in Border folklore," wrote [Américo] Paredes. "It has been extended to cover not only the Rangers but any other Americans armed and mounted and looking for Mexicans to kill." Adopting the Mexican point of view, scholars who came after Webb drew a different moral and political portrait of the Rangers. "The Anglo community," Julian Samore, Joe Bernal, and Albert Peña have written, "took it for granted that the Rangers were there to protect Anglo interests; no one ever accused the Rangers operating in South Texas of either upholding or enforcing the law impartially." The Rangers, moreover, kept up their traditional role in the twentieth century, lending a hand in strikebreaking and in cracking down on "Mexican-American activism in politics and education . . ."[46]

In this instance she achieves a multicultural view by relegating the historically dominant Anglo viewpoint to the status of myth and by presenting the Mexican viewpoint as the ultimate reality.

Limerick's discussion of a Native American point of view and voice illustrates the problems involved in achieving a multiperspectival history. Should a new Indian history merely reverse the old stereotypes of who is savage and who is civilized? Limerick argues that such a history would remain a flattened one because it would still homogenize Native Americans, with all their diverse languages, customs, religions, tribal governments, economies, localities, and experiences with Euro-Americans, into a "unitary thing." Concerns about intertribal rivalries and other native matters, for example, often loom larger in their own histories than the impact and implications of Euro-American contact. To speak of an "Indian side" therefore oversimplifies both the voices and viewpoints of Native Americans past and present.[47]

Limerick goes on to ask whether a changed perspective provides "a sufficient corrective to the ethnocentric conventions of the past." Is the traditional historian's "leap to the high ground of objectivity and neutrality" enough? "What if Indian people are now so certain of their injuries that they want condemnation and blame explicit in the writing of their history? How were white historians to respond when articulate and angry Indian people protested the fact that their history had been too long in the keeping of outsiders and invaders?" At first Limerick seems sympathetic to this point of view: "Much of what passed for objective frontier history was in fact nationalistic history, celebrating the winners and downgrading or ignoring the losers . . . The nationalism of conventional frontier history carried an assumption that history was itself a kind of property in which Americans deserved to take pride." In reaction to such white-centered history, "Indians have put forth a counterclaim: Indian history is not solely *about* Indians; it is history *belonging* to Indians, in which the owners should take pride and which should make them feel better about their inherited identity."[48] Such a claim, however, bothers her because corporations, governments, religions, and even individuals in the dominant society have asserted the same right to control and construct their own histories, and professional historians oppose such "authorized histories" as flagrantly partial and partisan.

Faced with the dilemma of whether each minority should write its own history in its own way, Limerick voices sympathy for both sides of the proposition. On one hand, each partial perspective cannot be taken for the whole by the professional historian. In arguing that all the various versions of Western history ought to be read, she writes:

> Of course, Indian people can and should write their own histories according to their traditions, just as pioneers and their descendants have every right to publish books enshrining their own version of the past. For the sake of national and regional self-understanding, however, there should be a group of people reading all these books and paying attention to all these points of view. In that process, Western historians will not reach a neutral, omniscient objectivity. On the contrary, the clashes and conflicts of Western history will always leave the serious individual emotionally and intellectually unsettled. In the nineteenth-century West, speaking out for the human dignity of all parties to the conflicts took considerable nerve. It still does.[49]

On the other hand, "historians of the American mainstream" can learn much from the "Indian perspective on the peculiar ways of white people," which frees one from "the intellectually crippling temptation to take white people's ways for granted." She proceeds to laud ethnohistory for resolving the dilemma she sees, because it "places actions and events in a carefully explored context of culture and worldview." Thus "ethnohistory reaches its peak when its techniques are applied across the board, when white people as well as Indians are cast as actors in complex cultural worlds, and when no point of view is taken for granted."[50]

As Limerick's discussion of the dilemmas of multiple viewpoints shows, she hopes to escape its relativistic implications for the Great Story as well as for a single historical text by incorporating both the actors' viewpoints and their context into the historian's own "larger" multiculturalist viewpoint. Such a solution may be an improvement over texts denying actors' viewpoints, but it does not answer all the challenges of multiculturalism to viewpoint in historical practice. In the end, she solves the multicultural challenge to hegemonic viewpoint in history safely from within the synoptic viewpoint customary to the paradigm of normal history even as she expands the number of viewpoints that normal history should embrace.

The paradigmatic limits as well as the moral implications of Limerick's approach are apparent in her discussion of the general problems of incorporating histories of minorities into the general history of the American West. Her ponderings illustrate the perplexities of combining multiple viewpoints with the historian's voice and viewpoint into a text and into history. First, the problems as she sees them:

> When the advance of white male pioneers across the continent was the principal concern of Western historians, the field had coherence to spare. But two or three decades of "affirmative action history" have made a hash of that coherence. Ethnocentricity is out, but what alternative center is in?
>
> When it comes to centers, Western history now has an embarrassment of riches—Indian-centered history, Hispanic-centered history, Asian-centered history, black-centered history, Mormon-centered history, and (discredited as it may be) white-American-main-stream history.[51] If historians were forced to choose one of these centers, hold to it, and reject all others, we would be in deep professional trouble. But that is by no means the only choice available.[52]

Her solution to the integration of multiple viewpoints into a history rests upon an analogy:

> Take, for instance, a thoroughly un-Western metaphor for a complicated phenomenon—a subway system. Every station in the system is a center of sorts—trains and passengers converge on it; in both departure and arrival, the station is the pivot. But get on a train, and you are soon (with any luck) at another station, equally a center and a pivot. Every station is at the center of a particular world, yet that does not leave the observer of the system conceptually muddled, unable to decide which station represents the true point of view from which the entire system should be viewed. On the contrary, the idea of the system as a whole makes it possible to think of all the systems at once—to pay attention to the differences while still recognizing their relatedness, and to imagine how the system looks from its different points of view.[53]

In applying this subway metaphor, she argues:

> What "system" united Western history? Minorities and majority in the American West occupied common ground—literally. A contest for control of the land, for the labor applied to the land, and the resulting profit set the terms of their meeting. Sharing turf, contesting turf, surrendering turf, Western groups, for all their differences, took part in the same story. Each group may well have its own, self-defined story, but in the contest for property and profit, these stories met. Each group might have preferred to keep its story private and separate, but life on the common ground of the American West made such purity impossible.[54]

Her solution resembles the effort by Thomas Bender to find a synthetic principle for U.S. history in the protracted conflicts over defining the public arena in American life. To explicate this analogy, she switches metaphors:

Everyone became an actor in everyone else's play; understanding any part of the play now requires us to take account of the whole. It is perfectly possible to watch a play and keep track of, even identify with, several characters at once, even when those characters are in direct conflict with each other and within themselves. The ethnic diversity of Western history asks only that: pay attention to the parts, and pay attention to the whole. It is a difficult task, but to bemoan and lament the necessity to include minorities is to engage, finally, in intellectual laziness. The American West was a complicated place for historical participants; and it is no exercise in "white guilt" to say that it is—and should be—just as complicated for us today.[55]

These are attractive metaphors, but do they provide the solution multicultural-ism seeks and needs to transform historical practice? Do they solve the problems of incorporating multiple viewpoints into a history text? How does Limerick know that the stations are all on the same subway system? Does someone still see the system as a whole? And if so, from what and whose viewpoint is that system to be ultimately organized and described? How can anyone know if it is a single system, let alone speak for it? Who is the System-Maker, let alone the Great Story-Teller? Her resolution resembles that of Joan Scott's poststructur-alist strategy. Both presume a (social) structure that permits their historical discourses to put multiple voices and viewpoints into their appropriate(d) places according to the underlying model and its Great Story.

In the end Limerick's advice on how to combine actors' and historians' viewpoints into a single text still privileges the historian's viewpoint over those of the actors through scripting the play, to use her analogy. Her method, laudable as some of its results may be, frequently draws an overall conclusion about the relationship among the multiple viewpoints apart from any one of them. Such a solution offers the historian's stance as the ultimate integrative viewpoint regardless of the actors' viewpoints. As Limerick admits, "the historian is obligated to understand how people saw their own times, but not obligated to adopt their terminology and point of view."[56] In this she agrees with Wallace Stegner, the famous novelist and authority on the American West, who proclaimed: "Unlike fiction, history can have only one voice, the historian's."[57]

Plural viewpoints therefore do not lead to plural pasts in Limerick's theory or practice. A variety of multiculturalist viewpoints can and ought to be combined by the historian because the very combination approaches ever more asymptotically to reality. Such an approach to historical reality, even if multiculturalist to some degree in practice, still conceives much of that reality according to the cultural and disciplinary conventions of historical realism—a reality seen from a single best synoptic viewpoint. Is, then, the lesson of Limerick's adherence to certain traditional tenets of normal history despite her multicultural ideals that the limits of multiculturalism in history are those of the paradigm of normal history itself?

The Reorientation of Anthropology

Recent efforts by some anthropologists to pluralize and historicize their disciplinary perspective offer an example of another approach to multiculturalism and multiple viewpoints. The discipline of anthropology had traditionally relied upon the Self/Other distinction translated as the Here and the There, with the consequent suppression of the Now and the Then. The so-called ethnographic present of a culture was substituted for the history of the people said to enact that culture. A crisis arose in the discipline as the Here and There was erased or blurred in a (post)modern world. The collapse of empires and the resultant loss of control by Western societies over other portions of the globe erased the previous scholarly as well as hegemonic divisions between the First and Third worlds. Others as scholars challenged in recent decades the ethnographic expertise of Western specialists. Whereas previous anthropological scholarship had rested upon the scholarly monopoly provided by asymmetrical power relationships, the self-proclaimed New Anthropology of the 1980s renounced sole control of the knowledge of the Other as the West's power decreased. No longer was scholarly expertise to be divided between the West and the Rest; all scholars now existed on spaceship Earth together. Thus, according to those anthropologists leading the movement, Self and Other needed to be renegotiated as selves and others and, in the process, reinvented. To achieve such a reinvention of Self and Other as merely selves and others interacting together, they argued for a fundamental change both in the Great Story and in the locus of ethnographic authority.[58]

To acknowledge the changed idea of power relationships in the discipline demands first a new Great Story that reinterprets Western history according to the present and the presumed (near) future. In the brief formulation of two scholars, the recent history of what was once hailed as the rise of the West must now be seen as a decline:

> Self-doubts within European liberalism, the outbreak of barbarism within the heartlands of "civilization," and the decline of the European states to the status of second-rate powers, all rendered out-of-date Victorian versions of historical teleology and racial anthropology. More recently, the economic decline of England, East Asia's high-tech prosperity, and the puncturing of boundaries between Europe East and West have further reshaped the familiar outline of (Western) "Civilization." As we approach the quincentenary of Columbus's collision with Asia/America, the conventions of "Western Civilization" *circa* 1900 have the quaint and odd look of a British Empire map of the World.[59]

In this version of the Great Story of the West, the West is displaced and decentered as the chief, let alone sole, actor of history.[60] The Great Story that interpreted Western imperial expansion as one of progress and reason for its spread of the ideal of universal liberal individualism is thrown over for a

Great Story that depicts not only the evils of capitalism on a worldwide scale but also the not-so-humane problems resulting from the ideal of liberal individualism. More important, the unidirectional thrust of cultural and social change in the earlier Great Story is exchanged for one that stresses the reciprocity and exchange among societies and cultures in terms of persons who interact as they encounter one another. Whereas the older Great Story viewed the West as the active source of change and the Rest as the passive recipients of those supposedly enlightened, if not necessarily benign, changes, the New Anthropology emphasizes the historically emergent and culturally creative qualities of the social and personal interaction. As Edward Said points out, "Partly because of empire, all cultures are involved in one another; none is single and pure, all are hybrid, heterogeneous, extraordinarily differentiated, and unmonolithic."[61]

According to this new Great Story, what is the case today was also the case in past times; the global intermixing and exchange of persons, ideas, and identities so prevalent today also occurred in previous centuries.[62] The strict separation of the Here and the There, the Self and the Other, was an ideology supporting the hegemony of Western scholars rather than an accurate description of what was happening in the history of actual encounters among peoples. To overcome that ideology requires a repudiation of the previous intellectual isolationism inherent in the old view of essentialized, autonomous cultures in favor of a long history of cultural exchange and invention, of global economic and social inter-, but unequal, dependence.

Such a transactional impression of ethnic identity demands a renunciation of the holism long considered fundamental to the definition of culture in the discipline. Just as cultures do not meet each other as autonomous wholes in the present, so they did not in the past. As the holism of an ethnographic present gave way to the innumerable transactions of an ethnographic past, anthropologists needed to portray ethnicity as "mixed, relational, and inventive," and culture as a "hybrid, often discontinuous inventive process" with (and in) a history.[63] As George Marcus and Michael Fischer argue in one manifesto of the New Anthropology:

> Most local cultures worldwide are products of a history of appropriations, resistances, and accommodations. The task for this subtrend in the current experimental moment is thus to revise conventions of ethnographic description away from a measuring of change against some largely ahistoric framing of the cultural unit toward a view of cultural situations as *always* in flux, in a perpetually historically sensitive state of resistance and accommodation to broader processes of influence that are as much inside as outside the local context.[64]

Therefore, anthropologists should renounce the essentialism and presumed universalism of the categories by which they previously measured change and continuity. As James Clifford argues: "All attempts to posit such abstract unities are constructs of monological power. A 'culture' is, concretely, an open-ended, creative dialogue of subcultures, of insiders and outsiders, of diverse factions," just as "a 'language' is the interplay and struggle of regional dialects, professional jargons, generic commonplaces; the speech of different age groups, individuals, and so forth."[65]

To produce a new ethnography according to new criteria, anthropologists must surrender their viewpoint on point of view in their discipline. They should repudiate, first, the whole totalizing, self-privileging ideology of the visualist or ocular representation of *a* point of view as *the* point of view. In the metaphors of Clifford, they should

> dislodge the ground from which persons and groups securely represent others. A conceptual shift, "tectonic" in its implications, has taken place. We ground things, now, on a moving earth. There is no longer any place of overview (mountaintop) from which to map human ways of life, no Archimedean point from which to represent the world. Mountains are in constant motion. So are islands: for one cannot occupy, unambiguously, a bounded cultural world from which to journey out and analyze other cultures. Human ways of life increasingly influence, dominate, parody, translate, and subvert each other. Cultural analysis is always enmeshed in global movements of difference and power. However one defines it, and the phrase here is used loosely, a "world system" now links the planet's societies in a common historical process.[66]

Does the evocation of place and time through those others' voices achieve this denial of any overall, synoptic viewpoint?

The introduction of new viewpoints into ethnography has challenged traditional notions of authorship, and therefore ethnographic authority, in anthropology. Anthropologists have long relied upon significant informants as their sources, but until recently they rarely acknowledged these persons as individuals with names, let alone as, what they were in effect, coauthors. Should the viewpoint and voices in a new ethnographic text be represented on the title page as well as in the acknowledgments? Should its viewpoint(s) be the cooperative outcome of a committee of native experts and outside anthropologists? In this case "native" informants would move from being objects of study to being coequal subjects in the construction of their "culture," just as their ancestors have moved from being passive objects to being active agents in their histories. Any self-privileging of the ethnographer's viewpoint over that (those) of her co-creative subjects in an ethnography would suggest that the author has not renounced the vestiges of power and cultural imperialism inherent in monological studies. Postcolonial anthropology has changed the power relationship in scholarship just as decolonization supposedly changed the power relationships in the former colonies. Any attempt to establish a normative or conceptual referent by which to represent the others appears as a measure set up to enforce discursive power over the others. Thus the original dialogue of the fieldwork should remain a dialogue conceptually in its final textualization, although its literary form need not be literally that of a dialogue.[67]

Changed viewpoints and voicing have necessitated a changed discursive or narrative site for the ethnographic analysis and story. The focus of the study and story must move from a Western to a multicultural viewpoint, one of transaction and negotiation among the participants as actors in an emerging, evolving (hi)story (but with no social evolutionary overtones). Even if the asymmetrical power relationships and politics favor the colonizers, the subordinated still have some control over their fate. They are agents as well as subjects in the developing story. The story tells not so much of super- and subordination in the power relationship as of the reciprocity and exchange that co-creates and reproduces the new social roles and cultural meanings in the continuing interaction. The constantly changing transculturative or transacculturative situation provides the new narrative site for the study and story—preferably on the aptly named "Middle Ground" of Richard White.[68]

Since a historicized cultural history posits a world of contestation, then what is European and Western happens as much on its margins as at its supposed center, and the actors at the so-called margins figure prominently in what happens at the center as well as in their homelands. Thus the New Anthropology postulates at base a dual (hi)story of macro- and microprocesses in interaction. Whereas the macroprocesses shaped the entire world during the past centuries, the microprocesses altered and individualized those processes in specific locales at specific times. A new ethnographic account must combine the dual processes by conveying the others' experience according to and in terms of their culture and yet take into account "world historical political economy" and thereby locate "knowable communities in larger systems."[69] Whether such a historicization of cultures escapes the Eurocentrism inherent in the Great Story of the Capitalist World System depends upon the skill with which the voices of those in the microprocesses are incorporated in the ethnographic discourse or how many of the larger determinants of the Great Story are omitted.

If there is to be no self-privileging of the author as authority through monological viewpoint or through traditional disciplinary modes, then what roles do the scholar's ontology, politics, and morality perform in and upon the text? Does the New Ethnography change the conception of and criteria for truth? These questions pose severe problems for those New Ethnographers who acknowledge with Derrida that (Western) epistemology is the white man's mythology and with Foucault that power hierarchies structure what is accepted as the "truth." In response to this criticism, Paul Rabinow declares that "epistemology must be seen as a historical event—a distinctive social practice, one among many others, articulated in new ways in seventeenth-century Europe." By being aware of "our historical practice of projecting our cultural practices upon the other," anthropologists can explore "how and when and through what cultural and institutional means other people started claiming epistemology for their own." To avoid "either economic or philo-sophic hegemony," anthropologists should "diversify centers of resistance: avoid the error of reverse essentializing; Occidentalism is not a remedy for Orientalism." To achieve such an outlook, (Western) scholars need "to anthropologize the West: show how exotic its constitution of reality has been; emphasize those domains most taken for granted as universal (this includes epistemology and economics); make them seem as historically peculiar as possible; show how their claims to truth are linked to social practices and have hence become effective forces in the social world."[70] These epistemologi-cal rules still privilege the Western conception of the problem of the other as central to understanding, to textualizing the other; reflexivity appropriates the other in the name of cross-cultural understanding.[71]

What if the others' viewpoints and moralities deny the basic postulates of the New Great Story? Or has the New Great Story become its own trans-acculturative narrative site for Western and non-Western scholars alike? Postorientalist scholarship and postmodernist anthropology suggest as much. Should plural Great Stories and Pasts become standard textual treatments for contradictory or contested ontologies? If not, who is to determine whether one Great Story or Past is better or more right than another?

All too often the New Anthropology seems to resort to an all-purpose call for historicization as a solution to all these many problems. To redefine culture from essentialist holism to historicist emergence only takes us back to square one, because history itself is not an essentialist given but an all-too-evident changing social and cultural construction, with its own history. "If culture is mediated by history, history is also mediated by culture," as the editor of a recent effort by symbolic anthropologists to bring their field into the current conceptual fashion reminds her readers.[72] If anthropologists need to historicize culture, they also need to culturalize history.

Is the Great Story that authorizes the historicization of culture in the New Anthropology constructed any differently from more traditional histories? Neither its ultimately singular viewpoint nor its predominantly single author-ial voice marks a departure from the old Great Story, although its scholarly politics and multicultural message are quite different. Even the outline of the Great Story of anthropology is treated too unproblematically as it traces the Western conception of culture from, first, the evolutionary whole of nine-teenth-century social biology to the cultural wholes of the earlier twentieth-century relativists to controvert the previous view. That approach is in turn repudiated for the nonevolutionary, systemic, one-world whole of those today who would historicize cultural contestations and ethnographic authority. Does not the New Ethnography still put a Eurocentric master narrative at the center of its drive to historicization?[73]

Not until postcolonial, postmodern anthropologists accept the others' thinking and worldviews as equal or superior to their own will their practice meet their dialogical, multiculturalist ideals, according to R. S. Khare. He accuses most New Anthropology works of still resisting a more open, co-creative approach to reforming the discipline. Unless the anthropologist surrenders the position (and viewpoint) of the "transcendental observer," no true reciprocity of knowledge and voice can occur between observer and observed. Otherwise, the other exists at the anthropologist's sufferance. If sharing of epistemologies and ontologies between selves and others is the goal, then the anthropologist-textualizer must no longer author-ize the other through the text, even through a dialogue, for such a text still allows the subject to speak only in terms of the intellectual interests and discursive practices of the author's paradigm. Such a paradigm, even a new ethnography, disassembles what the others consider whole about themselves in favor of its redistribution and disposition in the authorizing anthropologist's text. "It is as if the anthropologist's self requires the Other to 'sacrifice' itself, to let the anthropologist become a distinct 'text-maker.'"[74] In this view the anthropologist's context must inevitably distort the other's context.

For the New Anthropologists to allow the other to exist "side by side," as coequal in their representations, Khare argues that they must sustain "an earnest dialogue." Such a dialogue

> not only recognizes the Other's voice; it also accords intrinsically equal authenticity to the Other's existence and epistemology. A genuine dialogue consciously maintains a sense of *reciprocating advantage on all levels* of representation and communication (whether oral, descriptive, analytical, critical, or synthetic). A reciprocating "text" cannot consciously retain hidden—protected, unexamined, and unapproachable—notions of exclusivity, advantage, immunity, and superior rights when engaged in dialogue with the Other.[75]

Coequal contextualization of the other through "reciprocal knowledge" does not have "to achieve an absence of difference, but only its more complete, equipolar understanding and communication so as to avoid one-sided privileges, advantages, and immunities." As Khare explains in his final note: "Such a relationship involves reciprocal representation, persuasion, and evaluation, but it originates from *both* sides, without resulting in any built-in, long-term advantage of favor on either side."[76] Genuine reciprocity, in short, demands negotiated dialogues about what is known and how it is known, about how it is to be represented and then textualized as a discourse.

The culturalization of history would seem to demand, if the New Anthropology offers lessons, the renunciation of any essentialist notion of the past as history or of history as the past. The nature of both narration and historical authority come under question. Should a history be acknowledged as a cooperative effort between present author and past sources? Should viewpoints, like voices, multiply in proportion to the number of actors or social groups in the past? Such a cooperative effort diminishes the distinction between formal or professional history and oral or folk history. A less than cooperative effort becomes an arbitrary power ploy to boost the authority of the professional historian. Who, in the end, determines what Great Story serves as "middle ground" for the narrative site? Or should all Great Stories receive equal treatment and validity?

From this viewpoint, the greatest power grab of all in professional history is to draw the line between what is true and what is fiction (or myth or ideology). Drawing a line between truth and fiction in the past is even more important to historical construction and professional authority than the determination of who or what is part of history, for the former characterizes the latter. To deny, for example, the validity of witchcraft or prayer in one's own ontology shapes one's characterization of others' beliefs and behavior in one's own historical constructions. Who in the end defines what constitutes history is as much a question of politics and power as who appears in a history and how. What constitutes explanation or causation constrains historical construction as much as monological viewpoint, for in the end they are one and the same.[77] Worldview and viewpoint overlap, as their shared component word suggests and as the debates over multiculturalism in the curriculum attest.

Toward a Dialogic Ideal

The challenge of dialogism in historical discourses lies less in introducing additional voices into a text or even into a Great Story than in representing viewpoints beyond that of the historian. That polyvocality need not produce a pluralistic let alone a multicultural history seems plain from actual practice. Introducing multiple viewpoints into historical discourse requires both a revision of the normal history paradigm and a new vision of historical authority. A multicultural, dialogic ideal transforms not only the subject matter of histories but also the postulates of what a good history does and is. Ultimately, must multiple viewpoints issue forth in plural pasts and new approaches to textualizing histories?

Since any single viewpoint seems hopelessly partial by contemporary multicultural standards, the solution would appear to be the representation of the past and present from multiple viewpoints in a single text as well as in the Great Story and Great Past. At minimum, an ideal multicultural history should, as stated earlier, integrate multiple viewpoints as well as different voices (1) from within the represented world of the past, (2) from outside the represented world of the past in light of subsequent events, beliefs, and mores, and (3) from the conflicting or at least diverse viewpoints existing in the present. Nothing less seems sufficient in a multicultural history, if the author(s) seek(s) the fullest polyvocality and dialogy within the text. How does a historian or even a group of historians integrate the tensions of past and present societies into a single text? To what extent must such a text embody these tensions as well as represent them? Can a single text in the end be both multicultural and multiple viewpointed and still be understood by its readers as a "history"?

This multicultural ideal suggests a rough scale by which to measure polyvocality and multiple viewpoints in a given historical discourse. Such a range also allows classification of kinds of histories according to their treatment of the self/other problem. At one end lie those historical texts with only one voice and one viewpoint. At this end are also those that advocate the representation of multiple voices but do not employ multiple viewpoints in their own textualization. Although such works include others' voices, these are orchestrated to present the message for a transformed conception of the self/other relationship. A notable example is Edward Said's *Orientalism,* which objects to the stereotypes embodied in Western representations of Middle Eastern peoples. He uses many voices to exemplify the stereotyped view, but he makes no attempt to show how the new self/other relationship ought to be represented. Said's book does not practice what it preaches multiculturally.[78] At the same end of the range are the more general but similar calls for the reconception of the self/other relationship by Johannes Fabian, *Time and the Other: How Anthropology Makes Its Object;* Robert Young, *White Mythologies: Writing History and the West;* and Marianna Torgovnick, *Gone Primitive: Savage Intellects, Modern Lives*—all of whose titles express or suggest their purpose.[79] These books utilize history in the form of past representations to make their point about today's desired understanding of otherness. They quote past persons and paraphrase them to reveal their viewpoints as stereotyped and hegemonic. Regardless of their explicit message about multiculturalism, their point of view is single and univocal. Also located at this end of the spectrum are histories of anthropology or of the other social sciences that treat the self/other dichotomy as deficient ways of understanding or stereotypes in the past, and unproblematized versions of the changing Great Story of Western power in the world that adopt a traditional unified, overall viewpoint on the history of the World System.[80]

Existing in the middle of the range spanning the multicultural ideal are contemporary efforts like those of Patricia Limerick to introduce and to expound multiple viewpoints. Like those comparative histories that in the end integrate the various histories into a single framework, they incorporate the various others' viewpoints into an inclusive but ultimately predominant conceptual and political viewpoint. Even the extraordinary efforts of Carlo Ginzburg in *The Cheese and the Worms* or of Emmanuel Le Roy Ladurie in

Montaillou to evoke the worlds of the past belong here, as do the multiple reader-response efforts of Judith Walkowitz in *City of Dreadful Delight*.[81]

Also belonging in this middle range are Tzvetan Todorov's *The Conquest of America: The Question of the Other* and Sabine MacCormack's *Religion in the Andes: Vision and Imagination in Early Colonial Peru*.[82] Different as these two books are in terms of disciplinary method and discursive organization, both attempt to give voice to the other. Both authors derive images of the American natives as selves primarily from European descriptions of their otherness. MacCormack applies traditional intellectual history techniques to untraditional texts (and peoples). As a result she accepts the spiritual framework of her Spanish sources to derive the mutually interacting religious images of the Spanish and Andean peoples and how native religions changed over time as a result of the Spanish program of missionization. Through the literary analysis of certain Spanish texts, Todorov constructs a spectrum of Spanish perceptions of Meso-American peoples ranging from Columbus' monologic, ethnocentric view to the appreciation of them as others by the Dominicans Diego Durán and Bernardino de Sahagún through the dialogy of their texts. Ultimately Todorov seems more interested in making his presumably Eurocentric readers aware of their inherited provincial biases than in embodying in his text the cosmopolitan egalitarianism he avows. While MacCormack would not eschew such an aim, she states she searches for what really transpired so long ago in the Andes. Notable as their achievements are, both authors ultimately give voice to the others according to their own purposes and perspectives. Polyvocality is contained within their own texts by their own voices and viewpoints.[83]

What truly might exist at the other end of the spectrum has apparently not yet been textualized. For the moment it seems to be occupied by texts that are pure pastiches of quotations, pure evocations of others without an apparent privileging of the historian's voice or viewpoint over those of others—perhaps even without any apparent interjection of the historian's viewpoint. Can such discourses qualify as proper histories according to the standards of the profession? Even if the writer-compiler of such a text were not to impose an overall viewpoint, would not the reader project one onto it? Readers' responses to a text demand the security of expectations about genre. Anthologies of sources and textbooks of multiple interpretations correspond to postmodern fragmentation of the subject, of the author, and of viewpoint, but many historians and probably their readers would deny these texts status as proper histories. Postmodern books on multiculturalism all too often (re)solve the problem of multiple viewpoints and voices by collecting a group of symposiasts' supposedly different outlooks into a single volume. True experiments in multivocality are rare because they challenge the normal historical paradigm of an ultimately single authorial viewpoint. If the text is not to be a pastiche of quotations, a book of sources, what can it be? Ronald Fraser in his history of his childhood family home employs a collage of oral testimony from the manor's servants and his brother, his own journal entries about those persons in the past, and recollections of exchanges with his psychoanalyst about his upbringing among these people. The ambiguity of the main title, *In Search of a Past: The Manor House, Amnersfield, 1933–1945,* suggests the author's dual motivation to come to terms with his own past as he reconstructs a bygone era.[84] Through skillful juxtaposition of carefully edited materials, Fraser conveys the many voices and viewpoints of those persons who for a dozen years surrounded him while he recreates the history of class privilege and interwoven public and private lifestyles at the manor house during the 1930s and the Second World War. Although the purpose of the collage is to exorcize the psychological warping of the author's youth, it also provides a skillfully composed portrayal of insight and blindness among the privileged and subordinated alike in the English countryside during the final halcyon days of the aristocracy. This unusual combination of oral history and journal entry occupies a point far along the multicultural scale because of its attempt to present multiple perspectives of class and gender, the public and the private, as constituted and changed in those dozen years.

David Farber's history of the events surrounding the Democratic National Convention in Chicago in 1968 occupies a similar position on the multiculturalist scale.[85] In an experiment combining the multiple viewpoints of diverse historical actors and his own analysis, Farber first tells three separate stories of the events leading up to, culminating in, and resulting from the protest, from the perspectives of the Yippies, who created themselves to confront the old Democratic way of doing things at the convention; of the multiconstituent coalition under the name of the National Mobilization to End the War in Vietnam; and of Mayor Richard Daly and the police of Chicago. To convey in these narratives how each group perceived and represented matters in its own voice and viewpoint, he sometimes uses different typefaces for each. His three final chapters analyze from his viewpoint each of the three collective actors, focusing on the linkages between the politics of protest outside the American political system and the politics of information and media, between the politics of American radicalism and the politics of locality and social order.

Another important attempt to embody multiple viewpoints as well as voices is the historical anthropologist Richard Price's *Alabi's World.*[86] To convey the eighteenth-century history of the Saramaka maroons of Suriname, Price uses four voices, those of the German Moravians, the Dutch planters, the Saramakas, and his own as historian and anthropologist. He translates into English the various languages of the primary sources he reproduces, and he treats Saramaka oral history on a par with his documentary evidence. Throughout the book, including the notes, he accords each group, as well as himself, a different weight and face of type. But although all voices and viewpoints are supposedly equal, his own prevails in the end, as one reviewer noted.[87] Even though Price argues that the Saramaka possess a strong sense of linear history, ultimately it is his own views of history that organize the book, certify the authenticity of the various voices, and plot the dialogue of voices as diachronic and dialectic. Regardless of the problems of translation or of authorial viewpoint,[88] Price's book more than almost any other suggests the full potential of polyvocality and multiple viewpoints on the multiculturalist scale.

Although the ideal grounding this multiculturalist spectrum presumes equal representation of diverse voices and viewpoints, it does not specify how to construe the relationships that exist among the multiple voices and viewpoints or how to assemble them into a coherent, interrelated structure. This remains the issue that divides both theorists and practitioners of multiculturalism and pluralism. For those who stress the power relationships that prevail in all social networks, these inequalities provide the key to organizing the dialogue of the voices and viewpoints. For these scholars the pluralism of polyvocality and multiple viewpoints must never imply equal explanatory weight of all interests or conceal the hierarchy of power in human affairs that in their opinion constitutes the delusion of liberal politics. Plural textual representation should not lead the reader to assume plural political representation.[89]

But for those scholars who feel that only the full representation of all voices and viewpoints fulfills the goal of multiculturalism, such structured contextualization still represents the politics of the scholar as the univocal viewpoint of and on history. Like other aspects of historical methodology, multiple voices and viewpoints need contextualization, and that contextualization is constructed by the historian through and as an appropriate Great Story. From this perspective even a historical montage implies an omniscient narrator as the Great Organizer. For this position, to be polyvocal and multiple viewpointed in a historical text means to be plural in perspective and pluralized throughout the representation. How therefore to conceive and contextualize past voices depends as much upon the politics of the scholar as upon the nature of the evidence. In the end the politics of historical viewpoint determines the politics of multivocality and multiple viewpoints.

CHAPTER EIGHT

Politics and
Paradigms

To move from considering (a) discourse as (a) text(ualization) to considering discourse as a social practice, as part of a larger scholarly and political world, is to confront the politics of historical representations and professional practice in addition to any explicit, specific political messages contained in them. How these two meanings of discourse are related to each other is a central issue of many debates in history and other human sciences. In the case of history the debates range from the politics of viewpoint and of disciplinary authority, to the relation between text and context and between rhetorical and social construction of reality, to the very idea of what constitutes politics and the link between power and knowledge.

The dual but disparate meanings of discourse also raise the issue of reflexivity in the theorization of historical discourse and its politics. To take even a simple view of the ways of understanding a history (or history in general) as themselves ways of understanding quickly leads one into the realm of contradiction and mutual deconstruction, for the premises of the paradigms or the problematics of various ways of understanding challenge each other's validity. Asking how a problematic or paradigm conceives the role of language and social ontology or reality, how it explains itself, how it explains other ways of understanding, and how it explains history quickly reveals both the reflexive problems of plural paradigms in social understanding and the political and moral foundations of reflexivity itself as a way of understanding. Each mode of understanding seems to reduce the insights basic to other ways of understanding to its own premises and yet to remain unable to justify itself reflexively. This, perhaps, is the ultimate irony of metahistory as a way of understanding the past.

The Politics of Historical Practice

The Power in Discourse

How much of a role politics plays in historical discourse depends upon how discourse is defined. Discourse in this context possesses at least three different kinds of meaning or levels of application to professional practice. One level studies the political partisanship embodied in the explicit message of the text, which reveals the politics of the historian: does her interpretation embrace a certain ethics or politics? Another level investigates how a disciplinary discourse results in the text(ualization)s it does and how the politics of the profession shapes that outcome. What are the rules for objectivity and use of evidence? How does an anthology of sources or a historical novel differ from what is called a "history" in the profession? Still another level of application examines the socially based rules that make such a discipline and its mode of textualization possible in the first place. What rules determine the nature of history as a genre? What institutional arrangements in a society allow histories to take the form and content they do? These levels are described in the order of importance assigned them in traditional theorizations about historical practice.

Recently the importance of these levels has been reversed as a result of the influence of Michel Foucault's conception of disciplinary "discursive practices" or "discursive formations." A subject is constituted as an appropriate field of disciplinary study according to a network of discursive rules that specify its objects of study, the nature of its practices, the nature of its concepts, and the range of its theoretical options. The discursive formation comprises the joint sets of conditions that allow the discourse of the discipline to take place when, where, and how it does in regard to its subjects, practices, and concepts. The formation, in short, bounds what can be stated and done in a discipline and distinguishes one discipline from another. Although discursive formations come and go, their conditions of existence and their emergence, functioning, and transformation result less from personal acts than from collective, anonymous, impersonal actions. Disciplinary practitioners discourse according to the norms of their discursive practice, but these rules are more presumed than explicit in their maintenance of disciplinary boundaries, their prescription for an individual's behavior, their enactment as institutions, and their general effects for a society. For Foucault, such discursive formations and their associated discursive and institutional practices often embraced scattered objects, incompatible concepts, contradictory options, and unconnected institutional sites.[1]

As Foucault developed his notion of disciplinary practices and formations, he realized that they rested upon the exercise of power, polymorphous as that may be in his theory. In his model of history shifting discursive formations produce and enforce changing discursive practices as a consequence of symbolic, epistemic, and actual political conflict.

Truth is a thing of this world; it is produced only by virtue of multiple forms of constraint. And it induces regular effects of power. Each society has its regime of truth, its "general politics" of truth: that is the types of discourse it accepts and makes function as true; the mechanisms and instances which enable one to distinguish true and false statements; the means by which each is sanctioned; the techniques and procedures accorded value in the acquisition of truth; the status of those who are charged with saying what counts as true.[2]

From this viewpoint, then, to ask what truth is in a discipline or society is a vestige of transcendentalist rhetoric. Instead one should explore how "truth" functions in a discipline or in a society to regulate what can be thought about a subject. "Discourses constitute the truths they claim to discover and transmit."[3] Thus, "truths" are not only relative to a (socially) collective frame of disciplinary reference; they are also created as a function of that frame of reference. Such frames of reference as (and through) discursive formations delineate a subject field as appropriate, hence as meaningful. All discursive frameworks accordingly embrace some matters and outlooks as they suppress others—violently, Foucault would say, in line with his image of discourse as just another form of warfare. Power is both positive in what it constitutes as rational and real and negative in what it excludes and represses as irrational and unreal.

Under this approach, truth or knowledge is the effect of the set of discursive rules, with no transcendental signified to provide epistemological or ontological foundations—separate from the set of rules constituting a particular discourse. Norms of a discursive practice define a field as they constitute it, legitimate it as they generate it. Knowledge is a consequence of the discourse that creates, reinforces, and authorizes it. Such a set of rules in a discipline, often tacit and anonymous but always socially shared and enforced in specific ways for specific populations, classifies what is true and false, what is relevant to a given form of textualization, who is an "expert" or enunciator and enforcer of the rules, what the reader or audience should understand and how, and what is appropriate to think in the discipline, among other functions. Indeed such sets of rules are deemed necessary if producers and consumers of a set of resulting textualizations are to categorize them as history or fiction or otherwise.

In Foucault's theorization, if not always in his practice, the rules of a discursive formation were more implicit than explicit in the actual discourses. Although his theory condemned traditional "unities of discourse" as found in modern Western disciplines and governance, his own practice traced its own kinds of unities among the dispersed discursive formations he constituted through his genealogies. In his discourse such discursive unities linked power with knowledge, social and political institutions with academic and professional discourses, the logic of a system with its dissemination across disciplines and professions. Whereas Foucault preferred to focus on the microphysics of power situations, some of his latter-day disciples investigate the connections among intellectuals, discourses, and societal arrangements in the state. And although Foucault eschewed equating a set of discursive rules with class analysis as such, his followers, like him, try to tie specific kinds of discourses to specific social locations. Poststructuralist and postmodern theorists, inspired by Foucault's own supposed intellectual history, increasingly stress the institutional arrangements that generate and reinforce discourses about the textualized results of socially organized, collective practices. For them as for Foucault, the ultimate purpose of such discourse analysis is to criticize the systems of (conceptual) power in modern (bourgeois) society by tracing their genealogy, to challenge the "common sense" of our own time by pointing out the complicity between power and prevailing verities, to resist the subjugation of the individual as a subject constituted by discursive practice(s) and policed by professional experts.

That professional historians questioned whether Foucault's books could be considered histories and whether he should be called a historian demonstrates his notion of the power of discursive practice in a discipline.[4] According to Foucault's theory of discourse, it is to the policing of the historical profession that we must look for the nature of subject matter in the field, the methodologies by which historicization is accomplished, and the nature of its representation as textualization. Thus the guild of historians sanctions which changing interpretations are fashionable, the number of acceptable emplotments of history, the kinds of Great Stories that can be told, what is and is not proper history at any given time, and who is praised and promoted (or the reverse) as a result.

Beyond Objectivity and Relativism

Traditionally historians authorized themselves as historians and their textualizations as history through their professional credo. As Peter Novick summarizes that credo in his history of the American historical profession during the past century, it embraced two basic sets of ideas. One set centered upon the ideal of objectivity. By eschewing political partiality in favor of impartiality, the historical profession could claim that its products were above the heat of battles in the larger world of politics as well as the bickering over intellectual turf in academia. Even though many historians judged the morality of their subjects' activities and ideas, they still considered their treatment of the subject matter objective because they held to a second set of ideas basic to normal history, which Novick labels "objectivism," about the reality of a past independent of its interpretation. Adherence to these epistemological and ontological beliefs supposedly warranted the ideal of historical objectivity in the profession in the face of periodic threats of historical relativism and political relevance, at least as Novick tells the story.[5]

The quest for impartiality conducted according to the dual standards of objectivism as hyperrealism and objectivity as political impartiality produced such historical realist—one might say historical fundamentalist—mottoes as "letting the facts speak for themselves" or "studying the past for its own sake." Only by combining the principles of objectivism with the ideal of objectivity can these mottoes make sense. Those who voiced them feared "subjectivity" in the historian, "relativism" in historical discourse, and "present-mindedness" in histories.

Few historians today would avow such a simplistic understanding of their practice, but, as Novick points out, these principles and premises pervade normal historical practice far more than most members of the profession would admit. Allegiance to these principles can be found even in those who reject Novick's interpretation of today's professional credo. Some historians in reviewing Novick's book at length denied some of the principles while subscribing to others as necessary to the enterprise of history. Such a diversity of reviewer reaction illustrates the constraints of the normal historical paradigm as well as its approach to the problems of partiality in historical discourse and practice. In exploring these constraints, the reviewers also suggest their role in the foundation of professional authority in the discipline. A brief examination of two such critiques of Novick's philosophy as opposed to his practice in the book illustrates the relationship between objectivity and objectivism in authorizing history and, by extension, the profession. Both critics accepted some revision of the standard credo, but they castigated Novick's advocacy of historical relativism. They rejected the chief lesson he drew from the profession's alternation between objectivity and relativity during the last century.[6]

James T. Kloppenberg applauds the denial of "timeless truths and universal laws" resulting from the historicization of reason. Such historicization applied to history itself, he argues, need not catapult the historian into the abyss of relativism any more than into the cavern of objectivism. In fact such an option only strengthens historical practice:

> It is precisely because the indeterminacy of truth and the historicity of reason are now widely conceded that we can no longer claim to find objectivity—in science or history. It is, furthermore, precisely for that reason that historians must insist on the indispensability of historical studies as one of the most fruitful forms of inquiry in a world of uncertainty. We cannot have, nor should we want, the self-righteous smugness of earlier generations that we have "got it right" once and for all. But that should not cause us to despair about our prospects for making progress. Beyond the noble dream of scientific objectivity and the nightmare of complete relativism lies the terrain of pragmatic truth, which provides us hypotheses, provisional syntheses, imaginative but warranted interpretations, which then provide the basis for continuing inquiry and experimentation. Such historical writing can provide knowledge that is useful even if it must be tentative.[7]

In this encomium to the middle path between objectivism and relativism, a path he elsewhere christens "pragmatic hermeneutics,"[8] Kloppenberg avoids the pitfalls of radical historicization by affirming some of the tenets of historical realism found in objectivism. If historians are to advance beyond the dichotomies of knower/known and fact/value, they must still subscribe to the distinction between history and fiction and the prior reality of the past over its interpretation as grounds for judging the validity of Novick's own interpretations of past historians and intellectuals, let alone historical works in general.

In the end, the middle path wends its way through the community of historians and is policed by their own ideal discursive practices. At issue is not the rejection or acceptance of objectivism but the extent of commitment to its tenets. Many of the tenets of objectivism are as vital to the historicism of the middle path as they are to those opposed to the historicization of the profession's ideals. Kloppenberg, accordingly, praises Novick's actual practice of history in *That Noble Dream* as opposed to his philosophical stance in favor of relativism, because the practice confirms the larger principles of objectivism governing the professional community.[9]

In another long review praising Novick for his actual historical "practice" as opposed to his philosophical "rhetoric" on methodology, Thomas Haskell writes in favor of both objectivity and political commitment. As he asserts in his title, "Objectivity Is Not Neutrality,"

> I see nothing to admire in neutrality. My conception of objectivity (which I believe is widely, if tacitly, shared by historians today) is compatible with strong political commitment. It pays no premium for standing in the middle of the road and it recognizes that scholars are passionate and as likely to be driven by interest as those they write about. It does not value even detachment as an end in itself, but only as an indispensable prelude or preparation for the achievement of higher levels of understanding—higher not in the sense of ascending to a more spiritual plane, where the concerns of the soul displace those of the body, as an earlier generation might have understood it, but higher in [the philosopher Thomas] Nagel's sense of being more complete, more cognizant of that most powerful of all the world's illusory appearances, which is that the world centers on me (or those with whom I choose to identify) and that what matters to me (to us) is paramount.[10]

As he summarizes his ideal of objectivity for professional historians: "What we demand of them is self-control, not self-immolation . . . The demand is for detachment and fairness, not disengagement from life."[11]

For historians to escape the bad influences of their own social and political context on their texts would seem to demand nothing less—and nothing more!—than a monastic adherence to the ideals of their professional community. The social basis of the desired detachment is the discipline of the professional historical community itself:

Detachment functions in this manner not by draining us of passion, but by helping to channel our intellectual passions in such a way as to insure collision with rival perspectives. In that collision, if anywhere, our thinking transcends both the idiosyncratic and the conventional. Detachment both socializes and deparochializes the work of the intellect; it is the quality that fits the individual to participate fruitfully in what is essentially a communal enterprise. Objectivity is so much a product of social arrangements that individuals and particular opinions scarcely deserve to be called objective, yet the social arrangements that foster objectivity have no basis for existence apart from individual striving for detachment.[12]

But for such an intersubjective process to work to best effect demands a certain political climate as its basis: "The kind of thinking I would call objective leads only a fugitive existence outside of communities that enjoy a high degree of independence from the state and other external powers, and which are dedicated internally not only to detachment, but also to intense mutual criticism and to the protection of dissenting positions against threat of majority tyranny."[13] At bottom, then, detached and objective but still committed history can be achieved only in a certain liberal democratic atmosphere, which is dependent in turn upon a certain kind of compatible political and economic system. As a consequence Haskell's approach to objectivity naturalizes naturalism as it mystifies the ideological foundations of professional historical practices.

That both Kloppenberg and Haskell praise Novick's practice over his seeming philosophical commitment to and commentary on the issues of objectivity suggests that Novick's practice speaks to them more powerfully than his words of advice. They agree that Novick's own text gives the lie to his seeming preachments, and that therefore the lesson of his book is to do what he does and not what he says. Both Haskell and Kloppenberg admit that they, like he, practice a history well within the bounds of the traditional paradigm as judged by that paradigm. Both support the political uses of objectivity if the practice ranges within the limits of normal history as set by historians operating within a free (= our?) society.[14]

The lessons of Novick, Kloppenberg, and Haskell are the issues they suggest about the role of politics in disciplinary practice in addition to politics in and of historical texts themselves. Thus historians must consider the politics of interpretation as an intellectual process as well as what politics show up in those interpretations, the politics behind certain methods as well as what politics are explicit in the results of those methods, the politics of historical methodology in general as well as what is fostered by that methodology. Attention to these possibilities will alert historians or their critics to how the paradigmatic foundations of normal historical practice presume political stances despite whether historians profess partisanship or objectivity. They must explore the politics of how a Great Story is constructed as well as what is told in that Great Story, the politics of the ideal of the Great Past as well as what politics were practiced in the Great Past. To examine the politics of history as a way of study as opposed to discussing politics in history as a study of the past, historians must attend to the politics grounding professional authority as well as to skirmishes over politics in the profession. To be aware of the politics of approaches they share with other modern human science disciplines requires interest in the political debates in and among the disciplines. All these issues connect to and are influenced by the larger political world(s) in which historians live. Many of these issues are framed and debated in terms of such dualisms as textualism or contextualism, social or rhetorical construction of reality, poetics or politics.

The Politics of Viewpoint

Situating the Normal Viewpoint

As Kloppenberg and Haskell illustrate, one seeming challenge to the normal historical paradigm is mounted by those who seek to redefine the place of objectivity in the discipline and its discourses. Although they would admit the impossibility of some transcendental objectivity, hence the desirability, even necessity, of advocacy, they still seem to claim, if their own practice is any guide to their premises, that historical facts and Great Stories can exist beyond the relativism of a particular, hence partial, framework. At the same time as they denounce objectivism in favor of partiality of politics and of perspective, they argue for an alternative to relativism grounded in "situated knowledges," to borrow Donna Haraway's term.[15]

Knowledge is situated when it is connected to its social locations in a society presumed divided by access to power. Since the sites of contestation multiply in proportion to social fissures along the lines of sex, race, ethnic origin, region, religion, generation, and other groupings, it is not class or occupation alone that determines social location but rather the multiple interacting processes involved in power relationships. Therefore, according to Haraway, "objectivity turns out to be about particular and specific embodiment and definitely not about the false vision promising transcendence of all limits and responsibilities. The moral is simple: only partial perspective promises objective vision." She repudiates the all-seeing, all-knowing, godlike position traditional to objectivity as a single best or right viewpoint in favor of the partial perspectives of subgroups, particularly those in opposition to the power structure(s) of their society. "The alternative to relativism is partial, locatable, critical knowledges sustaining the possibility of webs of connections called solidarity in politics and shared conversations in epistemology." If a multiplicity of viewpoints is natural to a society of contestation, then, she argues, "it is precisely in the politics and epistemology of partial perspectives that the possibility of sustained, rational, objective inquiry rests." Thus for her "relativism is a way of being nowhere while claiming to be everywhere equally," but such a pretense of equiperspectivalism masks the necessarily specific location(s) of all knowledge(s) in a society presumed structured by inequalities. Relativism, according to her outlook, is just another form of liberal political pluralism that overlooks the inequities of power relationships in producing knowledge just as in affording political access.[16] In fact in the strongest version of this approach to partiality in viewpoint, the unequal social relationships produce the forms and kinds of knowledge and sanction what is true.[17]

This point of view on point of view in historical practice refers us back to the paradigm of normal historical practice. In other words, we must reconsider the foundations of historical practice from the perspective of the political implications of the very way normal historians textualize their stories and arguments through voicing and viewpoint as discourses. Ultimately, we must ask once again about the politics of the historian as (a) Great Story-Teller and how that shapes the viewpoint from which the Great Past is represented as History.

Normal histories as textualizations embody a political stance or partisanship as fundamental to their discourses in two closely related ways. First, when they pretend to be "natural" in their transparency, they may also pretend to be politically neutral to their subject matter in its textualization. Does repeating what was said in the past, however, convey acceptance of that point of view on matters? Does it imply accepting past categories and views as the author's own, if they are not explicitly disavowed in the text? Even the vocabulary of histories shows these effects. An example is the current argument over whether the once seemingly neutral word "discovery" should be applied to Columbus' exploits. Likewise, does "Progressivism" still seem appropriate for the decades straddling 1900 in the United States in light of the failure of Populism and the maturation of corporate industrialism? And can "revolution" be applied to European social movements before the eighteenth century?

The semantics of these examples imply that might makes history as well as right and to the victor belongs history as well as the spoils. The many examples of such vocabulary in the profession demonstrate that politics provide plots and morals determine methods in normal historical practice far more pervasively than the more obvious political uses and explicit messages of historical syntheses that historians confess in their perfunctory, often prefatory, full disclosure statements. Texts not only present stories and arguments about power in a society; they also represent it by how they textualize history according to the normal paradigm. Thus even those historians who do not argue explicitly for a political point of view argue from an implicit political point of view in their synthetic expositions.[18]

Histories also embrace politics when they pretend to be mimetic to some "natural," that is, customary, social order according to its own mode of mystification. The more historians justify the obviousness (transparency) of their productions by asserting a "natural" order of understanding, the more likely they are to assert that the social and political arrangements they talk about are also a "natural," that is, normal, social or political order. Such naturalization was particularly the target of revisionist women's history in its opposition to the classic dichotomies of culture versus nature, work versus family, public versus private, reason versus emotion, and even providing versus nurturing that until recently grounded descriptions of male/female relationships in Western societies.[19]

In these two senses most normal history-telling is implicitly ideological, for historians cannot discuss relationships in a society apart from some perspective within a network of political and social arrangements either then or now. They take a position (quite literally as well as figuratively) on such arrangements according to some viewpoint associated with a class, group, sex, or stratum in that past society and in a present one. Does writing as if what happened had to happen (or was inevitable in some sense) favor some political ideologies or moral outlooks over others in the past or the present? This was the fundamental political difference between Richard Hofstadter's and Lawrence Goodwyn's treatment of the Populists. Likewise, does writing as if the status quo was normal in a past era also seem to justify it as the morally right or natural way of doing things in that context regardless of today's ethics?

Central to such criticism of historical discourse are current conceptions of ideology and cultural hegemony. Just as the fundamental idea of ideology relates (or relativizes) ideation to its social location(s), so the notion of hegemony holds that dominant social and political arrangements generate conceptual structures to warrant those arrangements and their intellectual offspring as "natural," even inevitable, to many or most persons in the society. Cultural hegemony is from this point of view, as Nancy Fraser so aptly worded it, the "discursive face of power," and as such, "it is the power to establish the 'common sense' or 'doxa' of a society, the fund of self-evident descriptions that go without saying." As she points out, "this includes the power to establish authoritative definitions of social situations and social needs, the power to define the universe of legitimate disagreement, and the power to shape the political agenda. Hegemony, then, expresses the advantaged position of dominant social groups with respect to discourse."[20] Ultimately, discursive hegemony asserts a single best and right viewpoint about what constitutes "reality" for a society. It narrows the choice of representations to the preferred one(s) to the exclusion of others. "Hegemony becomes the successful representation of a representation, of any representation as real—as the only possible representation."[21] Even opponents in a society to a (the?) hegemonic view frequently express their dissent according to basic premises of the dominant discursive paradigm. Hence the need for semiotic and rhetorical iconoclasm, in the opinion of Roland Barthes, to unmask the "common sense" of the culture for what it is and whom it supports politically.[22]

These views of ideology and hegemony postulate a society riven actually or potentially by conflict and division, whether by sex, class, race, or other cleavage. Theorists of hegemony see it as a dynamic process of reproducing the standing order and the resistance that reproduction generates. Such dynamism results in a field of contestation, negotiation, modification, and even appropriation and innovation, hence a plurality of discourses and their social sites. Contesting ideologies and cultures coexist in shifting and unstable discursive formations over time.[23] As Stuart Hall argues:

> The important thing about systems of representation is that they are not singular. There are numbers of them in any social formation . . . Ideologies do not operate through single ideas, they operate in discursive chains, in clusters, in semantic fields, in discursive formations . . . So a variety of different ideological systems or logics are available in any social formation . . . They contest one another, often drawing on a common, shared repertoire of concepts, rearticulating and disarticulating them within different systems of difference or equivalence.[24]

In an effort to represent the dynamics of contestation and conflict, some theorists classify ideologies as "dominant," "accommodationist," or "oppositional,"[25] and cultures as "dominant," "residual," and "emergent,"[26] depending upon who is doing what to whom and how in a social system. In line with these dynamics, texts and their discourses can be classified according to the same terminology to show the politics they espouse as explicit argument and interpretation. Texts and discourses also exemplify the politics of their societies through their silences, for omissions also reveal commitment or, more probably, repression. Last, a text can incorporate the very tensions of a society, because hegemonic discourse must presume what it suppresses just as oppositional discourse must address what it challenges.

These conceptions of ideology and hegemony implicate historical practice in the discursive formations of the larger society in at least three ways. First, what is the effect on sources: who and therefore what appears among the sources in archives? Second, historians, like other members of their societies, have several or more social locations that shape their viewpoints and their histories. Historians' histories, like other discursive practices, must therefore take sides, knowingly or unknowingly, in the conflicts of their societies. Thus both seemingly apolitical reportage and partisan polemics, whether their message is radical or conservative, are alike in the mystification of their ideological origins in normal historical practice. Whether historians present their synthetic expositions as stories or arguments, as explicit or implicit political fables, all their writings presume a political subtext.[27] Such a subtext can be framed according to some hope of a future utopian society or an ideology justifying a present social arrangement, to use Karl Mannheim's terms—but both are ideologies because they are relativized to some rank or class or other kind of grouping within some social order and see the world and all history from a perspective within that rank, class, or grouping.[28]

Reinforcing this political subtext are the very ways in which the past is conceived as history and then represented as story and argument in the text in line with normal historical practice. To the extent that historians conceal their inventive or constructive operations, their very practice mystifies the political subtext in the name of reality and objective existence. Their texts present the political subtext and its partisanship as referentiality, and the political lessons are reinforced through the pretense of the presumed transparency of the medium. Such paradigmatic practice entails the concealment of all or part of their political viewpoint (bias?) as historians read sources as political Ur-texts and ground their Great and partial stories on and in political metahistories. Histories from the bottom up, like those from the top down, postulate their own teleologies as bases for the Great Stories contextualizing their facts.

All history, like all theory, can therefore be said to be interested, for it is produced according to some interest, whether that of the powerful or the dispossessed or even the professional, from the top down or the bottom up or the in-between. This relationship between politics and history goes beyond the obvious one of historians' use of overt political paradigms in their formal arguments; rather it is built into the disciplinary practice of history itself as it mystifies authority and power throughout the metastory and metasource as a natural mode of understanding the world past and present. In the end, then, plots and politics, methods and morals are obvious and collusive partners throughout the paradigm of normal history.

If the very foundations of normal historical practice are pervaded by the possibilities of political partisanship and moral judgments—all relevant to the present—even when applied to times and societies long ago, then the old warning about the evils of present-mindedness needs rethinking.[29] Although the doing of history is clearly partisan when it pretends to be mimetic of some natural social and political order in recent times, how relevant is such an accusation when the period or the society seems far in the past? If the social order is long ago and far away from present-day or recent societies, cannot the past be studied for its own sake without the political repercussions so evident in histories of modern times? Although historians of ancient societies may deem the social order of their subjects irrelevant to today's political battles, they cannot avoid taking positions on topics vital to the foundations of any political ideology. They presume models of human behavior, human agency, or the nature of human nature, and they offer them implicitly if not explicitly as the lessons of history for today's understanding of the world. Whether humans prefer peace or war, whether human nature is a constant or culturally emergent, what the human will can achieve in the face of adverse circumstances and social structures, what are the nature and roles of the sexes, and even what constitutes causation and proof, are among a multitude of questions whose answers necessitate taking positions basic also to political stances.[30]

Even to those historians who argue that they study the past for its own sake or that they show how the past differs from the present, one can ask: why study the past for its own sake, and what do you prove in the present knowingly or unknowingly? Why show how the past differs from the present? For what and whose purposes does the past look different from or the same as the present? What are the various political uses of ethnocentric universalism or radical relativism? In the end even the long, long ago must be textualized according to present-day historical practice with all the political implications embodied in that form of discourse; otherwise the reader will not understand the story or argument. From the viewpoint of its emplotment, all history is present-minded, since it is not only done in the present but also arranged in light of what occurred later than the past that is the ostensible topic of the text. In order for readers in the present to understand the ideas and actions of peoples in the past, historians must commit anachronism insofar as they must translate the language(s) of the past into the language(s) of the present.[31] Extreme historicism, like any radical relativism, would deny that historians could understand what they claim to understand as other societies or other times. It certainly would deny their ability to translate from past languages into present ones.[32]

Critical History as Oppositional Viewpoint

Radical and multiculturalist historical discourses in their opposition to the standing social order highlight how political viewpoints pervade normal historical texts and practice. In so doing they provide valuable lessons on the various ways in which normal historical textualizations and practices implicate political viewpoints as part of professional discourse and disciplinary methodology. Historians promoting minority or radical political representation in historical discourse condemn the viewpoint adopted in many normal histories as hegemonic, for it supports the traditional or dominant power structure as the "natural" way of viewing things social and political. It thus co-opts the minds of would-be opponents by concealing the alternatives proposed in the past as a way of censoring the alternatives to the present. The editors of an anthology of interviews with radical historians describe the problem succinctly:

> We live in a society whose past is given to us in images that assert the inevitability of the way things are. In more or less subtle ways, politicians and the media invoke history to show that the contemporary distribution of wealth and power

is at once freely chosen and preordained. By the same token, past efforts to contest prevailing social and political arrangements disappear from dominant versions of our history—when they are not simply labeled as foreign and dismissed as utopian. Yet there is a tradition of radical history writing that has worked to overcome this kind of historical amnesia. It has sought to rescue from oblivion the experiences and visions of past movements against social and political domination, and to analyze historically the structures and dynamics of domination today.[33]

For the same reasons, multiculturalist historians expounding the role of gender, race, ethnicity, and class in history also point out the frequent political partiality as well as professional partialness in textualizing the past according to the normal history paradigm.

Many who espouse multiculturalist or political revisionist ideals in historical discourse therefore do not fear partisanship and present-mindedness. Rather they proclaim their merits as a balance to the hegemonic viewpoints and politics that dominate normal historical discourse. If, in the end, all supposedly objective and neutral viewpoints are from someone's position and therefore partial, why not admit it? Linda Gordon, for example, argues that the pose of objectivity is worse than explicit partisanship, because those who claim neutrality are misleading people about their actual positions, and, worse from her outlook, they lack a viewpoint from which to be critical of their own culture.[34] Presuming a society of conflict and division, with power permeating every relationship, these historians see themselves as being more honest than those they oppose about their own discursive positions, even if their own arguments are not always entirely representative of their own location(s) in that society. Their scholarship becomes oppositional to the hegemonic common sense of their professional colleagues as they seek to demystify present conceptual and cultural categories and destabilize social and political institutions through exposing their history in their representations of the past. History is part of a larger emancipatory mission as it seeks a discourse that would empower those who are taken in and thereby oppressed by the prevailing system. For these dissenting scholars, classrooms and texts should be devoted not to the reproduction and transmission of the dominant culture but instead to the critique, renovation, and even transformation of that culture. As Myra Jehlen states: "As a principle of analysis, I would propose the view that conflict and contradiction shape the world more fundamentally than convergence and agreement." Thus scholars, according to her, should "disassemble" the systems that society presents as knowledge and actuality.[35]

The more radical a transformation historians desire in (a) society, the more history that pursues an oppositional point of view is critical for changing society through showing how fundamental the inequalities of power are to every instance of ideation and interaction in that society. So critical, in this view, is history to the struggle over power and ideas that radical history ought to be history critical of the standing order. Its chief purpose is to demystify and denaturalize past and present discourses to reveal the asymmetry of power that converts sex into gender, ethnicity into race, rankings into class, others into Others, and discourse into hegemony. Part of that agenda includes current historical practice itself, so that for self-proclaimed radical historians historical criticism is critical history applied to the discourses of their fellow historians to reveal how they naturalize the hegemonic categories of the present to discuss the past. Through self-critique, moreover, they hope to police the politics of their own professional discourse.

Howard Zinn in his generation-old essay "What Is Radical History?" provided a gloss on this viewpoint in his list of explicit goals for raising the political consciousness of the readers of history. First, radical history ought to "intensify, expand, sharpen our perception of how bad things are, for the victims of the world." As part of this goal a history should dissolve the separation between the "us" of the historian's and reader's world and the "them" in the victims' worlds. Second, such a history must "expose the pretensions of governments to either neutrality or beneficence." The reader must be convinced that the government will not right many of the wrongs exposed in the first goal, and may even cause or exacerbate the plight of the victims. Third, radical history should "expose the ideology that pervades our culture" so that the reader doubts the "rationale for the going order." Fourth, a history with these aims can "recapture those few moments in the past which show the possibility of a better way of life than that which has dominated the earth so far."[36]

Few histories achieve Zinn's third aim of defamiliarization more effectively for the United States past than Alan Trachtenberg's *The Incorporation of America: Culture and Society in the Gilded Age*.[37] The "incorporation" of the title refers not only to the emergence of large corporations as part of the industrialization of the United States in the last three decades of the nineteenth century but also the physical integration of the nation through transportation, communication, and social hierarchization. According to Trachtenberg, accompanying and enabling these two kinds of incorporation was the incorporation of people's values and perceptions. The final incorporation entails present-day Americans' understanding of all the other meanings as the inevitable and natural history of the period. To retrieve the conflict that was part of that history and, more important, to convince his readers of an alternative possible history, he juxtaposes the often ambivalent or ambiguous myths of late nineteenth-century Americans about the West, capital and labor, the city, and the machine and industrialism against what he describes as the actual social facts. As part of such juxtapositions, Trachtenberg shows how those myths themselves functioned as social facts in concealing the increasingly hierarchical and conflicted nature of nineteenth-century American society. As aspects of the hegemony of the period, they were, as one chapter title phrases it, the "fictions of the real." Thus he contrasts the dominant culture of plutocrats and the "genteel" culture of the middle class with the oppositional culture of labor unionists and Populists, the unions of labor uniting against exploitation with the Union of the United States as incorporated, the myth of equality with the actuality of hierarchy. The reader leaves the book conscious of how the dominant mythology of the earlier period still conceals the actual social facts of today. Ultimately, these social myths that purport to be "reality" are perpetrated through history books in today's society.

Although Trachtenberg's book is not as obvious as Lawrence Goodwyn's on the Populists in declaring who are the heroes and villains of the story, it too portrays those in opposition to the emergence of an incorporated America as the hope for social equality and the presumed pleasures of a more humane (cooperative?) commonwealth. Thus his book in a more general way than Goodwyn's achieves Zinn's fourth goal for radical history of persuading the reader that a possible alternative direction existed for history to the one that was taken in the late nineteenth century. On the other hand, Goodwyn's book is more specific about what was done then and, by analogy, what could be done now to achieve an alternative society. Trachtenberg, however, like Goodwyn urges his reader to consider that an alternative direction is still needed. Thus the last of Trachtenberg's several meanings of culture is that of social critique. As he states in another book, "Ordering facts into meaning, data into history . . . is not an idle exercise but a political act, a matter of judgment and choice about the emerging shape of the present and the future."[38]

From the viewpoint of current multiculturalist ideals, Zinn's first two principles emphasize the victimization of the other too much and need to be superseded or augmented by new ones. In either case, one of the new principles would stress an appreciation of others or the oppressed on their own terms rather than as victims, since the latter approach still represents them in hegemonic terms. Craig Calhoun advocates thematizing and appreciating "not only differences of value but the positive value of differences . . . [for] cultural difference among human societies and differences among people within societies or communicative communities is in itself desirable," on the grounds that "there is an intrinsic advantage to the production of cultural variation" for the maintenance of freedom and the encouragement of creativity. In his opinion, social and cultural diversity, like biological diversity, is good for the species.[39] In the end the good society of so many radical historians and other scholars is the democracy of a diverse community of differences. What assumptions that entails for multiculturalist scholarship is outlined succinctly by Joan W. Scott in her criteria for what any "blueprint for the reconceptualization of community in the age of diversity" must include:

- Differences are often irreducible and must be accepted as such.
- Differences are relational and involve hierarchy and differentials of power that will be constantly contested.
- Conflict and contest are therefore inherent in communities of difference. There must be ground rules for coexistence that do not presume the resolution of conflict and discovery of consensus.
- Communities cannot be based on conformity but on an acceptance and acknowledgement of difference.[40]

What she outlines as desirable is mixed with what she considers as typical of the way in which any society operates past and present.

Still other principles augmenting Zinn's ideology of victimization would emphasize the resistance of the oppressed to the hegemonic efforts of the established in discourse and politics and, as a result, the agency of the other in creating their past (and present). The dialectic of resistance is always presumed as being generated by efforts at domination. Such a representation of history, if the narrative and argument grant too much agency to the efforts of the oppressed against the structure of their oppression, risks creating the impression that the oppressed are collaborating in their own oppression. To avoid undue emphasis on structure or agency, radical, like other, historians must find their own middle ground on which to situate narrative and argument.

As radical history seeks to demystify the politics of domination through the self-representation of experience of the powerless and the oppressed, the historian has a moral and political obligation to introduce more voices (and presumably more viewpoints) as implicit or explicit criticism of the existing order. From the warnings against misappropriation and misrepresentation of others' experiences mentioned in the previous chapter and the aims of radical and multiculturalist history may be derived eight political principles of viewpoint regarding the self/other connection:

The asymmetry of power always grounds the relationship.

That asymmetry is not only the grounding of the relationship but also its chief story.

As the chief story, asymmetrical relationships should be made the primary focus of the explicit discourse.

Those who can tell the story best are those who wield the least power in the story.

Objectivity is best represented from the viewpoint of the oppressed. Jesse Lemisch, the first historian of the American past to urge viewing the

American experience from the "bottom up," stated this principle thus: "sympathy for the powerless brings us closer to objectivity."[41] More recently Haraway expressed the same principle: "'Subjugated' standpoints are preferred because they seem to promise more adequate, sustained, objective, transforming accounts of the world."[42] From this political viewpoint on point of view in history, the larger view of both the center and the margins comes from the margins, since those viewpoints of necessity include both the center and the margins.[43]

Polyvocality in the past, as in the present, should not be presented as if all the players were equal on some pluralistic playing field, because the real world of voices, viewpoints, and discourses is structured by power, hierarchy, and social conflict.[44] For every (hegemonic) discourse, there is an opposite but not equally powerful counterdiscourse. As the symbolic resistance of the counterdiscourse attempts to find an alternative way of representing "reality" in a society, the dominant discourse seeks to subvert it through absorption or repression, sometimes in the same text.[45]

The purpose of history texts is to empower the oppressed and the dispossessed through their understanding of their disadvantaged position vis-à-vis the powerful in a society.

The purpose of theory in scholarship is to demystify, denaturalize, defamiliarize power in aid of resistance and destabilization, whether in a classroom, a society, or the world.

Many postmodernists would add as a corollary to the last principle opposition to totality or totalization, whether found in the textualization practices of societies in general or of historians in particular. Totality or totalization as a concept has its own history, but the notion rejects conceiving society or history as an aggregation of isolated parts. Rather it stresses the history and society as totalities, as systems of interrelationships, as wholes. Its critics today condemn totalization as overemphasizing coherence and unity instead of conflict, reducing the actual workings of society and history to a preconceived holism. The term as used by today's theorists is heavily influenced by Foucault.[46] Foucault, for example, criticized periodization practices in traditional historical discourse for presuming "to reconstitute the overall form of a civilization" by appeal to some spiritual or material principle that was supposedly "common to all the phenomena of a period, the law that counts for their cohesion." Such a misguided method of periodization depends upon two or three "hypotheses":

> it is supposed that between all the events of a well-defined spatio-temporal area, between all the phenomena of which traces have been found, it must be possible

to establish a system of homogeneous relations; a network of causality that makes it possible to derive each of them, relations of analogy that show how they symbolize one another, or how they all express one and the same central core; it is also supposed that one and the same form of historicity operates upon economic structures, social institutions and customs, the inertia of mental attitudes, technological practice, political behavior, and subjects them all to the same type of transformation; lastly, it is supposed that history itself may be articulated into great units—stages or phases—which contain within themselves their own principle of cohesion.[47]

His archeological or genealogical approach to historical textualization was his attempt to avoid the problems of totalization that he condemned in the normal discourses of intellectual history or the history of *mentalités*.[48]

Those following Foucault's lead oppose the overcoming of contradictions in a society or the disjunctions in a history through omission or spurious unity in the process of textualizing them. As Lyotard urges, "let us wage war against totality."[49] Universalizing, categorizing, thematizing, normalizing, naturalizing, synthesizing, systematizing, marginalizing, and excluding are totalizing processes. Coherency, continuity, unity, system, and univocality are the hallmarks of textualized totalization. The good postmodernist prefers fragmenting, differentiating, specifying, particularizing, deconstituting practices to deconstruct the spurious unities and reveal the contradictions of social and textual practices.[50] Totalization in a text is a way of gaining control, perhaps power, over rebellious subjects and fractious subject matter through control of their textualization, especially by using traditional narrative techniques. If the textualization of society and history ought not to be unified, what of the textualization of that kind of textualization? Can antitotalization texts avoid their own form of totalization in making their cases or producing their histories? If normal textualization techniques in historical discourse repress, even commit violence against, the diversity and differences among their subjects, then what new forms of representation need to be used to represent the subject matter? Even Foucault's own textualization practices were accused of totalization.[51]

Foucault and other scholars gathered under the loose rubric of poststructuralism or postmodernism betray a romantic's fondness for diversity and polyvocality as opposed to what they represent as the Enlightenment enterprise to unify all thought and reshape society as a whole. Just as they deny the possibility of the liberal, humanist notion of the free individual because of organized surveillance and the coercive nature of modern society, they favor the resistance they believe inevitably arises to confront the many manifestations of power in that society to contain and constrain the varieties of persons as bodies, minds, and spirits. Picturing modern society as tending to total control through dispersed and localized as well as centralized power(s), they sought in their own texts, according to Eve Tavor Bannet, "to unmask and to displace the determinism and the domination, the rational coherence and the control of structural systems and to subvert all attempts to impose the alienating stamp of invariable sameness."[52] Since these thinkers were against totalization, or generalization through the appeal to transcendental truth and hierarchical imposition of unity, whether social or textual, whether political or narrative, they provided theory for a kind of poststructuralist radicalism. According to Bannet's description of this goal,

> They also sought to replace such systematic structures with structures of their own—structures which define new spaces of non-conformity and freedom. Different as they are from one another, Lacan, Barthes, Derrida and Foucault all developed structures of language and thought characterized by gaps, discontinuities and suspensions of dictated meanings in which difference, plurality, multiplicity and the coexistence of opposites are allowed free play. Implicitly or explicitly, they all tried to present these non-deterministic and non-determining structures as alternatives to the deterministic and determining structures inherent in the society, in the university, in the field of knowledge and in the language they had inherited.[53]

For these thinkers and those who follow them, unity and universality, whether in a text or in a nation, was an illusion that needed demystification and deconstruction because it was inherently oppressive. Ever seeking to suppress the local and the contingent or cultural differences and personal desires was power that was also dispersed and localized and that worked in a thousand ways to bring the appearance, if not the reality, of unity and homogeneity to Western societies since the eighteenth century. Such powers were as omnipresent on the micro level as on the macro level in a society. The quest for rationality, especially as codified in a positivist, scientistic discourse, was the conceptual ally of these forms of power.

Whether in textualizations, societies, or histories, poststructuralists prefer heterogeneity and discontinuity to coherence and holism. Although they portray power as omnipresent, they believe that society is not so monolithic that the resistances inevitably generated by hegemonic social arrangements and discourses cannot be efficacious at times. Surely, for them, ubiquitous power deserves the ubiquitous resistance it produces. Although they demystify the liberal, humanist notion of the free individual as an illusion perpetrated by the bourgeois quest for power, they still write as if human agency (of their readers and themselves) can undo as well as unmask hegemonic social and discursive structures. Whether or not they postulate in the end the desirability, if not the possibility, of a society characterized by differences that result in "a harmonious plurality of unmediated perspectives," as one scholar claims, they advocate resistance to hegemony of all kinds and the proliferation of ideologies to do so.[54]

With such romanticist notions of what is desirable, it is not surprising that so many of these scholars look to history to vindicate—and embody—their visions of domination and resistance, local and located knowledge(s), and differences and diversity. All too often in these circumstances the admonition to historicize culminates in a new Great Story that exposes previous Great Stories as attempts to represent the world as a totality, a goal represented as both illusory and historically specific to Western society. At the same time, this new Great Story shows that such an illusion was a power ploy in the construction of a world system of domination by the Western powers. This was the Great Story that Foucault started telling through his histories of discipline, sexuality, and epistemes. Whether or not such a Great Story violated his own admonitions about unifying the discontinuities and contingencies of the past and present in conveying its political message, Foucault's own books as argued and plotted stressed the disruptions as genealogies rather than as the customary unified totalizing histories.[55]

From this view of power as ubiquitous there arise certain overlapping dilemmas for historical practice. First, what does the notion of ubiquitous power imply about the nature of sources and archives as evidence?[56] At its most obvious, what remains as evidence from the past, what is "saved," what is in an archive is a function of the power relations in past and present societies. Historical methods have long tried to compensate for the selective provenience of sources and their preservation in archives as the product of past and later power, but who can discover and represent the voice of the other if the survival of evidence is constrained, even determined, by power? If the other cannot truly speak for itself because dominated, then who in fact speaks for the other in surviving texts purporting to represent that other? Likewise, if those who claim to speak for the dominated are constrained by the powerful in a society, then are the voices of the oppressed what they claim to be, or are they only another appropriation of another's representation?

Other dilemmas center upon the problems of contextualizing the (hi)story of power and knowledge in their many manifestations. At the least these problems include the relationships among social practices, concepts or other ideational entities, and appropriate(d) frameworks. On one level, these relationships are examined and explicated in terms of societal arrangements and social practice. How are micropractices to be connected to macroprocesses in a society and vice versa, past to present and vice versa? Is it possible to describe microprocesses without assuming that they affect the totality of a society, and vice versa? On another level, the relationships among social practices, concepts, and frameworks are explored as problems of frameworks and societal arrangements. How can one connect models of human behavior and society grounding the human sciences as discourses to specific existing societal arrangements without presuming the connection in one's own discourse? How strong a correlation exists between the politics of a society and the politics of a text, and how does a historian demonstrate that connection according to what (= whose?) framework? On still another level, the question arises how scholars' texts exploring the many filiations of power and knowledge can escape the paradoxes and reflexive problems of the power/knowledge nexus in their own discourses on those filiations. What frameworks allow/determine the subjects/objects of such studies? What sort of historical textualization is needed/allowed in historical discursive practice(s) to represent these matters? Whose framework? In the end, must not those who point out the ubiquity of power in present social arrangements and intellectual disciplines presume their own escape from that ubiquity in order to make their case?[57]

Foundations of Authority

The Politics of the Great Story

Regardless of the dilemmas about textualizing histories, both those who favor poststructuralist or postmodernist goals and those who situate all knowledges and demystify the power relations inherent in all interactions continue to present or presume a Great Story that explains the past and present domination and justifies an oppositional stance in order to work for a (the?) better future. For them previous Great Stories were truly "Master" Stories or Interpretive Codes that concealed the workings of patriarchy, imperialism, capitalism, heterosexism, or other totalizing systems in creating—or should one say coercing?—the world(s) of yesterday and today. Though theorized as a provisional truth contingent to present times, this new Great Story presumes to be the single best, most correct metanarrative of past power relationships as prelude to understanding present oppressions and future remedies. The widespread contemporary appeal of this Great Story is clear from the frequency with which it provides macrohistorical context across disciplines.

We have already seen the role played by a Great Story in both justifying and contextualizing the New Anthropology. That change in interpreting others was encapsulated by the anthropologist Edmund Bruner under his notion of the "dominant narrative" for understanding Native Americans during the twentieth century. The dominant narrative that anthropologists told or presumed about Native Americans in the 1930s was one in which "the present was disorganization, the past was glorious, and the future assimilation." In the 1970s the prevailing story became one in which "the present was resistance, the past was exploitation, and the future was ethnic resurgence." Bruner doubted that such dominant narratives "necessarily reflect or mirror actual experience, either anthropological field experience or Indian life experience."[58] As a correlate of this changing Great Story, the history of anthropology itself changed from a Great Story of hero-anthropologists encountering isolated peoples and constructing autonomous cultures to a tale of colonial encounters in the service of modernization and Western hegemony.[59]

The very notion of postmodernism presumes a Great Story at the same time as it denies the credibility of metanarratives in today's world.[60] According to the influential formulation of Jean-François Lyotard in *The Postmodern Condition,* modern societies face a "crisis of narratives." He applies the term "modern" to any body of knowledge that still "legitimates itself with reference to a metadiscourse," which makes "an explicit appeal to some grand narratives, such as the dialectics of Spirit, the hermeneutics of meaning, the emancipation of the rational or working subject, or the creation of wealth." Thus "rational minds" is an "enlightenment narrative, in which the hero of knowledge works toward a good ethico-political end—universal peace." Another Enlightenment metanarrative features the "hero of liberty" seeking some universal justification for emancipation of the people. "Simplifying to the extreme," he summarizes the postmodern as "incredulity to narratives."[61] The metanarratives that Lyotard condemns as no longer credible are those grand narrative discourses that summarized huge portions of modern history according to a single interpretive theme and culminated in utopian prophecies of human emancipation, such as those of the autonomous individual, the classless society, and the transcendental signified that grounded liberal and Marxian political and economic theories alike, and even supposedly empirical social sciences.[62]

Such a version of recent history depends upon its own Great Story if not metanarrative. Although Lyotard might deny that his implied history itself constituted a metanarrative, Warren Montag accuses Lyotard of a return to totalism through reducing such diverse modern phenomena as he gathered under the term "postmodernism" to "a single essence" and thereby writing his own "metanarrative of the end of metanarratives in politics, art, criticism, philosophy and science [all] in a mere eighty pages."[63] Likewise, Ernst Behler argues that Jürgen Habermas has constructed a new metanarrative of emancipatory reason to defend the Enlightenment project against the French attack.[64] Although Lyotard and Habermas differ over what should be done about the postmodern state of affairs, both agree upon the outlines of its development if not upon the details of that history.[65]

In postmodernist theorists' construction of European intellectual history, the outmoded metanarratives and their allied metadiscourses and metatheories arose in the Enlightenment. As Habermas himself summarizes the Enlightenment project:

> The project of modernity formulated in the 18th century by the philosophers of the Enlightenment consisted of their efforts to develop objective science, universal morality and law, and autonomous art according to their inner logic. At the same time, this project intended to release the cognitive potentials of each of these domains from their esoteric forms. The Enlightenment philosophers wanted to utilize this accumulation of specialized culture for the enrichment of everyday life—that is to say, for the rational organization of everyday social life.[66]

Accordingly, Habermas argues, "Enlightenment thinkers of the cast of mind of Condorcet still had the extravagant expectation that the arts and sciences would promote not only the control of natural forces but also the understanding of the world and of the self, moral progress, the justice of institutions and even the happiness of human beings." Thus both Habermas and Lyotard agree on the nature of the Enlightenment in their Great Stories.[67]

Those both for and against postmodernist trends historicize recent times as antithetic to the grand old emancipatory myths. As Habermas puts it:

> The twentieth century has shattered this optimism. The differentiation of science, morality, and art has come to mean the autonomy of the segments treated by the specialist and their separation from the hermeneutics of everyday communication. This splitting off is the problem that has given rise to efforts to "negate" the culture of expertise. But the problem won't go away: should we try to hold on to the *intentions* of the Enlightenment, feeble as they may be, or should we declare the entire project of modernity a lost cause?[68]

In accord with this Great Story, then, postmodernists repudiate as irrelevant to, if not destructive for, modern times the universalism, progressivism, and optimism that supposedly characterized or symbolized the Enlightenment project of utopian emancipationism, whether eventuating in liberalism or Marxism, in scientism or humanism. In their Great Story they favor the postmodern, postcolonial world of localism over universalism, the decentered over the centered, multiplicity and diversity over the unified and homogeneous.

Despite such seeming agreement in outline, postmodernism as a Great Story has its own problems of emplotment. Should it be plotted as rupture and discontinuity or as evolution and continuity? One need not be a devotee of Foucault's episteme to see the predicament of the relationship of postmodernism to modernism. Proponents of postmodernism as a conception can no more agree upon when it started than they can agree upon what it is. Although most theorists of postmodernism date its rise to the second half of the twentieth century, some see intellectual ancestors scattered throughout previous centuries. Although postmodernism in cultural productions correlates with multinational corporations and international capitalism as well as with modern mass communications and the so-called global village, how is postmodernism as a cultural phenomenon related specifically to the social and economic systems of our recent times? Scholars debate whether postmodernism, like postindustrialism, is a new stage of culture and society or merely an extension or later stage of capitalism, industrialism, and modernism. Is it, in short, POSTmodernISM or only postMODERNism?[69] Are pastiche, parody, irony, and reflexivity characteristic only of postmodernism or of modernism itself?[70] Even the politics of postmodernism hinges on whether the Great Story is one of continuity or rupture. Does a postmodern breakthrough herald a new vibrant liberation arising from the ruins of the old modernism, or is postmodernism a repudiation of the liberatory mission of the earlier modernism? If the latter, is it a reactionary movement complicit in the late industrial capitalism of consumer culture and society of spectacle it exposes and decries? Does it tacitly celebrate late modernist trends as it explicitly condemns them?[71]

Theories of postmodernism differ not only over when it actually begins but also over how it ends as a Great Story. According to the not very sympathetic description of Terry Eagleton,

> Postmodernism signals the death of such "metanarratives" whose secretly terror-istic function was to ground and legitimate the illusion of a "universal" human history. We are now in the process of waking from the nightmare of modernity, with its manipulative reason and fetish of totality, into the laid-back pluralism of the postmodern, that heterogeneous range of lifestyles and language games which has renounced the nostalgic urge to totalize and legitimate itself . . . Science and philosophy must jettison their grandiose metaphysical claims and view themselves more modestly as just another set of narratives.[72]

Deconstructionist postmodernism declares the end of the subject, of representation, and of teleology as they have been known since the Enlightenment. This version owes much to poststructuralism.[73] Whether the repudiation of traditional subjectivity and individualism or the crisis of representation and mimetic responsibility also entailed the end of cultural and social emancipation depends upon the theorist.[74]

Such an extreme view of the postmodern project produces its own reflexive problems. If postmodernism is a self-consciousness of a culture's own historical relativity with the consequent loss of the absoluteness of any Western account of history,[75] then what about the history assumed in the Great Story of postmodernism? How can a postmodernist of this persuasion plot history? Is it a narrative of epistemological and ontological innocence lost or of epistemological and ontological sophistication gained? Should the story be emplotted as irony or as tragedy? If pastiche or montage is the preferred postmodernist mode, should not its Great Story, like all history, be plotted accordingly? Must not the narrative, like the subject, be fragmented and mimetic realism be subverted in and through the discourse?[76]

As the plotting of the Great Story of postmodernism indicates, whether or not to generalize or totalize may not be the crucial problem it appears in historical textualization. Is an explicit antitotality position any less totalizing implicitly or subtextually than a totalizing one? An explicit position against totalization warns that any viewpoint is specific and not general and universal, but as I have argued in the previous chapter, most multiculturalists find it difficult to embody multiple viewpoints in a single text(ualization) produced by a single author or teacher. If totalization with a goal of objectivity presumes an omniscient or omnipresent viewpoint, then does not antitotalization assume likewise under the guise of situating all knowledge(s) and exposing all power relationships? The political and narrative subtext of such historicization presumes unities of subject and totalization that the explicit text may even deny. Regardless of any political goal avowed by the historian, normal historicization imposes holism and unity in and on the text; or, if the author leaves it undone, the reader will do so, as the disciplinary assimilation of Foucault's texts demonstrates.[77] Thus postcolonial, anticapitalist, antipatriarchal histories tend to resemble their opposites in how they go about textualizing their stories. Resistance histories, like other forms of resistance according to theories of hegemony, all too often operate within the hegemonic framework that contains and limits their opposition. To naturalize the narrative of poverty and oppression is to accept the telos as well as the methodology of normal history.[78]

Must not every political viewpoint use a Great Story textualized in the normal way as grounding for its political judgments?[79] Is not every Great Story a "narrative with a moral intent"?[80] Regardless of the politics of the historian, the Great Story provides the context for the history that can be told. If metanarratives, like words, have lost their meaning in today's scholarly discourses, then have Great Stories become foundational, even if directed against the possibility of other, older metanarratives? Even the most deconstructive postmodernists presume a Great Story to ground their case and bolster their politics. For Derrida to condemn the logocentrism inherent in Western thought, must he not only use the canon of Western thinkers but also presume a Great Story linking them?[81]

Proclaiming the death of the grand metanarratives has not meant the death of Great Stories. Which and what Great Story matters greatly from the viewpoint of a person's politics, but from the politics of viewpoint all Great Stories present the same problems of textualization. Who is the Great Story-Teller? From whose viewpoint is the Great Story told and emplotted either explicitly or subtextually?

The Politics of Authority

Historians establish their authority through obeying the rules of their profession, and those principles in turn justify the autonomy and authority of historians. Historians defend the authority as well as the autonomy of their profession both at its boundaries with other disciplines and at its core through their adherence to the basic principles of the normal historical paradigm. Although the defense is phrased in conceptual terms, it has political implications for the fight over intellectual turf in departments, in academia, and in the larger world.

Even the internal boundaries historians draw within the discipline bolster the authority of some enterprises at the expense of others. Proper history does not embrace historiography no matter how defined. If historiography is the history of history, then it undermines the authority of proper history through its historicization of all histories to their times, and thus suggests their cultural and political arbitrariness. If historiography is the theory of history or methodology, then once again the principles of proper history appear subordinated to other conceptual concerns and even perhaps relativized with the same consequences as the history of history. If historiography is the discussion of a set of interpretations of a set of events as opposed to the interpretation of those events, then once again proper history is subverted by the suggestion of conceptual or political arbitrariness. To avoid the radical ramifications of historicism, even one not reinforced by textuality, many historians to the left, right, and in between agree on the standard, normal paradigm of historical practice as the best way of policing and preserving their discipline in addition to being the best mode of historical practice.

In setting boundaries between their own and other disciplines, historians carefully divide the nature of proper history from the similar or contiguous subject matter of other disciplines, such as historical sociology and philosophy of history, in order to set disciplinary bounds. Likewise, most historians distinguish between professional histories and lay histories, between formal and folk histories, between oral and documentary histories, between learning and memory, between historical sources, source books, and "proper" histories as such to promote the authority of the profession and themselves. Although multiculturalist historians may be reluctant to admit or allow distinctions between folk and formal or oral and documented histories, in practice they often rely on them to justify the authority of their own texts as the single best and most valid interpretation. That even revisionists who propose alternative voices and viewpoints in historical discourse still operate according to the normal paradigm of historical practice and authority reveals the limits of both the new and the old approaches to objectivity and authority in the profession. Similarly, oppositional discourses ground their validity according to the principles of the hegemonic normal paradigm and the normative ideal of a single, if different, Great Story. The ultimate conceptual defense, hence justification, of the historical profession, like that of historical authority itself, is the line between fiction and history, of course, and the allied attempt to distinguish proper history from speculative philosophy of history and metahistory. That the lines between fiction and history, metahistory and history appear eroded in postmodernist theory prompts virulent attacks from traditional historians, whether radical, liberal, or conservative in political orientation. In the end, a single Great Past comprehended through a single Great Story derived according to proper historical methods and presented according to normal discursive practice must remain the goal of the profession in order to preserve its authority against other scholars and lay persons.

Since the politics grounding history as a professional discipline pervade, because they constitute, historical text(ualization)s, we can look to historical methodology itself for the political foundations of historical authority. The politics of the profession embedded in disciplinary practices reinforce and are in turn reinforced by the political subtext embraced in the theory of viewpoint as univocal and universal and ultimately objective. Historical texts mystify as they neglect to represent the political foundations of the discipline as a discipline. Texts therefore represent not only power relations in their content but also disciplinary power relations through their textualization according to the poetics and rhetoric of their construction, by how they are put together as opposed to what they talk about. The historian through the voice and viewpoint of the text authorizes its (and her) disciplinary, self-constituted authority.

Normal history essentially orders the representation of the past for the sake of historians' power over the audience. What is suppressed (repressed?) in normal historical exposition, whether narrative or nonnarrative, whether in so-called new or old histories, whether conservative, liberal, or radical, is the ultimate personal, hence political and inventive, production of that history. Each new kind like each old kind of history still claims to map, if not mirror, the past, even if multiculturally conceived. The function of normal historical principles is to conceal the true extent of the historian's intervention. The author tries to disappear behind the robes of an omniscient Clio as recorder of the past, for it is through the ideal of an ultimately single best or right viewpoint that professional authority is claimed. Historical authority, like all authority, depends upon a single voice speaking for all others as if no other voice(s) existed to do so.

Whatever the explicit viewpoint or voices in the actual text, the subtext's "official" viewpoint as represented in the Great Story and therefore the Great Past is one of omniscience and omnipresence. By assuming an official third-person voice and omniscient viewpoint, authors assert their power over their readers in the name of Reality, for they claim to know what actually happened: what all the characters did and why, what all the events were and why, what were the real implications and lessons. Such self-privileging of one's own interpretation through the devices of normal history is its own form of power, for it pretends to be outside the realm of its own discourse. It privileges its own givens and presuppositions as it *must* to claim professional authority over the reader.[82]

The impression of and claims to textual authority, hence discursive historical authority, are reinforced by the presumption of realism basic to the normal history paradigm. By collapsing the structure of interpretation into one appearing to be only referential, historians distinguish history from fiction and therefore enhance the Reality of the historical production by concealing its fictiveness. To the extent that normal historians mystify their inventive interventions or structures of interpretations as (f)actual representations, their very practice reinforces the political foundations of the discipline through subtext in the name of reality and gives it a seemingly objective existence through the contents of the text. The paradigmatic quest for objectivity and the "real" all reinforce the politics and authority of the discipline. Historians assert their authority over the real through the ideology of realism. Accordingly, Marxian-inspired history and its supposed bourgeois opposite rest upon the same assumptions of realism, of referentiality. One could say that the interpretive superstructure of Marxian history pretends to rest upon a base of referentiality, for otherwise the conceptual basis of materialist history would make no sense.[83] From this perspective, Marxian and bourgeois history are both bourgeois, if realism and referentiality are habits of the bourgeois mind-set.

Foundational to normal historical authority as an ideology of realism is the naturalization of social time presumed in—and represented by—history. According to Elizabeth Deeds Ermarth, "one cannot oppose history to foundationalism because history *is* foundationalism." History has become its "own commanding metanarrative, perhaps *the* metanarrative in Western discourse," because normal history has become the preferred single right and best way of representing the past as time. For the late modernist historian as would-be social scientist, "the methodology of history entails the relativization of every system *except history* which itself remains beyond the system."[84] In normal practice chronology and even narrative reduce the multiple and conflicting voices, events, and viewpoints to the single measure of chronology or story plot and therefore homogenize the variety of possible textualizations. The operation of narrative, at least in its normal (modernist?) forms, subverts the very multiple realities it tries to portray. In the end, then, does the very idea of (normal) history participate in and collude with hegemonic discourses through its use of narrative and chronology according to standard, seemingly commonsensical, ways of representing matters?[85]

Plural pasts, as opposed to plural interpretations, thus undermine the whole legitimating processes of normal historical discursive practice. The authority of the discipline is asserted through the stress on the single best or right story and the denial of equality among plural interpretations. Although there are many mediators in actuality between the past and the present, there is only one ideal mediation in each Great Story.[86] Normal historians supposedly act as mere surrogates for that ideal Great Story-Teller in their text(s). Multiple voices, even multiple viewpoints, may be included in historical textualization, but multiple viewpoints as the basic framework or interpretation of the partial and Great stories once again subvert the authority of historians, their works, and their discipline.

The quest for a single metastory or Great Story to organize the synthetic representational side of historical discourse only abets the political project of the discipline through the normal history paradigm. Authorial, hence professional, power over the reader is also asserted through the normal history presupposition of a single metastory to contextualize the synthetic, representational side of history-doing. Left, center, and right seem to take similar positions on this matter. Those inspired by Karl Marx seek a single interpretive code or master story, although they may disagree among themselves as to just what the key may be in interpreting the Ur-text.[87] Liberal and conservative like radical historians must also contextualize their cases by a single metastory, a single interpretive coding of the past. Otherwise, the arbitrary nature of the produced history becomes easily evident to the audience, and history loses its intended naturalizing effect.

Thus to explore the political grounding of the synthetic practices of the normal historian is to demystify all or most of the presuppositional framework of the normal history paradigm as both political and methodological. To the very extent that the conventions of normal history are discursively determined, hence in the end culturally arbitrary, they are political, an act of will and desire that affects the choice of tropological prefiguration and emplotment.

The Politics of Paradigms

Conflicting Problematics

Historians seem to be caught between the competing claims of fictional construction versus historical reconstruction, partisanship versus objectivity, plural interpretations versus a single real past, diverse voices and multiple viewpoints versus historical and disciplinary authority, and the other dilemmas they try to finesse or mediate in their discursive practice. Some members of the profession would like to find a middle-of-the-road or centrist stand on the issues, but other disciplines and even some historians challenge whether such a stand can exist. The debate, therefore, is not only conceptual but political within the profession and between disciplines. Translating some of the issues into such common categories of literary analysis as voice and viewpoint, content and form, and reference and representation clarifies the issues, but these very terms raise in too many historians' eyes the specter of the linguistic turn with its dangers for all understanding, let alone historical practice.[88]

Where the middle of the road lies depends upon how wide the road is conceived to be, but the issue of width is at the center of the contest over problematics basic to history-doing. Objectivism and hyperrealism constitute one edge of the road; a strong version of the linguistic and rhetorical turns comprises the opposite edge. Scholars have long questioned any simple linkage between language and texts and the (re)construction of historical reality and thereby challenged any simple understanding of history as overall context. The new intellectual currents from the European continent, however, seemed to mount a more basic challenge to the understanding of context as (social) reality and the relation between language and the constitution of social reality by calling for an increased awareness of history itself as text and discourse. Since the linguistic and rhetorical turns had important conceptual implications for writing histories or teaching history, they also possessed important political implications for the profession of history.

To show the possible paths such a middle course hopes to follow, one must consider what lies at the edges of the conceptual highway. Many of these issues today are discussed in dichotomous terms: textualism or contextualism, the social or the rhetorical construction of reality, politics or poetics, power or knowledge. In the end, incompatible premises, methodologies, or implications of theory in the human sciences pose major problems of mediation between text and context as subjects of discourse, between textualism and contextualism as ways of representing the past as context, and between poeticizing and politicizing in the present as the proper context of conducting current scholarship. As a consequence of this conceptual conflict there are also contests within and between disciplines which in themselves are open to interpretation as context and textualism.

The efforts of anglophone intellectual and other historians to fight off the reduction of reality to texts and language (the strong version of the linguistic turn) just as they earlier opposed the reduction of ideas to social context (the strong version of social construction) signify (represent?) the political battle over—and for—the conceptual foundations of historical practice itself. At bottom, the fight is a last-ditch stand to preserve the foundational premises of the normal history paradigm as the commonsense ideology of the profession and to retain the hegemony of one kind of textualization over another.[89] The contest of paradigms centers upon what is presumed as given or what is privileged as foundational in regard to (1) what is to be explained and (2) what explains and how one goes about explaining and representing by that mode.[90]

Competing methodologies founded on conflicting problematics can contextualize (con)text according to either a social or the rhetorical construction of reality. These conflicting problematics contest each other on all levels of historical methodology: first, how to contextualize the historical world of the past and its remains as sources in the present; second, how that contextualization of that past should be represented in and through histories produced in the present; and third, how such represented contextualizations should be judged in bolstering the authority of the historical profession. When social construction of reality is the preferred methodological strategy for contextualization, then the social construction of ethnicity, race, gender, class, power, society, the state, and culture supplies the various contexts past and present.

From this viewpoint, cultural analysis will emphasize ideation as ideology, discursive practices as hegemonic or oppositional, and the location of ideas according to what we might term a broadly conceived sociology of knowledge. Historical texts as both produced and consumed in the past and in the present are therefore categorized as ideological representations, their contextualization is by social construction, and their messages are best analyzed through a broadly conceived sociology of knowledge. When the preferred methodological strategy for contextualizing is through poetics and rhetoric, then the various contexts, past and present, will be analyzed or interpreted according to what might be called the rhetoric or poetics of ethnicity, race, gender, class, society, the state, power, and culture. The poetics or rhetoric of culture stresses the application of interpretive techniques to ideation as textualization. The rhetoric and poetics of history stress textualist approaches to the production and consumption of histories today just like the texts of yesterday. In the end, the disciplinary context of the present is studied as part of the rhetoric of the human sciences. This approach, in short, studies context as the poetics of context (to show the problematic) and the poetics of history (to reveal the methodology).

That social and rhetorical approaches to context usually compete as methodologies means they frequently oppose each other as politics within and across disciplines and academia. Advocates of both approaches recognize the social nature of rhetoric and the rhetorical construction of society, but in the last resort they take opposite paths in relating them to each other. For the determined contextualist, all meaning is constrained by lived social experience; ultimately social experience determines linguistic constructions. For the dedicated textualist, all experience is ultimately mediated by cultural meaning; linguistic conventions constitute social reality. These basic but incompatible premises ground the intuitions underlying the social versus the rhetorical construction of reality. The oppositional problems of contestation derive from differences over basic approaches to or models of human psychology and behavior, society and culture, explanation and epistemology, and theories of language and ontology.

What so many historians see as "common sense" denies the more radical conceptual implications of the linguistic turn for a form of realism that allows a mild cultural pluralism without various skeptical relativisms. At the heart of the controversy over the role of realism in historical practice is the relation between a traditional construal of the past grounded mainly on referentiality as opposed to its construal primarily as a(nother) form of representation. If historians do not hold to their traditional claims to the primacy "in the last resort" of social reality over rhetoric, that is, of experience over meaning, then they cannot assert the superiority of context over text and of reference over representation. As a result of these latter losses they would also lose their claims to certainty over relativism, history over fiction, and content over form. Consequently, they would lose their (interdisciplinary) legitimacy as well as their (disciplinary) authority, their very grounds for existence in today's scholarly world. How, otherwise, can they assert the "truth" in both their social and political ontology and the politics of their disciplinary authority? In implication, then, the debate over problematics is as political as it is conceptual in (and for) the discipline.

Mutual De(con)struction

Contested, even contradictory, definitions of key vocabulary reveal the opposing problematics in the very understanding of texts and their contexts, for they postulate—and therefore constitute—relationships among language, behavior, and social reality, including the nature of the state and society with their relationships of power and domination. Contested methods result from opposing methodologies, which depend upon contradictory presuppositional frameworks about textualizations and their relation to contexts. In turn contested methodologies and contradictory problematics provide the focus and the medium for the political contests over, and for, the control of meaning in a discipline, between disciplines, and beyond them.

Social construction and politics not only reduce the traditional viewpoint and authority of history to ideology; they also question the understanding of history as poetics, for they reveal the social, hence political, foundations of the language games underlying representational analysis. In the end this argument centers on the relation of power to knowledge and knowledge to power in the past and in the present. The political critique of history and poetics as (strong) textualism, and thus as modes of understanding, asserts its own ability to comprehend power and social relations outside the language games that constitute these texts or discourses. Proponents of social construction and political analysis contextualize their textualist opponents according to their own ideology of realism, which purports to know that their constructed context corresponds to the real world. They claim, in other words, that they can operate outside the postmodernist universe of hegemonic discourse that they argue textualists inhabit.

They use a basic Great Story both to explain and to justify their position. Thus literary critic Fredric Jameson argues that the transformation of reality into signs and texts occurs necessarily in a society that values consumerism and hides the mode of production that makes for such a spectacle. The arbitrary value of the sign conceals its production in a social context just as consumer goods mystify their own production and seem therefore mere arbitrary choice. Hence a strong textualist program of representational analysis reinforces the logic of consumer capitalism as it reproduces it. History is lost in postmodern society because it is transmuted into a series of perpetual presents as synchronic analysis is substituted for the dynamics of diachronic analysis. History loses its meaning as it is transformed into text, as the signified (past) is transformed into the signifier (history), and as the referent is disconnected from the real worlds of its original and subsequent production.[91]

The same Great Story is advanced by Jon Stratton in *Writing Sites: A Genealogy of the Postmodern World,* in which he too argues that privileging representation over presence is not only the measure but also the product of a postmodern consumer society.[92] Thus he shows how the theories of Foucault, Derrida, and Baudrillard and others both describe and exemplify postmodern times. This version of Great Story is expounded still more bluntly by Bryan Palmer, who argues that postmodernism is the condition of contemporary society at this moment in history and poststructuralism is its ideology, hence "why the descent into discourse is happening now."[93] Blunter still is the criticism of those who point out that the postmodernist "claim that verbal constructs do not correspond in a direct way to reality" arose among elite white males at exactly the time "when women and non-Western people have begun to speak for themselves, and, indeed, to speak about global power differentials."[94]

Such a critique of those who would urge a poetics of historical practice presupposes that it itself is grounded in the referential world that it says the poetics people pretend to lose. It postulates that the contemporary world's mode of social production is such that its system of cultural and language production makes poetics seem its natural mode of understanding. In other words, textualist poetics in general and the poetics of history in particular are the homologues of bourgeois history in the latest mode of production, labeled postmodern, late capitalism, consumer society, society of spectacle, or whatever. Poetics is thus bourgeois criticism to go along with bourgeois history. They defend their arguments about postmodernism through the construction of a Great Story about past and present reality that supposedly supports their case as it contextualizes their points. As Linda Hutcheon summarizes this historical "metanarrative": "market capitalism begat realism; monopoly capitalism begat modernism; and therefore multinational capitalism begets postmodernism."[95] Their arguments about others' metanarratives are "proved" by the construction of another one by them. Perhaps such a paradoxical metanarrative proves best Fredric Jameson's notion of the "political unconscious."

If such a critique constitutes the challenge of contextualist politics to textualist politics, the favor is returned by the textualist poetical deconstruction of the premises of the contextualist urge to historicize. Textualist poetics appears no kinder to post-Marxian inspired history than to its predecessor or to bourgeois history. The poetics of Marxian analysis can be said to transmute the base like the superstructure into a representational mode. Classes are codings of the metastory just as the mode of production is claimed to be the key to the Marxian-inspired metastory. Thus when the (neo)Marxian critic Fredric Jameson is called on to show why history is not just another code among many, he replies classically that history hurts and therefore is (represents?) necessity.[96] Such necessity determines the master code as opposed to the master code's constituting both the referent and the object of study. Marxian-inspired history cannot be textually arbitrary and still be true to its source of inspiration. Neither can such a history be presumed merely representational and still prove its lessons politically.[97] In this assertion neo- and post-Marxists are joined by their political opposites in the academy and society.

Proof for normal historians, be they bourgeois, Marxian, or otherwise, depends upon their assumption of referentiality. Their view of language presumes the existence of relatively direct connections among words, world-views, and the world. Their metastory postulates the reality of power and social relationships, past and present, and their stories relate how power and social arrangements shape events, ideas, and behavior. Those in opposition to these views postulate the antithesis about the nature of language, the comprehension of the social world, and the ability of humans to see beyond the mirrors of their own mind-sets. Both construct the appropriate Great Stories to justify their contentions, which, paradoxically, must presume as the basis of each story the very relationships they seek to disprove by their metanarrative.

Ultimately, defining text and context in a discipline is intertwined with contentions within the discipline itself considered as text(ualist analysis) and context(ualist premises). For the strong (basic) contextualist the fundamental issue seems to center upon the relation postulated between power and knowledge, while for the strong (basic) textualist the whole issue seems to depend upon the relation between language and the world. Hence the opposing positions taken by the two camps on the possibility of distinguishing between signified and referent, text and discourse, meaning and experience, ideology and social reality. The perspectivalism of the textualists leads, in the eyes of their opponents, to self-defeating relativisms that vitiate any secure foundations for political critique grounded upon principles offering explanatory and interpretive security; while to the textualists the theory and the politics of the contextualists appear to produce naught but more (inter)texts or ideology.

Does historical practice reduce merely to a matter of language and who prefers what, or does it become only a matter of power and social relations and who can assert what? Is the role of power in a society as tautologically omnipresent for the contemporary contextualist position as the role of language is tautologically self-referential for today's textualist stance? While the linguistic and rhetorical turns all too often seem at base to be self-referential in their problematics, the contextualist definitions of hegemony, power, and domination seem all too often self-fulfilling because the status quo is presumed by definition to prove the case.[98] At worst, the terminology of power is borrowed from Foucault and used more as metaphorical given than as something to be explained outside its omnipresence.[99]

The politics of (con)textualism and contextualization not only in but of the human sciences eventuates in the contestation of even the definition of politics. If politics might be defined as the struggle for control of the structures of meaning in a discipline, in a society, in the world,[100] then how resolve the ambiguities of the words "meaning" and "structure" when they are at the heart of the controversy between textualists and the contextualists? Textualists examine how meaning is structured, that is, construed textually in a poststructuralist, postmodernist world; contextualists investigate who controls the (social) structure determining meaning, that is, construed contextually in a post-Marxist world. Even this definition of politics, therefore, takes a stance on the issues, for it too centers upon the power/knowledge dilemma. The fundamental questions that seem to identify the camps in historical discourse and their loyalties are patent. Why do things take the form they do? marks a textualist. Why do the forms arise when they do? distinguishes a contextualist.[101] Of course, both camps answer both questions in their own way. One can answer, mediate, reduce these questions by conceptual and political choices, but in the end they remain grounded by either textualist or contextualist postulates about words, worldviews, and worlds.

Any understanding of context necessitates contested methodologies, hence contested histories, as part of the political struggles over both the nature of social reality and the ways of understanding it. The clash of interpretive principles and therefore communities—or vice versa—in the opposing approaches to context shows the lack of agreement among the players and their problematics on the very nature of what constitutes the (a?) game, as it were, let alone what are the rules of the game, which games are to be played, by whose (= what?) rules, and what (= whose?) plays count.[102] If the answers come from how or who or what decides, then they must be sought in the politics within and of a profession. Such an approach would seem to account for the recent popularity of the histories of professional discourse, especially in literary criticism and literary theory.[103] But how these histories should be constructed, plotted, and so on raises the very specter they were meant to dispel: what form should contextual representation take or whose definition of context should prevail in these histories of context?

In the end, then, determining the width of the historiographic road determines where the middle lies, but the very issue of the width of the road involves contesting positions on (con)textualism and therefore results in the politics of conflict over the nature of historical practice itself as opposed to what kinds of politics historical texts espouse. The more the road is widened to include the linguistic turn and a textualist approach to context, the more most normal historical practice moves off center to the right of that road. To the opponents of textualism, such a broadening of the roadway seems to destroy the customary authority and legitimacy of history as a discipline. From their standpoint, whether Anglo-American epistemology should allow Continental ontologies reduces to a matter of politics as much as to conceptual differences. That epistemology is seen as primarily or purely political undermines the contextualist side in spite of its preference for the social production of all knowledge (except its own essential premises?). Is history therefore nothing but an ideology from both the contextualist and textualist viewpoints?

The Politics of the Medium versus the Message

New Great Stories discredit old Great Stories, but do their messages take new forms and plots or make new use of the medium? Moving beyond a hegemonic political viewpoint in a normal history text does not entail moving beyond the normal approach to viewpoint in historical textualization. Adopting a viewpoint favored by those seeking radical political transformation of academia and society is not the same as a radical textualizing of (a) history. Thus the new historicization associated with the historic turn normally follows old ways of historicizing. In fact, the more recent texts represent contested, socially located ideas and conflicted social activities and movements, the more their textualization resembles traditional, even old-fashioned, history in the denial or concealment of explanatory models and the ways in which narrative is presented. Thus, to use an earlier distinction, critical reading and reviewing should distinguish between politics as the content of the discourse itself and the politics of that discourse as a mode of expression or representation.

As in textualizations in general, the nature of the political message presented explicitly by the text can be separated analytically from how that message is conveyed through and by the nature or form of the textualization itself. The latter may embody its own kind of political implications according to the paradigmatic presuppositions of historical practice. Thus, for example, the explicit message of a historian's text may be quite radical politically but the use and form of the medium quite traditional, even conservative, as the gap between the espousal of multiple voices and viewpoints by historians and the actual achievement of polyvocality in their texts demonstrates. The radicalness or conservativeness of the political message rarely correlates with the radicalness or conservativeness of the use of the medium.[104]

This distinction between understanding politics as the content of an explicit message and its implicit conveyance through the means of expressing that message applies in many areas of historical practice. Just as it clarifies the role of politics in professional discourse in contrast to the politics of the discipline as a profession, so it points up the difference between politics as the subject of the text as opposed to the politics of the textualization as discursive practice itself. Thus readers and reviewers must consider the politics of interpretations as intellectual activities in addition to the politics espoused or advocated in those interpretations, the politics behind certain methods in addition to what politics are explicit in the use of those methods, the politics of methodologies in general in addition to the politics fostered by those methodologies. Attention to these issues will alert historians to how the presuppositions of normal historical practice presume political stances in addition to, and in spite of, any professions of objectivity *or* advocacy.

Critical reading and reviewing explores the politics of the implicit paradigmatic premises of normal history while critical history opposes the hegemonic messages conveyed by that history. Critical reading and reviewing investigates the politics of how the Great Story is told while critical history exposes the politics of what is told in the Great Story. Critical reading and reviewing focus on the politics of the ideal of a Great Past in historical practice while critical history concentrates on the politics practiced in and as the Great Past. To examine the politics of history as a way of studying the past in contrast to discussing politics in history through the study of the past, historians must attend to the politics grounding professional authority as well as to the skirmishes over real-world politics in the profession. Likewise, they should look to the politics of modern disciplinary approaches themselves as opposed to political debates in and among the disciplines. All these issues connect to and are influenced by the larger political world, but that larger world is interpreted as much through the methods of textualization and discursive practices in the historical profession as a guild or community of scholars as through the explicit arguments over "facts" and interpretations.

The differences this distinction makes between the politics of medium and message can be seen in some examples. Although a consensus appears to exist in many recent works in both history and literature on the advantages (desirability) of a conflictual social and political model for understanding and depicting the past, conflict still prevails over how to apply a conflictual model to past texts and how to textualize those contexts in the present. That conflict over the role of conflict highlights the distinction between the politics of the message and the politics of the medium and how they are used in historical practice and normal contextualization.

The difference between an explicit discussion and use of politics as the message in the discipline versus an explicit examination of the politics or implicit presuppositions of historical practice itself is well illustrated by the articles in the *Journal of American History* in 1986 and 1987 debating the best way to find an overall context to serve as the (a?) synthesis of American history. For political as much as for conceptual reasons, demands arose for a new Great Story that would offer a new, more comprehensive unity beyond the plurality of partial histories of particular groups hidden by a previously unified, presumably hegemonic history. The debate focused on whether the evolution of a public realm in the American past provided the conceptual solution needed both to synthesize U.S. history as a subject and to supply the plot of the story. Thomas Bender, for example, suggested that the making of an American public culture, or the changing formations of a public arena resulting from the clash of classes and the interaction of groups, provided the basis in past social reality for present-day synthesis.[105] Although Bender allowed for contending groups and ideologies, his critics accused him of subscribing to an image of society and power based upon the theory and politics of (liberal) pluralism. One critic complained that Bender's model was just another history told from the top down that would continue to marginalize the victims of hegemonic history.[106] All at least implicitly advocated the replacement of Bender's competitive but still pluralistic model of politics by a more thorough conflict model of society and politics that created central and peripheral groupings not only in the past but also in the textualization of that history in the present.[107] The debate was about politics in the larger society not only then but also now and therefore about how the past should be conceived for what and whose purposes in the present.

Throughout this discussion all the scholars presumed a very traditional realist definition of context as the foundation of their practice and therefore of any historical synthesis. Whether they all subscribed to the ideal of a single Great Story as the only proper context is less clear but probable. No discussion of the problematic of history itself surfaced during this contest over politically correct thinking. Clearly, this omission was as political from the viewpoint of historical method as the proposed synthesis was in both its focus on the political arena and how that should be conceived or textualized. This program for synthesis must therefore be seen as both a political act and a judgment on contextualism versus textualism. "Bringing the state back in," as recent historiographical fashion has it, is combined moral and methodological advice.[108]

Another illustration of conflict over the politics of contextualization in explicating past politics comes from a comparison of Jean-Christophe Agnew's *Worlds Apart: The Market and the Theater in Anglo-American Thought, 1550–1750*, and Walter Benn Michaels' *The Gold Standard and the Logic of Naturalism: American Literature at the Turn of the Century*.[109] Both authors seem to be contributing to the same Great Story of the parallel rise of capitalism and the transformation of people's self-understanding of the world(s) they make and their relationship to it (them). The two texts, however, differ in their own representations of these past representations in their relation to their past contexts. The issue dividing their own texts is their position on the relations between textualism and contextualism in the present and therefore in the construal of the past. Agnew's diachronic treatment seems more wedded to normal historical practice than does Michaels' volume of New Historicist essays.[110]

Historian Agnew takes as his chief theme "the complex and mutually illuminating relation between the two ideas [of play(s) and market]—between the practical liquidity of the commodity form and the imaginative liquidity of the theatrical form." He argues that "commerciality and theatricality are inescapably dialectical ideas—labile, reflexive, deconstructive—and like the practices of which they are abstracted properties."[111] Despite this seeming espousal of reflexive deconstruction, Agnew, in his own representation of the spectacles of the market and the theater, assumes the pose of the grand spectator, that is, the Great Story-Teller, with one voice and viewpoint. His story is neither self-critical nor self-referring in its treatment of the reflexivity let alone the deconstruction of the supposed dialectic between work and play(s), capitalism and culture. In other words, he seems to construe texts almost solely from a basic contextualist viewpoint without worrying reflexively about the textualizing of his own account of texts and contexts. In his own textualization, demystification as social construction constrains deconstruction of contextualization.

Literary critic Michaels appears to agree with Agnew's approach when he argues about the connection between texts and their context in relation to naturalism as a literary convention and era:

> the only relation literature as such has to culture as such is that it is part of it. If I speak of the logic of naturalism, it is not to identify a specific ideological function of literature and the real. I want instead to map out the reality in which a certain literature finds its place and to identify a set of interests and activities that might be said to have as their common denominator a concern with double identities that seem, in naturalism, to be required if they are to be identities at all.[112]

In an approach common to other New Historicists (and Agnew), Michaels reveals how the contradictions of double identities inherent in the natures of corporations, currencies, and personalities in late nineteenth-century America stemmed from the same basic cultural premises in relation to the emerging industrial capitalist economy. However, he brings more of a textualist sensitivity to his own textualization as well as to past texts and therefore gives them a more problematical relationship to the contexts he constructs for them than does Agnew. In his essays the various versions of context combine to produce a more ambiguous stance on the underlying issues of textualism and representation. This difference shows in how he represents past representation(s), as, for instance, in his explication of the logic of naturalism:

> Why does the miser save? He saves to escape the money economy; he saves to reenact for himself the origin of the economy. How can metal become money? How can paint become a picture? One set of answers to these questions repeats

the escape from money: metals never did become money; they always were; hence they never are; a picture is just paper pretending to be something else. The logic of these answers is the logic of the goldbugs and Bryanites, trompe l'oeil, and a certain strand of modernism. The attraction of writing is that it escapes this logic. Neither a formal entity in itself nor an illusionistic image of something else, it marks the potential discrepancy between material and identity, the discrepancy that makes money, painting, and, ultimately, persons possible. But how are persons possible? Or, to put the question in its most general form, how is representation possible?[113]

The doubleness of past contradictory identities is replicated in the doubleness of their representation. Deconstruction of past doubleness goes hand in hand with the duality inherent in any historical reconstruction in the present as representation.

The issue dividing the two authors appears to be less politics than problematics, less disciplinary affiliation than the degree of commitment to realism as the basis for contextual construction. Whereas Agnew constructs too unproblematized a context from the viewpoint of postmodernist theorists, Michaels construes his texts too problematically from the standpoint of traditional or modernist historians. Whereas Michaels fuses his interpretations with those in his sources in such a way that traditional historians cannot tell which text is whose, Agnew, to the consternation of postmodernists, implies that the interpretations in, as well as of, his sources exist outside his textualization of their context.

Thus the search for a new historicized cultural studies still leads all too often to the old dilemmas even as the field tries to cope with the implications of the new trends in the human sciences. Even from a supposedly new contextualist position, historians' own texts continue to describe the relation of power to changing past times and to their own present-day professional conflicts according to old unproblematized contextualist premises. The conflictual model of society and politics that grounds the supposed mediation of the various versions of context in the new contextualism basic to so much of the new cultural studies in history frequently rests upon a very traditional form of historical textualization while propounding a radical message politically. From the textualist position the forms of these supposedly new textualizations seem as familiar as the forms of those produced by the old historical practice. Must all who would mediate between the polar positions in historicization therefore remystify as they demystify, reconstruct as they deconstruct, reify as they rematerialize, politicize as they poeticize according to traditional historical methodology? Or can—will—the new cultural studies create new varieties of historicization to match its efforts to resolve the seeming contradictions of the poetics of context?

CHAPTER NINE

Reflexive
(Con)Textualization

JUST as voice and viewpoint in histories ought to be multiple, so the practice of history as discourse ought to be reflexive. Any version of historical discourse should apply to itself at least as well as it does to those sources resulting in historical textualizations in the first place. Any theoretization of historical practice ought to explain itself as well as it does its oppositional discourses. Under a reflexive approach to the problems of historicization, the New Historicist motto "a reciprocal concern with the historicity of texts and the textuality of history"[1] or the anthropological advice about the historicization of culture and the culturalization of history take on a double meaning and, more important, a double application.[2] But the more reflexive historical textualization becomes, the more interesting and challenging it is to practice, whether as reading and reviewing or as writing and teaching. What reflexive (con)textualization entails as a discursive practice is easy enough to conceive. How to embody it in a new kind of textualization is far more difficult to envision. My use of parentheses around the first syllable is intended to indicate the double goal embraced by a reflexive representation of history.

A Basic Guide

A useful starting point in considering how reflexivity might apply to historical discourse is a list devised by James Clifford on the ways in which ethnographic writing is "determined."[3] Each element in the list at once complements and uses the others; all are implicated with one another. Each also has implications for both writing and teaching, reading and reviewing history.[4]

Context. Since context refers to both the context within constructed histories as they represent the past as history and the context of historians within their own time as they write these histories, should not historians in their works and teachers in their classrooms construct their textualizations so as to show their audience how these dual contexts constrain, maybe determine, or at least co-create each other through and in what is textualized? Even though in each case the context is author constructed in terms of both method and discourse, such textual decisions ought to be made manifest by how the various constitutions of context(ualization) relate to one another in a text. Reflexive contextualization requires multiple and explicit contexts in a history to represent the interaction between present-day intertextual ways of (con)textualizing and presenting the past contextualized as a history text. To what extent can this multiple contextualization be resolved through the inclusion of multiple viewpoints? Since contextualization denotes different methodologies depending upon choices about rhetorical and social construction of reality, poetics and politics, and the other reflexive dilemmas confronting, and confounding, the human sciences, should not historians and teachers discuss their choices explicitly as they constitute them in their textualizations? Any new forms of contextualization and narrativization demand that the Great Story and the subtext become a more explicit part of the actual textualization in practice.

Since a historical textualization both "draws from and creates meaningful social milieux," then the reader and reviewer must examine not only how the context is constructed within a history as explicit or subtextual past story or Great Story but also the degree to which and how the context of the historian's own time of writing is inscribed in the discursive practice(s) of the text. If context is constructed and (con)textualization is methodologically arbitrary, then how does an author or teacher go about it in each instance? Just as past histories serve as contextual sources for today's histories, present histories serve as intertextual sources as well as contextual dialogue for each other. What assumptions about the intra-, inter-, and extratextual as context does any given history make? Does the text image its own context(ualization) from a reflexive dual perspective?

Rhetoric. Rhetorical reflexivity would seem to demand more than the self-conscious self-revelation of choices of, and among, stylistic and persuasive possibilities in a text, important as that may be. The reflexive application of poetics and rhetoric to textualization requires their self-criticism at the same time as they shape the text(ualization). Historical textualization therefore requires the deconstruction of its story and argument by and through its (re)construction. New historicizations need to decompose their structures of expression for their readers at the same time as they compose a history as content. A reflexive textualization should incorporate its countertext as part of the created text.

If a textualization both "uses and is used by expressive conventions," then readers and reviewers must look to how the structures of expression shape as well as express the structures of argument and narrative in a text. Investigation of explicit expression employs such rhetorical categories as style, figuration, and order of the presentation, or what I have called the psychologic of presentation (in contradistinction to its logic). To read and review the role of narrative is to examine content and expression as narratology, rhetoric, and poetics. In the surface content of the narrative, the appropriate categories include analysis of plot, use and depiction of time, story line, event, actor, voice, viewpoint, and reader reception. Such analysis can combine formalist, more processual, and reader-oriented approaches. To examine the expression of the narrative in histories is to review how the story is presented or history is represented, not only through motifs, metaphors, choice of language and tenses, and other explicit aspects but also through more implicit prefigurative structures.

Since the deeper structure of the nonnarrative and narrative sides of history come together, because plots, stories, and metastories ground them either textually or subtextually, certain questions can be asked of both kinds of history. From whose viewpoint does the author tell the story or make the argument? How does the author emplot (or organize) the underlying narrative (conceived broadly)? What story or logic does the author employ to move the argument or narrative forward? Of what larger Great Story does the text or interpretation presume its story to be a part? Do the beginning and end points build in certain biases in the making of the argument?

At bottom, how does the author view the nature of history as a way or means of representing the past? The reader and reviewer cannot accept at face value what historians themselves announce is their degree of intervention between their own textual constructions and the pasts they postulate and construct. Both the extent and the theory of that intervention ought to be examined. Authors' full disclosure statements need to be compared with what their texts conceal as they construct arguments and stories. What foundational dilemmas show as tensions in a text? Is the subtext consistent with the text? Are Great Stories assumed but not avowed or explicated, let alone "proved"?

Genre. Since historians present their textualizations in such a way as to distinguish them from those of other genres, how does a text embody the conventions of the history genre? Genre conventions apply in two ways: first, among kinds of histories in the profession itself (such as economic, religious, and political or local, national, or other); and, second, between history and other kinds of textualizations in other disciplines or in the larger world. In the first case, does genre affect how discourses are represented as history? In the second instance, ought historical discourses to maintain strict separation between professional histories and other kinds of historicizations, including historical fiction and films as well as lay and oral histories? Or have teachers, students, and readers moved beyond such distinctions as artificial? Ought therefore every history to reveal how it constituted itself as a genre or specific subgenre? Does reflexive (con)textualization, like the incorporation of multiple voices and viewpoints, demand a new approach to historicization best served by a new narrative model? To what extent should narrativization of history draw inspiration from postmodern and metafictional novels and other genres and media?[5]

Readers and reviewers must inquire how a history constitutes itself as a genre. To what extent does a historical textualization draw on other genres as sources, and how are these other genres used? How is that history distinguished from those other genres? Does the history hierarchize these other genres in its own construction to enhance its own authority? How does any given history differentiate itself, say, from a historical novel or a diary or from the philosophy of history or historical sociology? Does the fact that major scholarly journals in history now review films, oral histories, and museum exhibitions in addition to books as historical representations mean that traditional distinctions among textualizations have been eroded or abandoned entirely? More important, in examining historical representations how far do these reviews depart from the traditional emphasis on referentiality?[6]

Institutions. If one writes, teaches, reads, and reviews "within, and against, specific traditions, disciplines, audiences," then what obligation does a text(ualization) have to reveal explicitly, in addition to incorporating implicitly, these social arrangements and cultural conventions in the text(ualization) itself? To what degree ought historians and teachers to make explicit the metahistorical foundations of their disciplinary practices and premises? Should writers and teachers confess their professional allegiances and their interpretive communities as part of their textualization? If historians seek to create a critical, that is, active, audience, what devices must be invented for writer and reader/reviewer, teacher and student to collaborate through the text itself? Can such cooperation provide the basis for new kinds of historical textualizations?[7]

Since "one writes within, and against, specific traditions, disciplines, audiences," then readers and reviewers should examine not only the interpretation of the text but also the interpretive community that makes "sense" of that way of interpreting matters. How do that interpretation and interpretive community relate to other interpretive communities in academia and in society? How, in short, is a history as a text determined by, and by what and whose, institutionally organized discursive practices? To what extent and how does a text reveal its author's multiple social locations? What textual forms and professional interpretations are resisted by argument, by example, or by silence?

Politics. If "the authority to represent cultural [and historical] realities is unequally shared and at times contested" within a profession, within a nation, and within the larger world, then how does a historical textualization handle these problems reflexively? Ought not the inequalities that ground that authority to become an explicit part of any historical representation? If politics pervades all aspects of historical textualization, then should not the full disclosure statement include the politics of historicization itself in addition to any customary confession of political choices according to the conventions of "real world" politics? Writers and teachers (and reviewers) should reveal their multiple social locations in addition to their political affiliation as pertinent to an understanding of their textualizations. Such statements include the roles of gender, generation, religion, ethnicity, and profession in the making of a text. Is such full disclosure possible, and what form ought it to take? At a minimum, the customarily perfunctory full disclosure statements in the prefaces of normal histories ought to be transformed into a major integral, dialectical, and explicit framework of the entire textualized enterprise of any new reflexive historicization. Should not the politics of historicization be the subject as much as the politics of the real world are the object of historical text(ualization)s?

With the distinctions drawn earlier between critical history and historical criticism, between the political uses of the medium and the politics of the message in the medium, we can begin to see what the job of the critical reader and reviewer entails. From this standpoint, the chief goal is to demystify normal historical authority as it is embodied in customary methods of textualization. To that end, critical reading and reviewing must explore a text's foundational premises and politics of disciplinary discursive practice in addition to its explicit or subtextual stories and arguments. Thus historians must consider the premises and politics of interpretation as an intellectual process as well as what politics and premises show up in those interpretations, the premises and politics behind certain methods as well as what politics and premises are explicit in the results of those methods, the premises and politics of historical methodology in general as well as what premises and politics are fostered by that methodology. They must explore how the premises and politics of a Great Story ground a history as well as what is told in the Great Story, and whether the premises and politics of the ideal of a Great Past pervade a text. To accomplish these aims, historians must be alert to the philosophy and politics grounding professional authority as well as skirmishes over philosophy and politics in the profession. To be aware of the politics of approaches that historians share with other modern human science disciplines requires interest in the political and philosophical debates in and among the disciplines.

History. Both multiculturalism and reflexivity remind us that the notion of history itself, particularly as professional history, is culturally provincial. To what extent should the debates I discuss in this book, and even this book itself, be labeled disciplinary, North American, anglophone, or Eurocentric? To enclose the word history in quotation marks to indicate its parochial provenience does not resolve the many problems of constructing a historical representation. Any historical textualization ought to situate itself historically as well as it does other histories or the past as history.

If "all of the above conventions and constraints are changing" and all historical practices and texts are specific to particular places and times, then must any reflexive historicization lead to an overt discussion of how a topic is contextualized, rhetoricized, and politicized as it is historicized in light of its own time in history? Does reflexivization of historical discourses lead to radical historicization as self-confessed, self-revealing text(ualization)s?

Because historical practices and texts are specific to particular places and times, reviews should situate a text in the context(s) of the many social sites that generated it. The reading and reviewing of histories must be as reflexive to their own times as they are alert to the reflexive problems of historicizing the past in general.

To Clifford's list let me add:

Ethics. Whereas politics emphasizes as it embraces the "is" of power and social relations, ethics stresses as it envisages the "ought" of those relationships. Systems of ethics deal with criteria for good and bad conduct of individuals and their institutions. Such individual and institutional ethical levels may be translated into the effects of micro and macro systems of power according to postmodernist theory, but the ethical question remains: what ought to be the role of power in the lives of people? As a result of concerns about macropower, ethics also embraces theories of what the state ought to be. In answering how one ought to live and what are the desirable modes of conduct for individuals and relations among individuals, should the historian promote oppositional efforts to hegemonic power and discourse and valorize multiplicity and otherness? To what degree are these ethical problems as well as political premises?

Historians particularly confront the dilemma of contextual versus absolute ethics. Should their texts espouse a transcultural, transhistorical ethics regardless of what their historical actors believed or practiced, or should they relativize ethical choices in texts to the times they represent? Whose system of ethics, then or now, should judge the horrors of slavery or the Holocaust? Ought not a commitment to freedom, equality, and diversity supersede any concern about present-mindedness in a history? Can historians espouse the social and cultural relativization of all knowledge through social location(s) and all institutions through social construction(s) and at the same time disavow ethical relativism?[8]

If multiculturalist ideals are to be realized, then ethics must embrace a set of questions about how justice and equity will be achieved in a new pluralistic or multiculturalist society. For communities to be based upon the acceptance as well as the recognition of diversity, how and what kinds of differences should be sanctioned? If, as Joan W. Scott argues, conflict need not be resolved and consensus need not be achieved in an ideal multicultural society, then what rules must be accepted by the members of a community to achieve that society?[9] Should there be no limits to efforts to achieve subgroup unity and representation in the name of the ideals of decentralization and self-determination? To what degree must a multicultural society depend upon a consensual etiquette of proper behavior to achieve its goals? As Jane Flax raises the issue of justice and power in terms of postmodernist theorizing, how can intergroup and intrasocietal let alone cross-societal conversations escape totalizing discourses? In discussing this problem, she raises questions about how to resolve conflicts among competing voices, how to give everyone a chance to speak, how to ensure that every voice counts equally, how to guarantee preference for speaking over force, and how to compensate for the unequal distribution and control of power.[10] How, in other words, can a middle ground be found between the center(s) and the margin(s) in a society? To what extent must historians erect their histories on such a middle ground between past practices and future hopes, if they are committed to multicultural ideals?

Reviewers and readers use their own ethics to evaluate those of others. What are the ethics of the text, and from whose perspective and interests do they proceed? Are ethical positions espoused from the center or the margins of a society? Do the ethics follow from the politics of the topic or from the social location of the author? Are the judgments explicit in the discourse or implicit in its textualization? Are the ethics absolute to all times or relative to those of past actors? Does the text criticize past actors and actions for their unethical practices or use past ideals to impugn present practices? Are there any connections among conceptual, cultural, and moral relativisms in the text? Is the text self-reflexive, hence self-revelatory of its ethical choices? Are the reader and reviewer aware and self-revelatory of their own ethical choices in exploring those of the text? Must readings and reviews of histories therefore be constructed upon the same middle ground of past politics and future hopes as those histories that would be multicultural?

Theories, Models, Images

Parallel to and implicated in the preceding list of ways in which reflexivity applies in and to a historical textualization is another one of what and how theory applies to and is applied in historical discourses. Theory, discursive practice, and historical representation are all intertwined, of course, and so their relationship(s) ought to be shown in a text.

The word "theory," however, conceals many kinds of theories in historical and other disciplinary practices. Theory therefore is not only divided by theory against theory but also by disciplinary genre. What literary critics call theory does not figure prominently in much of social science theory or vice versa, even when they at times carry the same general names. Literary theories are categorized under such rubrics as Russian formalism, reader reception or audience orientation, feminism, deconstruction, Freudianism, New Historicism, and genre theory.[11] Social theory, if we take those in sociology as an example, has such designations as conflict, exchange, functionalist, neofunctionalist, structurationist, evolutionary, symbolic interactionist, behavioral, human ecology, and ethnomethodology.[12] Even when various disciplinary schools of theory carry the same general designation and seem inspired by the same general outlook and assumptions, they differ greatly in content and application. Although critical theory, Marxist, post- and neo-Marxist, phenomenological, structuralist and poststructuralist, and even postmodernist schools exist in both literary and social theory, the resemblance between what is argued and how it is applied often extends little beyond the name. Likewise, what we might call philosophical theories embrace still another disciplinary genre and show quite other concerns, content, and application. Because of this variety, theories ought always to be reflexive in how and why they originated and are applied.[13]

Late or high modernists and postmodernists dispute the very role and nature of theory. Thus debate over the nature of theory generates its own theories. What is the status of the language in which a theory is expressed vis-à-vis the rest of language? Is it a superior metalanguage or on the same level as any other kind of language usage? Modernists enshrine scientific methods and explanatory models as the best way to produce knowledge. Postmodernists, in contrast, prefer story-telling and demystification as major ways of approaching knowledge; they deny that either Science or Literature is a privileged linguistic realm. High modernists idealize context-free theory and knowledge; postmodernists believe that all theory, like all knowledge, applies to, just as it is generated from, specific social and temporal locations. As a result of these differences, whether theory can exist is as much debated as what constitutes a theory. Must theory always be totalizing, univocal, and reductive, or can it embrace multiplicity, polyvocality, and contingency and still qualify as theory? Does theory have a referential basis in the end, or is it just another form of ideology?[14]

Since literary theorists more often presume basic social arrangements than discuss them explicitly or explain how they know what they are, let me supplement the preceding list of aspects of reflexive historicization with one inspired by and derived mainly from social theory and social explanation.[15] Although modernist and postmodernist approaches provide contradictory perspectives and the field of social theory is as contested as the nature of (a) society is said to be, nevertheless every historical textualization must embody the following kinds of theories, either as explicit models or as images and metaphors, of how past and present worlds work. Like the elements discussed in the preceding series, these too are interdependent in conception and implication.

Theories of social groupings and society. Whether theories of sociality are considered models, metaphors, or otherwise, they are important to historical representation as grounding for both the explicit description of historical context and the implicit grounding of the author's, hence the text's, whole approach to the way social arrangements work in the past and the present. For historical discourse these models serve at least three functions: they are represented as constructed supposedly from and according to the nature of the historical society under examination, they are often said to explain what happened and why in past societies, and they are basic to the implicit grounding of the author's whole approach to explanation in history and model the relationship between past and present politics and society.

Is anything not socially generated in today's theories, be they literary or social scientific? Some notion of the social matrix is employed in both modernist and postmodernist theorizing. But what is the social according to each? Is society a product, or is sociality a process? Is a society composed of social nexuses or networks, or is it cultural and discursive practices, or what? Are some parts of a society more determining than others of what happens in it? Can a society be viewed as whole or a totality? How does a society reproduce itself, and how was that arrangement produced in the first place? Should the history of a society be represented as stages, or can it only be compiled as a sum of what happened? Does the notion of a society have its own history just like the society itself? What relation exists between the social construction of what is social and cultural in the past and in the present of the historian in characterizing that society?[16]

Contextualization according to some theory or model of social matrix always presents the problem of aggregating individual actions, experiences, and the like into some grouping or subject position. Just who and what determines the membership of groupings or subject positions assumed along the social fissures of sex, class, generation, race, politics, and so on? How can the historian know of a grouping if it is truly repressed? Should counter-hegemonic statements be accepted at face value and as representative of a grouping or subject position? What relationship exists between past and present experience(s) and discourse(s)? How should historians organize their representations of the organization of society? These are more than problems of historical nominalism and methodological individualism or collectivism, relevant as they are to any social theorizing. Rather the problems arise from commitment to multiculturalism and multiple viewpoints.

Where modernism and postmodernism diverge most dramatically is in the application of viewpoint: from whose viewpoint is the social matrix, past as well as present, to be constructed in a textualization? Modernism generally seeks some (single) overview of the social field, whether it is conceived as contested terrain or otherwise. For postmodernism, such overviews ultimately proceed from someone's partial perspective. Multiculturalists prefer either the views from the margin or the juxtaposition of multiple views. Views from the margins, like those from the center, still are constructed as single, univocal models, no matter what their ostensible goal. How well any textualization of the social matrix can achieve multiplicity of voices and viewpoints in its representation of others as it represents the interplay of those voices and viewpoints remains to be seen. From whose viewpoint can a society be seen as a field of conflicting, usually unequal, forces, interests, ideologies, always volatile and contingent? Even if the notion of a social matrix is historicized, the problem remains. Is not the very notion of society as contested terrain ultimately only a construction of, and according to, a monological viewpoint? Such a monological viewpoint produces, as it lies at the heart of, totalization, a vision of a society as a total whole, even if represented as interrelated parts.

In exploring and critiquing a historical text for its models of society as groupings and institutional nexuses, the reader and reviewer might ask some of the following questions: What does the author presume about the nature of social, economic, political, religious, educational, familial, or other arrangements in the society being examined? How are social groupings and the subject positions and the relationships among them determined? Are social and economic or political and cultural arrangements considered more basic and determining in what happens historically? Does the historian presume a society completely homogeneous or heterogeneous, composed of interconnected or unrelated parts? Does the society have few or many sites of contestation? If multiple sites of contestation, does the text presume consensus or conflict within the subgroups? Does the society have classes as well as groups or subject positions? How does the author see the particular society, culture, or time as coming into being, and how does that society, culture, or time reproduce itself according to the author's arguments? Are the answers to these questions provided by representations of social and cultural arrangements as persons, practices, processes, or structures through time? Is social construction of the context in a text historically dynamic and yet reflexive at the same time?

Readers and reviewers should explore to what extent a theory or model of society is used as explanation for what happened in the text. How complex and explicit is the model? Does an author (or teacher) present supporting evidence or only theory in her or his exposition of these explanatory social arrangements? To ask what is presumed about the state, the economy, or the social organization in a text exposes political and moral uses as well as models, for they are often inextricably connected in an argument or a story.[17]

Theories of self/body/person. Not long ago these theories would have been designated theories of human nature and behavior. That the notion of human nature today is attributed to the Enlightenment project does not end a basic theoretical concern for how human beings operate as individual persons. Even those who repudiate any universalist or essentialist character to all humans alike, especially according to male-centered models, must still base their arguments on some theory of persons as individuals. These kinds of theories inquire into the psychology rather than the sociology of humans, the role of desire and will and agency in human behavior and affairs. To proclaim the death of the subject as author or originator of actions and thoughts denies bourgeois conceptions of the individual as the basic unit of political and ethical analysis. But does such a proclamation take adequate account of persons as self-constituted subjects, as agents critical of their own societies, or as actors seeking social change? Is there a prelinguistic or presocietal self that shapes human destinies and preserves some vestige of autonomy for persons as selves? Do the body and the heart have their own cunning, or is that an essentialist view? If individuals cannot make themselves, can they remake their society?[18]

Today it seems artificial to separate human beings as individuals from collections of them as groups, societies, and cultures. That individuals are considered projections of their society and its culture(s) problematizes such standard categories in historical discourse as experience, intention, motivation, and even memory and desire. This is true of individuals in and as subcultures or subgroups no matter how categorized along the social fissures of gender, race, class, and the like. Do scholars from both within or outside a given subgroup attribute experiences and motivations too common to the grouping as a social collectivity, making too little allowance for persons as individuals? If so, must some multiculturalist textualizations of groupings be revised? Is this a problem of vestigial humanism, as some argue, or is it a fundamental problem of methodological and theoretical choice, as others maintain?

Do multiple and conflicting locations of persons mitigate or problematize enough or too much the oversocialized model of human beings?[19] The problem becomes one of specifying the tightness of fit between individual persons multiply located in a society or culture, in a subgroup or subculture and what remains analytically after the socialization or enculturation—the social and cultural construction—of persons in the use of their bodies and any self-creation as individuals. Thus the (over)socialized image of humans not only questions the sources of individual persons' motivations but the efficacy of the resulting behavior and the ability to make themselves. Creative or outstanding individuals are reduced to the context that explains them. By reducing the Great Man or Hero in History to social explanation, the (over)socialized model challenges all who would seek the uniqueness of ideas, artifacts, and actions. The limitations of the oversocialized model concern not only those who investigate the creators of texts and other cultural artifacts as authors, artists, and scholars but even those who write political and other kinds of biographies. In the end, the issues seem not to be whether human beings are plastic or autonomous, socialized or self-created, diverse or common, but how much of each under what circumstances and according to whose theory. Arguing about such theories requires employing the very same theories as the basis of the argument or narrative.[20]

For those scholars who impugn the humanist model of the autonomous individual as a bourgeois social invention, what is their conception of the moral agency of their readers and students? To what extent can the persons they appeal to in their demystification and deconstruction of traditional theory read and, more important, act on their messages if they do not possess some individuality? Do not those antihumanist scholars who write of the social and discursive construction of individual motivation, intention, and experience direct their moral lessons to the very kind of individuals they deny can exist in their theory and politics? Are they not appealing to reason, feeling, imagination, or morals of individuals apart from those common to their groupings? Must not scholars seeking social transformation postulate an individual or group of individuals who can reason, make moral decisions, and act somewhat independently of their society in order for emancipatory politics to work?[21]

For readers and reviewers theories of self/body/person still sometimes show up in histories as attributions of human nature and behavior as opposed to social explanation. To what extent does a text assume that all human beings are alike over time in their interests, outlooks, and capacities or that they vary by gender, class, times, and cultures? Does the author, in other words, presume a human nature that is universal or one that is a cultural and temporal creation? Are certain desires, drives, and interests considered common to all or even to a group of human beings, or do these vary by individual, by culture, by time? Does, for example, a text assume that (most, all) human beings prefer to maximize happiness, minimize pain? Are subgroupings essentialized by gender, race, class, generation, or otherness? To what extent are humans constrained by their culture or society or times, and to what extent are they or at least some of them free to create what they will and desire? Does society, in the author's opinion, create human beings and their actions, or vice versa? What theories, models, or images ground the creation of individual selves or the control of their bodies in a text?

Theories of power/domination and the state. Theories of power, domination, and the state, as applied both to social theory in general and to politics and ethics in particular, emphasize political science and political theory, broadly conceived, as opposed to social and psychological theory. These themes focus on what is the political. Is it only the public realm, or is the personal also political, as early feminist theorists argued? Given the patriarchally imposed divisions between the male and female spheres, power and politics, like production and reason, were allocated solely to the male realm, and (male) historians sanctioned these dichotomies in their texts. That is why Foucault's notion of micro levels of power as opposed to the macrostructure of the state was so liberating to so many previously untheorized social groupings excluded under the old hegemonic dichotomies in human science theorization and historical textualization.

On the macro level, what is the polity or state? The relationship between micro and macro levels remains controversial, as Foucault's critics so often point out. To posit a connection among policy, police, knowledge, discipline, and disciplines in a society also presumes awareness and knowledge of the several levels of connections. All too many discussions of domination and hegemony fail to specify precisely how what they examine fits into any larger system, just as those who so often explicate macrostructures omit the micro levels that would lend their exposition complexity and credence. Disciplinary and other kinds of politics pervade political models of the state and the choice of macro versus micro systems of power. The most obvious models concern the various ways of picturing the state. For example, should capitalist states be depicted according to pluralist, managerial, or power elite models in the distribution of power among citizens/subjects?[22]

How to view the political remains in contention between modernist and postmodernist theorists. From what and whose perspective is politics or a political matrix to be represented? As with the notion of a social matrix in general, whether the view should come from center, margins, or outside divides the two camps. Postmodernists deny the possibility of any outside, Archimedean view of the system as a whole, while the modernists accuse the postmodernists of assuming what they ought to prove about the linkages they assert. To historicize the political does not specify the viewpoint from which to construct the (hi)story of a political matrix. Historical contextualization of politics and political systems ought to be reflexive in that not only does the present result from the past but also the theoreticizations of the past and present create each other as and through the political matrix and its levels.

Once again readers and reviewers must ascertain what an author or teacher argues explicitly or implicitly about the structures of power and the means of social control, domination, and cultural hegemony. What choices were made among models of micro and macro structures of power, and how do they affect or shape the argument and story? Does the author presume that consensual agreement or conflict is natural within social groups, among them, or in the overall workings of a society? Is the author a pluralist, viewing power as widely distributed throughout the society, or a power elitist, who sees a small, integrated group as dominating the society? Do theories or ethics ground an author's choice of pluralism or diversity in textualizing politics? What in a text's representation of these matters is univocal and political in discussing the political?

Theories of explanation/causation/motivation. Why something happened when it did and where it did is frequently explained by the what and how of social arrangements and the who of subgroups and individuals. In other words, explanation occurs through social causation or individual motivation. In the end, what kinds of explanation ought to be used in historical textualizations are also a matter of what constitutes proper forms and kinds of explanation. Although social and individual explanations depend upon the social sciences and psychology, what constitutes proper explanation is claimed as the province of philosophy. Is the only proper kind of explanation derived from universal generalizations issuing forth in lawlike statements, as was once argued, or do interpretation and narration also explain, as the opponents of the scientific model argue? High modernist theorists debated these issues, and older philosophy of history books framed their arguments accordingly.[23] In line with the criteria for scientific explanation, quantitative and social science historians foregrounded their explicit models and methodologies in their texts.[24] With the increasing return to narrative in history writing, explicit explanatory models of all kinds are all too often suppressed as they were earlier, woven into the story as foundational or as background without explicit discussion.

Some argue that the concept of causation is being lost in modern scholarship. The more societies are represented as multiple sites of contestation and the more knowledges are situated, the more difficult it is to aggregate historical agency and to explain connectedness. The more pluralized a society and the more fragmentary its groupings, the more difficult it is to characterize and explain connections. The more historically and spatially specific the description, the less general the explanation and the harder to provide a broader context. Indeterminacy results from conceiving diversity as pluralism because equal structural weights are given to multiple factors. To affirm or deny such explanatory equality is a political as well as a methodological decision. Determinacy, on the other hand, frequently presumes what it often fails to examine let alone prove.

Nevertheless connections, even if conceived only as chance and contingency, are as necessary in constituting emplotment by narrative as they are in providing explanation by argument. To value diversity without privileging a viewpoint among those in competition is to fall into narrative as well as explanatory and political relativism. Hence both multiple time series and micro/macro structures/processes pose narrative as well as conceptual and political problems, because they erode traditional approaches to causation. Both assert connections within a series but not across series. Accordingly, as I discuss below under new approaches to time, they challenge traditional narrative and explanation in historical discourses.

When readers and reviewers turn to matters of social and individual explanation in historical textualization, they investigate a series of basic questions.

One set concerns to what extent changes stemmed from willed human agency, that is, from goal-oriented human action individually or collectively. Such explanations center upon reason and rational actions, intention, motivation, or other explanations connected to persons acting as individuals and in groups. A second set looks to change coming from unanticipated consequences of deliberate actions or from larger forces or structures working upon or through human beings. Whether structures work through or upon humans collectively divides theorists even when they try to reconcile the two extremes. This second set uses explanations generated by the preceding models of society, culture, and politics. A third set centers upon images or models of human nature and causation. Does the author presume that human beings change their ways and outlooks easily or that they are fundamentally hostile to change? Can humans change their circumstances easily or only with difficulty? Philosophy of history books treat the theories of historical explanation in general, but those books discussing various models of explanation, causation, and motivation in the social sciences might prove the more useful guides if read with this larger purpose in mind. Does a text present some sort of big picture of what caused what, or does the author eschew such grand causation and explanation in favor of "description"? Whichever the option, how does the author know what is claimed or asserted?[25]

Theories of epistemology and ontology. Whether modernism stressed how we can know and postmodernism examines what we can know as one scholar claims,[26] both epistemology and ontology continue to pose problems for historical discourse in general and in particular. Are the kinds and conditions of knowing any more difficult in historical methodology than in other fields of knowledge because of the peculiar combination of an absent past and the intent to (re)construct it? To what degree can historical method obviate the well-known problems of adducing historical knowledge? In general, what theories of knowledge do historians share with other scholars as their approach to social reality? In this latter question epistemology and ontology concern not so much matters of evidence and proof or even of "facts" as what is accepted as given or needing no proof in a discourse and why. From this standpoint, then, it is epistemological and ontological concerns that ground the debates in the profession over rhetorical and social construction of reality and over the politics of poetics and vice versa. In both debates, postmodernists and modernists agree that it is difficult to practice history, but they invoke different reasons for the difficulty.[27]

In the end, any textualization, any discourse, any scholar must make some commitment about what is real, what is fictional, and what is hypothetical in a represented world. Such a commitment is never more obvious than in what is allowed and considered acceptable or proper as explanation—especially as seen in choices between secular or sacred causes, idealist or materialist models. Even those who deconstruct or deny traditional Western epistemologies and ontologies ground their cases upon some theory of how and what they can know or assert as the basis of their textualization.

Why privilege one's own explanation as the correct or best one over others in the competition of belief systems? What are the politics of a theory of knowledge from the perspective of social explanation? Social "facts" are not "out there" in the same sense as tables and chairs, even if one subscribes to a material basis for language. Rather, they are socially and culturally constructed, and it is this circumstance that produces the epistemological and ontological problems of historical discourse. Does social and cultural knowing in human societies manifest itself in performance, and is it therefore best studied as praxis? What implications does such a theory of practice have for historical texualization(s)? Even if the dialectical interplay between social subject and social object co-creates the knowledge, not all subjects are equal in the construction of societal knowledge, as the notion of hegemony implies. Controlling the construal of knowledge as "reality" or at least "common sense" grounds the conflict between hegemonic and counterhegemonic discourses. The idea of ideology once postulated a clear distinction between truth and those beliefs fostering the interests of the elite. That distinction presumed a more definite knowledge of a real world apart from social and cultural construction(s) of it than social explanation can now claim. Should scholars nevertheless privilege oppositional discourses and marginal groupings' knowledges as better epistemic guides to social reality? Such a viewpoint on the epistemology of social knowledge transforms social ontology into politics and discursive theory into ethics.

Once again, the basic divisions between modernist and postmodernist focus on viewpoint. Feminist theorists complained that traditional (male dominated) epistemology postulated a single godlike viewpoint as the consciousness proper to all knowers as perceivers and conceivers. They countered that a situated epistemology acknowledged multiple not single sites of knowledge, local not universal applications, fragmented not unified viewpoints, specific not general criteria of what constitutes knowledge. Postmodernist theorists deny the superiority of abstraction over concrete experience and of universality over historically and socially situated knowledges. In other words, the postmodernist view postulates diverse epistemic communities as various interpretive communities. These epistemic communities set the conflicting paradigmatic criteria of how to know and what to know.

Are standard approaches to epistemology peculiar to Western philosophy and history, part of the logocentrism that Derrida historicized and relativized by deconstructing its premises? If so, then does reflexive historicization investigate how past and present epistemologies and ontologies created each other as Western thinkers invented them? As part of the process, according to many feminist epistemologists, they divided fact from theory and value in the name of objectivity, defined abstraction as superior to the concrete, and valued the rational over the emotional—all in the name of advancing male-defined knowledge through male-dominated philosophy. Who writes this history, like who decides these questions, is a matter of hegemony. Must it only be a matter of politics, or can it also be a matter of ethics? Should the Great Story of this history of philosophy be told as philosophy or as history, as epistemology or as the history of ideas and concepts?[28]

If what one knows results from how one knows, then do multiple epistemic communities result in multiple realities? One of the dilemmas of multicultural textualizations stems from the relation of the ontological claims of others to those of the textualizer. In what one might call the Golden Rule of cross-cultural ontology, R. S. Khare argues that one must privilege others' truths as one would have others privilege one's own.[29] Such a rule demands respect for the authenticity, the validity, and the authority of others' knowledges, truths, and worldviews. Does such a principle also demand new forms of textualization as it denies the usual efforts to relativize others' beliefs to one's own in the textualization through overall viewpoint? Applied to history, does such a rule presume plural pasts?

Readers and reviewers of histories in the end juxtapose their theories of epistemology and ontology with those of the texts they explore. To what extent are past actors' truths accepted as true by the historian and by the reader and reviewer in turn? Are there universal ways of perceiving and knowing or only local and temporally specific ways of knowing? Whose way or what epistemic community is accepted as the basis for such judgments? Do all intellectual categories have their own histories and therefore pose reflexive problems in their use by historians? What does the text accept as given and needing no proof or argument in relation to reality, and how is historical reality divided from fictional history, ideology, and propaganda according to the author? What does the text assert explicitly in these matters, and what is implicit and silent but necessary to its representation of matters in the past? Is knowledge socially or rhetorically constructed and construed by the text, by the reader and reviewer? Must readers and reviewers accept multiple realities and conflicting perspectives as foundational to historicization if they would be multicultural? In the end, readers and reviewers must ask themselves the same question they put to the authors they read: how do they know what they assert and assume in their texts?

Theories of language. Historians use or presume a theory of language in all phases of their practice: in deriving facts from evidence, in combining facts into a synthesis, and in reading history as a Great Story. To what extent should the language of documents be read as directly representative, symbolically analogous, arbitrarily self-contained, or otherwise in constructing the context of the documents? What theory or theories of language prevailed in past worlds, and how does knowledge of those theories both aid and problematize the reading of evidence? What semiotic stand should historians take in their textualizations of histories and of history itself as a Great Story? How reflexive should such theories of language be in the presentation of the past as history? History as text signifies itself through its own constitution, as it is constructed as and through a discourse.

If the working fiction of (a) history is that it is true and factual, then the working fiction of (a) language is that all its categories are universal and timeless in application. If history is a construction about a past reality through language, then language is a construction about a present reality according to current usage in some group. Such paradoxes exacerbate the problems of reflexive historical discourse and textualization. If language cannot be a neutral medium, can historical reflexivity get beyond word games? Is the ultimate limit of reflexivity language itself? What are the reflexive implications of such a view for historical textualizations?

Should the nature of language be considered the proper or best model for theorizing the social world, a world that the proponents of such an approach say language cannot represent well or at all? Should linguistic models image systems of human knowledge and behavior as language loses its ability to refer?[30] Throughout most of the twentieth century, epistemological and ontological questions have been transmuted into problems about language and meaning. For example, F. R. Ankersmit in establishing the nature of the historical representation denies that any of the normal theories of truth—correspondence, coherence, pragmatic, or performative—apply in determining the "truth" of a historical narrative. These theories rest on what philosophers assume about the ability of language to convey knowledge and represent reality.[31] Thus modernists and postmodernists alike debate whether the nature of facts, structures of interpretations, and Great Stories in historical discourse should or can be modeled on systems of language as they differ over the relations among signifiers, signified, and referents.

The paradox of language talking about language comes down to the ability of a language to represent the world. Hayden White summarizes four general possibilities of relating words, worldviews, and the world: "(1) a *manifestation* of causal relationships governing the world of things in which it arises, in the mode of an index; (2) a *representation* of that world, in the mode of an icon (or mimesis); (3) a *symbol* of that world, in the mode of an analogue, natural or culture-specific, as the case might be; (4) simply another among those things that populate the human world, but more specifically a *sign system*, that is, a code bearing no necessary, or 'motivated' relation to that which it signifies."[32] Might not these different theories of language and referent apply differently to the realms of the physical, social, and conceptual worlds—or at least in different ratios when referring to physical objects, social conventions, and symbols?

Whether the scholar combines these theories to the extent possible or repudiates them for another approach, a theory of language is still relevant to how a text itself is put together in terms of what it purports to represent. Even an attempt to have language and social reality create each other through their mutual othernesses does not resolve the problems proceeding from language talking about language talking about reality in a text, historical or otherwise. If language is not simply a matter of referents, as some theorists maintain, then neither is it merely a matter of internal relations, as their arguments prove by their implied use of the medium if not by their explicit message.

Must a reflexive history become a history of semantics as it tries to represent a past world with words from both the present and the past? For example, the very words we employ for our categories of conceiving and describing our subject matter carry their own burden of conceptual baggage and political implications as a result of present interests combined with their historical development.[33] Are the same words, let alone different words, as employed in different or oppositional political paradigms translatable into the same larger context as (meta)story, or must even the same words mean different things according to which (meta)story they are embedded in as they represent it? Must therefore crucial (critical?) words and all representations demand as many (meta)stories as there are paradigms for understanding them?[34]

It is easier for readers and reviewers to examine what theories of language are used and how in a text than to use language to textualize their own efforts. What choices did an author make about the relation between language and its ability to represent the world? Neither readers nor reviewers (nor this writer) can step outside the universes of discourse that others inhabit. Ought readers and reviewers to reveal their own theories of language in addition to critiquing others' theories?

Theory of theories. Theories pose their own genre problems, including that of translation across genres. If the theories are considered incommensurate, then translation appears impossible. What is considered incommensurate, however, is also a matter of theory. Thus any theory should be reflexive, applying to and explaining itself at least as well as it claims to apply to and explain others.

All the kinds of theories underlying historical discourse are as interconnected in the conceptualization as in the practice of textualization. Even though some scholars today repudiate theory as totalizing or universalist when used explicitly, theories of various kinds implicitly ground even this new (anti)theory. Ought not historical textualizations therefore to make explicit the various problematics employed in explaining and narrating histories? Ought historians not to theorize about theories insofar as their texts exemplify them?[35]

Greg Dening accomplishes a quite explicit reflexive interweaving of description and theory in *Islands and Beaches: Discourse on a Silent Land,*

Marquesas, 1774–1880. Each chapter contains not only a chronological and topical history but also a "reflection" on a more abstract and general topic or model relevant to that history.[36] Thus the chapter "Priests and Prophets" also contains a reflection "On Religious Change," while the chapter on "Captains and Kings" includes a reflection "On Dominance."

Suzanne Gearhart's reflexive approach to theory in *The Open Boundary of History and Fiction: A Critical Approach to the French Enlightenment* offers another textual model as she explores the interaction between past and present in creating the forms of history. She complains that historians and other scholars historicize some "concepts," "events," "methods," and "theories" while they accept uncritically and unhistorically others as givens, most notably "history" itself. Accordingly, she historicizes the boundary between history and fiction by comparing eighteenth- and twentieth-century theorizing about what constitutes rationality, genre, narrative, nature, idealism, empiricism, and other categories and concepts. In each chapter she discusses a French Enlightenment thinker and one or more modern "theorists" to compare their approaches to and thus destabilize the current paradigmatic premises underlying current historical practice. Thus she juxtaposes Voltaire with Foucault on reason and the irrational and with Hayden White and Gérard Genette on genre, and Montesquieu with Lévi-Strauss on the Other and with Althusser on origins.[37]

Since the nature and value of theory are at issue between modernists and postmodernists, how can historians evaluate the usefulness of theory, whether as model, image, metaphor, or otherwise, apart from this debate? Modernist criteria for a single best and right theory include comprehensiveness of application, descriptive richness, abstraction, conceptual generation, and perhaps quantifiability. Postmodern theorists challenge why theory should be defined as cognitive and therefore as knowledge while moral and aesthetic reasons are denied equal validity and authority; why scientistic and universal approaches should be preferred over local stories and narrative histories; or why a single theory should be proclaimed the only right one. If theory cannot be as context-free as natural science pretended and the philosophy of science idealized as the scientific method, does disciplinary custom provide only the context of an interpretive community to gauge what is appropriate theory? To the extent that radical postmodernists treat the search for a metalinguistic theory as part of hegemonic discourses, then radical postmodernist theory ought to allow for multiple theories of what can constitute theory. The existence of multiple good theories seems to subvert good politics, however, in the eyes of those who believe that the only good theory is one critical of, even oppositional to, established (capitalistic) society. Can an antitotalizing theoretical stance depend upon a totalizing political stand?[38]

If the status and nature of theory are at issue, ought not even the theory of theory to be reflexively explicit in the text? If theory is not cross-cultural or transhistorical, then is any use of theory therefore a topical or local convenience, a "guerrilla tactic," as one scholar argues?[39] Must it be either oppositional to or complicit with prevailing social arrangements? Must such guerrilla theorists accept certain kinds of theory to ground even their arguments about theory? If the content of a theory is considered cultural or historical, can this theory about the status of theory transcend its own demystification and historicization? If theory is denied transcultural and transhistorical foundations, can it be rescued as "orienting strategies" or sets of paradigmatic assumptions?[40]

How these issues are resolved in a text constitutes the inquiry of readers and reviewers who would be reflexive in their theorization of others' theories. How explicit are the texts on the theories that ground them? What kind of theory or theories are used? How systematic, how general, how comprehensive or inclusive, how testable and "objective" are they? Does the text employ theory on an ad hoc orientational basis, as local guerrilla tactics, or as transcultural, transhistorical generalizations? Readers and reviewers should make implicit theories, models, and metaphors explicit, and they should explore silences on social theories and images that are foundational to a historical textualization. What academic and other political purposes do theories serve in the contest over the status of theory, in the role of knowledge as power in modern society? What, in short, is a text's ideology of theory? How explicit a role should readers and reviewers give their own theories of theory, if they would be reflexive in applying to and explaining their own textualizations about theories in others' texts?

Toward New Historicizations

To these two series should be added at least one more, one that discusses what forms of representation a textualization might take in any new kind of reflexive historicization. The goal of this series, like that of the previous ones, is to make explicit the theories and practices of representation as they might be employed and exemplified in transformed historical discourses. This series therefore explores the possibilities of how medium and messages might combine to produce new forms of textualization in which the items in the previous two series come together in new ways. To the degree that a crisis of representation exists today, then theories of it as textualization ought to be reflexive also.

New options. If modernism and postmodernism, poetics and politics, textualism and contextualism question, even at times contradict, each other in their implications for historical discourse in the profession, they also reinforce each other in discrediting traditional historical practice. These contradictory implications not only suggest the limits of normal historical practice as well as of each other; they also point to some of the options available to those who would take a historic turn. Historians and others who would historicize in new ways face at least three basic options.

First, new historicizers can develop options along the axes of the textualist/poetics problematic. One choice within this option is to collapse history into metahistory and practice it as a form of historical criticism. Would that entail a revision of Carl Becker's old slogan to read "every man his own metahistorian"?[41] Certainly the historian can explore the rhetorical configurations of historical texts and the modes of representation in and for themselves. It is unclear, however, that such an approach encompasses all that might be included under the rubric of what historicization embraces, important as it may be to understand the general implications of metahistorical concerns for general historical practice. The question therefore becomes: how can we go beyond the study of metahistory to the textualization of history itself as a newly self-aware discipline through its newfound reflexive understanding? This would seem to be both the challenge issued and the burden bestowed by Hayden White and others.

Historical practice according to the textualist/poetics paradigm can become a version of intellectual or conceptual history as historiography. White's own *Metahistory* transforms history into conceptual or representational history, as his subtitle, "The Historical Imagination in Nineteenth-Century Europe," suggests. In the same vein are such recent historiographical works as Stephen Bann, *The Clothing of Clio: A Study of Representation of History in Nineteenth-Century Britain and France;* Linda Orr, *Jules Michelet: Nature, History, and Language;* and Ann Rigney, *The Rhetoric of Historical Representation: Three Narrative Theories of the French Revolution,* whose titles signal their goals.[42]

Conceptual, intellectual, or cultural history can follow this lead by exploring the history of representations or modes of representation in general in a society or culture. As Linda Hutcheon observes, "In a very real sense, postmodernism reveals a desire to understand culture as the product of previous representations. The representation of history becomes the history of representations."[43] Much of the history of the body, for instance, describes its various representations over time.[44] Notwithstanding its title, the journal *Representations* contains articles that belong under the next option as well as this one.[45] Likewise, the New Historicism can be classified both ways. Perhaps Foucault's pronouncements demand and his productions demonstrate the most radical reorientation of history as conceptual history, for they challenge so many of the working fictions of doing intellectual history according to the normal history paradigm.[46]

Just as historians can reorient history practice and production through the textualist/poetics paradigm, so too can they develop the options derived from the contextualist/politics paradigm, which investigates the social and political generation of the subject matter under study. The most obvious strategy explores what we might call the sociology of historical knowledge itself and would result in a history of the political and social bases of modes of historical conceptualization and representation, including the turn to textualism and poetics and maybe even the historic turn itself. Such a subdiscipline of the profession would operate according to the normal history paradigm to connect knowledge and power and the larger society: the why to be answered by normal methods of contextualization. Thus, as mentioned in Chapter 4, Peter De Bolla urges that Hayden White's rhetoric of history be historicized as historical rhetorics. Which tropes dominated which periods, and why?[47] What can be done for the representation of history can also be done according to the same paradigmatic presuppositions for the social and political generation of ideas, concepts, and cultural representations in general in a society. Joan W. Scott, in conclusion to her arguments about experience, similarly urges a conceptual history that "takes all categories of analysis as contextual, contested, and contingent."[48] Both De Bolla and Scott stress the axis of contextualist/politics premises as opposed to that of textualist/poetics. To the extent that historians can establish the relations of power and social structure for ideas and the like, they can also determine them for all of the subject matter that the profession traditionally studies under the rubrics of political, economic, and social history.

Both of these options accept the limitations of their own paradigms of understanding, because the historian accepts the limits of the operative problematic itself. Both basic options also try to operate from within the traditional paradigm of history, although they may transform the nature of the subject matter and how it is approached. The problems of attempting to operate from within the respective paradigms and that of normal history too became clear even in this brief presentation of possibilities. The questions raised in this and previous chapters reveal some of the problems involved in trying to understand what such practices entail in the ways of conceptualization and representation for each other and themselves reflexively. The options, in general, transform history practice either into what the profession calls historiography and intellectual history (modified according to recent trends) or into social and political history (with greater awareness of poetic and textualist consequences), but mainly from within the normal history paradigm with its associated perplexities.

The last and most interesting option asks those who would historicize to rise to the seemingly insuperable challenge of moving beyond problematics of textualism and contextualism, poetics and politics, to reflexive historicization and postmodern textualization, of transcending the limitations of the basic problematics while preserving their insights. How can historians achieve such new histories when the exemplars in the field are few or nonexistent? Should (can?) the historian incorporate a plurality of viewpoints and stories within the same textualization? Should the historian show how a textualized history is constructed from interpretive contextualization of the sources while showing how the transformation of those interpretations into representations of the past as history are created from processes and systems of meaning at the same time?

Such a vision of what history as a disciplinary practice and form of representation might achieve attempts to break the conceptual barrier posed by the dilemma of representationalism. One cannot explicate how a representation represents something, or produces its effects, at the same time as one tries to comprehend what is represented, its effects and message, for their own sake: examining the means of representation downplays or even conceals the message; examining the message downplays or hides the medium.[49] A new form of reflexive history would resolve the dilemma by doing both together, seeking to operate in the conceptual spaces posed by the contradictions between textualism and contextualism, between social and rhetorical construction of reality, between normal history and metahistory. Thus both practice and production would accept the challenges facing the profession and incorporate them into new ways of doing history in line with late modernist or postmodernist ways of understanding. Such a vision of professional history should change the ways in which historians write articles and review books in the professional journals, conduct sessions and argue cases in professional meetings, and teach and examine in classrooms.

Does this vision of what history might be subvert all history-writing or only traditional ways of representing the past? Does it suggest the limits of the paradigm that constitutes the very possibility of doing history as we define it in the Western world? Do the competing definitions of history embody unresolvable, essentially contested problematics and conflicting, incommensurable paradigms? Should plural paradigms lead to coexisting, even conflicting, plural histories? Should—can—multiculturalism, social constructionism, deconstruction, and textualism issue forth in new kinds of histories based upon new ways of writing history? Can Clio embrace radically different ways of representing the past under the rubric of history? That is, can history be multicultural or only pluralistic, to use today's loaded terminology, about incorporating multiple viewpoints and stories? Can any one exemplar of history combine many viewpoints and (hi)stories? Do plural histories point to plural pasts? Can historians go beyond an ironic stance if they practice a self-conscious or reflexive mode of historicization?

New problematics. Textual experimentation in historical discourse can be aided by a new problematic that incorporates reflexively its own constitutive processes as part of its construction of representation. While old ways of constructing history are being challenged by the recent intellectual and political trends as a way of providing overall context, there is a call in literary criticism and the social sciences for a (re)new(ed) historicism or historicization to mediate the conflicting meanings of context, to move beyond the mutually deconstructing problematics of poetics and politics, of textualism and contextualism. The energetic role proposed for a new historicization is in part an effort to sidestep the incompatibilities of the premises and problems introduced from the human sciences, particularly as inscribed in literary and rhetorical theory. To escape the skepticism produced by the free play of interpretations and to avoid the essentialism associated with reified concepts and categories, scholars look to the history of the cultural, if not also the social, construction of these categories and their signifieds (or referents, for contextualists). The (a?) history of how the concepts and categories came about can reveal how they became essentialized and mystified and at the same time expose the political uses of the foundationalism and reification of concepts and the mystification of the social production of knowledge through both deconstruction and political critique. Such a new historicization seeks to avoid the problems of poststructuralist, postmodernist textualist criticism of contextualism while using those results, its critique, to provide a new, more reflexive context for contextualization without the problems of the old.

The new trends to historicization, particularly in what is called cultural studies in both literature and history, therefore seek a construction of the past that would provide a firm foundation to bound (constrain) the free play of interpretations while remaining sensitive to the problems of representation and textualization that form so important a part of the new trends. Whereas simple contextualism presumed that the construction of (a) history is transparent to its supposed referent, universal or omniscient in viewpoint, and self-evidently "realistic" in narrative construction of the "Great Story," the new trend to historicization must try to reconcile the dilemmas introduced by the premises of the specific social location of all texts, including its own textualization, the denial of referentiality and essentialism in historical discourse itself, and the constructedness of narrative as a basis for representing the past in the present.

But what then can Fredric Jameson's advice to "always historicize" mean in these postmodern times?[50] His own dilemmas of interpretation reveal all too well the problems of one who would be contextualist but sees the claims of textualism in a post-Marxist, poststructuralist, postmodernist world.[51] Surely the effort must advance beyond the recent flood of new but normal histories of methodologies, disciplines, and schools of criticism if it is to serve as the basis for a new contextualism.[52] It must at least mediate between—if not proceed beyond—textualism and contextualism as versions of context, between poetics and politics as textual versions of social reality. It cannot accept and base its narrative upon a transparent social history as normally narrativized for grounding its own analysis of social production and consumption of texts for the purposes of demystification. It cannot rehierarchize or reessentialize some basic social and cultural categories as it poeticizes the contextualization of other concepts and categories. It cannot move the margins to the center in the guise of the other but still resort to the traditional paradigm for constructing the past as a single Great Story. And it ought not to pretend to offer a middle way if it narrows the road to achieve it.

These many goals seem to ground Sacvan Bercovitch's summary of the new problematic of historicization espoused in *Reconstructing American Literary History:*

> that race, class, and gender are formal principles of art, and therefore integral to textual analysis; that language has the capacity to break free of social restrictions and through its own dynamics to undermine the power structures it seems to reflect; that political norms are inscribed in aesthetic judgment and therefore inherent in the process of interpretation; that aesthetic structures shape the way we understand history, so that tropes and narrative devices may be said to use historians to enforce certain views of the past; that the task of literary historians is not just to show how art transcends culture, but also to identify and explore the ideological limits of their time, and then to bring these to bear upon literary analysis in such a way as to make use of the categories of culture, rather than being used by them.[53]

With the change of a few words specific to literary history, this statement could constitute one methodological call, if not program, for all of a new culturalized and reflexive history. That Bercovitch's path seems quite different from that usually traveled, let alone called for, by most historians, even those advocating the so-called new cultural history, indicates all too well the hegemonic boundaries of the normal history problematic.

That other problematics might satisfy equally well the demand for a new reflexive basis for experimental historical discourses is not as important to my argument at this point as what Bercovitch's effort suggests for that goal. To achieve a new form of historicization demands a new, more reflexive problematic for historical textualization and disciplinary practice than is afforded by the normal professional paradigm. Just as reflexivity and multiculturalism reveal the limits of the normal history paradigm, they also suggest the potentiality of new approaches to historical discourse, approaches that incorporate both a new reflexive contextualization and a multiviewpointed narrative into the same text(ualization). To accept the dualisms and relativisms inherent in the various problematics, historians should incorporate the conflictual dilemmas explicitly into the very message of the text and not just implicitly through the process of textualization. A reflexive (con)textualization tries to surmount the basic dilemma of representation itself by incorporating texts and countertexts, discourses and counterdiscourses into the same textualization. New historicizations ought to show self-awareness of their own problematics or modes of representation, exhibiting them as basic to the construction of their textualization.

New viewpoints. To introduce multiple viewpoints into historical discourse would seem to require both a revision of the normal history paradigm and a new vision of what a historical text can be. A multicultural, dialogic ideal transforms not only the subject matter of histories but also the postulates of what a good history does and is. Ultimately, must multiple viewpoints result in plural pasts in a single text(ualization) as well as in new approaches to the narrativization of histories?

At the least, one narratologist suggests, such a multicultural textualization must abandon the third-person viewpoint for a combination of first-person perspective as creator of the representation and an effort to engage the subjects as co-creators. Such a "second-person" dialogue dissolves the subject–object relationship into a subject-to-subject discourse. The new narrative site becomes one of multiple conversations in the overlap among first, third, and second persons. Both what knowledge is and how it is represented proceed from the interplay of voices and viewpoints in such conversations. To what extent such an ideal demands new textual forms remains to be negotiated in the discipline.[54]

The ideal of multiple viewpoints challenges the very idea of representation as mimesis, for it substitutes a kaleidoscope for a telescope or microscope. Most certainly, it repudiates the omniscience of a Panopticon for the particular perspectives of situated viewpoints.[55] Does the model of pastiche or collage provide better forms of multiculturalist exposition than the normal unified text? As always, the question centers upon whether the contested terrain can be textualized as and through the politics of structured interplay if no one can play observer but all are only participants. Univocal and unitary points of view give way to heterogeneity of viewpoints and temporal locations. Texts deny homogeneity of author and reader and presume no transcendental author/reader, interpretive community, or referent. Textualizations presume that they exist within conflicting and contradictory world(s) and ought to represent themselves accordingly.

Dialogically, neither reader nor reviewer can accept at face value the supposed voices and viewpoints ascribed in a text to past actors or present observers. What choices of structure did a text make to organize the interplay of voices? Where along the multiculturalist spectrum presented in Chapter 7 is a textualized representation? What forms of representation are used to show the voices and viewpoints? Would montage or pastiche or some other form show better what the text represents as unitary, univocal, or transcendental?

New times. For the representation of time to be reflexive in any new historicization, the various kinds of temporal ordering in the text should be made as evident as possible. Time is textualized both explicitly, through overt argument and story in the text, and implicitly, through discursive organization, privileging presuppositions, and subtext. Periodization is the most obvious way of showing time, by segmenting it to measure it and to exhibit its contents. Should not any textualization discuss what ways are used and why, even what are not used and why? Should not the mode(l)s of imaging time and methods of temporal ordering in a text be made the subject of the text as much as any other topic textualized in it?

Would other than normal paradigmatic conceptions of time result in new ways of representing it in and through histories? Although the authors of a series of articles on "Narratives and Social Identities" in *Social Science History* are sensitive to various kinds of self-constructed historical narratives among past individuals, groups, and institutions, they assimilate these histories according to the professional construal of time in their own textualizations. Despite acknowledging various notions of time in narratives of identity, they still contextualize these other histories according to normal conceptions of time in the discipline and thus make that conception of time seem natural and universal to all kinds of histories.[56] How in a reflexive history should the personal and subjective experience of time by past actors or the collective experience of memory and popular history be represented as opposed to the chronology and formal time of professional history? How does oral history, for example, differ from its professional, written cousin, and should that make a difference in constructing a formal history?[57] In some cases oral histories have led to new forms of textualization, as did, for example, Ronald Fraser's reconstruction of his childhood days at Amnersfield Manor House, mentioned in Chapter 7. In the textual representation of history should present and past notions and constructions of time co-create as they implicate each other? Foucault made the past serve the present in his books, but in *The Open Boundary of Fiction and History* Suzanne Gearhart makes the relationship reciprocal in and through her textualization.

The concept of multiple viewpoints suggests a multiplicity of times and therefore of histories. Fernand Braudel proposed perhaps the most widely known conception of history as multiple, coexisting sequences of time. In his preface to *The Mediterranean and the Mediterranean World in the Age of Philip II,* he asserted that all history can be divided into three kinds.[58] In his well-known tripartite formulation, traditional history concentrates on "the history of events" or "a history of short, sharp, nervous vibrations" often framed and told in terms of the "contemporaries who felt it, described it, lived it." This history focuses on individuals and relates to "the rhythm of their brief lives," often centering on politics. The second kind, "a history of gentle rhythms, of groups and groupings," involves a longer span of time and receives its form from the "conjunctures" of trends and social structures in the form of collective institutions depicted as economies, societies, states, and civilizations. The third kind, the famed *longue durée,* encompasses "a history that is almost changeless, the history of man in relationship to his surroundings . . . a history that unfolds slowly and is slow to alter, often repeating itself and working itself out in cycles which are endlessly renewed." Covering very long-term demographic and ecological trends, it exists "almost out of time." According to Braudel, historians all too often take one of these kinds of time as the sole framework for history rather than using all three.[59]

How the three times relate to one another, or even whether they can relate to one another, receives different answers depending upon the lesson to be learned about the nature of time in historical representation. In the volumes of *The Mediterranean* Braudel argued that they are separate levels or series that interact with each other only now and then, and he devoted separate sections to each kind. Elsewhere, however, he asserted that they form a unity through interdependence and conjuncture, and both his goal of total history and his practice suggest as much.[60] It is the former possibility that excites postmodernists and supposedly inspired Foucault in his approach to events.[61] Whether as archaeology or as genealogy, Foucault enunciated the past in terms of discontinuities, ruptures, displacements, transformations, and chance occurrences. He accused traditional intellectual historians of forcing preconceived unities, continuities, and teleologies on the past through their normal discursive approach to time. Differences in the approaches to time are not a matter of calendars and dating or even of treating time as social activity and cultural construction but rather of the construal and construction of those very notions in (a) historical textualization. Should several modes of time be brought together into one multitemporal text?

What is at issue in exploring new ways of representing time can be seen in the gendering of historic time. Much of the reorientation of women's history has rested upon the different ways in which men and women spend and use time, and therefore in how their history should be represented and narrated. Since the patriarchal division between public and private time relegated (Western? bourgeois?) women to the private side, their lives were omitted from histories and history as being outside of what counted in history. As a result, male time emerged as the basis of histories of production, power, the professions, and even of reason and aesthetics as history recounted only what happened in the public, that is the male-defined and -dominated, sphere. To historicize past women's experiences and activities therefore demanded a transformation, or at least a transvaluation, and supplementation of what counted as worthy of being the subject of history, so that it could include both women's and men's time as creating history.[62]

But did such transvaluation and supplementation transform how women's pasts were contextualized as history? Were new subjects argued and narrativized according to old chronologic modes and temporality, or did new histories develop new ways of representing time as their bases? Julia Kristeva, in her article "Women's Time," maintains that a female subjectivity emphasizes time as cyclic and recurrent, as eternal and monumental, governed essentially by rhythm.[63] According to her scheme, then, men emphasize the linearity of time as direction and teleology, departure and arrival, genetic growth and progression. Regardless of its seemingly essentialist nature, her scheme highlights the issue of whose and what conception of time is authorized as professional history. What alternative histories might arise from other social constructions of time? Susan Deeds Ermarth in raising this same issue denies all representational history in favor of a rhythmic figural approach to time as a solution. Since she uses modern novels as examples of the new approach, it is unclear just how she envisions history as a genre.[64]

The theories and practices of Braudel and Foucault, like feminist histories and postmodernist metafiction, challenge assumptions about time and its representation in and as normal historicization. Such reflexive consideration of time in historical practice is reinforced by postmodernist critiques of temporality in general. The greater the emphasis on contingency and chance as central to how the world works, the smaller the role of causation—and the more in some ways historicization comes to resemble the one-fact-after-another school of historiography. To the extent that causation is vital to traditional historical narrativization, then the existence of simultaneous or discontinuous time series undermines the normal paradigm of historical discourse. Although Braudel and Foucault or those who follow their examples might be able to construct a series or even a series of series of events, like modern novelists they lose the big picture of connections as they renounce the larger framework of causation in their texts.[65] In the end, the idea of multiple times involves surrendering the idea(l) of a single past for many histories, even giving up the metaphorical growth of time as genetic connections that transform events into episodes, chronologies into histories. Such an orientation challenges the notion of origins as some form of continuous growth from some originary point. Whether represented as subject/author, as originator of ideas and actions, or as the present and future arising from the past as if the connections were intrinsic to the real world, hence to history itself, such devices ought to be shown for what they are: the historicizer's construction of the story.

Readers and reviewers should observe the many ways in which a text uses and represents time. How does a text divide time explicitly in its argument or story? What conventions of profession or culture does the author follow in approaching time in history as the past and as textualized? What periodization does the author presume or explicate, and how does the author know it or argue it? Is time represented through synchronic or diachronic organization of events, as process or stasis, as rupture or continuity, as dialectic or conjunction? To what extent does the author presume progress, decline, cycles, or other basic modes of comprehending time?[66] Is the chronologic framework of the text one of complete rupture, small shifts, continuity as growth, or transformation? Is time represented as stochastic and arbitrary or as ordered and structured, even as dialectical? If a text represents events and ideas as developing from some point in the past, does the text subscribe to some simple originary source or idea of origins? How are beginnings and endings handled? How is time shown through use of tense, imagery, periodization, and general discursive organization?[67]

New represents. That reflexive contextualization of history demands additional or new ways of representing time also implies that new ways of representing are needed for what occurs in it. If past and present create each other in a reflexive text, how should the historian represent their contents when either set of concepts or categories is chronologically specific? If concepts, categories, or other methods of description are not transcultural or transhistorical, what language can the historian use to describe her subjects? The quandary manifests itself even in what to name this category. I considered "actants," "existants," "representemes," and other semantic concoctions before settling on "representeds" to designate the "what" of what is referred to or represented in a textualization. All these neologisms are meant to embrace the various elements or entities that constitute the subject matter and topics making up the textual content of the narrative and arguments of historical discourses. The problem is what and how, on what level, and by what explicit or implicit methods to specify or individuate the subjects, objects, events, structures, trends, and other elements/entities of a history, if they themselves are subject to historicization for their understanding. How, that is, should historians code and represent the events, elements, entities, topics, and so on that constitute the subject matter of their historicizations if their designations possess no stable and persisting meaning over time but are locally specific and temporally contingent? The historicization of what is represented must incorporate present meaning as product of past process, just as the past processes are defined and constituted by present semantics. If the past and present co-create each other, the task of translation becomes doubly difficult. Although new fields of interest and so-called new histories treat new topics and subjects, they need not employ new ways of representing the representeds in stories and arguments. That all models of society, polity, and persons, like theories of explanation, language, and ontology, are time-bound and in contention complicates their use as referents/representeds in historical discourse.

The multiform nature of this problem can be demonstrated by several questions. How should the subject/object be represented in histories in these postmodern times? How did a series of events/structures/trends get constituted, and according to and from whose conception and viewpoint, in the past, and how should the historian translate these as subjects in a discourse? Should historians follow Foucault's lead in dissolving the subject/object into signifying and discursive practices?[68] The historian must not only investigate how individual subjects, the polity and structures of power, and the social axes of race, gender, and class come into being and who constituted and named them but also decide how to represent them now in a text. Who specifies their temporal and spatial location, how, and when? From the perspective of this rubric, then, how the various topics or subject matters came into being and through whose eyes, through whose actions, with what effects according to whom must be combined with the same questions asked of the historian's present-day textualization of them. Reflexive contextualization cannot just accept ethnocontextual or present-day answers to these questions; it must supplement or transform the traditional subject/object, entity/event, structure/trend in historical discourses.

The reflexive constitution of subject matter must deconstruct the seeming naturalness of social subject/object, entity/event, structure/trend in their very construction as and through historicization. To argue that social and cultural construction or even historicization of these topics resolves the problem misses the point, for such an answer does not say how that answer itself will be constructed and according to what and whose categories. Moreover, such an answer accepts either the ethnocontextual or current contextual construction of categories, classifications, interpretations, and metanarratives too much at face value. In each case, the problem concerns how the historian should code or textualize the categories for describing the subject matter or represent the relationships and the story when both past and present are relative to their times. How might the relationship between past and present be characterized and in what kinds of words? In sum, must new historicizations explore a new semantics of what is represented in them in order to convey their new reflexive ideals?

The questions that readers and reviewers must pose about representeds center upon how the various subjects/objects, persons/groups, events/structures, trends/periods, and other categorizations come to be distinguished as such in a text. What is accepted as seemingly natural or normal as an entity? Does a specific historical discourse designate matters according to the names and categories it says the actors employed, or does it construct new categorizations to give new meaning to the past through its representation? Does a text assume that its classifications are natural and transhistorical categories derived from some universal scheme, or are the representeds invented to render problematic even modern categories in the present discourse? To be themselves reflexive, must readers and reviewers construct historicized countercategories of their own to explicate those of historical texts?[69]

New textualizations. The primary goal of reflexive contextualism is to create new forms of discourse in the writing and teaching, the reading and reviewing of histories, not only by professional historians but also by those scholars who espouse the new historicisms in other disciplines. Thus all the prescriptive items in this and the preceding series are meant to come together under this rubric. No one best or right way exists to combine all the items in the three series; no one problematic, approach to subject matter, or experimental textualization is necessarily preferred. Although some approaches are probably more fruitful than others, we will not know what can be achieved without more experimentation.

These series constitute a catalogue, itself a form of representation. I am not advocating such a form for textualizing historical representations. My catalogue artificially divides what must be united in any historical representation. Any new historicization should embody these elements in new forms. Whether the combination in a single textualization of multiple criteria, deconstructive reconstruction, and theoretical reflexivity can take only such postmodern forms as a kaleidoscope, pastiche, or collage remains to be seen. Certainly a book of multiauthored essays does not solve the problems of form. Late modernism and postmodernism alike demand new approaches to narration, argument, explanation, and description as textualized.

Such a textualization should establish and sustain a conversation between subject and subject then and now and between author and reader, teacher and student. If all representation is self-representation, then surely full disclosure of the role of author as intervener must expand from a few sentences into a fully self-revelatory text. How overt, then, must the author's role be? Can a self-revelatory textualization ever be more than a self-advertisement of virtuosity? Surely the goal is some sort of cooperative conversation among voices and viewpoints of the past and present. But in the end, any postmodern historicization "calls attention, overtly or covertly, to the fact that it is a text first and foremost, that it is a human construct made up of and by words."[70]

To meet reflexive and dialogic goals, a new textualization must combine multiple contexts with novel ways of contextualizing them through their representations. It must combine metahistory and history, Great Stories and historiography while historicizing itself as it historicizes its subject matter; the postulated evidential past and the multifarious present should create each other as they problematize each other. It must combine discourses and counterdiscourses about poetics and politics, texts and textualization, and the other dilemmas historicization tries to resolve as it embodies them. It must theorize about what it theorizes as it theorizes and exemplify its models as explicitly as possible. Such textualization deconstructs itself as it (re)constructs history through its representation. It ought to broaden the genre even as it challenges it by breaching conventions and crossing or combining genres. How many rooms the house of history holds remains to be explored. Ultimately, such new textualizations challenge the dilemmas of representation and language as they try to talk about themselves as they talk about things. Since paradigms and their premises are not compatible, conflicting discourses will result in different approaches for different purposes—but all, it is to be hoped, in reflexive dialogue.

In the end, must incommensurable paradigms be given separate metanarratives, or can they be incorporated into the same Great Story as dissimilar modes of understanding power and social relations? Should oppositional viewpoints be incorporated into a single mode of representation? How can historians incorporate multiple voices and viewpoints from and about social and political conflicts into a narrative text in a fundamental and central way of structuring the expression in addition to the explicit content of the story and argument? Would the explicit inclusion of competing problematics and perspectives in formal historical narratives demand new literary forms?

Must all experimental efforts to transform historical discourse resort to postmodern fragmentation of a unified story line in order to avoid the subjection of the other through the imposition of a totalized point of view? Must they necessarily embody the eclecticism of montage or pastiche as they blur genres by crossing the customary boundaries of the discipline between philosophy of history and historical sociology, between oral and documentary history, between folk and professional history?[71] They point to a new way of narrativizing the past as partial and Great Stories. They forgo customary closure through holism, continuity, and consistency of authorship. Normal historicization constrains diversity of viewpoint and authority; so-called post-modern historicization surrenders an Archimedean overview for being just another participant in the dialogue(s) among the voices and viewpoints, just another text in time among other textualizations, another discourse among other discursive practices. By abandoning a totalized overview, postmodern historicization surrenders its claim to a superior Great Story as the foundation of disciplinary and historical authority. Thus any attempt to practice such postmodern history would appear to demand not only recanting and renouncing traditional approaches to historicization but also reconceiving representation in and of history and the nature of historicization itself.[72]

One historian's quite self-conscious attempt to meet many of these criteria is Greg Dening's *Mr. Bligh's Bad Language: Passion, Power and Theatre on the Bounty*.[73] This book exemplifies one postmodernist approach to reflexive (con)textualism in its self-conscious attempt to make explicit the interaction among the process of converting evidence into sources, the interpretation of events as historical, the organization of history as narratives, the application of various kinds of theories, and the choice and nature of representation. The book takes the reader along on the author's voyage to collect historical evidence and infer historiographical meaning, just as the book reconstructs and re-presents the voyage of the *Bounty* before and after the famed mutiny that made these episodes part of anglophone, and perhaps global, historical memory and culture. Dening reflexively considers in his own representations the interaction among various kinds of representations then and since of Captain Bligh, Fletcher Christian and the other mutineers, Tahitians and other Pacific islanders, and other actors and events. He plays with the power of words and words of power throughout the book. As his subtitle suggests, he depicts the spectacle of these events as theater for both English and islanders according to their various ways of demonstrating power and understanding each other through warfare, religion, systems of rank, or placing each other as others into their own histories as they made and remade them. He occasionally uses previous fictional representation to make factual points, and at the same time he makes clear the overall construction of his representation as a representation.

To convey the fictive invention of factuality as well as the theatricality of history then and now, Dening very explicitly organizes his main text into a prologue, three acts, two entr'actes, and an epilogue. The prologue contains three versions of a prologue written upon various bicentennial anniversaries of the events of the mutiny and outlining those events for the reader. Each of the three acts is divided into sections called "narrative" and "reflection." The narrative of the first act, "The Ship," tells of the ship's culture of power and rank in relation to British society and the world capitalist system and what therefore was wanted of the Pacific islanders and how the British interacted with them. The reflection muses on the amount of flogging on naval ships, the implications of violent discipline for the world of the ship's society, and the relation in general between law and force, among other matters. Subsequent acts narrate and reflect on the relations between sailors and Tahitians in terms of how they understood each other through religion, violence, sexuality, and other modes of connection; how the sailors went "native" before and after the mutiny; the trial and its aftermath; and finally, how these dramatic events have been represented in a series of twentieth-century motion pictures. The first entr'acte conveys the appropriateness of the Tahitian designation of Englishmen as "sharks that walk the land," given the islanders' cosmology of what happens on the beach and comes from the ocean; the second depicts (in the sense of double representation) the first actor portraying Captain Bligh on the English stage. In the epilogue Dening describes his own thirty-year quest for what happened on the *Bounty* and how that quest was and is memorialized and historicized as coinciding with the end of the Enlightenment project. Even the notes extend the reflexive arguments of the main text. Thus the endings, like the beginnings, are several. The reader leaves the book convinced of the factuality of what Dening represents and aware of the many textual layers involved in representing the dialogues of past and present, self and other, first and third person experience, the constructedness of memory and history. In this case a postmodernist exercise has eventuated in multiple viewpoints of the actors and those who interpreted them then and now, while the fragmented and juxtaposed textual pieces still sum up to Dening's organized theater of power as his historical representation.

Readers and reviewers, then, must ask a basic question about any history: how does its textualization put it all together? How reflexive are the self-references to the process of constructing the text? In this they seek not how facts are derived but how they are synthesized in and through what forms. How are they constituted as story and argument and Great Story(ies)? How are the layers of a text put together as a discursive representation? How many of the criteria for reflexive contextualization are met, and in what ways? What form does the text take to embody these criteria? Does the textualization employ new forms or only use one standard in the genre? Ought not readers and reviewers who favor new forms of historical discourse to praise experiments in form or point out new possibilities as they review old ones? Can historians with their help devise new forms that expand the genre?

New experiments. Whether and what new forms of historical textualization have appeared in recent years is a matter of how one conceives of the width of that metaphorical road some historians travel in search of a middle way. The more narrowly the road is conceived, the more innovative recent historical works seem, and the more they are seen as expanding historical practice and changing its direction. The more broadly the road is envisioned, the less the supposedly new historical forms seem to accomplish in any effort to move beyond normal historical discourse and practice. The question is not whether experimentation is occurring—it is—but rather, how far does it go? How many of the current new historicizations attempt to meet many or all the reflexive criteria discussed in this chapter? Measured by this standard, the experimentation seems small or nonexistent—if the point of a new historical practice is to meet all the many criteria or goals in one text, be it a partial history or a Great Story. To what extent do so-called new histories meet even the general goals of reflexivity and dialogy? Have the many new histories of recent times led to new forms of textualization in both representation of content and modes of expression? Although some *Annalistes* eschewed histories of events for those of the long durations, their textualizations of such structural histories adopted the old conventions of viewpoint and voice if not of story-telling. Even those *Annalistes* who moved to exposition of *mentalités* did not abandon old ways of contextualization for new ways. A comparison of the works of Fernand Braudel and Emmanuel Le Roy Ladurie and even Todorov's *Conquest of America* with the many postmodernist opportunities still to be explored by historians reveals that the former supply a limited range of options.[74]

Let us turn to some of the new histories to see if they provide the examples we need. In one of the more promising surveys, *New Perspectives on Historical Writing,* the essays cover such relatively new areas and topics as the history of reading, images, the body, and microhistory or review new trends in the histories of women, political thought, oral history, and "from below." Valuable and even exciting as such new histories are in terms of methods or subject matter, they frequently textualize in old ways. Some essays discuss new subject/object categories as appropriate to new fields or to transform old ones, but most show that advocating a broadened approach to what history should include as areas of interest need not lead to any fundamentally new forms of historical representation of their entities as subjects or in their textualization as context. Even those new narrative histories mentioned by the editor, Peter Burke, as harbingers of the future often fail to push very far beyond the bounds of normal history.[75]

Robert Rosenstone, in a short article in *Perspectives,* the newsletter of the American Historical Association, bemoans the lack of experimentation in historical forms among anglophone professional historians.[76] Among the few examples he can find, several have already been mentioned in these chapters as challenging and extending normal historical practice: Richard Price on multiple voices and viewpoints in *Alabi's World;* Elinor Langer on use of the personal voice in her biography of Josephine Herbst; David Farber on separating chapters on various viewpoints and voices in narration from analytical ones about the 1968 Democratic Convention in Chicago; and Simon Schama on pastiche and the division between history and fiction, discussed below. Rosenstone's own *Mirror in the Shrine: American Encounters with Meiji Japan* combines direct address both to his historical actors and to the reader, different voices represented as such through typeface and exposition, movielike fast cuts from one topic to another, and montage and self-confession—all in a reflexive effort to contradict and expand methods of historical representation as narration. His methods make the reader aware of *this* history as constructed artifact and of *this* historian as the grand organizer. He repudiates the usual discursive continuity, which patches over thin or nonexisting evidence, in favor of direct address to the reader about the problems of evidence and connectedness. Throughout the book Rosenstone seeks to collapse the usual rigid distinctions between the past and present of historical realism in a text and among author, actors, and reader in the textualization.[77]

Outside the discipline, New Historicism in literary studies offers less than its promise to textualize history as it historicizes textuality. Whether or how the New Historicism can resolve or mediate the dilemmas intrinsic in its dual goal is as uncertain as whether it is either new or historical.[78] Likewise, the models offered by anthropologists as they culturalize history in the process of historicizing culture are interesting so far as they go, but few examples of their work fulfill many of the criteria for a thoroughly reflexive and dialogic textualization of (a) history.[79] Nevertheless, examples from ethnohistory broadly conceived suggest the most important models for possible future historical textualizations.[80]

Such efforts will constitute their own genre(s) as they increasingly explore and try to exceed the limits of contemporary approaches to historical representation. The chief task of writer and teacher pursuing reflexive contextualization and multivocality is to expand the forms of historical representation across or beyond what is endorsed by the various interested epistemic and interpretive communities, across boundaries of genre regardless of politics in and out of the profession. As part of the new textualizations, experiments must also push the envelope of realism, for they must try to exist in the conceptual and expressive space between the magic realism of Latin American novelists and the objectivist realism of traditional histories.[81]

How far the boundaries of historical realism and representation can be extended and still be called history is the issue Simon Schama has forced upon the profession in his recent books. Although Schama says he is inspired by the great nineteenth-century narrative historians, his recent books betray postmodernist traits. *Citizens: A Chronicle of the French Revolution* lives up to its billing as a chronicle in a peculiarly (post)modern way, for his discourse eschews overall survey for a supposedly simple chronologically arranged series of vignettes.[82] By making pastiche his organizational device, he says he hopes to restore human agency to history. Through that means, structure both as interpretive framework and as explanation is deemphasized or hidden in the text. Schama's *Dead Certainties (Unwarranted Speculations)* is presented as an experiment in historical narration.[83] He not only proliferates voices and viewpoints in telling stories about the death of General James Wolfe at the battle of Quebec in 1759 and the disappearance in 1849 of George Parker, a Boston gentleman; he also crosses the line between fiction and fact by inventing a diary and entering into the inner consciousness of some of his characters like a novelist. He fragments the narrative unity in this book even more than in *Citizens;* indeed, one reviewer complained of the "cacophony" of his polyvocality.[84] Schama's "unwarranted speculations" nudge the boundaries of normal historical practice in a postmodernist direction, but his quest for "dead certainties" shows that he measures history by the presupposition of a knowable past according to an objectivist model of historical realism.

The issue in any reflexive (con)textualization resides less in empirical fact versus fictional invention than in what can be "legitimately" juxtaposed to constitute a context in what purports to be a historical representation. From the viewpoint of many historians, the problems of the New Historicism concern not their frequent use of unusual anecdotes nor even their juxtaposition of diverse kinds of documentary or other evidence but rather their crossing what historians postulate as different, even isolated, epistemic and interpretive communities for those materials without proving that such connections actually existed in the past. To read old texts with present-day theory may be inevitable in historical practice, but to textualize all past interpretations of those texts across classes, societies, and cultures without meticulous proof of those crossings unsettles professional historians. If magical realism and metafiction exceed the limits of historical representation on the fictional side, much of the new Historicism pushes the limits of historical representation on the factual side according to the normal paradigm of historical practice. Regardless of how broad a spectrum historical realism will and can eventually accommodate, contention will focus on the problems of juxtaposition in constructing the context in a history. The broader—some would say wilder—and more unlikely the connections across times, societies, and cultures, the greater the challenge to normal reading and interpretation of the past. The greater the challenge, the more the new textualizations will have to "prove" their cases by reference to the evidence. In the end, however, the history of historical practice suggests that what is accepted as proper juxtaposition is connected in its own way to the social and cultural contexts of the times and what a profession can police as part of those social arrangements and cultural premises. Experimentation must be seen as "legitimate" and encouraged if the bounds of the profession are to expand.[85]

Transforming Historical Practice

Reflexive Reading and Reviewing

Achieving new forms of historicization depends upon new ways of reading and reviewing historical texts as discursive practices. Under normal paradigmatic rules, readers and reviewers are supposed to deal only with the explicit arguments and narratives of histories. Active reading and criticism supplement these normal rules by also investigating the "inner workings," how a text goes about constructing itself as a history.

According to this goal, the fundamental tasks of historians as reflexive readers and reviewers are to demystify and deconstruct what historians as authors or teachers have combined or fused in a text as history; to explore and reveal the structure of interpretation and the means of representation for what they are; to show how a history is a multilayered text of evidential interpretation, argument, narrative, and Great Story; to apply the rhetoric and poetics of history in explicating the stylistic figuration, tropological prefiguration, and structures of expression in general; to expose how discursive practices have both enabled the textualization and suppressed other representations; to evaluate how well a discourse achieves reflexive and dialogic goals; and to uncover implicit politicization as well as explicit politics. The active reader and critical reviewer make a historical text a collaborative effort through their reading and reviewing, even to the extent of creating a countertext. Thus reviewers ought to devote as much effort and space to explicating historians today as intellectual historians devote to explicating historians of yesterday. In fact, these books can be considered models for extended reviews as their authors move toward the historical equivalent of literary criticism.[86]

Another important task of reviewers is to help build a poetics and rhetoric of historical discourse. By pointing out how a text exemplifies a poetics and a rhetoric as it constructs a representation, readers and reviewers help establish a general poetics of various subjects and modes of expression in the profession. As part of this goal, reader and reviewer explore the relationships among emplotments, structures of expression, and Great Stories to categorize them and probe their limits. A third goal is to prepare fellow readers and reviewers for new kinds of histories by appreciating them as experiments. When new historicizations breach paradigms and problematics; cross epistemic, interpretive, and political communities; and invent new forms of expression, critical reading and reviewing can foster reflexive contextualization and multicultural ideals as they (re)construct and (re)construe what a textualization achieved and how. Ultimately, the task of the active reader and the critical reviewer is to exhibit the same reflexivity that any new historicization ought to manifest. How did they themselves put it all together? Like critiques of historical textualizations, readings and reviews reflexive to their own construction help to indicate how a new historicization might proceed in these postmodern times. Thus becoming active readers and critical reviewers is as challenging in its way as producing a new kind of history is for writers and teachers.

Reflexive Writing and Teaching

Given the tasks before the profession as outlined in this chapter, this book ends at a new beginning. Building upon the criteria offered here or upon other, more comprehensive surveys from a greater range of perspectives than this one person can provide, others must continue to explore and exemplify the potential direction and scope of a new reflexive historicization. Most important and most difficult, more experimental textualizations exemplifying new problematics and forms of exposition are needed. The challenge is clear; the appropriate responses, less so. Both writers and teachers should work toward new forms of history as reflexive and multicultural (con)textualizations, but how to achieve this goal poses problems.[87] How can they incorporate the irony of metahistory, mutual deconstructions of problematics, and radical historicization without letting reflexivity paralyze their ability to produce textualizations at all, let alone ones comprehensible to their readers and students? Would the goal of a multiplicity of voices, viewpoints, methodologies, (Great) stories, deconstructive criticism, and reflexive construction in the same text dumbfound an audience expecting a history to be constructed according to normal discursive practice? Or will new reviewing practices lead to new reading practices?

Moving beyond normal history is more easily sought than achieved. Accomplishing this goal entails nothing less than overcoming the four crises of historical representation. First, historians must surmount the dilemma of representationalism or the semiotic absolute; any new historical textualization must show how it goes about achieving its representation at the same time as it represents the past as history. Second, historians must solve the problem of multicultural representation; any new historical textualization must include multiple viewpoints in addition to as well as according to the author's viewpoint in genuine dialogue in the very textualization itself. Third, historians must find new ways of overcoming the traditional dilemma of anachronism: how can the present scholar represent the past in its own terms and categories when those terms and categories must be retroapplied from present readings of sources and (re)translated into modern texts? Finally, historians must authorize new forms of representation without creating new rules of historical practice about what constitutes proper history itself; but adopting new rules entails breaking current prescriptions for distinguishing history from other genres and disciplines and therefore what authorizes the profession. Each of these dilemmas reveals the limits of normal historicization as representation and as discursive practice.

If the great challenge of a dialogic and reflexive contextualization culminates in the creation of new forms of historical representation, then the great question becomes whether the new rhetoric and poetics of history will actually issue forth in new kinds of experimental textualizations as historical representations. Or does the very conception of what constitutes formal and scholarly history in our society limit the degree of experimentation? Only further textual experimentation will answer this question. Only openness to such experimentation will allow the answers to be interesting. What might be the goals of any historic turn or drive to historicize should therefore not be judged by what has been practiced so far in the profession or produced up to this point as discourse. Rather the goals themselves should be part of the experiment.

Notes

1. The Postmodernist Challenge

1. The terms "linguistic turn" and "interpretive turn" may be found in Richard Rorty, ed., *The Linguistic Turn: Recent Essays in Philosophical Method* (Chicago: University of Chicago Press, 1968); and Paul Rabinow and William M. Sullivan, "The Interpretive Turn: Emergence of an Approach," in Rabinow and Sullivan, eds., *Interpretive Social Science: A Reader* (Berkeley: University of California Press, 1979), pp. 1–21. Herbert W. Simons coined the expression the "rhetorical turn" in his introduction to *Rhetoric in the Human Sciences* (London: Sage, 1989), p. 1, although in his preface to *The Rhetorical Turn: Invention and Persuasion in the Conduct of Inquiry* (Chicago: University of Chicago Press, 1990), p. vii, he credits Richard Rorty with having suggested all three turns earlier. For one intellectual historian's brief history and evaluation of the linguistic turn, see Donald R. Kelley, "Horizons of Intellectual History: Retrospect, Circumspect, Prospect," *Journal of the History of Ideas,* 48 (Jan.–March 1987), 143–169. Rabinow and Sullivan updated their reader as *Interpretive Social Science: A Second Look* (Berkeley: University of California Press, 1987). See also John S. Nelson, Allan Megill, and Donald N. McCloskey, eds., *The Rhetoric of the Human Sciences: Language and Argument in Scholarship and Public Affairs* (Madison: University of Wisconsin Press, 1987).

2. Richard Harlan, *Superstructuralism: The Philosophy of Structuralism and Post-Structuralism* (London: Methuen, 1987), offers one introduction; but see also Jonathan Culler, *Structuralist Poetics: Structuralism, Linguistics, and the Study of Literature* (Ithaca: Cornell University Press, 1975) and *On Deconstruction: Theory and Criticism after Structuralism* (Ithaca: Cornell University Press, 1982). A succession of anthologies gives some idea of the promulgation of these French intellectual trends and their timing in the anglophone world: Richard Macksey and Eugenio Donato, eds., *The Structuralist Controversy: The Languages of Criticism and the Sciences of Man* (Baltimore: Johns Hopkins University Press, 1970); Jacques Ehrmann, ed., *Structuralism* (Garden City, N.Y.: Doubleday, 1970); Michael Lane, ed., *Introduction to Structuralism* (New York: Basic Books, 1970); Josué V. Harari, ed.,

Textual Strategies: Perspectives in Post-Structuralist Criticism (Ithaca: Cornell University Press, 1979); Robert Young, ed., *Untying the Text: A Post-Structuralist Reader* (Boston: Routledge & Kegan Paul, 1981); and William V. Spanos, Paul A. Bové, and Daniel O'Hara, eds., *The Question of Textuality: Strategies of Reading in Contemporary American Criticism* (Bloomington: Indiana University Press, 1982).

3. For a now standard version of this story see Vincent Descombes, *Modern French Philosophy,* trans. L. Scott-Fox and J. M. Harding (Cambridge: Cambridge University Press, 1980), esp. pp. 27–32, 180–186. See also Lutz Niethammer, *Posthistoire: Has History Come to an End?* trans. Patrick Camiller (London: Verso, 1992); and Julian Pefanis, *Heterology and the Postmodern: Bataille, Baudrillard, and Lyotard* (Durham, N.C.: Duke University Press, 1991). I am not referring to the newer debate initiated by Francis Fukuyama's article "The End of History?" *National Interest,* 16 (Summer 1989), 3–18, or his book *The End of History and the Last Man* (New York: Free Press, 1992).

4. Terrence McDonald, of the Department of History at the University of Michigan, invented the expression "the historic turn" for a conference called "The Historic Turn in the Social Sciences," held at the University of Michigan on October 5–7, 1990, and sponsored by the Program for the Comparative Study of Social Transformations. The papers are being published by University of Michigan Press under the title of the conference. Jonathan Rée uses the term "historic turns" in his article "The Vanity of Historicism," *New Literary History,* 22 (Autumn 1991), 962–963, 976–978. Whether the turn should be called "historical" rather than "historic" depends upon stylistic choice and perhaps on how its participants saw their efforts to transform their disciplines in the light of creating history themselves.

5. The sociologist C. Wright Mills invented the term "grand theory" to condemn the goal of systematic theory in the social sciences at the time he wrote *The Sociological Imagination* (New York: Oxford University Press, 1959). See also Quentin Skinner's introduction to *The Return of Grand Theory in the Human Sciences* (Cambridge: Cambridge University Press, 1985).

6. In addition to McDonald, *The Historic Turn,* see Theda Skocpol, ed., *Vision and Method in Historical Sociology* (Cambridge: Cambridge University Press, 1984); and Emiko Ohnuki-Tierney, ed., *Culture through Time: Anthropological Approaches* (Stanford: Stanford University Press, 1990), among others.

7. Murray Krieger, in his introduction to *The Aims of Representation: Subject/Text/History* (New York: Columbia University Press, 1987), plots the history of changing critical concerns in the United States, from a focus on the author, to writing itself, and now, as the subtitle suggests, the social and political context producing the text. For an introduction to the New Historicism see H. Aram Veeser, ed., *The New Historicism* (New York: Routledge, Chapman and Hall, 1989); Brook Thomas, *The New Historicism and Other Old-Fashioned Topics* (Princeton: Princeton University Press, 1991); and "New Historicisms, New Histories, and Others," special issue of *New Literary History,* 21 (Spring 1990).

8. The relationship in current scholarship between poststructuralist theory and postmodernism is a vexed one. Although postmodernism and poststructuralism have different genealogies because they started out in different disciplines, they now overlap greatly, especially when feminist and cultural studies are added to the mix. See, for example, Linda Hutcheon, *The Politics of Postmodernism* (London: Routledge,

1989); Joe Doherty, Elspeth Graham, and Mo Malek, eds., *Postmodernism and the Social Sciences* (New York: St. Martin's Press, 1992); Jane Flax, *Thinking Fragments: Psychoanalysis, Feminism, and Postmodernism in the Contemporary West* (Berkeley: University of California Press, 1990); Vincent B. Leitch, *Cultural Criticism, Literary Theory, Poststructuralism* (New York: Columbia University Press, 1992).

9. The words "reflexive" and "reflexivity" occur frequently in this book. To be reflexive is to be more than self-aware; it is also to be self-conscious and self-critical in theoretical outlook and practice. In the end, such reflexivity results in texts that refer to their own construction as they go about it; in other words, they are self-referring as well as self-reflecting.

10. Have "paradigm" and "problematic" come to possess similar meanings in current scholarly discourse, even though they derive from different political and conceptual contexts? Although "paradigm" was adumbrated by Thomas Kuhn and "problematic" comes from Louis Althusser, both seem to refer today to the set of presumptions that frame the questions and circum(in)scribe the answers. See, for example, the definition of problematic offered by Ellen Rooney, *Seductive Reasoning: Pluralism as the Problematic of Contemporary Theory* (Ithaca: Cornell University Press, 1989), p. 50: the "historically determinate structure of presuppositions that constitute a discourse, its enabling conditions . . . a conceptual matrix that defines objects within a field, fixes lines of inquiry, sets problems, and thereby determines the 'solutions' that can be generated within its limits."

11. This list does not pretend to be definitive or unbiased. For a different possible brief list, compare Ihab Hassan, "Pluralism in Postmodern Perspective," *Critical Inquiry*, 12 (Spring 1986), 503–520; and Madan Sarup, *An Introductory Guide to Post-structuralism and Postmodernism* (New York: Harvester Wheatsheaf, 1988), esp. pp. 1–5. Other lists could be compiled from the books cited in the preceding note. F. R. Ankersmit, "Historiography and Postmodernism," *History and Theory*, 28, no. 2 (1989), 137–153; Linda Hutcheon, *A Poetics of Postmodernism: History, Theory, and Fiction* (New York and London: Routledge, 1988); and John Toews, "Intellectual History after the Linguistic Turn: The Autonomy of Meaning and the Irreducibility of Experience," *American Historical Review*, 92 (Oct. 1987), 879–907, discuss some of the implications of postmodernism for historical practice.

12. Compare the usage of "plastic" and "autonomous" in Martin Hollis, *Models of Man: Philosophical Thoughts on Social Action* (Cambridge: Cambridge University Press, 1977). This argument is allied to but not identical with the one over human agency versus structural explanation in interpreting social behavior; see, for example, Anthony Appiah, "Tolerable Falsehoods: Agency and the Interests of Theory," in *Consequences of Theory*, ed. Jonathan Arac and Barbara Johnson (Baltimore: Johns Hopkins University Press, 1991), pp. 63–90.

13. Or so argues Harlan, *Superstructuralism*, pp. 67–68. Of these trends to denaturalization, those of feminist theory are most advanced in conceptualization, but even in this field not all problems are resolved to everyone's satisfaction. Compare in literature, for example, Toril Moi, *Sexual/Textual Politics: Feminist Literary Theory* (New York and London: Methuen, 1985); and Janet Todd, *Feminist Literary History* (New York and London: Routledge, 1988). In history see, for example, Joan Wallach Scott, *Gender and the Politics of History* (New York: Columbia University Press,

1988), esp. pts. 1 and 2; and Karen Offen, Ruth Roach Pierson, and Jane Randall, eds., *Writing Women's History: International Perspectives* (Bloomington: Indiana University Press, 1991), esp. pt. 1, "Conceptual and Methodological Issues."

14. Roland Barthes, *Mythologigues,* trans. Annette Lavers (New York: Hill and Wang, 1972), p. 141.

15. As do, for example, so many of the essays in Lawrence Grossberg, Cary Nelson, and Paula Treichler, eds., *Cultural Studies* (New York: Routledge, 1992).

16. Hence the popularity of Pierre Bourdieu, *Distinction: A Social Critique of the Judgement of Taste,* trans. Richard Nice (Cambridge, Mass.: Harvard University Press, 1984). See, for example, Richard Johnson, "What Is Cultural Studies Anyway?" *Social Text,* 16 (Winter 1986–87), 38–80.

17. Robert D'Amico, *Historicism and Knowledge* (London: Routledge, 1989), p. 147, but his book draws intellectual comfort from this conclusion. Compare the main title of Donna Haraway, "Situated Knowledges: The Science Question in Feminism and the Privilege of Partial Perspective," *Feminist Studies,* 39 (Fall 1988), 575–599.

18. Elizabeth Deeds Ermarth, *Sequel to History: Postmodernism and the Crisis of Time* (Princeton: Princeton University Press, 1992), p. 66.

19. See, among others, Brian Rigney, *Popular Culture in Modern France: A Study of Cultural Discourse* (London: Routledge, 1991); Graeme Turner, *British Cultural Studies: An Introduction* (Boston: Unwin Hyman, 1990); Anthony Easthope, *British Post-Structuralism since 1968* (London: Routledge, 1988); and Stanley Aronowitz, *Roll over Beethoven: The Return of Cultural Strife* (Hanover, N.H.: University Press of New England for Wesleyan University Press, 1993).

20. Terry Eagleton, *Literary Theory: An Introduction* (Oxford: Basil Blackwell, 1983), p. 205.

21. Bourdieu, *Distinction,* is the new classic study on these matters.

22. As quoted in Ellen K. Coughlin, "Growing Success and Conservatives' Attacks: Cultural Studies Scholars Ponder Future Directions," *Chronicle of Higher Education,* Jan. 18, 1989, p. A4.

23. Essentialism claims that a word or concept contains an essential core of meaning irrespective of a specific social or temporal context. Accordingly, words carry the same basic meaning from one text to another. The word "foundational" possesses an allied meaning when it refers to an assumption or proposition so fundamental to a conceptual system that the system could not exist without that premise.

24. The whole idea of this history is summarized in the title of Lawrence Levine's book: *Highbrow/Lowbrow: The Emergence of Cultural Hierarchy in America* (Cambridge, Mass.: Harvard University Press, 1988).

25. The theme of Coughlin, "Growing Success and Conservatives' Attacks," but see also Grossberg, Nelson, and Treichler, *Cultural Studies.* On the long tradition of combining cultural and political criticism see, for example, Giles Gunn, *The Culture of Criticism and the Criticism of Culture* (New York: Oxford University Press, 1987); and Tobin Sievers, *The Ethics of Criticism* (Ithaca: Cornell University Press, 1988).

26. Karl Mannheim, *Ideology and Utopia: An Introduction to the Sociology of Knowledge,* trans. Louis With and Edward Shils (New York: Harcourt, Brace, 1936), pp. 67–68, 239–275; and noted again more recently by Anthony Giddens in *Central*

Problems in Social Theory: Action, Structure, and Contradiction in Social Analysis (Berkeley: University of California Press, 1979), pp. 168–174; but see his whole chapter on the reflexive problems of ideological analysis.

27. Cathy N. Davidson, *Revolution and the Word: The Rise of the Novel in America* (New York: Oxford University Press, 1986), pp. 255–256; the ellipses mark words omitted as specific to literary history.

28. Richard Rorty, *Philosophy and the Mirror of Nature* (Princeton: Princeton University Press, 1979), was important for this movement in the United States.

29. This has been a major goal of the University of Iowa Project on the Rhetoric of Inquiry, for which see Nelson, Megill, and McCloskey, *The Rhetoric of the Human Sciences;* and Simons, *Rhetoric in the Human Sciences* and *The Rhetorical Turn.*

30. Leitch, *Cultural Criticism, Literary Theory, Poststructuralism,* p. 37.

31. Barthes, *Mythologigues,* p. 75.

32. No social scientist in the United States argued earlier and more persistently for a transformation of his discipline's orientation than Richard H. Brown; the title of his most recent book, *Society as Text: Essays on Rhetoric, Reason, and Reality* (Chicago: University of Chicago Press, 1987), conveys the general idea, as does his earlier *A Poetic for Sociology: Toward a Logic of Discovery for the Human Sciences* (Cambridge: Cambridge University Press, 1977). In history the seminal American thinker is Hayden White, with *Metahistory: The Historical Imagination in Nineteenth-Century Europe* (Baltimore: Johns Hopkins University Press, 1973), *Tropics of Discourse: Essays in Cultural Criticism* (Baltimore: Johns Hopkins University Press, 1978), and *The Content of the Form: Narrative Discourse and Historical Representation* (Baltimore: Johns Hopkins University Press, 1987).

33. Easthope, *British Post-Structuralism,* pp. 187–188, lists five definitions of deconstruction, but see all of chap. 12. The difference between the nature of deconstruction in France and in the United States is the major theme of Art Berman, *From the New Criticism to Deconstruction: The Reception of Structuralism and Post-Structuralism* (Urbana: University of Illinois Press, 1988). Compare, among many in English on deconstruction, Jonathan Culler, *On Deconstruction: Theory and Criticism after Structuralism* (Ithaca: Cornell University Press, 1982); Vincent B. Leitch, *Deconstructive Criticism: An Advanced Introduction* (New York: Columbia University Press, 1983); Christopher Norris, *Contested Faculties: Philosophy and Theory after Deconstruction* (New York and London: Methuen, 1985); Danny J. Anderson, "Deconstruction: Critical Strategy/Strategic Criticism," in *Contemporary Literary Theory,* ed. G. Douglas Atkinson and Laura Morrow (Amherst: University of Massachusetts Press, 1989), pp. 137–157.

34. Whether Derrida's oft-quoted words meant he believed that nothing existed outside its textualization and that therefore everything could and must be interpreted as a(nother) text is debated, perhaps paradoxically given the supposed loss of signification in deconstruction itself.

35. Raymond Tallis, *Not Saussure: A Critique of Post-Saussurean Literary Theory* (London: Macmillan, 1988), discusses this problem from a perspective in opposition to much of recent literary and rhetorical theory.

36. I use this expression complete with parentheses to indicate both text as product and textualization as the process of producing one. Although in historical practice "text" and "textualization" refer both to sources from the past and to the

synthetic work the historian produces in the present, my use of this term throughout my own text usually refers to the latter.

37. See Berman, *From the New Criticism to Deconstruction;* and Frank Lentricchia, *After the New Criticism* (Chicago: University of Chicago Press, 1980).

38. For an early statement in this vein see Paul Ricoeur, "The Model of the Text: Meaningful Action Considered as Text," in *Interpretive Social Science: A Reader,* ed. Paul Rabinow and William M. Sullivan (Berkeley: University of California Press, 1979), pp. 73–101. Compare Brown, *Society as Text,* esp. chap. 6, "Social Reality as Narrative Text: Interactions, Institutions, and Polities as Language."

39. H. Stuart Hughes, *History as Art and as Science: Twin Vistas on the Past* (New York: Harper & Row, 1964), was one such assessment.

40. White, *Metahistory,* p. 2.

41. A. J. Greimas and J. Courtés, *Semiotics and Language: An Analytical Dictionary,* trans. Larry Crist and Daniel Patte et al. (Bloomington: Indiana University Press, 1982), p. 143.

42. Ibid., p. 353.

43. Sande Cohen, *Historical Culture: On the Recoding of an Academic Discipline* (Berkeley: University of California Press, 1986), p. 329.

44. Harry Ritter, *Dictionary of Concepts in History* (Westport, Conn.: Greenwood Press, 1986), p. 193; but for other views compare his brief essays on "Constructionism," "Constitution," "Interpretation," and "Relativism."

45. For a good statement of this dilemma and its implications for radical politics, see Ellen Somekawa and Elizabeth Smith, "Theorizing the Writing of History, or 'I Can't Think Why It Should Be So Dull, for a Great Deal of It Must Be Invention,'" *Journal of Social History,* 22 (Fall 1988), 145–161.

46. Gertrude Himmelfarb, "Some Reflections on the New History," *American Historical Review,* 94 (June 1989), 665.

47. As is suggested in the title of her article, "Telling It as You Like It: Post-Modernist History and the Flight from Fact," *Times Literary Supplement,* no. 4672 (Oct. 16, 1992), 12–15. See also the complaints of Perez Zagorin, "Historiography and Postmodernism: Reconsiderations," *History and Theory,* 29, no. 3 (1990), 263–274; and a reply by F. R. Ankersmit, ibid., pp. 275–296.

48. Toews, "Intellectual History after the Linguistic Turn," pp. 901–902. Compare Gabrielle M. Spiegel, "History, Historicism, and the Social Logic of the Text in the Middle Ages," *Speculum,* 65 (Jan. 1990), 59–68.

49. Bryan D. Palmer, *The Descent into Discourse: The Reification of Language and the Writing of Social History* (Philadelphia: Temple University Press, 1990), p. 188.

50. Linda Orr, "The Revenge of Literature: A History of History," *New Literary History,* 18 (Autumn 1986), 1–26, quotation from p. 1.

51. As G. R. Elton, *Return to Essentials: Some Reflections on the Present State of Historical Study* (Cambridge: Cambridge University Press, 1991), esp. pp. 27–73, shows in his reiteration of old arguments and the refusal to understand what is at issue or even to read much of what he condemns. Notable exceptions are Nancy Partner, "Making Up Lost Time: Writing on the Writing of History," *Speculum,* 61 (Jan. 1986), 90–117; and Lynn Hunt, "History as Gesture; or, The Scandal of History," in Arac and Johnson, *Consequences of Theory,* pp. 91–107; idem, "History beyond

Social Theory," in *The "States of Theory": History, Art, and Critical Discourse,* ed. David Carroll (New York: Columbia University Press, 1990), pp. 95–111; plus her books on the French Revolution. These implications were not addressed by the journal of the American Historical Association until David Harlan, "Intellectual History and the Return of Literature," *American Historical Review,* 94 (June 1989), 581–609; David Hollinger, "The Return of the Prodigal: The Persistence of Historical Knowing," ibid., pp. 610–621; and reply by Harlan, ibid., pp. 622–626; and Joyce Appleby, "One Good Turn Deserves Another: Moving beyond the Linguistic: A Response to David Harlan," ibid. (Dec. 1989), 1326–32. Whether and to what extent there was a crisis in current historical practice was the subject of a plenary session of the American Historical Association meetings in December 1988, the content of which was published in *American Historical Review* under the title "The Old History and the New," 94 (June 1989), 654–698. See Peter Novick, *That Noble Dream: The "Objectivity Quest" and the American Historical Profession* (Cambridge: Cambridge University Press, 1988), chaps. 15–16, for developments in the historical profession in the United States. See also the brief comments under the heading "History and Postmodernism" in *Past and Present* by Lawrence Stone (no. 131, May 1991, 217–218), Patrick Joyce (no. 133, Nov. 1991, 204–209), and Catriona Kelly (ibid., pp. 209–213).

52. The debate in the profession about whether or not Foucault wrote history indicates both the possibilities and limits of contemporary historical assumptions in professional discourse. See, for example, Allan Megill, "The Reception of Foucault by Historians," *Journal of the History of Ideas,* 48 (Jan.–March 1987), 117–140. Hayden White has always been cited more by scholars outside his discipline than by those inside it, according to Wulf Kansteiner, "Hayden White's Critique of the Writing of History," *History and Theory,* 32, no. 3 (1993), 272–295. Dominick LaCapra has been accused of subverting intellectual history by arguing the importance of Derrida and Bakhtin for the field. For example, Russell Jacoby, "A New Intellectual History," *American Historical Review,* 97 (April 1992), 405–424; and reply by LaCapra, "Intellectual History and Its Ways," ibid., pp. 425–439. LaCapra, *Soundings in Critical Theory* (Ithaca: Cornell University Press, 1989), pp. 5–7, explains his relationship to Derrida and Bakhtin, but see all of his chap. 1.

53. Among the first to write books about Foucault and other continental thinkers or about their ideas and implications are Allan Megill, *Prophets of Extremity: Nietzsche, Heidegger, Foucault, Derrida* (Berkeley: University of California Press, 1985); and Mark Poster, *Foucault, Marxism and History: Mode of Production versus Mode of Information* (Cambridge: Polity Press, 1984). One intellectual historian, Michael Ermarth, mockingly titled his condemnation "Mindful Matters: The Empire's New Codes and the Plight of Modern European Intellectual History," *Journal of Modern History* (Sept. 1985), 506–527.

54. Toews, "Intellectual History after the Linguistic Turn," pp. 881–882. The good multiculturalist will immediately ask: whose experience is preferred as the determiner of the meaning of experience? Joan W. Scott, "The Evidence of Experience," *Critical Inquiry,* 17 (Summer 1991), 787–790, criticizes Toews for never defining experience and argues that it is shaped and conveyed through socially determined discursive practices. Most important, she accuses him of being unhistorical about the changing experiences of persons and how the history of a society shapes experience and gives it meaning in that society.

55. Toews, "Intellectual History after the Linguistic Turn," p. 882.

56. Ibid., p. 907.

57. Sharing Toews's resolution, for example, are Ermarth, "Mindful Matters"; and Spiegel, "History, Historicism, and Social Logic" and the responses it evoked in *Past and Present* under the heading "History and Postmodernism"; Saul Cornell, "Early American History in a Postmodern Age," *William and Mary Quarterly,* 3rd ser., 50 (April 1993), 329–341; and the impressive survey by John Zammito, "Are We Being Theoretical Yet? The New Historicism, the New Philosophy of History, and 'Practicing Historians,'" *Journal of Modern History,* 65 (Dec. 1993), 783–814.

58. Palmer, *Descent into Discourse,* p. xiv.

59. See, for example, Steven Watts, "Academe's Leftists Are Something of a Fraud," *Chronicle of Higher Education,* 38, no. 34 (April 29, 1992), A40. Compare idem, "The Idiocy of American Studies: Poststructuralism, Language, and Politics in the Age of Self-Fulfillment," *American Quarterly,* 34 (Dec. 1991), 625–660, with responses in ibid., 44 (Sept. 1992), 439–458, and his reply, pp. 459–462. Likewise, Christopher Norris, "Postmodernizing History: Right Wing Revisionism and the Uses of History," *Southern Review,* 21 (July 1988), 123–140, feared that extension of then current literary theory played into the hands of conservatives.

60. Himmelfarb, "Telling It as You Like It," pp. 15, 12.

61. See, among others, Donald Morton and Mas'ud Zavarzadeh, eds., *Theory/Pedagogy/Politics: Texts for Change* (Urbana: University of Illinois Press, 1991); Hutcheon, *The Politics of Postmodernism;* Michèle Barrett, *The Politics of Truth: From Marx to Foucault* (Cambridge: Polity Press, 1991); Eve Tavor Bannet, *Postcultural Theory: Critical Theory and the Marxist Paradigm* (New York: Paragon House, 1993); and Charles Altieri, "Temporality and the Necessity for the Dialectic: The Missing Dimension of Contemporary Theory," *New Literary History,* 23 (Winter 1992), 133–158. Opponents of both poststructuralism and postmodernism accuse the proponents of each movement of taking stands on both sides of the political spectrum. See, for example, Joe Doherty on the paradoxes of politics in Doherty, Graham, and Malek, *Postmodernism and the Social Sciences,* pp. 196–220. Donald Morton, "The Crisis of the Narrative in the Postnarratology Era: Paul Goodman's *Empire City* as (Post)Modern Intervention," *New Literary History,* 24 (Spring 1993), 408–409, divides the late and postmodernist theorists into "ludic" and "resistance" camps.

62. See the overlap between cultural poetics and cultural materialism in essays collected in Veeser, *The New Historicism;* and the critique of what Altieri calls the first generation of New Historicists in "Temporality and the Necessity for the Dialectic."

63. Whether or not poststructuralism renders historiography impossible is the topic of the essays in Derek Attridge, Geoff Bennington, and Robert Young, eds., *Post-Structuralism and the Question of History* (Cambridge: Cambridge University Press, 1987).

64. For a spectrum of differing approaches to (con)text ranged very roughly from one end to the other of the scale in terms of what they either advocate or summarize, see Giovanni Levi, "On Microhistory," in *New Perspectives on Historical Writing,* ed. Peter Burke (University Park: Pennsylvania State University Press, 1992), pp. 106–108; David Boucher, *Texts in Context: Revisionist Methods for Studying the History of Ideas* (Dordrecht: Martinus Nijhoff, 1985); James Tully, ed., *Meaning and Its*

Context: Quentin Skinner and His Critics (Princeton: Princeton University Press, 1988); Mark Bevir, "The Errors of Linguistic Contextualism," *History and Theory*, 31, no. 3 (1992), 276–298; Dominick LaCapra, *Rethinking Intellectual History: Texts, Contexts, Language* (Ithaca: Cornell University Press, 1983), pp. 35–59; Martin Jay, "The Textual Approach to Intellectual History," in *Fact and Fiction: German History and Literature, 1848–1924,* ed. Gisela Brude-Firnau and Karin J. MacHardy (Tübingen: Francke, 1990), pp. 77–86; Hutcheon, *A Poetics of Postmodernism,* pp. 154–156.

65. "Interpretive community" comes from Stanley Fish, *Is There a Text in This Class? The Authority of Interpretive Communities* (Cambridge, Mass.: Harvard University Press, 1980); "reading formation" is from Tony Bennett, "Texts in History: The Determinations of Readings and Their Texts" in Attridge, Bennington, and Young, *Post-Structuralism and the Question of History,* p. 70.

66. See the references cited in note 2 above on early approaches to textualism in the anglophone world, especially Harari, *Textual Strategies;* Young, *Untying the Text;* Spanos et al., *The Question of Textuality,* for the diversity of its proponents. Cesare Segre with collaboration of Tomaso Kemeny, *Introduction to the Analysis of the Literary Text,* trans. John Meddemmen (Bloomington: Indiana University Press, 1988), presents an encyclopedic introduction to textualism; while John Mowat, *Text: The Genealogy of an Antidisciplinary Object* (Durham, N.C.: Duke University Press, 1992), provides a history of some its proponents and their theories.

67. As this brief paragraph implies, textualism embraces diverse approaches ranging from formalist models to polyvocal discursive models. In general, these approaches ranged historically from earlier formalist, structuralist models to later poststructuralist, dialogical, and discursive models. See Mowat, *Text.* Two important articles on the problems of textualism as theory are Edward Said, "The Problem of Textuality: Two Exemplary Positions," *Critical Inquiry,* 4 (Summer 1978), 673–714; and Nancy Fraser, "The Uses and Abuses of French Discourse Theory for Feminist Politics," in *Revaluing French Feminism: Critical Essays on Difference, Agency, and Culture,* ed. Nancy Fraser and Sandra Lee Bartky (Bloomington: Indiana University Press, 1992), pp. 177–194.

68. Much of Spiegel, "History, Historicism, and Social Logic," esp. pp. 68–78, wrestles with the problems of distinguishing text and context from both the linguistic and historic turns before she takes a position congenial to anglophone historians.

69. The term "intertextuality" comes originally from Julia Kristeva. My usage of the word broadens its original technical definition, but I believe this accords with scholarly practice today. See, for example, the definition given in Chris Baldick, *The Concise Oxford Dictionary of Literary Terms* (Oxford: Oxford University Press, 1990), p. 112.

70. See again Ricoeur, "The Model of the Text"; Brown, *Society as Text* and *A Poetic for Sociology;* plus Clifford Geertz, *The Interpretation of Cultures* (New York: Basic Books, 1973), chap. 1.

71. Berman, *From the New Criticism to Deconstruction,* p. 169.

72. Richard Rorty calls textualism a latter-day form of idealism in his *Consequences of Pragmatism (Essays: 1972–1980)* (Minneapolis: University of Minnesota Press, 1982), chap. 8, "Nineteenth-Century Idealism and Twentieth-Century Textualism."

73. Myra Jehlen, "Patrolling the Borders," *Radical History Review,* 43 (Winter 1989), 34–35, discusses the "linguicizing of history" as "vulgar linguicism." Palmer, *Descent into Discourse,* p. 165, picks up this phrase as well as the complaint.

74. On the popularity of crisis as a mode of historical description, see Ritter, *Dictionary of Concepts in History,* pp. 79–84. Harvey J. Kaye, *The Powers of the Past: Reflections on the Crisis and the Promise of History* (New York: Harvester Wheatsheaf, 1991), begins his book with a chapter titled "The Crisis of History," which he sees as the evaporation of faith in the "grand governing narrative." Simon Schama, "Clio Has a Problem," *New York Times Magazine,* Sept. 8, 1991, pp. 30–34, laments the decline of great narrative history and the consequent loss of an audience for history.

75. Few historians discuss what would constitute a new kind of history and what it would look like. Peter Burke, *History and Social Theory* (Cambridge: Polity Press, 1992), pp. 121–129, makes a similar point; but see for some suggestions idem, ed., *New Perspectives on Historical Writing* (University Park: Pennsylvania State University Press, 1991), chap. 11; Robert A. Rosenstone, "Experiments in Writing the Past—Is Anybody Interested?" *Perspectives* (newsletter of the American Historical Association), 30, no. 9 (Dec. 1992), 10, 12, 20; and Stephan Yeo, "Whose Story? An Argument from within Current Historical Practice in Britain," *Journal of Contemporary History,* 21 (April 1986), 295–320. For more on this topic see Chapter 9.

76. For two such complaints, see Watts, "The Idiocy of American Studies"; and Elizabeth Fox-Genovese, "Literary Criticism and the Politics of the New Historicism," in Veeser, *The New Historicism,* pp. 213–24. Milder criticism comes from Hayden White in ibid., pp. 293–302; Spiegel, "History, Historicism, and Social Logic," pp. 70–75; and Hunt, "History as Gesture." Thomas, *The New Historicism,* on the other hand, maintains that the New Historicism is just traditional historicization in literary studies under a new name.

2. Narratives and Historicization

1. Lawrence Stone, "The Revival of Narrative," *Past and Present,* no. 85 (1979), 3–24, reprinted in idem, *The Past and the Present* (Boston: Routledge & Kegan Paul, 1981), pp. 77–96. William Palmer, "Lawrence Stone and the Revival of Narrative," *South Atlantic Quarterly,* 85 (Spring 1986), 176–182, offers important emendations to Stone's claims and story. Compare Mark Phillips, "The Revival of Narrative: Thoughts on a Current Historiographical Debate," *University of Toronto Quarterly,* 53 (Winter 1983–84), 149–165. See also Peter Burke's concluding essay, "History of Events and the Revival of Narrative," in *New Perspectives on Historical Writing,* ed. Peter Burke (University Park: Pennsylvania State University Press, 1991), pp. 233–248.

2. Savoie Lottinville, *The Rhetoric of History* (Norman: University of Oklahoma Press, 1976), pp. 49–50.

3. See Paul Ricoeur, *Time and Narrative,* trans. Kathleen McLaughlin Blamey and David Pellauer, 3 vols. (Chicago: University of Chicago Press, 1984–88), vol. 1, pp. 99–111, for comments on the *Annales* school and "the eclipse of the event in French historiography." Compare among others Traian Stoianovich, *French Histori-*

cal Method: The Annales Paradigm (Ithaca: Cornell University Press, 1976); Georg G. Iggers, *New Directions in European Historiography,* rev. ed. (Middletown, Conn.: Wesleyan University Press, 1984), pp. 43–79; Peter Burke, *The French Historical Revolution: The Annales School, 1929–1989* (London: Polity Press, 1990); Lynn Hunt, "French History in the Last Twenty Years: The Rise and Fall of the *Annales* Paradigm," *Journal of Contemporary History,* 21 (April 1986), 209–224. Philippe Carrard, *Poetics of the New History: French Historical Discourse from Braudel to Chartier* (Baltimore: Johns Hopkins University Press, 1992), provides a literary critic's approach to the *Annales* school.

4. I borrow the term "social science history" from the name of the Social Science History Association and its journal, *Social Science History* (1976–). It was chiefly associated with quantification and statistical analysis, but its methodological philosophy and its goals were far broader than the movement's critics allowed. For one explication of this philosophy, see Robert Fogel, "'Scientific' History and Traditional History," in Robert W. Fogel and Geoffrey R. Elton, *Which Road to the Past? Two Views of History* (New Haven: Yale University Press, 1983), pp. 5–70. Compare the covering law argument in philosophy and "the eclipse of understanding" in Ricoeur, *Time and Narrative,* vol. 1, pp. 111–120.

5. Both Carrard, *Poetics of the New History,* pp. 62–70; and Palmer, "Lawrence Stone and the Revival of Narrative," question whether Stone was correct in attributing narrative to those *Annalistes'* works that he does.

6. Stone, "The Revival of Narrative," pp. 3–4.

7. The idea of "normal history" derives from Thomas Kuhn, *The Structure of Scientific Revolutions* (Chicago: University of Chicago Press, 1962), who used the term "normal science" to designate the fundamental premises, the various practices, and the basic products of the scientific enterprise in any given era. I use "normal history" throughout this book to indicate the paradigmatic assumptions of historical scholarship in our time (but the term could be applied to earlier eras of historical practice also). I employ this term in preference to "traditional history" because historians labeled both "nontraditional" and "traditional" practice their crafts using the same larger set of assumptions. "Normal historians" is my shorthand for historians applying the normal paradigm in their practice.

8. F. R. Ankersmit, *The Reality Effect in the Writing of History: The Dynamics of Historiographical Topology* (Amsterdam: Koninklijke Nederlandische Akadamie van Wetenshaften Noord-Hollandische, 1989), pp. 5–6. As Ankersmit observes, these two postulates both presuppose and contradict each other from the standpoint of recent literary and rhetorical theory.

9. For example, compare chaps. 8–11 and chaps. 3–7 in Louis Gottschalk, *Understanding History: A Primer of Historical Methods,* 2d ed. (New York: Alfred A. Knopf, 1969). See also parts 2 and 3 in Jacques Barzun and Henry F. Graf, *The Modern Researcher* (New York: Harcourt, Brace and World, 1957). An exception to this generalization is Lottinville, *The Rhetoric of History.*

10. Perhaps the best proof of this point is afforded by a comparison of the diagrams in Robert F. Berkhofer, Jr., *A Behavioral Approach to Historical Analysis* (New York: Free Press, 1969), pp. 21, 23, 25, with the ones in this text.

11. Thomas L. Haskell, *The Emergence of Professional Social Science: The American Social Science Association and the Nineteenth-Century Crisis of Authority* (Ur-

bana: University of Illinois Press, 1977), p. 20. Although Haskell argued this specifically in relation to Thomas Kuhn's conception of a paradigm, I trust the interpretation I give his sentence does not distort his larger meaning.

12. Charles Tilly, "Retrieving European Lives," in *Reliving the Past: The Worlds of Social History,* ed. Olivier Zunz (Chapel Hill: University of North Carolina Press, 1985), p. 12.

13. Henri-Irénée Marrou, *The Meaning of History,* trans. Robert J. Olsen (Baltimore: Helicon, 1966), p. 192.

14. This term, borrowed from Gilbert Ryle and popularized in the human sciences by Clifford Geertz, has its own context and therefore meaning in Geertz, *The Interpretation of Cultures* (New York: Basic Books, 1973), chap. 1, "Thick Description: Toward an Interpretive Theory of Culture." Geertz put forth this term as a way of describing culture "as interworked systems of construable signs . . . culture is not a power, something to which social events, behaviors, institutions, or processes can be causally attributed, it is context, something within which they can be intelligibly—that is thickly—described"; p. 14.

15. Although Hayden White, *Metahistory: The Historical Imagination in Nineteenth-Century Europe* (Baltimore: Johns Hopkins University Press, 1973), pp. 18–20, argues that contextualism is only one of four modes of formal argument available to historians, he also admits that it "can be regarded as a *combination* of the dispersive impulses behind Formism on the one hand and the integrative impulses behind Organicism on the other hand." Since it tries to avoid the abstraction of organicism and mechanism, he asserts, it is preferred in normal historical practice, along with formism.

16. Dominick LaCapra offers a stimulating list of six kinds of contexts in "Rethinking Intellectual History and Reading Texts," in *Modern European Intellectual History: Reappraisals and New Perspectives,* ed. Dominick LaCapra and Steven L. Kaplan (Ithaca: Cornell University Press, 1982), pp. 57–78; reprinted in Dominick LaCapra, *Rethinking Intellectual History: Texts, Contexts, Language* (Ithaca: Cornell University Press, 1983), pp. 35–59. Dale H. Porter's hierarchy of levels of abstraction in historical analysis, from the whole event and individuals through social groups, institutions, and ideational elements, to major forces or factors and the universal significance of the event(s), in *The Emergence of the Past: A Theory of Historical Explanation* (Chicago: University of Chicago Press, 1981), pp. 86–97, can also be read as kinds of context. He uses the Reform Bill of 1832 in England as his example in applying these levels, but one can just as well read the example as ways of contextualizing an event in normal history.

17. As E. P. Thompson argued, for example, in "Anthropology and the Discipline of Historical Context," *Midland History,* 1 (Spring 1972), 41–55. As Michael Kammen observes, "a scrupulous attention to context" is one of the "most distinctive attributes" of the historical craft; *Selvages & Biases: The Fabric of History in American Culture* (Ithaca: Cornell University Press, 1987), p. 36.

18. Mark Cousins, "The Practice of Historical Investigation," in *Post-Structuralism and the Question of History,* ed. Derek Attridge, Geoff Bennington, and Robert Young (Cambridge: Cambridge University Press, 1987), p. 127, calls anachronism the temporal equivalent of ethnocentrism, or "chronocentrism." Compare my term "temporocentrism" in *A Behavioral Approach to Historical Analysis,* pp. 144–145. That

the ideal of historicity demands the very notion of anachronism, however, is the argument of Jonathan Rée, "The Vanity of Historicism," *New Literary History,* 22 (Autumn 1991), 978–981, for the present could not describe or explicate the past without committing anachronism.

19. David Boucher, *Texts in Context: Revisionist Methods for Studying the History of Ideas* (Dordrecht: Martinus Nijhoff, 1985), discusses standard arguments of the issues by intellectual historians. James Tilly, ed., *Meaning and Its Context: Quentin Skinner and His Critics* (Princeton: Princeton University Press, 1988), offers less of relevance on this issue than the title would indicate; but see Mark Bevir, "The Errors of Linguistic Contextualism," *History and Theory,* 31, no. 3 (1992), 276–298.

20. William H. Walsh, "Colligatory Concepts in History," in *The Philosophy of History,* ed. Patrick Gardiner (Oxford: Oxford University Press, 1974), p. 136. See also idem, *An Introduction to the Philosophy of History,* 3rd ed. (London: Hutchinson, 1967), pp. 59–64, for another discussion of what he means by the term "colligation." The notion is discussed and clarified in L. B. Cebik, "Colligation and the Writing of History," *Monist,* 53 (Jan. 1969), 40–57; C. Behan McCullagh, "Colligation and Classification in History," *History and Theory,* 27, no. 3 (1978), 267–284; and William H. Dray, *On History and Philosophers of History* (Leiden: E. J. Brill, 1989), chap. 2. Other references are given under the entry "Colligation" in Harry Ritter, *Dictionary of Concepts in History* (Westport, Conn.: Greenwood Press, 1986), pp. 50–55. Compare the notion of configuration as the basis of historical understanding in Louis Mink, "History and Fiction as Modes of Comprehension," *New Literary History,* 1 (Spring 1970), 541–558; and the elaboration of this idea as part of emplotment by Ricoeur, *Time and Narrative,* esp. vol. 1, chap. 2, and vol. 2. I discuss emplotment in Chapter 5.

21. White, *Metahistory,* pp. 18–19.

22. Ritter, *Dictionary of Concepts in History,* pp. 183–188, surveys the differing meanings of "historicism" and provides a brief bibliography to this much-discussed topic. The philosopher Robert D'Amico discusses the implications of the concept in *Historicism and Knowledge* (London: Routledge, 1989).

23. White, *Metahistory,* pp. 17–18.

24. Only social scientific historians seem to have tried to apply what is called the covering law model of historical explanation to their analysis of evidence and the building of models. Many of the important articles are reprinted in Patrick Gardiner, ed., *Theories of History* (Glencoe, Ill.: Free Press, 1959), pp. 344–475. See Ricoeur, *Time and Narrative,* vol. 1, pp. 110–155, for exposition and analysis of the issues between the covering law model exponents and their narrativist opponents. Contextualism poses conceptual problems for the social scientific historian because it seems to be a case of all—that is, only—dependent variables without any independent ones to explain the phenomena under investigation.

25. Walsh, "Colligatory Concepts in History," pp. 143–144, uses this formula, borrowed from Hegel's "concrete universal," as proper to colligation.

26. Walsh, *Introduction to the Philosophy of History,* pp. 23–24; compare ibid., pp. 62–63.

27. I maintain this despite the arguments by McCullagh, "Colligation and Classification in History," and Walsh, "Colligatory Concepts in History," on the use of general classificatory terms for colligation, such as "revolution" and "renaissance."

28. Paul Veyne, *Writing History: Essay on Epistemology,* trans. Mina Moore-Rinvolucri (Middletown, Conn.: Wesleyan University Press, 1984), p. 124.

29. Raymond Grew, "The Case for Comparing Histories," *American Historical Review,* 85 (Oct. 1980), 773; my emphasis.

30. George M. Frederickson, "Comparative History," in *The Past before Us: Contemporary Historical Writing in the United States,* ed. Michael Kammen (Ithaca: Cornell University Press, 1980), p. 473.

31. Ibid., p. 459.

32. George Frederickson, "Giving a Comparative Dimension to American History: Problems and Opportunities," *Journal of Interdisciplinary History,* 16 (Summer 1965), 109.

33. Grew, "The Case for Comparing Histories," p. 763.

34. Compare Walsh, "Colligatory Concepts in History"; McCullagh, "Colligation and Classification in History"; and Cebik, "Colligation and the Writing of History."

35. Robert R. Palmer, *The Age of the Democratic Revolution: A Political History of Europe and America, 1760–1800,* 2 vols. (Princeton: Princeton University Press, 1959–1964).

36. Ritter, *Dictionary of Concepts in History,* p. 457, argues that *Zeitgeist* and "climate of opinion" are closely associated with colligation. "Paradigm" is the well-known term of Thomas Kuhn, and "episteme" (my anglicization of *épistème*) the equally well-known term of Michel Foucault from *The Order of Things: An Archaeology of Human Sciences* (New York: Pantheon, 1970).

37. To emphasize that the presumption of rupture between present and past is foundational to historical discourse, Michel de Certeau, *The Writing of History,* trans. Tom Conley (New York: Columbia University Press, 1988), speaks of the dead and absent of history as the Other, for example, on pp. 2, 14, 38, 46–47, 99.

38. The words "narrative" and "narration" pose terminological problems for those who would be precise about the differences among a narrative as a product, narration as the process for its production, the principles governing both that product and its production, and the study of those principles. No one set of terms has gained total acceptance to clarify the distinctions, but I have tried in this book to use "narrative" only for the product. "Narration" is the telling of the narrative, or the recounting of a story, but seems inadequate to refer both to the overall process involved in producing narratives in general and to the principles involved in the practice. Those who discuss narratives employ "narrativity" to refer to the principles underlying narratives, or what accounts for their form and structure. To differentiate between narration as *narrating,* the telling of a story, and its principles, I have followed those scholars who employ "narrativization" as the term for the general processes of producing narratives and the principles underlying them. The explicit, formal study of the principles underlying narratives and narration is called "narratology"; narratologists seek, in short, a general theory of narrativity and narrativization. Gerald Prince, *A Dictionary of Narratology* (Lincoln: University of Nebraska Press, 1987), provides one introduction to these terms.

39. Roland Barthes glibly asserted that narrative was universal and transhistorical; quoted at the beginning of Ann Rigney, "Narrativity and Historical Representation," *Poetics Today,* 12 (Fall 1991), 591–605, who tries to categorize the

differing definitions of what constitutes narrative as part of her review of Hayden White's *The Content of Form: Narrative Discourse and Historical Representation.* Jack Goody, "The Time of Telling and the Telling of Time in Written and Oral Cultures," in *Chronotypes: The Construction of Time,* ed. John Bender and David E. Wellbury (Stanford: Stanford University Press, 1991), pp. 77–96, questions whether narrative is as universal as so many scholars assume.

40. William Cronon, "A Place for Stories: Nature, History, and Narrative," *Journal of American History,* 78 (March 1992), 1349, n. 3, claims that he will use story and narrative interchangeably as a result of the difficulty of differentiating the two, but he defines narrative on p. 1367. Thomas M. Leitch, *What Stories Are: Narrative Theory and Interpretation* (University Park: Pennsylvania State University Press, 1986), explores the difficulty in trying to specify his main title. The problem is especially exemplified in the effort to follow the same supposed narrative across media, for example, a novel or history made into a film.

41. I follow Ricoeur, *Time and Narrative,* vol. 1, pp. 178–179, in taking this position on the nature of narrative and plot. Compare the notion of emplotment in Chapter 5. This approach to sequence in narrative was taken by E. M. Forster in *Aspects of the Novel* (London: Methuen, 1927).

42. Seymour Chatman, *Coming to Terms: The Rhetoric of Narrative in Fiction and Film* (Ithaca: Cornell University Press, 1990), p. 9, specifies not only causality but also a special kind of contingency as crucial to the narrative.

43. This was the issue dividing those debating, first, the covering law model versus the narrative model in Anglo-American philosophy, for which see Ricoeur, *Time and Narrative,* vol. 1, pp. 111–155; Porter, *The Emergence of the Past,* pp. 24–62; and F. R. Ankersmit, "The Dilemma of Contemporary Anglo-Saxon Philosophy of History," *History and Theory,* 25, no. 4 (1986), an issue titled "Knowing and Telling History: The Anglo-Saxon Debate," pp. 1–27; and second, the nature of plot and narrative, for which see Ricoeur, *Time and Narrative,* vol. 2, and the works cited below in note 46.

44. See Hayden White on the difference customarily presumed between annal and chronicle on one hand and history on the other in "The Value of Narrativity in the Representation of Reality," in idem, *The Content of the Form: Narrative Discourse and Historical Representation* (Baltimore: Johns Hopkins University Press, 1987), pp. 1–25; but see his additional comments on the matter in ibid., p. 42.

45. Even in so-called postmodern narratives? See the conclusion of Chapter 7. Historians have long had problems with the idea of causation, as Ritter, *Dictionary of Concepts in History,* pp. 31–39, acknowledges. This concern about causation has been exacerbated in the debates over historical structure versus historical agency in post-Marxian theory and by the fusion of text and context in so much of poststructuralist and New Historicist theorizing.

46. In addition to Leitch, *What Stories Are,* Wallace Martin, *Recent Theories of Narrative* (Ithaca: Cornell University Press, 1986); Shlomith Rimmon-Kenan, *Narrative Fiction: Contemporary Poetics* (London: Methuen, 1983); and Mieke Bal, *Narratology: Introduction to the Theory of the Narrative* (Toronto: University of Toronto Press, 1985), survey modern theories of narratology. Prince, *A Dictionary of Narratology,* offers a guide to the vocabulary of the field as well as bibliography. For some indication of the different approaches to narrative in history these days, see the special issue on "The Representation of Historical Events," *History and Theory,* 26, no. 4

(1987). The three volumes of Ricoeur, *Time and Narrative,* represent one man's effort to reconcile the various theorists of narrative with his own worldviews. On one working historian's attempt to come to terms with these problems, see Cronon, "A Place for Stories."

47. Louis Mink, "Narrative Form as a Cognitive Instrument," in *The Writing of History: Literary Form and Historical Understanding,* ed. Robert H. Canary and Henry Kozicki (Madison: University of Wisconsin Press, 1978), pp. 129–149, but esp. pp. 135–141.

48. Compare, among others on the relationships among the experience of life, narrative as a mode of understanding and organizing life, and narrative as a constructed literary form, Ricoeur, *Time and Narrative;* F. R. Ankersmit, *Narrative Logic: A Semantic Analysis of the Historian's Language* (The Hague: Martinus Nijhoff, 1983); David Carr, *Time, Narrative, and History* (Bloomington: Indiana University Press, 1986); Andrew P. Norman, "Telling It like It Was: Historical Narratives on Their Own Terms," *History and Theory,* 30, no. 2 (1991), 122–128, but see the whole article; and T. Carlos Jacques, "The Primacy of Narrative in Historical Understanding," *Clio: An Interdisciplinary Journal of Literature, History, and the Philosophy of History,* 19 (Spring 1990), 197–214.

49. Simon Schama in a paper, "The Age of Innocence and Where It Went," delivered in a session on "Rescuing Narrative from Narrative Theory" at the meeting of the Organization of American Historians, April 3, 1992. Sharing these views are those authors contributing to "Narratives and Social Identities," *Social Science History,* 16 (Fall 1992), 479–537, and (Winter 1992), 591–692.

50. The ideas of "whole" and "total" present problems that are discussed under emplotment and patterning in Chapter 5 and under totalization and politics in Chapter 8.

51. In addition to Mink, "Narrative Form as a Cognitive Instrument," see Peter Munz, *The Shapes of Time: A New Look at the Philosophy of History* (Middletown, Conn.: Wesleyan University Press, 1977), chaps. 7–8, on story in history.

52. "Master interpretive code" comes from Fredric Jameson, "Marxism and Historicism," *New Literary History,* 11 (Autumn 1979), 46. "Grand governing narrative" is from Harvey J. Kaye, *The Powers of the Past: Reflections on the Crisis and the Promise of History* (New York: Harvester Wheatsheaf, 1991), chap. 2. *Meta-récit,* or metanarrative, comes from Jean-François Lyotard, *The Postmodern Condition: A Report on Knowledge,* trans. Geoff Bennington and Brian Massumi (Minneapolis: University of Minnesota Press, 1984). Compare the term "dominant narrative" of Edmund Bruner, "Ethnography as Narrative," in *The Anthropology of Experience,* ed. Victor W. Turner and Edmund Bruner (Urbana: University of Illinois Press, 1986), pp. 139–155.

53. Does this mean that historians have what might be termed a "big picture" of history as plenitude, one that postulates a surplus of "facts" that are not completely narrativized by any story at all? Does this notion of surplus unnarrativized facts lie at the base of the historical profession's preference for specialization in a "field" and "period" in order to get the "in-depth" knowledge needed for a big picture of an era?

54. W. H. Walsh distinguished between modern *critical* philosophy of history and the older *speculative* philosophy of history in his *Philosophy of History,* pp. 13–28. See the distinction at work in the entry "Philosophy of History" in Ritter, *Dictionary of Concepts in History,* pp. 319–324. Because of the particular meaning given

"metanarrative" first by the speculative philosophers of history and, more recently, by Jean-François Lyotard as the grand stories of emancipation, progress, etc., I do not equate metanarrative with Great Story. In essence the metanarratives of Lyotard and the histories postulated by the speculative philosophers of history serve the same intellectual and ethical ends. Karl Popper condemned such speculative metanarratives as historicism and devoted *The Poverty of Historicism* (Boston: Beacon Press, 1957) and *The Open Society and Its Enemies,* 4th ed. rev., 2 vols. (New York: Harper Torchbooks, 1963), to their refutation. See also Burleigh T. Wilkins, *Has History Any Meaning? A Critique of Popper's Philosophy of History* (Ithaca: Cornell University Press, 1987); and D'Amico, *Historicism and Knowledge,* esp. chaps. 1–2.

55. Richard Hofstadter, *The Progressive Historians: Turner, Beard, Parrington* (New York: Alfred A. Knopf, 1968), provides a survey of the so-called Progressive school of American history.

56. The school received its name from John Higham, "The Cult of the 'American Consensus': Homogenizing Our History," *Commentary,* 27 (Feb. 1959), 93–100; idem, "Beyond Consensus: The Historian as Moral Critic," *American Historical Review,* 77 (April 1962), 609–625. See also Marian J. Morton, *The Terrors of Ideological Politics: Liberal Historians in a Conservative Mood* (Cleveland: Press of Case Western University, 1972); and Bernard Sternsher, *Consensus, Conflict, and American Historians* (Bloomington: Indiana University Press, 1975).

57. Eric Monkkonen, "The Dangers of Synthesis," *American Historical Review,* 91 (Dec. 1986), 1146–57, defends this fragmentation as a necessary stage preceding a more social scientific history of the United States.

58. Novick, *That Noble Dream,* chaps. 13–16, presents one version of this history. Allan Megill, "Fragmentation and the Future of Historiography," *American Historical Review,* 96 (June 1991), 693–698, raises interesting questions about efforts to move beyond fragmentation in historical discourse.

59. Thomas Bender, "Wholes and Parts: The Need for Synthesis in American History," *Journal of American History,* 73 (June 1986), 120–136; quotation from p. 130.

60. Ibid., p. 131.

61. Ibid., p. 132.

62. Ibid., p. 131.

63. "A Round Table: Synthesis in American History," *Journal of American History,* 64 (June 1987), 107–130.

64. Michael Geyer and Konrad H. Jarausch, "The Future of the German Past: Transatlantic Reflections for the 1990s," *Central European History,* 22 (Sept.–Dec. 1989), 229–259.

65. Albert Borgmann, *Crossing the Postmodern Divide* (Chicago: University of Chicago Press, 1992), p. 5.

66. Could not the essays in Theda Skocpol, ed., *Vision and Method in Historical Sociology* (Cambridge: Cambridge University Press, 1984), be read with this point in mind?

67. The terms respectively of Wolfram Eberhard, "Problems of Historical Sociology" in *State and Society: A Reader in Comparative Political Sociology,* ed. Reinhard Bendix (Boston: Little, Brown, 1968), pp. 25–28; Charles Tilly, *Big Structures, Large Processes, Huge Comparisons* (New York: Russell Sage Foundation, 1984), p. 2;

Theda Skocpol, *States and Social Revolution: A Comparative Analysis of France, Russia, and China* (Cambridge: Cambridge University Press, 1979), p. 4; and (I could not resist including) Karl Polanyi, *The Great Transformation* (New York: Farrar and Rinehart, 1944).

68. These two terms from among the several used by Wallerstein come from the titles of two of his books: *The Modern World-System: Capitalist Agriculture and the Origin of the European World Economy in the Sixteenth Century* (New York: Academic Press, 1974) and *The Capitalist World-Economy: Essays* (New York: Cambridge University Press, 1979). Charles Ragan and Daniel Chirot, "The World System of Immanuel Wallerstein: Sociology and Politics as History" in Skocpol, *Vision and Method in Historical Sociology,* pp. 276–312, provide guidance not only to Wallerstein's ideas but also to the bibliography by and about him.

69. Tilly, *Big Structures,* pp. 80–84; Skocpol, *Vision and Method in Historical Sociology,* pp. 362–386.

70. Tilly, *Big Structures,* pp. 7–10.

71. Skocpol, *States and Social Revolution,* p. 4.

3. Historical Representations and Truthfulness

1. Claudia L. Bushman, *America Discovers Columbus: How an Italian Explorer Became an American Hero* (Hanover, N.H.: University Press of New England, 1992), provides some historical background for the topic. Compare the recent debate with that of two hundred years ago as given in Henry Steele Commager and Elmo Giordanetti, eds., *Was America a Mistake? An Eighteenth-Century Controversy* (New York: Harper Torchbooks, 1967).

2. "Interpretation" is a much-used but poorly defined word in historical practice. It possesses multiple meanings depending upon the philosophical affiliations and political purposes of the user, and it has gained new meaning and importance as a result of the so-called interpretive turn in the human sciences. See, for example, the brief history of the profession's usage given in Harry Ritter, *Dictionary of Concepts in History* (Westport, Conn.: Greenwood Press, 1986), pp. 243–250. Compare, for literary theory, Steven Mailloux, "Interpretation," in *Critical Terms for Literary Study,* ed. Frank Lentricchia and Thomas McLaughlin (Chicago: University of Chicago Press, 1990), pp. 121–134. Two attempts from different perspectives to clarify the term in relation to history are Hayden White, "Interpretation in History," in idem, *Tropics of Discourse: Essays in Cultural Criticism* (Baltimore: Johns Hopkins University Press, 1978), pp. 51–80; and Marvin Levich, "Interpretation in History: Or What Historians Do and Philosophers Say," *History and Theory,* 24, no. 1 (1985), 44–61.

3. Although the overall purpose of the distinctions may be the same, the actual implications for the three fields of study are quite different. Story and discourse are discussed in Chapter 4. Other important aspects of interpretation, bias and the problems of partiality, are discussed in Chapter 6.

4. In my scheme, a Great Story may include one or more interpretations, just as an interpretation may depend on two or more Great Stories.

5. Jerald A. Combs, *American Diplomatic History: Two Centuries of Changing Interpretations* (Berkeley: University of California Press, 1983), p. xi.

6. Peter Novick, *That Noble Dream: The "Objectivity Quest" and the American Historical Profession* (Cambridge: Cambridge University Press, 1988), p. 2.

7. Elizabeth Deeds Ermarth, *Sequel to History: Postmodernism and the Crisis of Time* (Princeton: Princeton University Press, 1992), warns scholars that their naturalization of history is a timeless approach to the representation of time.

8. Dominick LaCapra, "Rhetoric and History," in idem, *History and Criticism* (Ithaca: Cornell University Press, 1985), p. 17.

9. For the argument between Davis and the challenger, Robert Finlay, see *American Historical Review,* 93 (June 1988), 553–603; quotation from Finlay p. 571. Similarly, Paul Hirst, "The Necessity of Theory—A Critique of E. P. Thompson's *The Poverty of Theory,*" in idem, *Marxism and Historical Writing* (London: Routledge and Kegan Paul, 1985), p. 78, accuses Thompson of believing that the facts of history constitute a court in which theories of history are tried. Likewise, G. R. Elton, *Return to Essentials: Some Reflections on the Present State of Historical Study* (Cambridge: Cambridge University Press, 1991), esp. pp. 50–62, presumes that evidential facts create their own history.

10. Ritter, *Dictionary of Concepts in History,* p. 366; but see the whole entry, pp. 366–372.

11. Novick, *That Noble Dream,* p. 1.

12. Peter Gay, *Style in History* (New York: Basic Books, 1974), p. 210.

13. Ibid., p. 211.

14. As quoted in Novick, *That Noble Dream,* p. 611.

15. Jack N. Rakove, ed., *Interpreting the Constitution: The Debate over Original Intent* (Boston: Northeastern University Press, 1990), provides a convenient compendium of essays and a bibliography on this very American matter.

16. Much of what is in contention and therefore argued in Saul Friedlander, ed., *Probing the Limits of Representation: Nazism and the "Final Solution"* (Cambridge, Mass.: Harvard University Press, 1992), is of direct relevance to what is discussed here specifically and what is argued in general in this and later chapters. Michael Geyer and Konrad H. Jarausch, "The Future of the German Past: Transatlantic Reflections for the 1990s," *Central European History,* 22 (Sept.–Dec. 1989), 229–259, discuss various Great Stories advanced to explain modern Germany's history.

17. Linda Orr, "The Revenge of Literature: A History of History," *New Literary History,* 18 (Autumn 1986), 7, 9, 11, illustrates the historian's use of asymptote as metaphor.

18. This issue often arises in the work of the philosopher of history William Dray, for which see *On History and the Philosophers of History* (Leiden: E. J. Brill, 1989), esp. pp. 239–257; and in the work of some of his students, for which see W. J. van der Dussen and Lionel Rubinoff, eds., *Objectivity, Method, and Point of View: Essays in the Philosophy of History* (Leiden: E. J. Brill, 1991), esp. pp. 97–111, 133–153, and Dray's commentary, pp. 181–182, 185–187. The problem of a single best interpretation in literary theory is argued (and supported) in P. D. Juhl, *Interpretation: An Essay in the Philosophy of Literary Criticism* (Princeton: Princeton University Press, 1980). See the earlier defense of the case by E. D. Hirsch, Jr., *Validity in Interpretation* (New Haven: Yale University Press, 1967). Compare Paul B. Armstrong, *Conflicting Readings: Variety and Validity in Interpretation* (Chapel Hill: University of North Carolina Press, 1990), on the problems of trying to limit the proliferation of interpretive

pluralism. Ellen Rooney, *Seductive Reasoning: Pluralism as the Problematic of Contemporary Theory* (Ithaca: Cornell University Press, 1989), argues against the political implications of such interpretive pluralism.

19. Michael Krausz, "Ideality and Ontology in the Practice of History," in van der Dussen and Rubinoff, *Objectivity, Method, and Point of View*, pp. 97–99, clarifies the relationship between the notion of pluralism of historical interpretations and what he terms singularism and multiplism. The singularist ideal postulates one best or right interpretation, while the multiplist ideal recognizes the incommensurability of two or more right interpretations. A pluralist ideal can mean the latter, or it might postulate that the variety of interpretations ought to and can be reconciled to produce one best or right interpretation. The elephant analogy is the latter, of course; I would like to argue for the former usage. Compare the terms "uni-perspectivism" and "trans-perspectivism" (borrowed from William Dray) and "inter-perspectival" in Lionel Rubinoff, "Historicity and Objectivity," ibid., pp. 139–141, which describe respectively the transcendental authority of one particular viewpoint, various viewpoints approaching (one) reality asymptotically, and mutually constituted and interacting viewpoints that may converge.

20. William Cronon, "A Place for Stories: Nature, History, and Narrative," *Journal of American History*, 78 (March 1992), 1347–76; quotations from pp. 1347, 1348, 1374. The two books are Paul Bonnifield, *The Dust Bowl: Men, Dirt, and Depression* (Albuquerque: University of New Mexico Press, 1979); and Donald Worster, *Dust Bowl: The Southern Plains in the 1930s* (New York: Oxford University Press, 1979).

21. Cronon, "A Place for Stories," pp. 1350–51. Most of this chronicle is cast in sentences that are minimal narratives in themselves. See the definition of minimal narrative in Chapter 5.

22. Ibid., pp. 1370–71.

23. Ibid., p. 1371.

24. Ibid., pp. 1371, 1372.

25. I take considerable liberty with his second criterion by offering what I consider the general implications of his specifically environmentalist approach to nature as material, hence ultimate, reality.

26. For this second set of criteria see Cronon, "A Place for Stories," pp. 1372–74.

27. Armstrong, *Conflicting Readings*, pp. 13–16; quotations from pp. 13, 15.

28. Ibid., p. 13.

29. On the connection between power in a society and the nature of knowledge and its dissemination, see Steven Mailloux, *Rhetorical Power* (Ithaca: Cornell University Press, 1989), chaps. 1, 2, and 6.

30. Armstrong, *Conflicting Readings*, pp. 12–19; but see the whole volume as relevant to the problems discussed not only in this section but throughout my book. In connection with some of Cronon's and Armstrong's criteria compare "scope-maximilization" and fertility in F. R. Ankersmit, *Narrative Logic: A Semantic Analysis of the Historian's Language* (The Hague: Martinus Nijhoff, 1983), pp. 224–225, 238–239, 241–247; and the criteria of unity and coherence in idem, "The Use of Language in the Writing of History," in *Working with Language: A Multidisciplinary Consideration of Language Use in Work Contexts*, ed. Hywel Coleman (Berlin: Mouton de Gruyter, 1986), pp. 76–78. See also C. Behan McCullagh, "Can Our Understanding

of Old Texts Be Objective?" *History and Theory,* 30, no. 3 (1991), 302–323, for criteria for assessing the correctness of what he calls primary and secondary interpretations of a text, especially on such notions as a basic meaning and key ideas.

31. See, for example, the forum in *American Historical Review,* 97 (April 1992), 487–511, devoted to the film *JFK,* directed by Oliver Stone. The collapse of the Weimar Republic refers to the notorious "David Abraham case," of which Novick, *That Noble Dream,* gives one version, pp. 612–621; but see Joseph M. Levine, "Objectivity in History: Peter Novick and R. G. Collingwood," *Clio,* 21 (Winter 1992), 111–113.

32. See "Fact," in Ritter, *Dictionary of Concepts in History,* pp. 153–160.

33. Compare "Event," ibid., pp. 138–142; and the idea of colligation as a collective noun in note 79 below. See also the concept of the *narratio* as developed by Ankersmit in *Narrative Logic* and summarized in "The Use of Language in the Writing of History," pp. 64–78. That historical evidence comes already interpreted is also argued by Carlo Ginzburg, "Checking the Evidence: The Judge and the Historian," *Critical Inquiry,* 18 (Autumn 1991), 79–92.

34. I derive sentences 7 and 8 from Seymour Lipset, *The First New Nation: The United States in Historical and Comparative Perspective* (New York: Basic Books, 1963), pp. 16–23.

35. Compare Eugene Genovese, *Roll, Jordan, Roll: The World the Slaves Made* (New York: Pantheon Books, 1974); and Eugene Genovese and Elizabeth Fox-Genovese, *Fruits of Merchant Capital: Slavery and Bourgeois Property in the Rise and Expansion of Capitalism* (New York: Oxford University Press, 1983); with James Oakes, *The Ruling Race: A History of American Slaveholders* (New York: Alfred A. Knopf, 1982).

36. In *The Bounds of Race: Perspectives on Hegemony and Resistance,* ed. Dominick LaCapra (Ithaca: Cornell University Press, 1991), pp. 104–133.

37. Probably few historians in these multicultural times would assert such a generalization as "fact," given the revised view of how little emancipation and Reconstruction accomplished for African Americans, let alone for Native Americans and other minority Americans. But even in this regard this revisionist view must also be constructed and contextualized in accordance with other Great Stories. Both Charles and Mary Beard, *The Rise of American Civilization,* vol. 2 (New York: Macmillan, 1930), chap. 18; and Eric Foner, *Reconstruction: America's Unfinished Revolution, 1863–1877* (New York: Harper and Row, 1988), pp. xxiii–xxiv, speak of the Civil War as the "Second American Revolution," but with quite different emphases. What the Beards saw as the most revolutionary aspect of the war—the "silent shift of social and material power" from a Southern plantation aristocracy to Northern capitalists and free farmers—is subordinated by Foner to the "transformation of slaves into free laborers and equal citizens," particularly the active role of African Americans in achieving that transformation.

38. Ankersmit, *Narrative Logic,* pp. 58–66, argues that analysts of historical narratives miss the point if they reduce a *narratio* to mere conjunctions or sequences of sentences (p. 59).

39. Ibid., pp. 66–78. His theory of the relationship among a *narratio,* language, and reality is summarized in "The Use of Language in the Writing of History," pp. 71–78.

40. Ankersmit, *Narrative Logic,* pp. 138–139. Compare ibid., pp. 218–219.

41. As pointed out by Linda Hutcheon, *A Poetics of Postmodernism: History, Theory, and Fiction* (London: Routledge, 1988), p. 57; and argued by W. J. van der Dussen, "The Historian and His Evidence," in van der Dussen and Rubinoff, *Objectivity, Method, and Point of View,* pp. 154–169.

42. Paul Christianson, "Patterns of Historical Interpretation," ibid., pp. 47–71, proposes the notion of historical frameworks and levels of factuality.

43. Krausz, "Ideality and Ontology in the Practice of History," p. 99.

44. Sean Wilentz, *Chants Democratic: New York City and the Rise of the American Working Class, 1788–1850* (New York: Oxford University Press, 1984), chap. 9.

45. For some indication of the complexity of realistic representation in the visual and dramatic arts, see, among a huge bibliography, Paul Hernadi, "Re-Presenting the Past: A Note on Narrative Historiography and Historical Drama," *History and Theory,* 15, no. 1 (1976), 45–51; Patrice Pavis, "Production, Reception, and the Social Context," in *On Referring in Literature,* ed. Anna Whiteside and Michael Issacharoff (Bloomington: Indiana University Press, 1987), pp. 122–137; and Robert A. Rosenstone, "History in Images/History in Words: Reflections on the Possibility of Really Putting History onto Film," *American Historical Review,* 93 (Dec. 1988), 1173–85, and the four commentaries that follow, pp. 1186–1227. The classic study on realism and art is E. H. Gombrich, *Art and Illusion: A Study in the Psychology of Pictorial Representation* (London: Phaidon Books, 1960); but see Norman Bryson, *Vision and Painting: The Logic of the Gaze* (New Haven: Yale University Press, 1983), for an important critique.

46. As Savoie Lottinville advises the beginning historian in *The Rhetoric of History* (Norman: University of Oklahoma Press, 1976), chaps. 1–6.

47. Compare Donald N. McCloskey, *The Rhetoric of Economics* (Madison: University of Wisconsin Press, 1985) and *If You're So Smart: The Narrative of Economic Expertise* (Chicago: University of Chicago Press, 1990).

48. In *Tropics of Discourse: Essays in Cultural Criticism* (Baltimore: Johns Hopkins University Press, 1978), pp. 121–134. Among many works on the relation of forms of representation to "reality," W. J. T. Mitchell, "Representation," in *Critical Terms for Literary Study,* ed. Frank Lentricchia and Thomas McLaughlin (Chicago: University of Chicago Press, 1990), pp. 11–22; and Oswald Ducrot and Tzvetan Todorov, *Encyclopedic Dictionary of the Sciences of Language,* trans. Catherine Porter (Baltimore: Johns Hopkins University Press, 1979), pp. 259–263, provide an introduction. The classic on its subject is Erich Auerbach, *Mimesis: The Representation of Reality in Western Literature* (1946), trans. Willard Trask (Princeton: Princeton University Press, 1953).

49. These principles are inspired by Jonathan Culler's discussion of conventions and *vraisemblance* in *Structuralist Poetics: Structuralism, Linguistics, and the Study of Literature* (Ithaca: Cornell University Press, 1975), pp. 138–160, with some assistance from Elizabeth Deeds Ermarth, *Realism and Consensus in the English Novel* (Princeton: Princeton University Press, 1983), chaps. 1–3.

50. Ruth Roach Pierson, "Experience, Difference, Dominance, and Voice in the Writing of Canadian Women's History," in *Writing Women's History: International Perspectives,* ed. Karen Offen, Ruth Roach Pierson, and Jane Randall (Bloomington: Indiana University Press, 1991), pp. 79–80. That practicing historians base their prac-

tices on many of these postulates of realism can be seen in E. P. Thompson's credo, for example, as given in his argument with Althusser, "The Poverty of Theory, or an Orrery of Errors," in Thompson, *The Poverty of Theory and Other Essays* (London: Merlin Press, 1978), esp. pp. 217–242. That a more extended commitment to realism is perhaps necessary in Marxian-inspired history is argued in Gregor McLennan, *Marxism and the Methodologies of History* (London: Verso Editions and NLB, 1981), chap. 2. Compare, among others on realism in historical practice, Lionel Gossman, "History and Literature: Reproduction or Signification," in *The Writing of History: Literary Form and Historical Understanding,* ed. Robert H. Canary and Henry Kozicki (Madison: University of Wisconsin Press, 1978), pp. 3–39; Christopher Lloyd, *Explanation in Social History* (Oxford: Basil Blackwell, 1986), esp. pp. 96–177; and F. R. Ankersmit, *The Reality Effect in the Writing of History: The Dynamics of Historiographical Topology* (Amsterdam: Koninklijke Nederlandische Akadamie van Wetenshaften Noord-Hollandishe, 1989). For another view see the revisionist arguments of Derek Layder, *The Realist Image in Social Science* (London: Macmillan, 1990).

51. F. R. Ankersmit, "Historical Representation," *History and Theory,* 27, no. 3 (1988), 205–228, argues that representation rather than interpretation is basic to what historians achieve in their practice. Compare Roger Chartier, *Cultural History: Between Practices and Representation,* trans. Lydia G. Cochrane (Cambridge: Polity Press, 1988), pp. 6–10, on meanings of representation.

52. Roland Barthes, "The Reality Effect" (1968), in *French Literary Theory Today: A Reader,* ed. Tzvetan Todorov, trans. R. Carter (Cambridge: Cambridge University Press, 1982), pp. 11–17; see p. 16 for the term "referential illusion." See also Barthes's "Historical Discourse," translated and reprinted in Michael Lane, ed., *Introduction to Structuralism* (New York: Basic Books, 1970), p. 154, for the term "reality effect." Ankersmit, *The Reality Effect in the Writing of History,* provides important clarification of this notion.

53. See, for example, the definition under "Hi/story" in *Semiotics and Language: An Analytical Dictionary,* ed. A. J. Greimas and J. Courtés, trans. Larry Crist et al. (Bloomington: Indiana University Press, 1982), pp. 143–144; Hutcheon, *A Poetics of Postmodernism;* the books by Hayden White; and Hans Kellner, *Language and Historical Representation: Getting the Story Crooked* (Madison: University of Wisconsin Press, 1989).

54. Ferdinand de Saussure uses these two examples in his *Course in General Linguistics* (translated in Lane, *Introduction to Structuralism,* pp. 43–45) to explain the terms "sign," "signifier," and "signified." The terms "signifier," "signified," and "referent" are defined variously by scholars depending upon their premises about the relationship between language and the world. These premises vary by academic specialty and by whether they are inspired by the francophone or the anglophone schools of thought. On the use of these terms in the former school, see, under the appropriate entries, Greimas and Courtés, *Semiotics and Language;* and Ducrot and Todorov, *Encyclopedic Dictionary of the Sciences of Language.* For a recent effort to cope with the perplexities of the referent in literary texts, see the essays in Whiteside and Issacharoff, *On Referring in Literature,* especially the conclusion, pp. 175–204; and Uri Margolin, "Reference, Coreference, Referring, and the Dual Structure of Literary Narrative," *Poetics Today,* 12 (Fall 1991), 516–542. If my own usage in this complicated matter reflects any consistency of position, it would be similar to that of

Robert Scholes, "Language, Narrative, and Anti-Narrative," in *On Narrative,* ed. W. J. T. Mitchell (Chicago: University of Chicago Press, 1981), pp. 200–205.

55. On interpreting Ranke's dictum, compare Peter Munz, *The Shapes of Time: A New Look at the Philosophy of History* (Middletown, Conn.: Wesleyan University Press, 1977), p. 84; and Ankersmit, *Narrative Logic,* p. 86.

56. See Munz, *The Shapes of Time,* chap. 7, on sources.

57. For example, Jerzy Toploski, "Conditions of Truth of Historical Narratives," *History and Theory,* 20, no. 1 (1981), 47–60, agrees with this conclusion about the difference between the factuality *of* a historical work and factuality *in* a historical work, but in his view of the relation of language to the world he differs substantially from those who advocate what we might call a radical constructionist position on the nature of historical practice. For a sample of the debate on constructionism, see articles gathered together under the title "The Constitution of the Past," *History and Theory,* 16, no. 4 (1977). Compare Ankersmit's definition of the *narratio* in "The Use of Language in the Writing of History," pp. 71–78; and Michael E. Hobart, "The Paradox of Constructionism," *History and Theory,* 28, no. 1 (1989), 42–58.

58. On the rhetorical artistry of social science history, see the example explicated by Donald N. McCloskey, "The Problem of Audience in Historical Economics: Rhetorical Thoughts on a Text by Robert Fogel," *History and Theory,* 24, no. 1 (1985), 1–22.

59. That *res gestae* equals *historia rerum gestarum* in normal historical practice is also the point of Munz, *The Shapes of Time,* chap. 8; and Barthes, "Historical Discourse," pp. 145–155, among others.

60. The generalizations in this paragraph hold even if we substitute "a" for "the" before Great Story and Great Past throughout.

61. Oscar Handlin et al., eds., *Harvard Guide to American History* (Cambridge, Mass.: Harvard University Press, 1954), p. 15. Of course, historians might be able to discover or corroborate factual information they might not have otherwise. The argument is given a more sophisticated turn in the notion of the "ideal chronicle" as advanced by Arthur Danto, *Narration and Knowledge,* expanded ed. of *Analytical Philosophy of History* (New York: Columbia University Press, 1985), pp. 149–182. For more on this idea see Paul Roth, "Narrative Explanations: The Case of History," *History and Theory,* 27, no. 1 (1988), 1–13.

62. Notable among the advocates of fusion in the United States, for example, are Hayden White and Hans Kellner. For some indication of the reaction to such an approach to history, see F. R. Ankersmit, "Historiography and Postmodernism," *History and Theory,* 28, no. 28 (1989), 137–153; the reply by Perez Zagorin, "Historiography and Postmodernism: Reconsiderations," ibid., 29, no. 3 (1990), 263–274; and Ankersmit's reply to Zagorin, ibid., pp. 275–286.

63. See once again the complaints of Gertrude Himmelfarb against postmodernist history in "Telling It as You Like It: Post-Modernist History and the Flight from Fact," *Times Literary Supplement,* no. 4672 (Oct. 16, 1992), 12–15.

64. Much of this discussion is premised, of course, on realistic novels. Suzanne Gearhart, *The Open Boundary of History and Fiction: A Critical Approach to the French Enlightenment* (Princeton: Princeton University Press, 1984), problematizes the distinction between history and fiction by comparing the differing views of eighteenth-century thinkers and twentieth-century theorists on what constitutes the

boundary. David Carroll, *The Subject in Question: The Languages of Theory and the Strategies of Fiction* (Chicago: University of Chicago Press, 1982), argues that the distinction has been further eroded in recent decades by those metafictional novelists who deliberately subvert the boundaries through conscious appropriation of recent literary theory.

65. C. Vann Woodward makes and applies this distinction in his review, under the headline "Gilding Lincoln's Lily," of William Safire's *Freedom*, in *New York Review of Books*, 34 (Sept. 24, 1987), 23–26.

66. Cushing Strout, *The Veracious Imagination: Essays on American History, Literature, and Biography* (Middletown, Conn.: Wesleyan University Press, 1981), pp. 192–193. In contrast, although both fictional and historical persons appear in John Dos Passos' *Big Money* (1937), he maintained the historical integrity of his real historical figures through separate sections devoted to the biographies. Although the lives of fictional characters paralleled or symbolized those of the real biographees, they did not meet and interact in the ways in which modern novelists manipulate the historic record. For a more favorable reading of Doctorow's work by a literature scholar, see Christopher D. Morris, *Models of Misrepresentation: On the Fiction of E. L. Doctorow* (Jackson: University Press of Mississippi, 1991). Among those books putting historical novels into their historical context are the classic Georg Lukács, *The Historical Novel*, trans. Hannah Mitchell and Stanley Mitchell (London: Merlin Press, 1962); and Barbara Foley, *Telling the Truth: The Theory and Practice of Documentary Fiction* (Ithaca: Cornell University Press, 1986).

67. Compare, on genre, Paul Hernadi, *Beyond Genre: New Directions in Literary Classification* (Ithaca: Cornell University Press, 1972); and Adena Rosmarin, *The Power of Genre* (Minneapolis: University of Minnesota Press, 1985). What should historians make of the "magic realism" of Latin American authors?

68. Matt F. Oja, "Fictional History and Historical Fiction: Solzhenitsyn and Kis as Exemplars," *History and Theory*, 27, no. 2 (1988), 111–124, suggests the spectrum as a way of looking at the subject. Linda Hutcheon provides context for this subject in "Metafictional Implications for Novelistic Reference," in Whiteside and Issacharoff, *On Referring in Literature*, pp. 1–13. Compare the approach of Michel de Certeau, "History: Ethics, Science, and Fiction," in *Heterologies: Discourse on the Other*, trans. Brian Masumi (Minneapolis: University of Minnesota Press, 1986).

69. Marie-Laure Ryan, "Possible Worlds and Accessibility Relations: A Semantic Typology of Fiction," *Poetics Today*, 12 (Fall 1991), 553–576, offers a sophisticated interpretation of fictional reference in terms of actual worlds, textual actual worlds, textual reference worlds, and possible alternative worlds. See also Margolin, "Reference, Coreference, Referring."

70. Simon Schama, *Dead Certainties (Unwarranted Speculations)* (New York: Alfred A. Knopf, 1991). See especially Gordon S. Wood's review essay in *New York Review of Books*, 38 (June 22, 1991), 12–16. Compare Gore Vidal's defense of his "novel" *Lincoln* against the charges of errors by Don Fehrenbacher in a letter to the *American Historical Review*, 96 (Feb. 1991), 324–326; and the reply by Fehrenbacher, ibid., pp. 326–328, about the boundary between fact and fancy.

71. For a sampling of opinion on the differences between narrative in history and in fiction, see Paul Ricoeur, *Time and Narrative*, trans. Kathleen McLaughlin Blamey and David Pellauer, vol. 3 (Chicago: University of Chicago Press, 1988), chaps. 6, 8;

Wallace Martin, *Recent Theories of Narrative* (Ithaca: Cornell University Press, 1986), chap. 3; Roger G. Seamon, "Narrative Practice and the Theoretical Distinction between History and Fiction," *Glyph*, 16 (Fall 1983), 197–218; Linda Hutcheon, *A Poetics of Postmodernism*, esp. chaps. 6–7, 9; Thomas M. Leitch, *What Stories Are: Narrative Theory and Interpretation* (University Park: Pennsylvania State University Press, 1986), chaps. 9–10; Norman Hampson, "History and Fiction: Where Does the Difference Lie?" *Manchester Literary and Philosophical Society, Memoirs and Proceedings*, 106 (1963–64), 64–73; Dorrit Cohn, "Signposts of Fictionality: A Narratological Perspective," *Poetics Today*, 11 (Winter 1990), 775–804.

72. Martin, *Recent Theories of Narrative*, p. 71.

73. Ibid., pp. 71–72.

74. The essays in Whiteside and Issacharoff, On *Referring in Literature,* argue and illustrate the problems of referring and reference peculiar to fictional as opposed to nonfictional texts. See also Ryan, "Possible Worlds and Accessibility Relations"; and Margolin, "Reference, Coreference, Referring."

75. Clues to this context are often supplied by such paratextual matter as dust-jacket descriptions, advertisements, introductions, and stylistic conventions.

76. Ankersmit, *Narrative Logic*, pp. 19–27, argues that historical fiction is applied historical point of view rather than its creation.

77. As Hayden White admits in "'Figuring the Nature of the Times Deceased': Literary Theory and Historical Writing," in *The Future of Literary Theory*, ed. Ralph Cohen (New York and London: Routledge, 1989), p. 20. See also his position as expressed in "Historical Emplotment and the Problem of Truth," in Friedlander, *Probing the Limits of Representation*, pp. 37–53.

78. Roman Jakobson, "Closing Statement: Linguistics and Poetics," in *Style in Language,* ed. Thomas Sebeok (Cambridge, Mass.: MIT Press, 1960), pp. 350–377. According to Roland Barthes in *S/Z*, trans. Richard Miller (New York: Farrar, Straus and Giroux, 1974), novels can be coded in one of five ways, of which the referential is under the cultural code as opposed to hermeneutic, proairetic, semic, and symbolic codes. Douwe W. Fokkema, "The Concept of Code in the Study of Literature," *Poetics Today*, 6, no. 4 (1985), 643–656, warns against applying Barthes's five codes to literature as opposed to language and offers five different codes. Sande Cohen, *Historical Culture: On the Recoding of an Academic Discipline* (Berkeley: University of California Press, 1986), offers an alternative way of looking at how a historical text is coded.

79. Compare the notion of collective nouns as colligatory terms in William H. Walsh, "Colligatory Concepts in History," in *The Philosophy of History*, ed. Patrick Gardiner (Oxford: Oxford University Press, 1974), pp. 127–144; C. Behan McCullagh, "Colligation and Classification in History," *History and Theory*, 17, no. 3 (1978), 267–284; and William Dray, *On History and Philosophers of History* (Leiden: E. J. Brill, 1989), chap. 2.

80. As Richard Rorty argues in "Nineteenth-Century Idealism and Twentieth-Century Textualism," in *Consequences of Pragmatism (Essays, 1972–1980)* (Minneapolis: University of Minnesota Press, 1982), pp. 139–159; but see also Michael Ermarth, "Mindful Matters: The Empire's New Codes and the Plight of Modern European Intellectual History," *Journal of Modern History*, 42 (Sept. 1985), 506–527; and James T. Kloppenberg, "Deconstruction and Hermeneutic Strategies for

Intellectual History: The Recent Work of Dominick LaCapra and David Hollinger," *Intellectual History Newsletter,* 9 (April 1987), 3–22. This debate over problematics in historical practice is discussed in Chapter 8.

81. For example, note the dichotomy posed in the title as well as in the text itself of Gordon Wood's oft-cited article, "Rhetoric and Reality in the American Revolution," *William and Mary Quarterly,* 3rd ser., 23 (Jan. 1966), 3–32.

82. For example, see Edmund Morgan's apologetic prose on whether or not to call ideological concepts "fictions," for they are political "make-believe," in *Inventing the People: The Rise of Popular Sovereignty in England and America* (New York: W. W. Norton, 1988), pp. 13–15. Compare Daniel Rodgers, *Contested Truths: Keywords in American Politics since Independence* (New York: Basic Books, 1987), pp. 5 and 227, n. 4, on why he substitutes the term "metaphors" for what Morgan calls "fictions."

83. The ethnocentrism, indeed cultural hubris, of contemporary industrial societies as embodied in normal or professional historical practice was the main target of Claude Lévi-Strauss in the last chapter of *The Savage Mind* (Chicago: University of Chicago Press, 1966).

84. See the classic article by David M. Potter appropriately titled "The Historian's Use of Nationalism and Vice Versa," *American Historical Review,* 97 (July 1962), 924–950.

85. See especially his conclusion to *Metahistory: The Historical Imagination in Nineteenth-Century Europe* (Baltimore: Johns Hopkins University Press, 1973).

86. Mario J. Valdés, *World-Making: The Literary Truth-Claim and the Interpretation of Texts* (Toronto: University of Toronto Press, 1992), esp. chap. 3, inspired this approach to the criteria for truth claims in historical texts.

87. Lynn Hunt, "History as Gesture; or, The Scandal of History," in *Consequences of Theory,* ed. Jonathan Arac and Barbara Johnson (Baltimore: Johns Hopkins University Press, 1991), pp. 102–103. See also her introduction to *The New Cultural History* (Berkeley: University of California Press, 1989) and "History beyond Social Theory," in *The "States of Theory": History, Art, and Critical Discourse,* ed. David Carroll (New York: Columbia University Press, 1990), pp. 95–111, for her effort to cope with the challenge to historicization in these (postmodern) times. See also the perplexity expressed by Ellen Somekawa and Elizabeth Smith in "Theorizing the Writing of History; or, 'I Can't Think Why It Should Be So Dull, for a Great Deal of It Must Be Invention,'" *Journal of Social History,* 22 (Fall 1988), 145–161.

4. *The New Rhetoric, Poetics, and Criticism*

1. See "Criticism," in Harry Ritter, *Dictionary of Concepts in History* (Westport, Conn.: Greenwood Press, 1986), pp. 84–88. A notable exception to historians' eschewal of historical criticism in the sense employed here is Dominick LaCapra in his aptly titled *History and Criticism* (Ithaca: Cornell University Press, 1985); and idem, *Soundings in Critical Theory* (Ithaca: Cornell University Press, 1989). For a traditional view of what criticism entailed, compare Oscar Handlin, *Truth in History* (Cambridge, Mass.: Harvard University Press, 1979), chaps. 5–6.

2. Savoie Lottinville, *The Rhetoric of History* (Norman: University of Oklahoma Press, 1976), chap. 8, esp. pp. 171–172, gives typical reviewers' rules. For older advice

on book reviewing see, for example, Oscar Handlin et al., eds., *The Harvard Guide to American History* (Cambridge, Mass.: Harvard University Press, 1955), pp. 49–51. For more recent advice see, for example, Steven Stowe, "Thinking about Reviews," *Journal of American History*, 98 (Sept. 1991), 590–595. James O. Hoge, ed., *Literary Reviewing* (Charlottesville: University Press of Virginia, 1987), provides an introduction to the varieties of literary reviewing.

3. Cesare Segre with the collaboration of Tomaso Kemeny, *Introduction to the Analysis of the Literary Text,* trans. John Meddemmem (Bloomington: Indiana University Press, 1988), offers a recent version of a textualist approach.

4. The distinction becomes the very basis of the title of Seymour Chatman, *Story and Discourse: Narrative Structure in Fiction and Film* (Ithaca: Cornell University Press, 1978). This distinction takes various forms and terminology in narrative theory; Wallace Martin, *Recent Theories of Narrative* (Ithaca: Cornell University Press, 1986), pp. 107–109, gives a brief overview of the competing terminology. Defenses of this now traditional distinction against newer theories of narratology in a contextualist mode include Seymour Chatman, "What We Can Learn from Contextualist Narratology," *Poetics Today,* 11 (Summer 1990), 309–328; Thomas Pavel, "Narrative Tectonics," ibid., pp. 349–364; and Gérard Genette, "Fictional Narrative, Factual Narrative," ibid., pp. 755–774.

5. Garrett Mattingly, *The Armada* (Boston: Houghton Mifflin, 1959). See the appreciation of Mattingly's approach to narrative history in J. H. Hexter, *Doing History* (Bloomington: Indiana University Press, 1971), chap. 6.

6. Paul Boyer and Stephen Nissenbaum, *Salem Possessed: The Social Origins of Witchcraft* (Cambridge, Mass.: Harvard University Press, 1974.)

7. William Cronon, *Changes in the Land: Indians, Colonists, and the Ecology of New England* (New York: Hill and Wang, 1983).

8. David H. Fischer, *Historians' Fallacies: Toward a Logic of Historical Thought* (New York: Harper and Row, 1970).

9. Despite titles like J. H. Hexter, "The Rhetoric of History," in *Doing History,* pp. 15–76; and Lottinville, *The Rhetoric of History.* Hayden White's various books and articles offer many valuable suggestions but not extended and comprehensive guidance. This is also true of Hans Kellner's articles collected in *Language and Historical Representation;* Nancy Struever, "Historical Discourse," in *Handbook of Discourse Analysis,* ed. Teun A. van Dijk, vol. 1 (London: Academic Press, 1985), pp. 249–271; and Allan Megill and Donald N. McCloskey, "The Rhetoric of History," in *The Rhetoric of Human Sciences: Language and Argument in Scholarship and Public Affairs,* ed. John S. Nelson, Allan Megill, and Donald N. McCloskey (Madison: University of Wisconsin Press, 1987), chap. 13.

10. Robert Fogel, *Railroads and American Economic Growth in the Nineteenth Century: Essays in Econometric History* (Baltimore: Johns Hopkins Press, 1964).

11. Donald N. McCloskey, "The Problem of Audience in Historical Economics: Rhetorical Thoughts on a Text by Robert Fogel," *History and Theory,* 24, no. 1 (1985), 1–22; extensively revised with comments quoted from Fogel in idem, *The Rhetoric of Economics* (Madison: University of Wisconsin Press, 1985), chap. 6, quotations from p. 126.

12. For what such an approach entails, see Paolo Valesio, *Novantiqua: Rhetoric as a Contemporary Theory* (Bloomington: Indiana University Press, 1980); Chaim

Perelman and L. Olbrechts-Tytecca, *The New Rhetoric: A Treatise on Argumentation,* trans. John Wilkinson and Purcell Weaver (Notre Dame, Ind.: University of Notre Dame Press, 1969); Kenneth Burke, *A Rhetoric of Motives* (Englewood Cliffs, N.J.: Prentice-Hall, 1950); and Stephen Toulmin, *The Uses of Argument* (Cambridge: Cambridge University Press, 1958).

13. This and subsequent tables are inspired by Seymour Chatman, *Story and Discourse,* chap. 1, who borrowed from Louis Hjelmslev. These common distinctions receive various names, as is quickly apparent in the chart provided in Martin, *Recent Theories of Narrative,* p. 108; but see the "mild protest" to this equation by Gérard Genette, *Narrative Discourse Revisited,* trans. Jane E. Lewin (Ithaca: Cornell University Press, 1988), pp. 13–15, and the observation of Michael J. Toolan, *Narrative: A Critical Linguistic Introduction* (London: Routledge, 1988), pp. 9, 11. Jonathan Culler, "Fabula and *Sjuzhet* in the Analysis of Narrative: Some American Discussions," *Poetics Today,* 1 (Spring 1980), 27–37, points out the contradictory assumptions of this distinction.

14. This definition reflects the textualist side as opposed to the contextualist side of the competing definitions of discourse.

15. See the essays in Anna Whiteside and Michael Issacharoff, eds., *On Referring in Literature* (Bloomington: Indiana University Press, 1987).

16. Even if it may be argued that synchronic histories as opposed to diachronic histories do not present a narrative as their explicit content, their argument and their larger context presume such a narrative as either partial or Great Story.

17. Although my employment of "subtext" in the chart broadens its original technical definition, this usage seems to accord with current scholarly practice. See, for example, the definition given in Chris Baldick, *The Concise Oxford Dictionary of Literary Terms* (Oxford: Oxford University Press, 1990), p. 216.

18. Kenneth Lockridge, *A New England Town: The First Hundred Years* (New York: W. W. Norton, 1970). Cronon, *Changes in the Land.* My discussion of these two books does not pretend to be a definitive analysis. My use of the authors' names to refer to their texts is, of course, not meant to imply I know their actual thinking. It is the inferred author or the author imputed from the text to which I am referring, a conception discussed in Chapter 6.

19. I ignore the "Afterword" in the later edition (New York: W. W. Norton, 1985).

20. Cronon, *Changes in the Land,* p. 161; but see his efforts to make this argument more complex (or less definite) throughout pp. 160–162.

21. Ibid., p. 13.

22. See his own long and somewhat confusing note on p. 89 about the relationship between idealistic and materialistic explanations of human behavior.

23. Marshall D. Sahlins, *Culture and Practical Reason* (Chicago: University of Chicago Press, 1976).

24. An extensive literature surrounds the debate whether or not Puritan subsistence farmers were capitalistic and market-oriented. A recent effort to resolve the issue as part of a reexamination of New England's ecological history is Carolyn Merchant, *Ecological Revolutions: Nature, Gender, and Science in New England* (Chapel Hill: University of North Carolina Press, 1989), chap. 5. Her long note 3 on pp. 308–310 provides a brief history of the debate with bibliographical references on the topic.

25. Merchant, *Ecological Revolutions,* addresses this omission as she provides an interpretation for the present intellectual generation.

26. How the dual lenses of narrative and argument analysis provide new perspective on other approaches to historical practice may be seen through example. Thus Allan Megill charts four important dimensions of the "historiographic enterprise" in "Recounting the Past: Description, Explanation, and Narrative in Historiography," *American Historical Review,* 94 (June 1989), 627–653. As his title suggests, he argues that recounting some aspect of historical reality is as important to historical practice as the explaining of it. To the extent that "telling what was the case" is significant in a text, then recounting will take an implicit if not also explicit form of a narrative in that text. The second task is connecting what is to be explained with what explains it. Since Megill argues, in line with current trends, that universalistic, omniscient, "scientific" forms of explanation are no longer the only models of explanation, then the rhetoric as well as the logic of inquiry lie at the root of such connections. The third task is argument or justification to validate either the evidentiary sources or the interpretation as best or true. Megill's last task is interpretive viewpoint or perspective that connects the text's world to its author's world. Explanation and argument can be investigated as part of rhetoric as argumentive theory and discourse analysis. From a textualist orientation, recounting and viewpoint can be studied under narratology as poetics. Seymour Chatman, *Coming to Terms: The Rhetoric of Narrative in Fiction and Film* (Ithaca: Cornell University Press, 1990), chaps. 1–2, argues strenuously, however, for not collapsing description into narrative and argument. See also Philippe Carrard, *Poetics of the New History: French Historical Discourse from Braudel to Chartier* (Baltimore: Johns Hopkins University Press, 1992), pp. 87–88, for the significance of commentary to historical exposition.

27. For introductions to narrative theory see Martin, *Recent Theories of Narrative;* Toolan, *Narrative;* Shlomith Rimmon-Kenan, *Narrative Fiction: Contemporary Poetics* (London: Methuen, 1983); Mieke Bal, *Narratology: Introduction to the Theory of the Narrative* (Toronto: University of Toronto Press, 1985); Steven Cohan and Linda M. Shires, *Telling Stories: A Critical Analysis of Narrative Fiction* (London: Routledge, 1988). Classic longer comprehensive introductions to the field include, among many, Wayne Booth, *The Rhetoric of Fiction,* 2d ed. (Chicago: University of Chicago Press, 1983); Chatman, *Story and Discourse* and *Coming to Terms;* Gérard Genette, *Narrative Discourse: An Essay in Method,* trans. Jane E. Lewin (Ithaca: Cornell University Press, 1980); idem, *Narrative Discourse Revisited;* Gerald Prince, *Narratology: The Form and Functioning of Narrative* (Berlin: Mouton, 1982); and Thomas M. Leitch, *What Stories Are: Narrative Theory and Interpretation* (University Park: Pennsylvania State University Press, 1986). The current state of the field is surveyed in the "Narratology Revisited" issues of *Poetics Today,* 11 (Summer and Winter 1990). Gerald Prince, *A Dictionary of Narratology* (Lincoln: University of Nebraska Press, 1987), provides a convenient guide to the terminology and concepts in the field.

28. See Carrard's preference for this phrase over rhetoric or discourse analysis in *Poetics of the New History,* pp. xiv–xv. See Struever, "Historical Discourse," pp. 249–271, for her usage.

29. To use the pertinent chapter titles of Jacques Barzun and Henry Graf, *The Modern Researcher* (New York: Harcourt, Brace and World, 1957), chaps. 12, 13.

According to Carrard, *Poetics of the New History,* pp. 8, 24–26, and 198–199, French manuals also enjoined new and old historians alike to adopt a plain, unembellished style to convey their facts.

30. Peter Gay, *Style in History* (New York: Basic Books, 1974), p. 3; my emphasis.

31. Ibid., p. 6. Louis Gottschalk, in his standard handbook *Understanding History: A Primer of Historical Method,* 2d ed. (New York: Alfred A. Knopf, 1969), pp. 17–19, saw the same gulf between "good style" and "good scholarship."

32. Hayden White, *Metahistory: The Historical Imagination in Nineteenth-Century Europe* (Baltimore: Johns Hopkins University Press, 1973).

33. Hayden White, *Tropics of Discourse: Essays in Cultural Criticism* (Baltimore: Johns Hopkins University Press, 1978) and *The Content of the Form: Narrative Discourse and Historical Representation* (Baltimore: Johns Hopkins University Press, 1987). Critical understanding of his first book is offered in "Metahistory: Six Critiques," *History and Theory,* 19, no. 4 (1980).

34. Hexter, "The Rhetoric of History," in *Doing History;* Lottinville, *The Rhetoric of History;* Hans Kellner, *Language and Historical Representation: Getting the Story Crooked* (Madison: University of Wisconsin Press, 1989). See "Style," in Ritter, *Dictionary of Concepts in History,* pp. 424–428, to get some inkling of the differences between older and newer approaches to the topic.

35. For one example, almost no essay in the comprehensive overview of historical practice in the United States during the 1970s, *The Past before Us: Contemporary Historical Writing in the United States,* edited for the American Historical Association by Michael Kammen (Ithaca: Cornell University Press, 1980), devotes any space to these matters. George Iggers and Harold Parker, eds., *International Handbook of Historical Studies: Contemporary Research and Theory* (Westport, Conn.: Greenwood Press, 1979), is an exception, with articles by Nancy Struever and Louis Mink. Even though the essays in Peter Burke, ed., *New Perspectives on Historical Writing* (University Park: Pennsylvania State University Press, 1991), cover such very up-to-date and nontraditional topical fields as history of the body and the history of reading, only the editor's last essay, "History of Events and the Revival of Narrative," treats at any length the problems of textualizing histories from the perspective of rhetoric or poetics.

36. In addition to White, LaCapra, Kellner, and Carrard, analyses of past historians' works by Stephen Bann, *The Clothing of Clio: A Study of Representation of History in Nineteenth-Century Britain and France* (Cambridge: Cambridge University Press, 1984); Linda Orr, *Jules Michelet: Nature, History, and Language* (Ithaca: Cornell University Press, 1976); and Ann Rigney, *The Rhetoric of Historical Representation: Three Narrative Theories of the French Revolution* (Cambridge: Cambridge University Press, 1990), exemplify what historical criticism might entail.

37. Recent histories of rhetoric show both the abandonment and revival of the field. For a brief overview of the history of rhetoric in this vein, see Renato Barilli, *Rhetoric,* trans. Giuliana Menozzi (Minneapolis: University of Minnesota Press, 1989). For a longer history focused more traditionally, see Brian Vickers, *In Defense of Rhetoric* (Oxford: Clarendon Press, 1988).

38. A suggestive essay on the trivialization and revitalization of rhetoric in and as a scholarly discourse since the eighteenth century is John Bender and David Wellbury,

"Rhetoricality: On the Modernist Return of Rhetoric," in *The Ends of Rhetoric: History, Theory, Practice,* ed. John Bender and David Wellbury (Stanford: Stanford University Press, 1990), pp. 3–39. Equally interesting are the articles in R. H. Roberts and J. M. M. Good, eds., *The Recovery of Rhetoric: Persuasive Discourse and Disciplinarity in the Human Sciences* (London: Bristol Classical Press, 1993), pts. 1 and 2, esp. Michael Cahn, "The Rhetoric of Rhetoric: Six Tropes of Disciplinary Self-Constitution," chap. 3.

39. Compare, for example, the brief definition of poetics in Carrard, *Poetics of the New History,* pp. xiv–xv.

40. For an overview of the field, see van Dijk, *Handbook of Discourse Analysis,* esp. vol. 1.

41. These categories are taken from such standard anthologies of literary theory as Raman Selden, *A Reader's Guide to Contemporary Literary Theory: A Comparative Introduction,* 2d ed. (Lexington: University Press of Kentucky, 1989); G. Douglas Atkinson and Laura Morrow, eds., *Contemporary Literary Theory* (Amherst: University of Massachusetts Press, 1989); Ann Jefferson and David Robey, eds., *Modern Literary Theory: A Comparative Introduction,* 2d ed. (London: B. T. Batsford, 1986); and Joseph Natoli, ed., *Tracing Literary Theory* (Urbana: University of Illinois Press, 1987). K. M. Newton, *Interpreting the Text: A Critical Introduction to the Theory and Practice of Literary Interpretation* (New York: Harvester Wheatsheaf, 1990), adopts a somewhat historical approach to most of these categories. For indications of the current state and its contending problematics see Ralph Cohen, ed., *The Future of Literary Theory* (New York: Routledge, 1989); Joseph Natoli, ed., *Literary Theory's Future(s)* (Urbana: University of Illinois Press, 1989); Peter Collier and Helga Geyer-Ryan, eds., *Literary Theory Today* (Cambridge: Polity Press, 1990); and David Carroll, ed., *The States of "Theory": History, Art, and Critical Discourse* (New York: Columbia University Press, 1990).

42. See, for example, the definitions of poetics, rhetoric, and stylistics in Oswald Ducrot and Tzvetan Todorov, *Encyclopedic Dictionary of the Sciences of Language,* trans. Catherine Porter (Baltimore: Johns Hopkins University Press, 1979); and A. J. Greimas and J. Courtés, *Semiotics and Language: An Analytical Dictionary,* trans. Larry Crist et al. (Bloomington: Indiana University Press, 1982). Compare the definition of poetics by Benjamin Hrushovski quoted in Rimmon-Kennon, *Narrative Fiction,* p. 2. Nancy Struever, "Historiography and Linguistics," in Iggers and Parker, *International Handbook of Historical Studies,* pp. 127–150, applies such a formalist linguistic model to historical discourse; but compare the broader approach of Carrard, *Poetics of the New History.*

43. Many scholars distinguish between text and discourse because the two terms follow from the differing premises of textualism and contextualism respectively. As Gunther Kress, "Ideological Structures in Discourse," in van Dijk, *Handbook of Discourse Analysis,* vol. 4, p. 27, states: "Discourse is a category that belongs to and derives from the social domain, and text is a category that belongs to and derives from the linguistic domain."

44. For brief introductions to the conflicting presuppositions among rhetorical theories, see Stanley Fish, "Rhetoric," in *Critical Terms for Literary Study,* ed. Frank Lentricchia and Thomas McLaughlin (Chicago: University of Chicago Press, 1990), pp. 203–222; Nancy Fraser, "The Uses and Abuses of French Discourse Theory for

Feminist Politics," in *Revaluing French Feminism: Critical Essays on Difference, Agency, and Culture,* ed. Nancy Fraser and Sandra Lee Bartky (Bloomington: Indiana University Press, 1992), pp. 177–194; and Edward Said, "The Problem of Textuality: Two Exemplary Positions," *Critical Inquiry,* 4 (Summer 1978), 673–714. Compare the difference in approaches of Paul Bové, "Discourse," in Lentricchia and McLaughlin, *Critical Terms for Literary Study,* pp. 50–65; and "Discourse," in Greimas and Courtés, *Semiotics and Language,* pp. 81–85.

45. Richard T. Vann, "Rhetoric and Social History," *Journal of Social History,* 10 (Winter 1976), 221–236.

46. On the relation between upper text and such lower text as notes, see also Struever, "Historical Discourse," p. 265; J. H. Hexter, *The History Primer* (New York: Basic Books, 1971), pp. 227–230; and Carrard, *Poetics of the New History,* pp. 158–165. I discuss paratext in Chapter 6.

47. A standard guide to terminology and concepts in the field is Richard A. Lanham, *A Handlist of Rhetorical Terms: A Guide for Students of English Literature* (Berkeley: University of California, 1968).

48. Donald N. McCloskey, *If You're So Smart: The Narrative of Economic Expertise* (Chicago: University of Chicago Press, 1990). See also idem, *The Rhetoric of Economics.*

49. White, *Metahistory,* esp. chap. 1. See Kellner, *Language and Historical Representation,* chap. 9, for an important view of the use of tropology by White in which he suggests that historical representation is better viewed as allegory than as structure. Peter De Bolla offers a critique of White's rhetorical theory through a comparison with LaCapra's rhetorical theory in a review of the two authors in "Disfiguring History," *Diacritics,* 16 (Winter 1986), 49–58; but see LaCapra, *History and Criticism,* chap. 1, for a statement of his own position vis-à-vis White. See also Lloyd S. Kramer, "Literature, Criticism, and Historical Imagination: The Challenge of Hayden White and Dominick LaCapra," in *The New Cultural History,* ed. Lynn Hunt (Berkeley: University of California Press, 1989), chap. 4.

50. Compare Paul Ricoeur, *Time and Narrative,* trans. Kathleen McLaughlin Blamey and David Pellauer, 3 vols. (Chicago: University of Chicago Press, 1984–88), vol. 1, pp. 161–168, for an analysis of White's approach to these levels.

51. In addition to the explication of this theory in *Metahistory,* see also his introduction to *Tropics of Discourse,* pp. 1–25. White defends tropology against his critics in "'Figuring the Nature of the Times Deceased': Literary Theory and Historical Writing." Wulf Kansteiner, "Hayden White's Critique of the Writing of History," *History and Theory,* 32, no. 3 (1993), 272–295, traces the modifications in White's theories as he contends with his critics.

52. E. P. Thompson, *The Making of the English Working Class* (New York: Pantheon, 1963), p. 11; White, *Tropics of Discourse,* p. 16.

53. Although Thompson divides his book into only three major parts, his own description of organization (*Making,* p. 12) adds an implicit fourth part, not unlike White's divisions.

54. White, *Tropics of Discourse,* pp. 15–19. For a quite different but still critical approach to Thompson's classic, see Joan Wallach Scott, *Gender and the Politics of History* (New York: Columbia University Press, 1988), chap. 4. Sande Cohen, *Historical Culture: On the Recoding of an Academic Discipline* (Berkeley: University of

California Press, 1986), pp. 195–228, provides an interesting interpretation of how Thompson's theory of narrative undercuts his political agenda through a close reading of *The Poverty of Theory*. Likewise, LaCapra, *Soundings in Criticism,* p. 198, n. 8, argues that Thompson's subtext subverts his explicit emplotment and thus shows as much about the "unmaking" as about the making of the English working class as a revolutionary subject. Harvey Kaye and Keith McClalland, eds., *E. P. Thompson: Critical Perspectives* (Oxford: Polity Press, 1990), offers more orthodox critiques according to standard disciplinary categories.

55. For example, Bryan D. Palmer, *The Descent into Discourse: The Reification of Language and the Writing of Social History* (Philadelphia: Temple University Press, 1990), pp. 67–78, but esp. pp. 68–69, not only accuses White of completely misrepresenting Thompson's work but also denies that tropology is useful to either historical practice or its criticism. Palmer raises the important problem of summary in historical and historiographic argument. After all, a summary is not the original of what it summarizes. (My summary is not even his summary, to paraphrase Magritte's important observation on his painting of a pipe.) He also defends Thompson against Joan Scott's criticism (pp. 78–86).

56. Struever, "Historical Discourse," pp. 262–263; Dominick LaCapra, "Rhetoric and History," in *History and Criticism,* pp. 34–35.

57. Especially Kellner, *Language and Historical Representation,* pt. 3.

58. To use Palmer's grudging formulation; *The Descent into Discourse,* p. 69.

59. On motifs and themes see Werner Sollors, ed., *The Return of Thematic Criticism* (Cambridge, Mass.: Harvard University Press, 1993).

60. White, *Tropics of Discourse,* chap. 11. Compare idem, "Michel Foucault," in *Structuralism and Since: From Lévi-Strauss to Derrida,* ed. John Sturrock (Oxford: Oxford University Press, 1979), pp. 61–115.

61. James Mellard, *Doing Tropology: Analysis of Narrative Discourse* (Urbana: University of Illinois Press, 1987), chap. 3.

62. Kellner, *Language and Historical Representation,* chap. 7.

63. Another suggestive essay along these lines is Richard Reinitz, "Niebuhrian Irony and Historical Interpretation: The Relationship between Consensus and New Left History," in *The Writing of History: Literary Form and Historical Understanding,* ed. Robert H. Canary and Henry Kozicki (Madison: University of Wisconsin Press, 1978), pp. 93–128.

64. Donald Ostrowski, "A Metahistorical Analysis: Hayden White and Four Narratives of 'Russian' History," *Clio,* 19 (Spring 1990), 215–236.

65. Carrard's book is cited in note 26 above.

66. De Bolla, "Disfiguring History." Suzanne Gearhart, *The Open Boundary of History and Fiction: A Critical Approach to the French Enlightenment* (Princeton: Princeton University Press, 1984), pp. 57–64, plays up the irony of White's use of an ahistorical formalist scheme to discuss the poeticity of history.

67. When Hayden White argues that Michel Foucault's sequence of epistemes in *The Order of Things* follows the sequence of tropes, he does concentrate upon what and how Foucault writes in the text on these matters. Nevertheless, he also discusses what tropes predominated in past discourses in the human sciences.

68. Struever, "Historical Discourse," pp. 249–271. Compare her critique of White's approach to rhetoric in idem, "Topics in History," *History and Theory,* 19,

no. 4 (1980), 66–79, as concentrating on tropology to the neglect of topology, hence emphasizing a narrow textualist poetics over the broader contextualist approach of rhetoric as she defines these terms. See the comments by John S. Nelson on this article, ibid., pp. 80–101.

69. See Chapter 8 for more on Foucault's theory of disciplinary discourse.

70. Michel de Certeau, "The Historiographical Operation," in *The Writing of History*, trans. Tom Conley (New York: Columbia University Press, 1988), chap. 2; but see also chap. 1.

71. Compare Michel Foucault, *The Archaeology of Knowledge*, including "The Discourse on Language" in an appendix, trans. Alan Sheridan (New York: Harper Colophon, 1972), esp. pp. 126–131; and idem, "Politics and the Study of Discourse," in *The Foucault Effect: Studies in Governmentality*, ed. Graham Burchell, Colin Gordon, and Peter Miller (Chicago: University of Chicago Press, 1991), pp. 59–60, on archives.

72. De Certeau, *The Writing of History*, p. 64.

73. John S. Nelson, "Seven Rhetorics of Inquiry: A Provocation," in Nelson, Megill, and McCloskey, *The Rhetoric of the Human Sciences*. This essay is itself an extraordinarily succinct, often apothegmatic synopsis of a very large area and a great many topics. My summary of his summary must necessarily omit much of Nelson's argument, stinting the contextualist side in favor of its textualist side. See what one might call a rehearsal for this article in idem, "Tropal History and the Social Sciences: Reflections on Struever's Remarks," *History and Theory*, 19, no. 4 (1980), 80–101.

74. Nelson, "Seven Rhetorics of Inquiry," p. 413.

75. Ibid., p. 415.

76. Ibid., p. 417.

77. Consult Lanham, *Handlist of Rhetorical Terms*, for definitions.

78. Nelson, "Seven Rhetorics of Inquiry," p. 419. Is my fabricated normal historian a trope in this sense?

79. Ibid., p. 422.

80. Paul Veyne, *Writing History: Essay on Epistemology*, trans. Mina Moore-Rinvolucri (Middletown, Conn.: Wesleyan University Press, 1984), pp. 218–224, offers some topoi common in historical writing. Nelson, "Tropal History and the Social Sciences," points out the relation between tropics and topics as he sees the matter.

81. Nelson, "Seven Rhetorics of Inquiry," p. 424.

82. Ibid., p. 426.

83. Ibid., p. 427.

84. More traditional approaches to hermeneutics are outlined in Richard E. Palmer, *Hermeneutics: Interpretation Theory in Schleiermacher, Dilthey, Heidegger, and Gadamer* (Evanston: Northwestern University Press, 1969); and Josef Bleicher, *Contemporary Hermeneutics: Hermeneutics as Method, Philosophy and Critique* (London: Routledge and Kegan Paul, 1980); but see David Couzens Hoy, *The Critical Circle: Literature and History in Contemporary Hermeneutics* (Berkeley: University of California Press, 1978).

85. Nelson, "Seven Rhetorics of Inquiry," p. 429.

86. Note once again the plea of LaCapra, *History and Criticism*, esp. pp. 35–43, for a broadened approach to what rhetoric is and how it works dialogically and performatively in a text, whether it is one that historians read or one that they produce.

5. Emplotment

1. Historians use temporal ordering more than they theorize about it. See, for example, the lack of time-related concepts in Harry Ritter, *Dictionary of Concepts in History* (Westport, Conn.: Greenwood Press, 1986), with the exception of "Periodization." My discussion of time in *A Behavioral Approach to Historical Analysis* (New York: Free Press, 1969), chaps. 10–11, offers references until the date of publication. For more recent references see John Bender and David E. Wellbury, eds., *Chronotypes: The Construction of Time* (Stanford: Stanford University Press, 1991).

2. Jacques Le Goff, *History and Memory,* trans. Steven Rendall and Elizabeth Claman (New York: Columbia University Press, 1992), pp. 1–19, traces the evolution of the distinction between past and present in Western thought. He summarizes Emile Benveniste's tripartite division of time into natural or physical time, chronological or "event" time, and linguistic time as tense and enunciation (p. 6) and discusses calendars (pp. xix–xx). Reinhart Koselleck, *Futures Past: On the Semantics of Historical Time,* trans. Keith Tribe (Cambridge, Mass.: MIT Press, 1985), pp. 21–38, 88–115, 130–155, 231–266, discusses some historic ideas about the nature of time and its representation in histories.

3. Paul Veyne, *Writing History: Essay on Epistemology,* trans. Mina Moore-Rinvolucri (Middletown, Conn.: Wesleyan University Press, 1984), p. 65. Although my interpretation of that statement here is not in accord with what he writes on that page, it does fit well his emphasis throughout the book on the singular significance of plotting to historical practice.

4. Savoie Lottinville, *The Rhetoric of History* (Norman: University of Oklahoma Press, 1976), p. 133.

5. Hence Claude Lévi-Strauss' argument about the synchronicity of all forms of history, even diachronic and dialectical ones, in the famous final chapter of *The Savage Mind* (Chicago: University of Chicago Press, 1966).

6. Gérard Genette, *Narrative Discourse: An Essay in Method,* trans. Jane E. Lewin (Ithaca: Cornell University Press, 1980), pp. 33–160, provides a good introduction to varying ways of treating time in narrative; but see idem, *Narrative Discourse Revisited,* trans. Jane E. Lewin (Ithaca: Cornell University Press, 1988), pp. 21–40, for a reconsideration of this topic. See also Paul Ricoeur, *Time and Narrative,* trans. Kathleen McLaughlin Blamey and David Pellauer, 3 vols. (Chicago: University of Chicago Press, 1984–88), for narrative time in both fiction and history. Compare Meir Sternberg, *Expositional Modes and Temporal Ordering in Fiction* (Baltimore: Johns Hopkins University Press, 1978); idem, "Telling in Time (I): Chronology and Narrative Theory," *Poetics Today,* 11 (Winter 1990), 901–948; and idem, "Telling in Time (II): Chronology, Teleology, Narrativity," ibid., 13 (Fall 1992), 463–541.

7. Elizabeth Deeds Ermarth, *Sequel to History: Postmodernism and the Crisis of Time* (Princeton: Princeton University Press, 1992), esp. pt. 1, is good on the assumptions of time as a social construction. If the time of historical discursive practice is a social construction, then should not "the historicization of time" be called more accurately "the historicalization of time"?

8. See Philippe Carrard, *Poetics of the New History: French Historical Discourse from Braudel to Chartier* (Baltimore: Johns Hopkins University Press, 1992), pp. 10–15, for one such example and analysis.

9. Terminology defined in Gerald Prince, *A Dictionary of Narratology* (Lincoln: University of Nebraska Press, 1987).

10. On periodization see Berkhofer, *A Behavioral Approach to Historical Analysis*, pp. 226–229; and Ritter, *Dictionary of Concepts in History*, pp. 313–319.

11. Which way has important political implications. That the uses of process and stasis in historical emplotment are political is the argument of Thomas P. Slaughter, "The Historian's Quest for Early American Culture(s), c. 1750–1825," *American Studies International*, 24 (April 1986), 29–59, as he classifies nineteen books about the seventy-five years in his title according to whether they assume static or dynamic, homogeneous or heterogeneous models of American society during the period.

12. Jacob Burckhardt, *The Civilization of the Renaissance in Italy* (1860), trans. S. G. C. Middlemore (New York: Random House, 1954), p. 265. In fact the book does contain diachronic portions: part 1 explains how the conditions that made for the revival of art and learning came about, and part 5 on religion describes a process of collapse and disintegration.

13. Perry Miller, *The New England Mind: The Seventeenth Century* (New York: Macmillan, 1939); quotations from p. viii.

14. Emmanuel Le Roy Ladurie, *Montaillou: The Promised Land of Error*, trans. Barbara Bray (New York: George Braziller, 1978). The English edition was an abridgment of the French edition, published in 1975 as *Montaillou, village occitan de 1294 à 1324*. Le Roy Ladurie does provide in the English edition a brief introduction outlining the historical context of his study, pp. vii–xvii.

15. As Trygve R. Tholfsen noted three decades ago, the idea of a period is "the historicization of the concept of culture"; *Historical Thinking: An Introduction* (New York: Harper and Row, 1967), p. 262. Should much be made of the progressive diminution of the amount of time "frozen" by each author into synchrony, from two to one centuries to a quarter-century, as the publication dates approach the present?

16. Thomas Kuhn, *The Structure of Scientific Revolutions* (Chicago: University of Chicago Press, 1962). Imre Lakatos and Alan Musgrave, eds., *Criticism and the Growth of Knowledge* (Cambridge: Cambridge University Press, 1970); and Gary Gutting, ed., *Paradigms and Revolutions: Applications and Appraisals of Thomas Kuhn's Philosophy of Science* (Notre Dame, Ind.: University of Notre Dame Press, 1980), examine both the concept and its applications.

17. Michel Foucault, *Les mots et les choses*, translated as *The Order of Things: An Archaeology of the Human Sciences* (New York: Pantheon, 1970).

18. Michel Foucault, *The Archaeology of Knowledge*, including "The Discourse on Language" in an appendix, trans. Alan Sheridan (New York: Harper Colophon, 1972), p. 191; and he elaborates the notion in the rest of the paragraph. I know of no collection of essays in English that examines the notion of the episteme and its application as such, but see, among others, Hayden White, *Tropics of Discourse: Essays in Cultural Criticism* (Baltimore: Johns Hopkins University Press, 1978), chap. 11; idem, "Michel Foucault," in *Structuralism and Since: From Lévi-Strauss to Derrida*, ed. John Sturrock (Oxford: Oxford University Press, 1979), pp. 61–115; Patricia O'Brien, "Michel Foucault's History of Culture," in *The New Cultural History*, ed. Lynn Hunt (Berkeley: University of California Press, 1989), chap. 1; and Thomas R. Flynn, "Michel Foucault and the Career of the Historical Event," in *At the*

Nexus of Philosophy and History, ed. Bernard P. Dauenhauer (Athens: University of Georgia Press, 1987), pp. 178–200.

19. As Stephen Greenblatt, "Towards a Poetics of Culture," in *The New Historicism,* ed. Harold Veeser (New York: Routledge, Chapman, and Hall, 1989), chap. 1, explains why he prefers the term "cultural poetics" to "New Historicism" to designate a strategy pointing beyond the dilemmas of Marxism and poststructuralism, he contextualizes U.S. society synchronically in the name of history. Louis A. Montrose, "Professing the Renaissance: The Poetics and Politics of Culture," ibid., p. 17, charges that Greenblatt's New Historicism is formalist at bottom in substituting "the synchronic text of a cultural system" for the "diachronic text of an autonomous literary history"; but see the whole essay. That Greenblatt is not a cultural materialist and therefore cannot be historical is the opinion of Carolyn Porter, "Are We Being Historical Yet?" in *The States of "Theory": History, Art and Cultural Discourse,* ed. David Carroll (New York: Columbia University Press, 1990), chap. 1. Compare Brook Thomas, *The New Historicism and Other Old-Fashioned Topics* (Princeton: Princeton University Press, 1991).

20. Paul Johnson, *A Shopkeeper's Millennium: Society and Revivals in Rochester, New York, 1815–1837* (New York: Hill and Wang, 1978).

21. Oscar Handlin, *The Uprooted: The Epic Story of the Great Migrations That Made the American People* (Boston: Little, Brown, 1952). Idem, *Boston's Immigrants: A Study in Acculturation,* rev. ed. (Cambridge, Mass.: Harvard University Press, 1959), extended the last phase in the final chapter of the earlier edition from 1865 to 1880. Whereas the earlier book, first published in 1941, reflected the sociological studies of immigration in the 1920s and 1930s, the later one borrowed from the social psychology of its time.

22. Reed Ueda, "Immigration and Moral Criticism in American History: The Vision of Oscar Handlin," *Canadian Review of American Studies,* 21 (Fall 1990), 183–202, argues that Handlin saw the immigrant journey as a metaphor for the history of the contemporary human condition as Westerners experienced increasing existential angst during the transition from traditional institutions and values to modernity.

23. Irving Howe, *World of Our Fathers: The Journey of East European Jews to America and the Life They Found and Made* (New York: Simon and Schuster, 1976); John Bodnar, *The Transplanted: A History of Immigrants in Urban America* (Bloomington: Indiana University Press, 1985).

24. Werner Sollors, *Beyond Ethnicity: Consent and Descent in American Culture* (New York: Oxford University Press, 1986), argues that the immigrant narrative frequently takes the plot form of a saga, including the story of Superman as a typical immigrant.

25. On duration see Genette, *Narrative Discourse,* pp. 86–112.

26. Depending on measurement, of course: 1492 to 1776 versus 1776 to 1993 equals 284 years versus 267; 1588 to 1789 versus 1789 to 1993 equals 201 years versus 204. In ten college survey textbooks published from 1984 to 1991, the number of pages devoted to the period before the swearing in of George Washington as president in 1789 under the newly adopted Constitution ranged from 126 to 278 out of a total of 855 and 1,343 pages. In another instance, the number of pages covering the period from 1763 to 1789, or the era from the coming of the American Revolution

to the ratification of the Constitution, ranged from a low of 36 percent to a high of 113 percent of the pages treating the time from Native American settlements to 1763.

27. Karl Popper, *The Open Society and Its Enemies,* 4th ed. rev. (New York: Harper Torchbooks, 1963), vol. 2, pp. 269, 278. Of relevance is Burleigh T. Wilkins, *Has History Any Meaning? A Critique of Popper's Philosophy of History* (Ithaca: Cornell University Press, 1987).

28. W. H. Walsh, "Meaning in History," in *Theories of History,* ed. Patrick Gardiner (Glencoe, Ill.: Free Press, 1959), pp. 296–297.

29. Ibid., p. 296.

30. Ibid., p. 303. As Wilkins, *Has History Any Meaning?* pp. 18–19, points out, one could disapprove of the pattern found in all of history as well as approve of it. That history is meaningless is as much a philosophy of history as that it is meaningful. On the whole issue see J. F. M. Hunter, "On Whether History Has a Meaning," in *Objectivity, Method, and Point of View: Essays in the Philosophy of History,* ed. W. J. van der Dussen and Lionel Rubinoff (Leiden: E. J. Brill, 1991), pp. 87–96; and William Dray's response, ibid., pp. 178–181.

31. Hayden White offers an interesting interpretation of the distinctions among chronicle, annal, and proper history that most working historians accept in "The Value of Narrativity in the Representation of Reality," reprinted in *The Content of the Form: Narrative Discourse and Historical Representation* (Baltimore: Johns Hopkins University Press, 1987), esp. pp. 42–44. There is a danger of overdrawing these distinctions in theory as opposed to what practice shows. Even annals can convey great meaning, if one takes the widespread popularity of a song by the pop singer Billy Joel, "We Didn't Start the Fire," as evidence. Most of the song's verses recite the names of persons, places, and events in the news year by year from 1949, the year of the singer's birth, to 1989, the year the song was written. The names range from those of politicians to sports figures and movie stars to fictional and real places. The events are drawn from the real and media worlds without implying that there is any difference. Overall, the selection seems miscellaneous except for rhyme and year. The choruses, however, are another matter, since they offer in their way a historical interpretation of the chronicle from the viewpoint of the singer's generation ("The Lessons of Rock and Roll," *Newsweek,* Jan. 29, 1990, p. 76). Similarly, William Cronon's effort to write a bare chronicle of Great Plains history contained many sentences that could only be called minimal narratives themselves. Even as he tried to produce only a "chronological listing of events as they occurred in sequence" and to "remove as much sense of connection" as possible, he admitted that he introduced meaning and narrative (and Great Story) into his chronicle through the criterion of importance. William Cronon, "A Place for Stories: Nature, History, and Narrative," *Journal of American History,* 78 (March 1992), 1350–51. How little or how much sense and pattern an annal or chronicle contains would seem to be a matter of how much common meaning through shared Great Stories writers and readers (or singers and listeners) bring to the text as opposed to any universal reading of these stories by "outsiders." Nevertheless, the distinction is important in the historical profession's understanding and justification of its practices.

32. Historians borrow this distinction from E. M. Forster, for example, Lee Benson, *Toward the Scientific Study of History: Selected Essays* (Philadelphia: J. B. Lippincott, 1972), pp. 81–82. Forster in turn borrowed it from Aristotle, according to Ricoeur, *Time and Narrative,* vol. 1, p. 182.

33. No historian surpasses Paul Veyne, *Writing History,* in declaring plot basic to historical practice. According to him, even "a theory is only the summary of a plot," p. 118.

34. Prince, *A Dictionary of Narratology,* p. 71.

35. Ibid., p. 72. Compare with definitions under "Narrative," pp. 58–60.

36. Peter Brooks, *Reading for the Plot: Design and Intention in Narrative* (New York: Alfred A. Knopf, 1984), p. 10.

37. Ibid., p. xi.

38. On narrative theory, in addition to previously cited works by Genette, Prince, Ricoeur, and Brooks, see Seymour Chatman, *Story and Discourse: Narrative Structure in Fiction and Film* (Ithaca: Cornell University Press, 1978); Shlomith Rimmon-Kenan, *Narrative Fiction: Contemporary Poetics* (London: Methuen, 1983); Mieke Bal, *Narratology: Introduction to the Theory of the Narrative* (Toronto: University of Toronto Press, 1985); Wallace Martin, *Recent Theories of Narrative* (Ithaca: Cornell University Press, 1986); Thomas M. Leitch, *What Stories Are: Narrative Theory and Interpretation* (University Park: Pennsylvania State University Press, 1986); Michael J. Toolan, *Narrative: A Critical Linguistic Introduction* (London: Routledge, 1988); Steven Cohan and Linda M. Shires, *Telling Stories: A Critical Analysis of Narrative Fiction* (London: Routledge, 1988); and the "Narratology Revisited" issues of *Poetics Today,* 11 (Winter and Summer 1990).

39. Ruth Ronen, "Paradigm Shift in Plot Models: An Outline of the History of Narratology," *Poetics Today,* 11 (Winter 1990), 827–842, clarifies various approaches to plot.

40. These controversies on the nature of emplotment and narrative are important in their own ways, of course. Ricoeur is deeply interested in these matters throughout *Time and Narrative.* See Hayden White, "The Metaphysics of Narrativity: Time and Symbol in Ricoeur's Philosophy of History," in *The Content of the Form,* chap. 7. Compare the different approaches to narrativity and life in David Carr, *Time, Narrative, and History* (Bloomington: Indiana University Press, 1986); and idem, "Narrative and the Real World," *History and Theory,* 25, no. 2 (1986), 117–131; with F. R. Ankersmit, *Narrative Logic: A Semantic Analysis of the Historian's Language* (The Hague: Martinus Nijhoff, 1983), esp. pp. 79–88; Hans Kellner, *Language and Historical Representation: Getting the Story Crooked* (Madison: University of Wisconsin Press, 1989), esp. chap. 12. The articles gathered under the title "Narratives and Social Identities" in *Social Science History,* 16 (Fall 1992), 479–537 and (Winter 1992), 591–692, take the coincidence of the narrativity of life and history as basic to any redirection of historical practice.

41. Ricoeur, *Time and Narrative,* vol. 1, p. 65.

42. Quotations from ibid., p. 66. See pp. 67–68 for more on the paradox of time. Ricoeur acknowledges (pp. 155–161) that he derived the idea of narrativity as configural act from Louis Mink. J. P. Connerty, "History's Many Cunning Passages: Paul Ricoeur's *Time and Narrative,*" *Poetics Today,* 11 (Summer 1990), 383–403, discusses Ricoeur's attempts to overcome dualisms of form and content, prefiguration and figuration, and text and context in fiction and history.

43. Is that what the anthropologist Anthony F. C. Wallace claims to have discovered in *Rockdale: The Growth of an American Village in the Early Industrial Revolution* (New York: W. W. Norton, 1978)? P. xvi: "But what I did not really expect,

and found to my considerable surprise, was the presence of 'plot'—that is to say, an organized structure of conflict among the main participants in the story that required a period of time before strategies of the sides combined toward resolution. It is this structure of conflict, among named persons about whom considerable information is known, that has made the work a poignant chronicle of struggles between well-intentioned men and women all striving toward a better age."

44. Examine, for instance, the sentences in Cronon's Great Plains chronicle as minimal narratives, "A Place for Stories," pp. 1350–51. Compare the definitions of "minimal narrative" and "minimal story" in Prince, *A Dictionary of Narratology*, p. 53. Is a synchronic history a narrative strictly speaking if a narrative needs at the least two stages and a transition? Since any synchronic history presumes a similarly structured era before and after it as Great Story, it implicitly, if not explicitly, affirms its place in a narrative.

45. On the concept of crisis, for example, see Michael Kammen, *Selvages & Biases: The Fabric of History in American Culture* (Ithaca: Cornell University Press, 1987), pp. 10–12; Ritter, *Dictionary of Concepts in History*, pp. 79–84.

46. Frank Kermode, *The Sense of Ending: Studies in the Theory of Fiction* (New York: Oxford University Press, 1967), provides a useful guide to historians who would investigate the implications of endings for historical narrative. Edward Said, *Beginnings: Intention and Method* (New York: Basic Books, 1975), will not prove as useful for beginning a history, but he nevertheless raises important issues for historical practice. Of still less direct use to historians is A. D. Nuttal, *Openings: Narrative Beginnings from the Epic to the Novel* (Oxford: Clarendon Press, 1992), who is reacting to current literary criticism. On the political uses of happy endings as opposed to sad ones, see Michael Denning, *Mechanic Accents: Dime Novels and Working-Class Culture in America* (London: Verso, 1987), pp. 211–213.

47. Said, *Beginnings*, pp. 5–6, distinguishes between beginnings and origins.

48. Paul Kennedy, *The Rise and Fall of the Great Powers* (New York: Random House, 1987).

49. Richard White, *The Middle Ground: Indians, Empires, and Republics in the Great Lakes Region, 1650–1815* (New York: Cambridge University Press, 1991), p. xi.

50. Judith R. Walkowitz, *City of Dreadful Delight: Narratives of Sexual Danger in Late-Victorian London* (Chicago: University of Chicago Press, 1992), chap. 5.

51. Margaret R. Somers, "Narrativity, Narrative Identity, and Social Action: Rethinking English Working-Class Formation," *Social Science History*, 16 (Winter 1992), 590–630; the quotations are taken chiefly from pp. 590–598.

52. Cronon, "A Place for Stories," pp. 1351–52. These plot lines are fleshed out with variations and political subtexts on pp. 1352–67.

53. Herbert Butterfield, *The Whig Interpretation of History* (London: G. Ball and Sons, 1931).

54. Robert A. Nisbet, *Social Change and History: Aspects of the Western Theory of Development* (New York: Oxford University Press, 1969), provides a history of the notion in Western society. Compare Peter Burke, *History and Social Theory* (Ithaca: Cornell University Press, 1992), chap. 5, "Social Theory and Social Change."

55. For example, Nancy Struever, "Philosophical Problems and Historical Solutions," in Dauenhauer, *At the Nexus of Philosophy and History*, pp. 75–76, points out the prevalence of whiggism in histories of philosophy by philosophers.

56. Manifestos for new histories in particular employ such visions of the past and future of historiography as progress. See, for example, Ernst Breisach, "Two New Histories: An Exploratory Comparison," ibid., pp. 138–156.

57. Johannes Fabian, *Time and the Other: How Anthropology Makes Its Object* (New York: Columbia University Press, 1983), stresses how these typologies operated through temporal manipulation.

58. To what extent is this true of the idea(l) of moral community as developed by E. P. Thompson or Natalie Zemon Davis? See Suzanne Desan, "Crowds, Community, and Ritual in the Work of E. P. Thompson and Natalie Davis," in Hunt, *The New Cultural History*, chap. 2. Compare the similar approach to workers' corporate self-identification and practices by William Sewell, *Work and Revolution in France: The Language of Labor from the Old Regime to 1848* (Cambridge: Cambridge University Press, 1980).

59. Stanley Aronowitz, in his new edition of *False Promises: The Shaping of American Working Class Consciousness* (Durham: Duke University Press, 1992), pp. xxiii–xxxiv, writes about the (con)fusion between the social relations in the artisanal workshop and the republican vision of equality in studies of the working class in North American history, so important is the theme as moral and conceptual foundation to the Great Story of capitalism and industrialization in the United States.

60. Mary P. Ryan, for example, in the first and second editions of her popular textbook, *Womanhood in America: From Colonial Times to the Present* (New York: New Viewpoints, 1975, 1979), portrayed the preindustrial period of American women's history as a relative golden age. See Linda Kerber, "Separate Spheres, Female Worlds, Woman's Place: The Rhetoric of Women's History," *Journal of American History*, 75 (June 1988), 9–39. Jane Flax, *Thinking Fragments: Psychoanalysis, Feminism, and Postmodernism in the Contemporary West* (Berkeley: University of California, 1990), pp. 142–178, outlines four basic (proto)typical stories that explain gender relations from feminist viewpoints.

61. Stow Persons, *The Decline of American Gentility* (New York: Columbia University Press, 1973), argued that the alienated intellectuals of recent times in the United States were the successors to the gentry who criticized the emerging social system that rendered them functionally useless and powerless.

62. Edward Said, for one, in "The Problem of Textuality: Two Exemplary Positions," *Critical Inquiry*, 4 (Summer 1978), 680–681, pointed out Derrida's dependence upon the traditional approach to Western history in order to critique it through deconstruction.

63. Giles Gunn, *Thinking Across the Grain: Ideology, Intellect, and the New Pragmatism* (Chicago: University of Chicago Press, 1992), pp. 12–13.

64. Somers, "Narrativity, Narrative Identity, and Social Action," pp. 596–597.

65. Somers suggests her own alternative version of English history, ibid., pp. 615–616.

66. For example, compare the emplotments in outline offered by Jacques Lyotard, "The Sign of History," in *Post-Structuralism and the Question of History*, ed. Derek Attridge, Geoff Bennington, and Robert Young (Cambridge: Cambridge University Press, 1987), pp. 162–163; and Jeffrey Alexander, "General Theory in the Postpositivist Mode: The 'Epistemological Dilemma' and the Search for Present Reason," in *Postmodernism and Social Theory: The Debate over General Theory*, ed. Steven

Seidman and David G. Wagner (Cambridge: Basil Blackwell, 1992), pp. 324–346, with that of Gunn.

67. White, *The Content of the Form*, p. 65.

68. Richard Hofstadter, *The Age of Reform: From Bryan to F. D. R.* (New York: Alfred A. Knopf, 1955), pp. 23–130.

69. Kenneth Stampp, *The Era of Reconstruction, 1865–1877* (New York: Alfred A. Knopf, 1965), chap. 1, "The Tragic Legend of Reconstruction," points out the three-act drama of Reconstruction that had been traditional to that time. Did either he or Eric Foner, *Reconstruction: America's Unfinished Business, 1863–1877* (New York: Harper and Row, 1988), shake the basic tripartite treatment of Reconstruction even though they changed moral judgments on it?

70. E. P. Thompson, *The Making of the English Working Class* (New York: Pantheon, 1963), p. 12.

71. Thompson himself goes on to characterize his book as "a group of studies, on related themes, rather than a consecutive narrative" (ibid.).

72. Somers, "Narrativity, Narrative Identity, and Social Action," p. 595, lists Thompson under her typical end options for the classic master narrative of English working-class history. Dominick LaCapra, *Soundings in Critical Theory* (Ithaca: Cornell University Press, 1989), p. 197, likens the structure of the plot to that of the "older three-decker Bildungsroman."

73. Thomas Bender, *Community and Social Change in America* (New Brunswick, N.J.: Rutgers University Press, 1978), discusses the typology and its application to U.S. history. See another application in David J. Russo, *Families and Communities: A New View of American History* (Nashville: American Association for State and Local History, 1974).

74. David Grayson Allen, *In English Ways: The Movement of Societies and the Transferral of English Local Law and Custom to Massachusetts Bay in the Seventeenth Century* (Chapel Hill: University of North Carolina Press, 1982).

75. Louis Hartz, *The Liberal Tradition: An Interpretation of American Political Thought since the Revolution* (New York: Harcourt, Brace, 1955), offers a classic statement of this thesis.

76. White, *The Middle Ground*, p. ix, complains that even the so-called new Indian history followed this model. See Fabian, *Time and the Other*, for the theory behind this process.

77. The so-called New Immigration History repudiated this older emplotment by showing that immigration to the United States was an extension of changing economic and social situations in Europe rather than a reflection of changes in America. Bodnar, *The Transplanted*, is a synthesis of this scholarship and its new emplotment, esp. chap. 1.

78. No historian of the American past packed more "facts" into this typological framework for a period than Robert Wiebe in *The Search for Order, 1877–1920* (New York: Hill and Wang, 1967).

79. Synchronic histories attempt a one-stage periodization, although they may be emplotted by such a standard literary form as irony.

80. Carrard, *Poetics of the New History*, pp. 47–54.

81. What role does metaphor play in the stage theory of periodization? The four seasons and the seven stages of man, like the trinity, all hint at metaphorical founda-

tions for periodization by stages. Compare Alexander Demandt, *Metaphern für Geschichte: Sprachbilder und Gleichnisse im historische-politischen Denken* (Munich: Beck, 1978). See also Richard H. Brown, *A Poetics for Sociology: Toward a Logic of Discovery for the Human Sciences* (Cambridge: Cambridge University Press, 1977), chap. 4, on metaphors.

82. White lists the sources of his inspiration in "'Figuring the Nature of the Times Deceased': Literary Theory and Historical Writing," in *The Future of Literary Theory,* ed. Ralph Cohen (New York and London: Routledge, 1989), pp. 412–413, n. 18.

83. For introductory surveys of these efforts see Bal, *Narratology,* chaps. 11–12; Martin, *Recent Theories of Narrative,* chaps. 4–6; and Rimmon-Kenan, *Narrative Fiction,* chap. 9.

84. Edward Rothstein, "Hard Up for a Plot? Get with the Program," *New York Times,* September 22, 1991, sec. H, pp. 13, 18–19.

85. Werner Sollors, *Beyond Ethnicity: Consent and Descent in American Culture* (New York: Oxford University Press, 1986).

86. Dale Porter, *The Emergence of the Past: A Theory of Historical Explanation* (Chicago: University of Chicago Press, 1981), pp. 146–160. Porter's scheme actually employs, as he admits, Norman Friedman's elaboration of Crane's approach to plotting, for which see Friedman's *Form and Meaning in Fiction* (Athens: University of Georgia Press, 1975), chap. 5. Porter warns against applying his scheme too literally, pp. 156–159.

87. Ibid., pp. 180–190.

88. White, *Tropics of Discourse,* chap. 11. See also James M. Mellard, *Doing Tropology: Analysis of Narrative Discourse* (Urbana: University of Illinois Press, 1987), pp. 23–29.

89. In addition to his *Open Society and Its Enemies,* see *The Poverty of Historicism* (New York: Harper Torchbooks, 1964).

90. Linda Hutcheon, *A Poetics of Postmodernism: History, Theory, and Fiction* (New York and London: Routledge, 1988), suggests the possibility of differing assumptions about time in modern histories through her analysis of postmodern fiction. Compare Ermarth, *Sequel to History,* for an even more emphatic statement on the implications of a new kind of temporality in recent fiction for representing history. That traditional, professional versions of temporality may be inadequate for American Indian history is the argument of Calvin L. Martin in his introduction and epilogue to the essays collected in *The American Indian and the Problem of History* (New York: Oxford University Press, 1987), but see the other essays for varying opinions. Compare Bogumil Jewsiewicki and David Newbury, eds., *African Historiographies: What History for Which Africa?* (Beverly Hills: Sage Publications, 1986), for similar concerns. This theme is resumed in Chapter 9.

6. Partiality as Voice and Viewpoint

1. Although the basic argument of this chapter was drafted before the publication of Philippe Carrard, *Poetics of the New History: French Historical Discourse from Braudel to Chartier* (Baltimore: Johns Hopkins University Press, 1992), which contains important observations on voice and point of view, I was able to use some of his argument and examples for my purposes.

2. Peter Novick, *That Noble Dream: The "Objectivity Quest" and the American Historical Profession* (Cambridge: Cambridge University Press, 1988), p. 2. Compare "Objectivity," in Harry Ritter, *Dictionary of Concepts in History* (Westport, Conn.: Greenwood Press, 1986), pp. 302–308. See also "Interpretation," ibid., pp. 243–248.

3. Henry Steele Commager, *The Nature and the Study of History,* ed. Raymond H. Meussig and Vincent R. Rogers (Columbus, Ohio: Charles E. Merrill Books, 1965), p. 53.

4. Novick, *That Noble Dream,* p. 6, uses the term "full disclosure" as he warns his readers about his own philosophical commitments with regard to objectivity.

5. Stephen Vaughan, ed., *The Vital Past: Writings on the Uses of History* (Athens: University of Georgia Press, 1985), provides an anthology of texts discussing the purposes of history. What schoolchildren of various nations read in their history books about the pasts of their own and other societies is the subject of Marc Ferro, *The Use and Abuse of History; or How the Past Is Taught* (London: Routledge & Kegan Paul, 1984); and Frances Fitzgerald, *America Revised: History Schoolbooks in the Twentieth Century* (Boston: Little, Brown, 1979).

6. Joyce Appleby, *Capitalism and the New Social Order: The Republican Vision of the 1790s* (New York: New York University Press, 1984), esp. pp. 31, 105.

7. That a postmodernist approach to historical representation in general, and specifically that of Hayden White, poses moral dilemmas for such shared standards is the focus of Saul Friedlander, ed., *Probing the Limits of Representation: Nazism and the "Final Solution"* (Cambridge, Mass.: Harvard University Press, 1992).

8. David B. Davis, "Reflections on Abolitionism and Ideological Hegemony," *American Historical Review,* 92 (Oct. 1987), 810.

9. David B. Davis begins the first volume of his trilogy, *The Problem of Slavery in Western Culture* (Ithaca: Cornell University Press, 1966), p. 3, noting the incongruity, as does Peter Kolchin, *American Slavery, 1619–1877* (New York: Hill and Wang, 1993), p. 3. See also Carl Degler, "The Irony of American Negro Slavery," in *Perspectives and Irony in American Slavery,* ed. Harry P. Owens (Jackson: University Press of Mississippi, 1976), pp. 3–5.

10. Ernest R. May, *"Lessons" of the Past: The Use and Misuse of History in American Foreign Policy* (New York: Oxford University Press, 1973); and Richard E. Neustadt and Ernest R. May, *Thinking in Time: The Uses of History for Decision Makers* (New York: Free Press, 1986), are directed more to teaching high government officials how to use the lessons of history to formulate present policy than to enlightening the general public, as the preface to the latter makes plain.

11. Howard Zinn, *The Politics of History* (Boston: Beacon Press, 1970), pt. 1, provided some concise statements about the premises and goals of radical history, but see Chapter 8 of this volume on the politics of oppositional viewpoint and authority.

12. All three controversies are introduced in Novick, *That Noble Dream,* pp. 96–97, 588–589, 612–621. Richard Hofstadter, *The Progressive Historians: Turner, Beard, Parrington* (New York: Alfred A. Knopf, 1968), chaps. 5–8, discusses Beard's interpretation and the scholarly responses to it. In Paul A. David et al., *Reckoning with Slavery: A Critical Study in Quantitative History of American Negro Slavery* (New York: Oxford University Press, 1976), five historians respond to Fogel and Engerman.

13. For example, Irwin G. Wylie, *The Self-Made Man in America: The Myth of Rags to Riches* (New Brunswick, N.J.: Rutgers University Press, 1954); John Cawelti,

Apostles of the Self-Made Man: Changing Concepts of Success in America (Chicago: University of Chicago Press, 1965).

14. Stephan Thernstrom, *Poverty and Progress: Social Mobility in a Nineteenth-Century City* (Cambridge, Mass.: Harvard University Press, 1964). Stephan Thernstrom, *The Other Bostonians: Poverty and Progress in the American Metropolis, 1880–1970* (Cambridge, Mass.: Harvard University Press, 1973), presents his reconsideration of the issues and problems.

15. It is unclear whether many of his professional readers noted the skewed framework at the time. By using almost a reverse mirror image of Thernstrom's method of analysis, Gary Nash, *The Urban Crucible: Social Change, Political Consciousness, and the Origins of the American Revolution* (Cambridge, Mass.: Harvard University Press, 1979), arrives at the conclusion that democratic innovation in the Revolutionary era came from the great mass of people. He divides the population of colonial American cities into a small elite and everyone else and so, by combining a middling and bottom group together, implies that democratic innovation stemmed from the bottom group alone.

16. For example, Daniel D. Luria, "Wealth, Capital, and Power: The Social Meaning of Home Ownership," *Journal of Economic History*, 7 (Autumn 1976), 261–282.

17. The classic pluralist study was Robert Dahl, *Who Governs: Democracy and Power in an American City* (New Haven: Yale University Press, 1961). The classic power elite study was Floyd Hunter, *Community Power Structure* (Chapel Hill: University of North Carolina Press, 1953). David C. Hammack, "Problems in the Historical Study of Power in Cities and Towns of the United States, 1800–1960," *American Historical Review*, 88 (April 1978), 323–349, discusses both the pluralist and stratificationist theories of community power and their uses by historians.

18. James Henretta, "The Study of Social Mobility: Ideological Assumptions and Conceptual Bias," *Labor History*, 18 (Spring 1977), 167.

19. According to Michael B. Katz, "Social Class in North American History," *Journal of Interdisciplinary History*, 11 (Spring 1981), 583. Compare Raymond Williams, *Keywords: A Vocabulary of Culture and Society*, rev. ed. (New York: Oxford University Press, 1985), pp. 299–301, on "Status."

20. Lawrence Goodwyn, *Democratic Promise: The Populist Moment in America* (New York: Oxford University Press, 1976); Richard Hofstadter, *The Age of Reform: From Bryan to F. D. R.* (New York: Alfred A. Knopf, 1955), chaps. 1–3.

21. In presenting an interpretation of the Populist movement for the 1980s, Steven Hahn, *The Roots of Southern Populism: Yeoman Farmers and the Transformation of the Georgia Upcountry, 1850–1890* (New York: Oxford University Press, 1985), argues that popular radicalism was based in those areas where once herders had grazed their stock on common lands or petty producers had lived and farmed; and as the advance of the cotton economy, capitalism, and the marketplace transformed these people into tenants, they turned to Populism.

22. Cited in note 19 above. Compare Daniel T. Rodgers, *Contested Truths: Keywords in American Politics since Independence* (New York: Basic Books, 1987).

23. Hofstadter, *The Progressive Historians*, treated the school through its three founders.

24. John Higham's articles, "The Cult of the 'American Consensus': Homogenizing Our History," *Commentary,* 27 (Feb. 1959), 93–100, and "Beyond Consensus: The Historian as Moral Critic," *American Historical Review,* 67 (April 1962), 609–625, gave the school its name. Gene Wise, *American Historical Explanations: A Strategy for Grounded Inquiry* (Homewood, Ill.: Dorsey Press, 1973), preferred the term "Counterprogressive" for the school. Marian J. Morton, *The Terror of Ideological Politics: Liberal Historians in a Conservative Mood* (Cleveland: Case Western Reserve University Press, 1972); and Bernard Sternsher, *Consensus, Conflict, and American Historians* (Bloomington: Indiana University Press, 1975), examined the school's politics and assumptions.

25. See as an early example Barton Bernstein, ed., *Towards a New Past: Dissenting Essays in American History* (New York: Random House, 1968).

26. For an example of this school, see most of the essays gathered in Eric Foner, ed., *The New American History* (Philadelphia: Temple University Press, 1990). I offered the name "neoprogressive" in "The Two New Histories: Competing Paradigms for Interpreting the American Past," *OAH Newsletter,* 2 (May 1983), 9–12.

27. That recent enthusiasm to set straight earlier Eurocentric, whitewashed American Indian history for a native-centered history has generated a set of counter-myths is the argument of the provocative essays in James Clifton, ed., *The Invented Indian: Cultural Fictions and Government Policies* (New Brunswick, N.J.: Transaction Publishers, 1990).

28. William H. Walsh, *An Introduction to the Philosophy of History,* 3d ed. (London: Hutchinson, 1967), pp. 19–22, 94–118. See also William Dray, *On History and Philosophers of History* (Leiden: E. J. Brill, 1989), chap. 3; and idem, *Philosophy of History* (Englewood Cliffs, N.J.: Prentice-Hall, 1964), chap. 3.

29. See, for example, for theories of the state, Robert R. Alford and Roger Friedland, *Powers of Theory: Capitalism, the State, and Democracy* (Cambridge: Cambridge University Press, 1985), particularly the glossary, pp. 444–451; for the argument over structure versus agency, see Anthony Appiah, "Tolerable Falsehoods: Agency and the Interests of Theory," in *Consequences of Theory,* ed. Jonathan Arac and Barbara Johnson (Baltimore: Johns Hopkins University Press, 1991), pp. 63–90.

30. Given the seeming self-evident naturalness of ideology, full disclosure would be even harder than I have implied here. See Chapter 8 on the politics of viewpoint. Compare Gayatri Chakravorty Spivak, "The Politics of Interpretation," *Critical Inquiry,* 9 (Sept. 1982), 259–278.

31. See the various terms in Gerald Prince, *A Dictionary of Narratology* (Lincoln: University of Nebraska Press, 1987). See also Gérard Genette, *Narrative Discourse Revisited,* trans. Jane E. Lewin (Ithaca: Cornell University Press, 1988), pp. 15, 45–46; and Paul Ricoeur, *Time and Narrative,* vol. 1, trans. Kathleen McLaughlin Blamey and David Pellauer (Chicago: University of Chicago Press, 1984), esp. chap. 2.

32. In addition to Genette and Ricoeur, cited above, see Seymour Chatman, *Coming to Terms: The Rhetoric of Narrative in Fiction and Film* (Ithaca: Cornell University Press, 1990), pp. 109–115. For the problems of telling history through film see Robert A. Rosenstone, "History in Images/History in Words: Reflections on the Possibility of Really Putting History onto Film," *American Historical Review,* 93 (Dec. 1988), 1173–85, and the four commentaries that follow, pp. 1186–1227. On the nontransparency of photography see, for example, Alan Trachtenberg, *Reading*

American Photographs: Images as History, Mathew Brady to Walker Evans (New York: Hill and Wang, 1989). The classic work on pictorial representation is E. H. Gombrich, *Art and Illusion: A Study in the Psychology of Pictorial Representation* (London: Phaidon Books, 1960); but see also Norman Bryson, *Vision and Painting: The Logic of the Gaze* (New Haven: Yale University Press, 1983), for an important critique.

33. Seymour Chatman, *Story and Discourse: Narrative Structure in Fiction and Film* (Ithaca: Cornell University Press, 1978), suggests these and the following questions in his elaborate typology of the narrator, chap. 5. Equally suggestive for these questions and this chapter are Susan Sniader Lanser, *The Narrative Act: Point of View in Prose Fiction* (Princeton: Princeton University Press, 1981); and Boris Uspensky, *A Poetics of Composition: The Structure of the Artistic Text and Typology of a Compositional Form,* trans. Valetina Zavarin and Susan Wittig (Berkeley: University of California Press, 1973).

34. My use of scales is suggested by Lanser's use of spectrums in *The Narrative Act,* chap. 4. She in turn was inspired, as she acknowledges, p. 156, n. 7, by Chatman, *Story and Discourse.*

35. This scale omits the important hermeneutic problems of understanding the remains as a source or text itself. What sort of translation and interpretation do historians need to perform upon an artifact in order to transform it into a "text" for their methodological purposes?

36. The aims, rules, and techniques of documentary editing are given in Mary-Jo Kline, *A Guide to Documentary Editing* (Baltimore: Johns Hopkins University Press, 1987).

37. Laurel Thatcher Ulrich, *A Midwife's Tale: The Life of Martha Ballard, Based on Her Diary, 1785–1812* (New York: Alfred A. Knopf, 1990), pp. 7–8, points out the formulaic nature of Martha Ballard's religious statements in her diary. Compare Marilyn Ferris Motz, *True Sisterhood: Michigan Women and Their Kin, 1820–1920* (Albany: State University of New York Press, 1983), chap. 3, on the stylistics of nineteenth-century rural women's correspondence. This scale of intervention applies to artifacts as well; thus a photograph of a building, locale, etc. appears more mimetic than a verbal description of the object or place, but it too has its framing devices that suppress and enhance the viewpoint taken. See again Trachtenberg, *Reading American Photographs.*

38. Julian P. Boyd, ed., *The Papers of Thomas Jefferson,* vol. 6 (Princeton: Princeton University Press, 1952), p. 612, n. 26.

39. Cited in note 37 above.

40. Carlo Ginzburg, *The Cheese and the Worms: The Cosmos of a Sixteenth-Century Miller* (1976), trans. John Tedeschi and Anne Tedeschi (Baltimore: Johns Hopkins University Press, 1980). Emmanuel Le Roy Ladurie, *Montaillou: The Promised Land of Error* (1975), trans. Barbara Bray (New York: George Braziller, 1978).

41. For a sampling of criticism with further references, see Dominick LaCapra, *History and Criticism* (Ithaca: Cornell University Press, 1985), chap. 2; Renato Rosaldo, "From the Door of His Tent: The Fieldworker and the Inquisitor," in *Writing Culture: The Poetics and Politics of Ethnography,* ed. James Clifford and George E. Marcus (Berkeley: University of California Press, 1986), pp. 77–97; and Leonard E. Boyle, "Montaillou Revisited: *Mentalité* and Methodology," in *Pathways*

to *Medieval Peasants,* ed. J. A. Battis (Toronto: Pontifical Institute of Medieval Studies, 1981), pp. 119–140. Carlo Ginzburg offers one answer to these complaints in a long endnote to the English edition of *The Cheese and the Worms,* pp. 154–155, and another in "The Inquisitor as Anthropologist," in his *Clues, Myths, and Historical Method,* trans. John and Anne Tedeschi (Baltimore: Johns Hopkins University Press, 1989).

42. Natalie Zemon Davis, *The Return of Martin Guerre* (Cambridge, Mass.: Harvard University Press, 1983); idem, *Fiction in the Archives: Pardon Tales and Their Tellers in Sixteenth-Century France* (Stanford: Stanford University Press, 1987).

43. Although the discourse of Davis' book takes an argument form more than a narrative one. This is a good instance of the difference mentioned in Chapter 4 between the form of content as discourse and the actual content as the story moves from one genre into another. See Carlo Ginzburg's commentary on this book and on narrative history in general in "Proofs and Possibilities: In the Margins of Natalie Zemon Davis' *The Return of Martin Guerre,*" *Yearbook of Comparative and General Literature,* 37 (1988), 113–127.

44. Davis, *Fiction in the Archives,* p. 4.

45. Martin Jay, "Of Plots, Witnesses, and Judgments," in Friedlander, *Probing the Limits of Representation,* pp. 103–104. Carlo Ginzburg, "Checking the Evidence: The Judge and the Historian," *Critical Inquiry,* 18 (Autumn 1991), 79–92, also mentions prior narrativization in the evidence.

46. Margaret R. Somers, "Narrativity, Narrative Identity, and Social Action: Rethinking English Working-Class Formation," *Social Science History,* 16 (Winter 1992), 603–605. Compare George Steinmetz, "Reflections on the Role of Social Narratives in Working-Class Formation: Narrative Theory in the Social Sciences," ibid., p. 490, who divides individuals' stories into those about themselves as individuals, those about themselves as collectivities, and collective narratives which influence individuals' lives but which they do not comprehend as collective or influential. The third kind is revealed by the historian or social scientist.

47. Michel Foucault, ed., *I, Pierre Rivière, Having Slaughtered My Mother, My Sister, and My Brother . . .: A Case of Parricide in the 19th Century,* trans. Frank Jellinek (New York: Pantheon, 1975).

48. Robert Finlay, "The Refashioning of Martin Guerre," *American Historical Review,* 93 (June 1988), 553–571, complains that Davis was more inventive than her sources warranted; but see her reply, ibid., pp. 572–603.

49. Charles E. Rosenberg, *The Trial of the Assassin Guiteau: Psychiatry and Law in the Gilded Age* (Chicago: University of Chicago Press, 1968).

50. The more historians assume that past and present peoples organize their lives according to conscious narrativization, the less the intervention supposedly needed to historicize those lives. The more historians' narratives incorporate or build upon the historical actors' own narrative ways of organizing and understanding the world, the more the derivation of the historian's own narrative and its organization becomes one of mimesis according to traditional conventions of historical representation as literary realism. The historian's narrative becomes a synthesis of the various kinds of narratives that individuals, collectivities, and societies construct about themselves in combination with the ways in which historians understand themselves and their world(s). No wonder most of the articles in *Social Science History* on "Narratives and Social

Identities" (16 [Fall and Winter 1992], 479–537, 591–692) presume a correlation between actors' explicit use of narrative and the historians' use of narratives. No wonder Simon Schama, "The Age of Innocence and Where It Went" (paper delivered at a session on "Rescuing Narrative from Narrative Theory" at the meeting of the Organization of American Historians, April 3, 1992), believes that historians cannot operate without assuming a correlation between the narrativization of everyday lives and of history.

51. My efforts in this section and the rest of the chapter are restricted to suggesting some of the major implications of literary theory about voice and viewpoint to the theorist of historical practice. I try neither to cover the full utility nor to summarize the multitudinous literature for normal history. The whole topic in historical practice deserves its own book. The best we have about contemporary historical practice is Carrard, *Poetics of the New History*. Good starting surveys in literary theory in English on the issues are Wallace Martin, *Recent Theories of Narrative* (Ithaca: Cornell University Press, 1986), chap. 6; Shlomith Rimmon-Kenan, *Narrative Fiction: Contemporary Poetics* (London: Methuen, 1983), chaps. 6–8; Mieke Bal, *Narratology: Introduction to the Theory of the Narrative* (Toronto: University of Toronto Press, 1985), pp. 100–149; and Ricoeur, *Time and Narrative*, vol. 2, pp. 88–99. Chatman, *Story and Discourse* and *Coming to Terms*; Uspensky, *Poetics of Composition*; and Lanser, *The Narrative Act*, are more detailed but very useful. How far apart contextualist and textualist analyses of viewpoint are may be sampled in a comparison of the varying viewpoints of Lanser, *The Narrative Act*; Robert Weimann, *Structure and Society in Literary History: Studies in the History and Theory of Historical Criticism* (Charlottesville: University Press of Virginia, 1976), chap. 6; and Linda Hutcheon, *A Poetics of Postmodernism: History, Theory, and Fiction* (New York and London: Routledge, 1988). Comments germane to a postmodernist approach to voice and viewpoint are scattered throughout Elizabeth Deeds Ermarth, *Sequel to History: Postmodernism and the Crisis of Time* (Princeton: Princeton University Press, 1992).

52. Voice and viewpoint apply to historical practice in two different ways: in reading a historian's text and in reading the sources themselves. I treat only the former here, although in practice they are, of course, connected.

53. Thus my attribution throughout this book of thoughts, arguments, or stories to an author as I describe or analyze them is, of course, the author I infer from my reading of the text. What the real author intended by a text is, through my reading, transmuted into the goals of the textual author, just as the reader of this book imputes motive and thought to me and constructs me as the implied author. The term "implied author" originated with Wayne C. Booth, *The Rhetoric of Fiction* (Chicago: University of Chicago Press, 1961). Lanser, *The Narrative Act*, launched "textual author"; see her caveat, p. 120, n. 18, about Booth's implied author. In turn, see Chatman, *Coming to Terms*, chaps. 5–6, 8–9; and Genette, *Narrative Discourse Revisited*.

54. I am skipping the important issue of extrafictional clues to the author in the text, such as name and credentials, biography on the dustjacket, general reputation, preface, dedication, and even perhaps title. Lanser, *The Narrative Act*, pp. 121–131.

55. A good example of a scholar as author's denying how a scholar as reader construed his work is David B. Davis' challenge of Thomas Haskell's summation of

his work in "Reflections on Abolitionism and Ideological Hegemony." All authors have experienced the same feeling after reading learned reviews of their books.

56. Two anthologies provide an introduction to the various theories in the field as it was constituted earlier in the United States: Susan Suleiman and Inge Crosman, eds., *The Reader in the Text: Essays on Audience and Interpretation* (Princeton: Princeton University Press, 1980); Jane P. Tompkins, ed., *Reader-Response Criticism: From Formalism to Post-Structuralism* (Baltimore: Johns Hopkins University Press, 1980). For more recent theory see Robert C. Holub, *Reception Theory: A Critical Introduction* (London: Methuen, 1984); Stephen Mailloux, *Rhetorical Power* (Ithaca: Cornell University Press, 1989); Robert Scholes, *Protocols of Reading* (New Haven: Yale University Press, 1989), among many. Robert C. Holub, *Crossing Borders: Reception Theory, Poststructuralism, Deconstruction* (Madison: University of Wisconsin Press, 1992), chaps. 1–2, provides a brief history of the scholarly reception of German reception theory in the United States. Martyn P. Thompson, "Reception Theory and the Interpretation of Historical Meaning," *History and Theory*, 32, no. 3 (1993), 248–272, argues that historians should combine insights from both Anglo-American theorists of author-intended meaning and German theorists of audience-created meaning.

57. "Interpretive community" comes from Stanley Fish, *Is There a Text in This Class? The Authority of Interpretive Communities* (Cambridge, Mass.: Harvard University Press, 1980); "reading formation" was coined by Tony Bennett, "Texts in History: The Determinations of Readings and Their Texts," in *Post-Structuralism and the Question of History*, ed. Derek Attridge, Geoff Bennington, and Robert Young (Cambridge: Cambridge University Press, 1987), pp. 63–81, esp. p. 70. Theories of reader reception and reader formations can also be applied to the reading of sources. Thus Judith R. Walkowitz, *City of Dreadful Delight: Narratives of Sexual Danger in Late-Victorian London* (Chicago: University of Chicago Press, 1992), infers and constructs multiple readerships for the same newspaper articles.

58. Little investigation and much impressionism exist on the actual readership of history, but see Carrard, *Poetics of the New History*, pp. 133–148, for suggestions about the topic in general. Compare George E. Marcus and Dick Cushman, "Ethnographies as Texts," *Annual Review of Anthropology*, 11 (1982), 51–54, for readership in anthropology. They include a category of action-oriented government officials for that field that I feel is not as evident for history. There are, however, policy histories and the field of what is called public history in the United States.

59. For example, Simon Schama, "Clio Has a Problem," *New York Times Magazine*, Sept. 8, 1991, pp. 30–34.

60. Little has been done on these matters, but see again Carrard, *Poetics of the New History*, pp. 138–142, 158–164, for a start. Anthony Easthope, *British Post-Structuralism since 1968* (London: Routledge, 1988), p. 220, states that implied or model readers are interpretations derived from the text, while actual readers are "situated within social and historical practice," as if the latter were less a textualization than the former. In any case, he argues that inscribed readers as theorized by scholars all read the same way, whereas real readers all read differently.

61. On annotation see Nancy Struever, "Historical Discourse," in *Handbook of Discourse Analysis*, ed. Teun A. van Dijk, vol. 1 (London: Academic Press, 1985), p. 265; Carrard, *Poetics of the New History*, pp. 158–164. Gérard Genette, "Intro-

duction to the Paratext," *New Literary History*, 22 (Spring 1991), 261–272, offers what his title states. Hutcheon, *The Politics of Postmodernism* (London: Routledge, 1989), pp. 82–92, provides a brief commentary on paratext in metafiction.

62. The whole notion of the eye equaling "I" and vice versa in eyewitness accounts; for which see the introduction by John Carey, ed., *Eyewitness to History* (Cambridge, Mass.: Harvard University Press, 1987), on what constitutes good reporting.

63. Compare Samuel Eliot Morison's letters from the Harvard Columbus expedition in *By Land and by Sea* (New York: Alfred A. Knopf, 1953), chap. 4, with his *Admiral of the Ocean Sea: A Life of Christopher Columbus* (Boston: Little, Brown, 1942). David Farber felt that growing up in Chicago gave him added insight through firsthand experience into the riots surrounding the Democratic National Convention in 1968 for his book, *Chicago '68* (Chicago: University of Chicago Press, 1988).

64. Timothy H. Breen, *Imagining the Past: East Hampton Histories* (Reading, Mass.: Addison-Wesley, 1989). He also employs the first person plural frequently but most often uses the third person.

65. Elinor Langer, *Josephine Herbst* (Boston: Atlantic–Little, Brown, 1984), uses the first person pronoun to suggest her own empathic identification with her (self-proclaimed) heroine, notably in the introduction but also throughout the book. Since she quotes Herbst extensively, another frequent use of "I" occurs in the book. A bolder use of the first person occurs in Lillian Faderman, *Scotch Verdict: Miss Pirie and Miss Woods v. Dame Cumming Gordon* (New York: William Morrow, 1983), both to "present a modern perspective" on an early nineteenth-century trial and to indicate empathic identification with the two women accused of lesbianism. Faderman also confesses, pp. 9–10, to some (minor?) manipulation of the historical record to tell a better story.

66. The use of the first person features prominently in a review essay by Patricia Limerick, "The Multicultural Islands," *American Historical Review*, 97 (Feb. 1992), 121–135, and raises strong objections from Robert H. Zieger, ibid. (June 1992), 1001–03, who argues that such personal engagement could be signified by more traditional voicing than the intrusive use of "I." Carrard, *Poetics of the New History*, hypothesizes that the use of "I" increases in recent French historical writing as the historian becomes more famous and therefore speaks for as well as part of the French historical establishment (p. 99).

67. See, for example, the self-conscious quest for evidence and its construction as history in the essay of Greg Dening, *History's Anthropology: The Death of William Gooch* (Lanham, Md.: University Press of America, 1988), which combines autobiography and historiography with history.

68. Martin Duberman, *Black Mountain: An Exploration in Community* (New York: E. P. Dutton, 1972).

69. Savoie Lottinville, *The Rhetoric of History* (Norman: University of Oklahoma Press, 1976), p. 104. See Carrard, *Poetics of the New History*, p. 23, for earlier French advice to the same effect.

70. Is this different for the francophone historiographic world than for the anglophone historiographic world? Carrard, *Poetics of the New History*, suggests as much.

71. Paul Hernadi, "Clio's Cousins: Historiography as Translation, Fiction, and Criticism," *New Literary History*, 7 (Winter 1976), 252–253, argues that the implied

author and the narrator in historical narratives must be the same to make it a history, while the two must be different in fictional narratives. He maintains that this difference is one of the fundamental ways of distinguishing history from fiction. For similar arguments, see Gérard Genette, "Fictional Narrative, Factual Narrative," *Poetics Today,* 11 (Winter 1990), 763–770; and Dorrit Cohn, "Signposts of Fictionality: A Narratological Perspective," ibid., pp. 786–800. Carrard, *Poetics of the New History,* pp. 86–87, agrees on the whole.

72. For a strong statement that historians should read for the dialogic tensions in all texts, see LaCapra, *History and Criticism,* pp. 35–43.

73. Michel de Certeau, *The Writing of History,* trans. Tom Conley (New York: Columbia University Press, 1988), pp. 63–64, makes interesting observations about the use of "we," and the translator extends these thoughts to why the pronouns "I" and "you" are effaced for the third person in historical writing (pp. xix–xx). I omit discussion of the use of "one." On its use in French historical practice, see Carrard, *Poetics of the New History,* pp. 95–97.

74. Patricia Nelson Limerick, *The Legacy of Conquest: The Unbroken Past of the American West* (New York: W. W. Norton, 1978), p. 291.

75. See Prince, *A Dictionary of Narratology,* pp. 43–44, for definition and references. Lottinville, *Rhetoric of History,* p. 50, says that historians employ indirect discourse in lieu of dialogue.

76. Thus in *Chicago '68* Farber tries to give rhetorical due to each of his major collective historical actors by adopting their language and tone as closely as possible.

77. Compare Carrard, *Poetics of the New History,* p. 182.

78. Ibid., pp. 196–197.

79. This is the beginning of my attempt to translate some of the important but multiply interpreted ideas of Mikhail Bakhtin on polyvocality and the dialogue of socially situated subjects he called dialogism and heteroglossia, through the notions of multiple voices and multiple viewpoints. Michael Holquist, *Dialogism: Bakhtin and His World* (London: Routledge, 1990), offers a brief introduction to Bakhtin's ideas by the leading translator of his works into English. Robert Stam, "Mikhail Bakhtin and Left Cultural Critique," in *Postmodernism and Its Discontents: Theories and Practices,* ed. E. Ann Kaplan (London: Verso, 1988), pp. 116–145, provides another interpretation. For a sampling of recent opinion about Bakhtin's theories, see the two special issues of *Critical Studies:* 1, no. 2 (1989), "The Bakhtin Circle Today"; and 2, nos. 1–2 (1990), "Mikhail Bakhtin and the Epistemology of Discourse."

80. Quoted in Fritz Stern, ed., *The Varieties of History: From Voltaire to the Present* (New York: Meridian Books, 1956), p. 25.

81. Narrative theorists dispute whether to call perspective "viewpoint," "focalization," or something else. See "Point of View" and "Focalization," in Prince, *A Dictionary of Narratology,* pp. 31–32, 73–76. See Chatman for new terms to distinguish between narrator and character perspectives in "Characters and Narrators: Filter, Center, Slant, and Interest-Focus," *Poetics Today,* 7 (Summer 1986), 189–204, and *Coming to Terms,* chap. 9. William Nelles, "Getting Focalization into Focus," *Poetics Today,* 11 (Summer 1990), 365–382, also tries to clarify Genette on the terminology. Carrard, *Poetics of the New History,* uses the term "focalization" but titles the relevant section "Perspective," pp. 104–121.

82. I owe this quotation and its translation to my colleague Jonathan Beecher. See Norman Friedman, *Form and Meaning in Fiction* (Athens: University of Georgia Press, 1975), pp. 145–150, 153–156, on types of omniscience.

83. Lottinville, *Rhetoric of History*, p. 104.

84. Ibid., pp. 105–108.

85. What those advocating viewpoint call "omniscience" becomes "zero focalization" for those preferring other terminology. Elizabeth Deeds Ermarth, *Realism and Consensus in the English Novel* (Princeton: Princeton University Press, 1983), chap. 3, eschews point of view as too bound to a notion of individual consciousness; she prefers the term "perspective" to designate the supposedly faceless, omniscient narrator conventional to realism in literature.

86. De Certeau, *The Writing of History*, throughout part 1 makes much of rupture between the past and present as foundational to historical practice.

87. These planes or levels are derived from combining Chatman, *Story and Discourse*, pp. 151–152; Uspensky, *A Poetics of Composition*; Roger Fowler, *Linguistic Criticism* (Oxford: Oxford University Press, 1986), chap. 9. I leave out the phraseological plane of Uspensky and Fowler. Other systems are proposed by Prince, *A Dictionary of Narratology*, pp. 31–32, 73–76; Rimmon-Kennon, *Narrative Fiction*, chaps. 6–8; and Lanser, *A Narrative Act*. Friedman, *Form and Meaning in Fiction*, pp. 134–142, offers a brief history of the idea of point of view as an explicit concept.

88. In my scheme "multiple viewpoints" designates the perspectival aspects of multiple voices in Bakhtinian dialogism.

89. This simplification is similar to Lottinville's distinction between author and character viewpoint, but it allows for more viewpoints on each side of the representational world than his theory seems to encourage.

90. Uspensky, *A Poetics of Composition*, uses the term "bird's-eye view," but "panoramic" and "synoptic" are my terms and not those of literary theorists. See Dale H. Porter, *The Emergence of the Past: A Theory of Historical Explanation* (Chicago: University of Chicago Press, 1981), chap. 6, on synoptic view.

91. To borrow the title of John Chavez, *The Lost Land: The Chicano Image of the Southwest* (Albuquerque: University of New Mexico Press, 1984), which offers a brief polemical interpretation of the historical context of these terms and their meaning for the Spanish-speaking inhabitants of the area.

92. What Laura Mulvey in "Visual Pleasure and Narrative Cinema," reprinted in her *Visual and Other Pleasures* (Bloomington: Indiana University Press, 1989), chap. 3, christened the "male gaze" is cinematic voyeurism achieved through framing the scene in such a way that the image of the female is represented as a passive but erotic object for the active consumption of the male through observation. Likewise, the ideology of viewpoint in photography is explored by Trachtenberg, *Reading American Photographs*.

93. See, for example, the defense of the New Deal by William E. Leuchtenberg, "The Achievement of the New Deal," in *Fifty Years Later: The New Deal Evaluated*, ed. Harvard Sitkoff (New York: Alfred A. Knopf, 1985), pp. 211–231, as opposed to the other articles in the book.

94. To expose the moral bases and political foundations of the social sciences is a major goal of the rhetoric of human sciences project. See, for example, John S. Nelson, Allan Megill, and Donald N. McCloskey, eds., *The Rhetoric of the Human*

Sciences: Language and Argument in Scholarship and Public Affairs (Madison: University of Wisconsin Press, 1987); Herbert W. Simons, ed., *Rhetoric in the Human Sciences* (London: Sage, 1989) and *The Rhetorical Turn: Invention and Persuasion in the Conduct of Inquiry* (Chicago: University of Chicago Press, 1990); and R. H. Roberts and J. M. M. Good, eds., *The Recovery of Rhetoric: Persuasive Discourse and Disciplinarity in the Human Sciences* (London: Bristol Classical Press, 1993). For an extended critique of the political judgments grounding various social science methodologies, see, among many, Christopher Lloyd, *Explanation in Social History* (Oxford: Basil Blackwell, 1986).

95. Goodwyn, *Democratic Promise.*

96. If the historian provides enough quotations in the text, the reader and critic can construct an alternative version of the (hi)story based on a more dialogical representation of diverse socially situated viewpoints.

97. F. R. Ankersmit, *Narrative Logic: A Semantic Analysis of the Historian's Language* (The Hague: Martinus Nijhoff, 1983), pp. 216–224, argues the crucial importance of point of view to construction of what he calls the *narratio,* but he does not distinguish its many aspects. Thus some of his discussion (pp. 25–26) of the role of point of view in historical as opposed to fictional discourses needs augmentation. See also his concept of the "frame" in *The Reality Effect in the Writing of History: The Dynamics of Historiographical Topology* (Amsterdam: Koninklijke Nederlandische Akadamie van Wetenshaften Noord-Hollandische, 1989), p. 24.

98. Stephen Tyler, "Post-Modern Ethnography: From Document of the Occult to Occult Document," in *Writing Culture: The Poetics and Politics of Ethnography,* ed. James Clifford and George E. Marcus (Berkeley: University of California Press, 1986), pp. 130–131, is a vigorous presentation of this viewpoint. Compare Donna Haraway, "Situated Knowledges: The Science Question in Feminism and the Privilege of Partial Perspective," *Feminist Studies,* 14 (Fall 1988), 581, for a similar condemnation of the traditional ocular viewpoint, but see pp. 581–590 for her comments on vision in general. Compare the denunciation of traditional approaches to viewpoint in Ermarth, *Realism and Consensus in the English Novel,* esp. pt. 1, with her condemnation of traditional approaches to historical time in *Sequel to History,* esp. pt. 1.

7. Representing Multiple Viewpoints and Voices

1. Paula Rothenberg, "Critics of Attempts to Democratize the Curriculum Are Waging a Campaign to Misrepresent the Work of Responsible Professors," *Chronicle of Higher Education,* 37 (April 10, 1991), B3.

2. Ibid. That such documents are not self-interpreting lies at the center of the original-intent argument about what the founding fathers meant in the Constitution, for which see Jack N. Rakove, ed., *Interpreting the Constitution: The Debate over Original Intent* (Boston: Northeastern University Press, 1990).

3. Frederick Jackson Turner, *The Frontier in American History* (New York: Henry Holt, 1920), p. 1.

4. Reprinted in ibid., pp. 259–260, 266.

5. Ibid., p. 11. Note the use of "we" instead of the third person. Who is this "we" from a socioeconomic, ethnic, or sexual viewpoint?

6. Ibid., pp. 2–3, 38.

7. Ray Allen Billington, *Frederick Jackson Turner: Historian, Scholar, Teacher* (New York: Oxford University Press, 1973), pp. 435–443, gives some idea of Turner's politics; Richard Hofstadter, *The Progressive Historians: Turner, Beard, Parrington* (New York: Alfred A. Knopf, 1968), chaps. 1–4, places Turner's ideas in their general "American" setting. See also the rhetorical analysis of Ronald H. Carpenter, *The Eloquence of Frederick Jackson Turner* (San Marino, Calif.: Huntington Library, 1983).

8. Turner, *The Frontier in American History*, p. 3.

9. Patricia Limerick, *The Legacy of Conquest: The Unbroken Past of the American West* (New York: W. W. Norton, 1987), p. 21.

10. Ibid., p. 27.

11. Ibid., pp. 27–30.

12. That the New Western History presumes the Great Story of the expansion of European economies and nation-states in the "American frontier" is even more explicit in William Cronon, George Miles, and Jay Gitlin, eds., *Under an Open Sky: Rethinking America's Western Past* (New York: W. W. Norton, 1992), for example, pp. 8–10.

13. Both Ellen K. Coughlin, "Myth and History Clash as Scholars Question Anew the Traditional Story of the American West," *Chronicle of Higher Education*, 27 (Nov. 21, 1990), A4, A6; and Richard Bernstein, "Unsettling the Old West," *New York Times Magazine*, March 18, 1990, pp. 34, 56–59, mention Limerick and her book as prominent in the New Western History. Will some future historian write a book about Limerick's West as a summation of the mythology of her time as Henry Nash Smith did about Turner's West in *Virgin Land: The American West as Symbol and Myth*, 2d ed. (Cambridge, Mass.: Harvard University Press, 1970)? For other "new" approaches to the West, often with similar basic assumptions about the personnel and the processes, see Cronon, Miles, and Gitlin, *Under an Open Sky;* and Richard White, *"It's Your Misfortune and None of My Own": A New History of the American West* (Norman: University of Oklahoma Press, 1991).

14. Much of this and the section on the New Anthropology later in this chapter was inspired by the argument over orientalism, which started with Edward W. Said, *Orientalism* (New York: Pantheon, 1978). See his own updates: "Orientalism Reconsidered," in *Arab Society: Continuity and Change*, ed. Samih Farsoun (London: Croom Helm, 1985), pp. 105–122; "Orientalism Revisited," *Middle East Report*, no. 150 (1985), 32–36; and "Representing the Colonized: Anthropology's Interlocutors," *Critical Inquiry*, 15 (Winter 1990), 205–225. For an overview of the recent debate see also Gyan Prakash, "Writing Post-Orientalist Histories of the Third World: Perspectives from Indian Historiography," *Comparative Studies in Society and History*, 32 (April 1990), 383–408; the challenge to this article by Rosalind O'Hanlon and David Washbrook, "After Orientalism: Culture, Criticism, and Politics in the Third World," ibid., 34 (Jan. 1992), 141–167; and the reply by Gyan Prakash, "Can the 'Subaltern' Ride? A Reply to O'Hanlon and Washbrook," ibid., pp. 168–184. See also idem, "Postcolonial Criticism and Indian Historiography," *Social Text*, nos. 31/32 (1992), 8–19; and Lisa Lowe, *Critical Terrains: French and British Orientalisms* (Ithaca: Cornell University Press, 1991), esp. chap. 1.

15. Richard Bernstein, *The New Constellation: The Ethical-Political Horizons of Modernity/Postmodernity* (Cambridge: Polity Press, 1991), chap. 3, provides an ele-

mentary overview of the issues of both incommensurability and otherness. Compare what was once debated in philosophy under the rubric of other minds and relativism. Martin Hollis and Steven Lukes, eds., *Rationality and Relativism* (Oxford: Basil Blackwell, 1982), offer an introduction to this earlier debate.

16. Compare the questions posed by Tzvetan Todorov, *The Conquest of America: The Question of the Other,* trans. Richard Howard (New York: Harper and Row, 1984), pp. 3–4.

17. Bernard Cohn discusses why Westerners did not accept other people's histories as such because they applied their own conception of "real events" and the notion of an unmediated history, in "Anthropology and History in the 1980s: Toward a Rapprochement," in *The New History, The 1980s and Beyond: Studies in Interdisciplinary History,* ed. Theodore K. Rabb and Robert I. Rotberg (Princeton: Princeton University Press, 1988), pp. 245–249.

18. Johannes Fabian, *Time and the Other: How Anthropology Makes Its Object* (New York: Columbia University Press, 1983), explores how Westerners used temporalization to subordinate other societies as Others. Michel de Certeau, *The Writing of History,* trans. Tom Conley (New York: Columbia University Press, 1988), stresses the notion of a rupture between present and past as central to historical practice. He refers to the dead of the past not only as absent but also as other, for example, pp. 2, 14, 38, 99, 101.

19. Reinhart Koselleck, *Futures Past: On the Semantics of Historical Times,* trans. Keith Tribe (Cambridge, Mass.: MIT Press, 1985), pp. 159–197, discusses some of these earlier Self/Other divisions.

20. See, among other recent works, in addition to Said, *Orientalism;* and Fabian, *Time and the Other;* Adam Kuper, *The Invention of Primitive Society: Transformations of an Illusion* (London: Routledge, 1988); Marianna Torgovnick, *Gone Primitive: Savage Intellects, Modern Lives* (Chicago: University of Chicago Press, 1990); Robert Young, *White Mythologies: Writing History and the West* (London: Routledge, 1990). Bernard McGrane, *Beyond Anthropology: Society and the Other* (New York: Columbia University Press, 1989), offers a brief history of changing Western conceptions of the Other from the sixteenth century to the present.

21. In modern philosophy and psychology, even the inner person was divided between a superior self as ego or consciousness and a baser other as libido or unconsciousness. Michael Theunissen, *The Other: Studies in the Social Ontology of Husserl, Heidegger, Sartre, and Buber,* trans. Christopher Macann (Cambridge, Mass.: MIT Press, 1984), provides an introduction to the philosophical and psychological divisions of the self. Dominick LaCapra, *History and Criticism* (Ithaca: Cornell University Press, 1985), pp. 137–138, 140, argues that the alterity of history is not simply out there but "always already" in us as well.

22. To employ a title often used in revisionist histories, for example, in the history of sexuality and gender: Sheila Rowbotham, *Hidden from History: Rediscovering Women in History from the 17th Century to the Present* (London: Pluto Press, 1973); Martin B. Duberman, Martha Vicinus, and George Chauncy, Jr., eds., *Hidden from History: Reclaiming the Gay and Lesbian Past* (New York: New American Library, 1989).

23. As in the title of Eric Wolf, *Europe and the People without History* (Berkeley: University of California Press, 1982).

24. The point of Said, *Orientalism.*

25. Cited above in note 23.

26. Harry Liebersohn and Daniel Segal, "Introduction," in *Crossing Cultures: Essays in the Displacement of Western Civilization* (Tucson: University of Arizona Press, 1992), p. xiii.

27. Thomas Bender, "Wholes and Parts: The Need for Synthesis in American History," *Journal of American History,* 73 (June 1986), 120–136; and commentaries in ibid., 74 (June 1987), 109–122. Jim Sharpe, "History from Below," in *New Perspectives on Historical Writing,* ed. Peter Burke (University Park: Pennsylvania State University Press, 1991), pp. 24–41, discusses the aims of history from the bottom up; but compare Giovanni Levi, "On Microhistory," ibid., pp. 93–113.

28. See Gregory L. Ulmer, "Mystory: The Law of Idiom in Applied Grammatology," in *The Future of Literary Theory,* ed. Ralph Cohen (London: Routledge, 1989), pp. 304–323, for his much more complicated definition and argument.

29. Compare Gayatri Chakravorty Spivak, "Can the Subaltern Speak?" in *Marxism and the Interpretation of Culture,* ed. Cary Nelson and Larry Grossberg (Urbana: University of Illinois Press, 1988), who notes that "representation" possesses two quite different but related meanings: representation in the sense of "'speaking for,' as in politics"; and "'re-presentation,' as in art or philosophy." She uses this distinction in a more specific and political sense than I do here.

30. One of my Native American students refused to read William Cronon's *Changes in the Land: Indians, Colonists, and the Ecology of New England* (New York: Hill and Wang, 1983) beyond the first few pages, because, he argued, if the author could not understand so fundamental a fact as that Indians had not migrated across the Bering Strait but had always existed in North America, on what else could he be trusted?

31. Particularly on the whole issue of secularism versus religious fundamentalism. The problems of cross-cultural epistemologies and ontologies are discussed quite persuasively by R. S. Khare, "The Other's Double—The Anthropologist's Bracketed Self: Notes on Cultural Representation and Privileged Discourse," *New Literary Review,* 23 (Winter 1992), 1–23.

32. Clifford Geertz, "'From the Native's Point of View': On the Nature of Anthropological Understanding," in *Local Knowledge: Further Essays in Interpretive Anthropology* (New York: Basic Books, 1983), chap. 3, explores some of the problems of cross-cultural translation and understanding.

33. Clifford Geertz, *Works and Lives: The Anthropologist as Author* (Stanford: Stanford University Press, 1988), p. 144.

34. Chandra Talpade Mohanty, "Under Western Eyes: Feminist Scholarship and Colonial Discourses," in *Third World Women and the Politics of Feminism,* ed. Chandra Talpade Mohanty, Ann Russo, and Lourdes Torres (Bloomington: Indiana University Press, 1991), p. 52.

35. Ruth Roach Pierson, "Experience, Difference, Dominance and Voice in the Writing of Canadian Women's History," in *Writing Women's History: International Perspectives,* ed. Karen Offen, Ruth Roach Pierson, and Jane Randall (Bloomington: Indiana University Press, 1991), p. 90.

36. Ibid., p. 93.

37. Quoted in Giles Gunn, *Thinking across the American Grain: Ideology, Intellect, and the New Pragmatism* (Chicago: University of Chicago Press, 1992), p. 10.

38. Pierson, "Experience, Difference, Dominance," p. 94.

39. Ibid.

40. Joan W. Scott, "The Evidence of Experience," *Critical Inquiry,* 17 (Summer 1991), 773–797.

41. Ibid., pp. 777, 779, and 780.

42. Ibid., pp. 797, 793. Compare the similarities of the critique by O'Hanlon and Washburn of the post-Orientalism debate in "After Orientalism" with Scott's critique of the debate about experience. Does not Scott's argument also apply to the conceptions of desire and memory?

43. See Joan Scott's assessment of poststructuralist implications for women's history in "Women's History," in Burke, *New Perspectives on Historical Writing,* pp. 57–61.

44. Whether such parts presume a social whole may be left to discussion by others. Foucault has been criticized for sometimes presuming the overall working of a society without explicating it. More important for the purposes of my argument at this point is the criticism of Foucault's conception of discursive practice as being univocal. Craig Calhoun, "Culture, History, and the Problem of Specificity in Social Theory," in *Postmodernism and Social Theory: The Debate over General Theory,* ed. Steven Seidman and David G. Wagner (Cambridge: Basil Blackwell, 1992), pp. 281–282, n. 18, accuses Foucault of writing monologically even when critiquing it.

45. Limerick, *The Legacy of Conquest,* p. 257.

46. Ibid., p. 258.

47. Ibid., pp. 214–218.

48. Ibid., pp. 219, 220.

49. Ibid., p. 221.

50. Ibid., pp. 220—221.

51. Should she have called these "histories" to show conflicts within each group? This is the problem of aggregating a viewpoint: How many of whom agreed on what? How local is local? Why assume that subgroupings are more united than society as a whole?

52. Limerick, *The Legacy of Conquest,* pp. 291–292.

53. Ibid., p. 292.

54. Ibid.

55. Ibid.

56. Ibid., p. 25.

57. Quoted in Cushing Strout, "Border Crossings: History, Fiction, and *Dead Certainties,*" *History and Theory,* 31, no. 2 (1992), 156.

58. Leading theoretical works on the New Anthropology or Ethnography, usually called postmodern by those opposed to it, are George Marcus and Michael Fischer, *Anthropology as Cultural Critique: An Experimental Moment in the Human Sciences* (Chicago: University of Chicago Press, 1986); James Clifford and George E. Marcus, eds., *Writing Culture: The Poetics and Politics of Ethnography* (Berkeley: University of California Press, 1986); James Clifford, *The Predicament of Culture: Twentieth-Century Ethnography, Literature, and Art* (Cambridge, Mass.: Harvard University Press, 1988). For a more radical reflexive approach, see James A. Boon, *Other Tribes,*

Other Scribes: Symbolic Anthropology in the Comparative Study of Cultures, Histories, Religions, and Texts (Cambridge: Cambridge University Press, 1982); and *Affinities and Extremes: Crisscrossing the Bittersweet Ethnology of East Indies History, Hindu-Balinese Culture, and Indo-European Allure* (Chicago: University of Chicago Press, 1990); Stephen A. Tyler, *The Unspeakable: Discourse, Dialogue, and Rhetoric in the Postmodern World* (Madison: University of Wisconsin Press, 1987). Geertz, *Works and Lives*, chap. 6, offers a somewhat sarcastic description and evaluation of this movement. Francis E. Mascia-Lees, Patricia Sharpe, and Colleen Ballerino Cohen, "The Postmodernist Turn in Anthropology: Cautions from a Feminist Perspective," *Signs: Journal of Women in Culture and Society*, 15 (Autumn 1989), 7–33; and Marilyn Strathern, "Out of Context: The Persuasive Fictions of Anthropology," *Current Anthropology*, 28 (June 1987), 251–270, provide critical appraisals of the movement. See also Marc Manganaro, ed., *Modernist Anthropology: From Fieldwork to Text* (Princeton: Princeton University Press, 1990); and George Marcus, ed., *Rereading Cultural Anthropology* (Durham: Duke University Press, 1992).

59. Liebersohn and Segal, *Crossing Cultures*, pp. xii–xiii.

60. For a similar version of this Great Story, see Clifford, *The Predicament of Culture*, p. 22; and Marcus and Fischer, *Anthropology as Cultural Critique*, p. 114.

61. Edward Said, *Culture and Imperialism* (New York: Alfred A. Knopf, 1993), p. xxv.

62. See Liebersohn and Segal, *Crossing Cultures*, pp. xv–xvi, for the blunt statement that the "multicultural, creolizing world of the present is a consequence of a multicultural, creolizing past."

63. Clifford, *The Predicament of Culture*, p. 10. Compare the introduction and essays in Elizabeth Tonkin, Maryon McDonald, and Malcolm Chapman, eds., *History and Ethnicity* (London: Routledge, 1989).

64. Marcus and Fischer, *Anthropology as Cultural Critique*, p. 78.

65. Clifford, *The Predicament of Culture*, p. 46. Culture and society are constructs of whom? for whom? by whom? Compare once again Tonkin, McDonald, and Chapman, *History and Ethnicity*.

66. Clifford, *The Predicament of Culture*, p. 22. Compare the implications of these metaphors for viewpoint with the subway system of Limerick.

67. Or so argues Johannes Fabian, "Presence and Representation: The Other and Anthropological Writing," *Critical Inquiry*, 16 (Summer 1990), 763–765. Compare the conception of evocation and dialogue in Tyler, "Post-Modern Ethnography," pp. 122–140. Even a text in dialogue form might reproduce relationships of power, especially if languages need translation. Talal Asad, "The Concept of Cultural Translation in British Social Anthropology," in Clifford and Marcus, *Writing Culture*, esp. pp. 156–163, argues that translation imposes the viewpoint as well as the voice of the self on the other as a part of the power of imperialist language, because a language is both some group's orientation to the world and some group's mode of thought in a situation of unequal relationships. Compare Mohanty, "Under Western Eyes," p. 55.

68. Richard White, *The Middle Ground: Indians, Empires, and Republics in the Great Lakes Region, 1650–1815* (New York: Cambridge University Press, 1991), frequently uses quotations from Clifford, *The Predicament of Culture*, as epigraphs to his chapters. "Transculturation" is the usual anthropological term for the reciprocal processes involved in the cross-cultural exchange of roles, ideas, etc., but I propose

"transacculturation" to designate the transculturative (co)creation of a new culture to which two or more groupings involved must adjust since it has new roles, customs, etc. different from those of each of the contributing societies.

69. To borrow or paraphrase some chapter titles from Marcus and Fischer, *Anthropology as Cultural Critique*, chaps. 3–4. Marshall Sahlins both theorizes and illustrates the conjunction of macro and microhistories in terms of how they are given cultural significance by the participating parties in *Historical Metaphors and Mythical Realities: Structure in the Early History of the Sandwich Islands Kingdom* (Ann Arbor: University of Michigan Press, 1981) and *Islands of History* (Chicago: University of Chicago Press, 1985).

70. Paul Rabinow, "Representations Are Social Facts: Modernity and Post-Modernity in Anthropology," in Clifford and Marcus, *Writing Culture,* p. 241. Compare the issues discussed in Linda Alcoff and Elizabeth Potter, eds., *Feminist Epistemologies* (New York: Routledge, 1993).

71. As Khare claims in "The Other's Double." See also Tyler, "Post-Modern Ethnography" and *The Unspeakable.*

72. Emiko Ohnuki-Tierney, ed., *Culture through Time: Anthropological Approaches* (Stanford: Stanford University Press, 1990), p. 18; but see conflicting definitions of history within this author's work and among the symposiasts on pp. 6, 129, 164, 229, for example.

73. That postcolonial historicization still tends to rely on earlier historical forms and Great Stories and has not achieved the new narrative site it argues for seems one point of Prakash, "Postcolonial Criticism and Indian Historiography."

74. Khare, "The Other's Double," p. 13.

75. Ibid., pp. 15–16.

76. Ibid., pp. 16, 23, n. 44.

77. What of conflicting truth-claims resulting from different worldviews? For those Native Americans who deny any tribal migration over the Bering Strait, for example, do their stories of origins in North America become true for others as well as themselves in their histories? What others might call mythology was presented as (pre)history in the first volume of the Navajo History Project, *Navajo History,* ed. Ethelou Yazzie (Chinle, Ariz.: Navajo Community College Press for the Navajo Curriculum Center, Rough Rock Demonstration School, 1971), which reprinted with illustrations a version of that tribe's (hi)stories of previous worlds and the beginnings of the Navajo people themselves, their division into clans, and the peopling of neighboring regions by other tribes.

78. As he acknowledges in *Culture and Imperialism,* especially on p. xii, where he admits that he omitted the resistance that white advance invariably generated in the colonized countries. Vincent B. Leitch, *Cultural Criticism, Literary Theory, Poststructuralism* (New York: Columbia University Press, 1992), pp. 132–137, criticizes Said for assuming at times a humanist reality of authentic experience as opposed to the representation of the other as Other, a dichotomy he cannot know from a poststructuralist position on knowledge as relational.

79. Cited in notes 17 and 19 above.

80. Is this the basis of much historical sociology from that of Charles Tilly to Immanuel Wallerstein and beyond? See, for example, Immanuel Wallerstein, "World-Systems Analysis," in *Social Theory Today,* ed. Anthony Giddens and Jonathan

Turner (Stanford: Stanford University Press, 1987); the essays in Theda Skocpol, ed., *Vision and Method in Historical Sociology* (Cambridge: Cambridge University Press, 1984); and Philip Abrams, *Historical Sociology* (Ithaca: Cornell University Press, 1982).

81. Carlo Ginzburg, *The Cheese and the Worms: The Cosmos of a Sixteenth-Century Miller*, trans. John Tedeschi and Anne Tedeschi (Baltimore: Johns Hopkins University Press, 1980); Emmanuel Le Roy Ladurie, *Montaillou: The Promised Land of Error*, trans. Barbara Bray (New York: George Braziller, 1978); Judith R. Walkowitz, *City of Dreadful Delight: Narratives of Sexual Danger in Late-Victorian London* (Chicago: University of Chicago Press).

82. Todorov, *The Conquest of America*; Sabine MacCormack, *Religion in the Andes: Vision and Imagination in Early Colonial Peru* (Princeton: Princeton University Press, 1991).

83. Compare Rolena Adorno, "The Discursive Encounter of Spain and America: The Authority of Eyewitness Testimony in the Writing of History," *William and Mary Quarterly*, 3d ser., 49 (April 1992), 210–228; but see the whole issue, titled "Columbian Encounters," for how narrow the spectrum is in which the various authors handle the problem of textualizing otherness.

84. Ronald Fraser, *In Search of a Past: The Manor House, Amnersfield, 1933–1945* (London: Verso, 1984).

85. David Farber, *Chicago '68* (Chicago: University of Chicago Press, 1988).

86. Richard Price, *Alabi's World* (Baltimore: Johns Hopkins University Press, 1990). Compare his *First-Time: The Historical Vision of an Afro-American People* (Baltimore: Johns Hopkins University Press, 1983).

87. Michael Craton in *William and Mary Quarterly*, 3d ser., 49 (Oct. 1992), 697–703, offers a critical but sympathetic review that ends on this point.

88. That translation substitutes the author's worldviews and intellectual categories for those of the other as a part of the power of imperialist language as a mode of thought is the contention of Talal Asad, "The Concept of Cultural Translation in British Social Anthropology."

89. Mascia-Lees, Sharpe, and Cohen, "The Postmodernist Turn in Anthropology," warn that polyvocality may lead to a political pluralism that neglects power relationships, thereby reinforcing a liberal politics.

8. Politics and Paradigms

1. Foucault theorized his own discursive practice in *The Archaeology of Knowledge*, trans. Alan Sheridan (New York: Harper Colophon, 1972), esp. pp. 115–117, and in various essays and interviews, most notably in "Politics and the Study of Discourse," in *The Foucault Effect: Studies in Governmentality*, ed. Graham Burchell, Colin Gordon, and Peter Miller (Chicago: University of Chicago Press, 1991), chap. 2. That Foucault's ideas loom large in much recent discourse theory can be seen, for example, in Diane Macdonnel, *Theories of Discourse: An Introduction* (Oxford: Basil Blackwell, 1986), chaps. 5–6; Michèle Barrett, *The Politics of Truth: From Marx to Foucault* (Cambridge: Polity Press, 1991); Michael J. Shapiro, *Language and Political Understanding: The Politics of Discursive Practices* (New Haven: Yale University Press, 1981); Paul Bové, "Discourse," in *Critical Terms for Literary Study*, ed. Frank

Lentricchia and Thomas McLaughlin (Chicago: University of Chicago Press, 1990), pp. 50–65; and Richard Terdiman, *Discourse/Counter-Discourse: The Theory and Practice of Symbolic Resistance in Nineteenth-Century France* (Ithaca: Cornell University Press, 1985).

2. Michel Foucault, *Power/Knowledge: Selected Interviews and Other Writings, 1972–1977,* ed. Colin Gordon, trans. Colin Gordon et al. (New York: Pantheon, 1980), p. 131. As Foucault states in "Truth and Power" (ibid., p. 114), he prefers the model of warfare to one of language to describe the realm of symbolic discourse. Hubert L. Dreyfus and Paul Rabinow, *Michel Foucault: Beyond Structuralism and Hermeneutics* (Chicago: University of Chicago Press, 1982), pt. 1, provides a good introduction to Foucault's changing conception of discursive practice and power. See also Larry Shiner, "Reading Foucault: Anti-Method and the Genealogy of Power-Knowledge," *History and Theory,* 21, no. 3 (1982), 382–397; and Jan Goldstein, "Foucault among the Sociologists: The 'Disciplines' and the History of Professions," ibid., 23, no. 2 (1984), 170–192.

3. Bové, "Discourse," p. 56.

4. Allan Megill, "The Reception of Foucault by Historians," *Journal of the History of Ideas,* 48 (Jan.–Mar. 1987), 117–140. Foucault, of course, was not trained as a "professional historian."

5. Peter Novick, *That Noble Dream: The "Objectivity Quest" and the American Historical Profession* (Cambridge: Cambridge University Press, 1988), esp. pp. 1–2, where the two principles and their premises are outlined.

6. See the symposium "Peter Novick's *That Noble Dream: The Objectivity Question and the Future of the Historical Profession,*" *American Historical Review,* 96 (June 1991), 675–708, for another discussion of this book. The various reviews illustrate audience-reception theory about multiple readings' creating a countertext.

7. James T. Kloppenberg, "Objectivity and Historicism: A Century of American Historical Writing," *American Historical Review,* 94 (Oct. 1989), 1030.

8. James T. Kloppenberg, "Deconstruction and Hermeneutic Strategies for Intellectual History: The Recent Work of Dominick LaCapra and David Hollinger," *Intellectual History Newsletter,* 9 (April 1987), 3–22.

9. For similar praise of Novick's objectivity in practice despite his relativistic argument, see Joseph M. Levine, "Objectivity in History: Peter Novick and R. G. Collingwood," *Clio,* 21 (Winter 1992), 109–114.

10. Thomas L. Haskell, "Objectivity Is Not Neutrality: Rhetoric vs. Practice in Peter Novick's *That Noble Dream,*" *History and Theory,* 29, no. 2 (1990), p. 134. Note the opposition of rhetoric and practice in the subtitle. He quotes from Thomas Nagel, *The View from Nowhere* (New York: Oxford University Press, 1986), at some length at the beginning of his article.

11. Ibid., p. 139.

12. Ibid., p. 135.

13. Ibid.

14. For various views of its title subject, see the articles in Allan Megill, ed., "Rethinking Objectivity," *Annals of Scholarship: An International Quarterly in the Humanities and Social Sciences,* 8, nos. 3–4 (1991), and 9, nos. 1–2 (1992).

15. Donna Haraway, "Situated Knowledges: The Science Question in Feminism and the Privilege of Partial Perspective," *Feminist Studies,* 14 (Fall 1988), 575–599.

Sandra Harding, "Rethinking Standpoint Epistemology," in *Feminist Epistemologies,* ed. Linda Alcoff and Elizabeth Potter (London: Routledge, 1993), pp. 49–82, defends Haraway's position against relativism. Most of the essays are relevant, esp. chaps. 1–4.

16. Ibid., pp. 582–583, 584. For a critique of pluralism as both an intellectual and a political practice because it is "a strategy of power, for the powerful," see Ellen Rooney, *Seductive Reasoning: Pluralism as the Problematic of Contemporary Theory* (Ithaca: Cornell University Press, 1989), quotation from p. 203. Elizabeth Deeds Ermarth, *Sequel to History: Postmodernism and the Crisis of Time* (Princeton: Princeton University Press, 1992), p. 150, n. 12, describes pluralism as "merely one of the more seductive forms of historicist and transcendentalist thinking."

17. Do Haraway and those who subscribe to the same general position presume what they claim they cannot know? If Haraway and others repudiate a godlike view, must they still use a godlike view to assert the partialness and specific location of all knowledge? Situated knowledge and historicity, like other relativizations, are self-contradictory on their face from the viewpoint of traditional epistemology, as is the case with all social location and sociology of knowledge claims. Either the statement that all knowledge is local and historically specific is a general statement applicable across gender, class, racial, and other lines, or it is local and historically specific only to a certain group. Should one consider such generalizations as morally universal but epistemologically local? If all general statements serve ideological ends, then what political and ideological goals does Haraway's generalization foster or mask? Barbara Herrnstein Smith, "Unloading the Self-Refutation Charge," *Common Knowledge,* 2 (Fall 1993), 81–95, offers a defense of postmodernist positions against the common traditionalist epistemological charge of self-refutation.

18. Compare F. R. Ankersmit, *Narrative Logic: A Semantic Analysis of the Historian's Language* (The Hague: Martinus Nijhoff, 1983), pp. 241–245, on moral judgment as the very point that gives the view to viewpoint in the *narratio.* He quotes Michael Howard on "no bias, no book" (p. 242) to support his position.

19. Gisela Bok, "Challenging Dichotomies: Perspectives on Women's History," in *Writing Women's History: International Perspectives,* ed. Karen Offen, Ruth Roach Pierson, and Jane Randall (Bloomington: Indiana University Press, 1991), pp. 2–7.

20. Nancy Fraser, "The Uses and Abuses of French Discourse Theory for Feminist Politics," in *Revaluing French Feminism: Critical Essays on Difference, Agency, and Culture,* ed. Nancy Fraser and Sandra Lee Bartky (Bloomington: Indiana University Press, 1992), p. 179. The defining of ideology and hegemony is its own intellectual industry, an industry that illustrates the relationship between viewpoint and political interests and how they issue forth in conflicting theories and competing languages and definitions. One guide to recent theorists of ideology is John B. Thompson, *Studies in the Theory of Ideology* (Berkeley: University of California Press, 1984), but see his own attempt to theorize the field: *Ideology and Modern Culture: Critical Social Theory in the Era of Mass Communication* (Cambridge: Polity Press, 1990). Ernesto Laclau and Chantal Mouffe, *Hegemony and Socialist Strategy: Towards a Democratic Politics* (London: Verso, 1985), chap. 1, provide what they term a "genealogy" of the concept. See also Barrett, *The Politics of Truth;* Mike Cormack, *Ideology* (Ann Arbor: University of Michigan Press, 1992); Graeme Turner, *British Cultural Studies: An*

Introduction (Boston: Unwin Hyman, 1990), chap. 6, for recent treatments of the issues.

21. Jon Stratton, *Writing Sites: A Genealogy of the Postmodern World* (London: Harvester Wheatsheaf, 1990), p. 320.

22. Roland Barthes, in the two prefaces to *Mythologies*, trans. Annette Lavers (New York: Farrar, Straus and Giroux, 1972).

23. Hence the problem with the dominant ideology thesis, for which see Nicholas Abercrombie, Stephen Hill, and Bryan S. Turner, eds., *The Dominant Ideology Thesis* (London: Allen & Unwin, 1980).

24. Stuart Hall, "Signification, Representation, Ideology: Althusser and Post-Structuralist Debates," *Critical Studies in Mass Communications*, 26 (June 1985), 104–105.

25. To borrow from Novick, *That Noble Dream*, p. 62, who borrowed from Ira Katznelson and Mark Kesselman, who adapted from Frank Parkin.

26. To use Raymond Williams' terms, *Marxism and Literature* (Oxford: Oxford University Press, 1977), pp. 121–128.

27. To what extent should the notion of political subtext be equated with Fredric Jameson's idea of the political unconscious in *The Political Unconscious: Narrative as a Socially Symbolic Act* (Ithaca: Cornell University Press, 1981)?

28. Karl Mannheim classified political ideologies as part of his argument in *Ideology and Utopia: An Introduction to the Sociology of Knowledge* (New York: Harcourt, Brace, 1936), pts. 3–4. Compare Hayden White's four categories of "explanation by ideological implication": anarchism, conservatism, radicalism, and liberalism, in *Metahistory: The Historical Imagination in Nineteenth-Century Europe* (Baltimore: Johns Hopkins University Press, 1973), pp. 22–29. For quite another way of looking at political ideology, see Robert R. Alford and Roger Friedland, *Powers of Theory: Capitalism, the State, and Democracy* (Cambridge: Cambridge University Press, 1985).

29. For some recent discussion of this matter from the viewpoint of traditional historiography, see William Dray, "Comment," in *Objectivity, Method and Point of View: Essays in the Philosophy of History*, ed. W. J. van der Dussen and Lionel Rubinoff (Leiden: E. J. Brill, 1991), pp. 185–186; Jacques Le Goff, *History and Memory*, trans. Steven Rendall and Elizabeth Claman (New York: Columbia University Press, 1992), pp. 106–111. Compare Dreyfus and Rabinow, *Michel Foucault*, pp. 118–119, on Foucault and present-mindedness.

30. To take but one not-so-random example, that of sexual orientation, compare the views of John Boswell, David Halpern, and Robert Padgug on homosexuality in ancient Greece as given in Martin Duberman, Martha Vicinus, and George Chauncy, Jr., eds., *Hidden from History: Reclaiming the Gay and Lesbian Past* (New York: Penguin, 1989), pp. 17–64.

31. And that is why Jonathan Rée, "The Vanity of Historicism," *New Literary History*, 22 (Autumn 1991), 978–980, praises anachronism in its larger sense.

32. Paradoxically, for the past to prove any of these cases, it must be presumed different from the present. Compare the conclusions of David L. Hull, "In Defense of Presentism," *History and Theory*, 18, no. 1 (1979), 1–15. See also Michel de Certeau, *The Writing of History*, trans. Tom Conley (New York: Columbia University Press, 1988), pp. 38–40, on presuming rupture between past and present in order to see the

otherness of history; and Le Goff, *History and Memory,* pp. 1–19, on the relationship between "past/present."

33. Henry Abelove, Betsy Blackman, Peter Dimock, and Jonathan Schneer, eds., *Visions of History* (New York: Pantheon, 1984), p. ix.

34. Linda Gordon, "A Socialist View of Women's Studies: Reply to Editorial," *Signs: Journal of Women in Culture and Society,* 1 (Winter 1975), 565.

35. Myra Jehlen, "Patrolling the Borders," *Radical History Review,* 43 (Winter 1989), 36. In the process of that disassembly, she argues, scholars must not allow all life to be transmuted into representation or language.

36. Howard Zinn, *The Politics of History* (Boston: Beacon Press, 1970), pp. 36, 42, 45, 47; but see all of his chap. 3. For his own efforts along these lines, see idem, *A People's History of the United States* (New York: Harper and Row, 1980).

37. Alan Trachtenberg, *The Incorporation of America: Culture and Society in the Gilded Age* (New York: Hill and Wang, 1982).

38. Alan Trachtenberg, *Reading American Photographs: Images as History, Mathew Brady to Walker Evans* (New York: Hill and Wang, 1989), p. xiv. Compare Robert Scholes, "Language, Narrative, and Anti-Narrative," in *On Narrative,* ed. W. J. T. Mitchell (Chicago: University of Chicago Press, 1981), p. 205: "Narrative is not just a sequencing, or the illusion of sequence, . . . narrative is a sequencing of something for somebody."

39. Craig Calhoun, "Culture, History, and the Problem of Specificity in Social Theory," in *Postmodernism and Social Theory: The Debate over General Theory,* ed. Steven Seidman and David G. Wagner (Oxford: Basil Blackwell, 1992), p. 250; but see his whole argument on the need for cultural sensitivity in historical practice, pp. 247–258.

40. Joan W. Scott, "The Campaign against Political Correctness: What's Really at Stake," *Radical History Review,* 54 (Fall 1992), p. 77. Compare Iris Marion Young, "The Ideal of Community and the Politics of Difference," in *Feminism/Postmodernism,* ed. Linda J. Nicholson (New York: Routledge, 1990), chap. 12, for a defense of difference against the notion of community.

41. Jesse Lemisch, "The American Revolution Seen from the Bottom Up," in *Towards a New Past: Dissenting Essays in American History,* ed. Barton J. Bernstein (New York: Pantheon, 1968), p. 6.

42. Haraway, "Situated Knowledges," p. 584. To what extent does this principle presume that "the oppressed have a privileged, unitary, and not just different relation to and ability to comprehend a reality that is 'out there' waiting for our representation," as Jane Flax, *Thinking Fragments: Psychoanalysis, Feminism, and Postmodernism in the Contemporary West* (Berkeley: University of California, 1990), p. 141, argues? According to her, such a fundamental premise grounds certain feminist theory and presumes "knowing the whole as it really is."

43. Nancy Hartsook, "Foucault on Power: A Theory for Women?" in Nicholson, *Feminism/Postmodernism,* p. 171, argues that marginal groups are less likely to mistake themselves for "universal man" (her term) by assuming that their experience represents the experience of all peoples.

44. Francis E. Mascia-Lees, Patricia Sharpe, and Colleen Ballerino Cohen, "The Postmodernist Turn in Anthropology: Cautions from a Feminist Perspective," *Signs: Journal of Women in Culture and Society,* 15 (Autumn 1989), esp. pp. 22, 29,

complain that an enthusiasm for polyvocality must not allow the structured and unequal interplay of voices to be presented as if they were all equal according to some liberal pluralistic model of society. Similarly Marilyn Strathern, "Out of Context: The Persuasive Fictions of Anthropology," *Current Anthropology*, 28 (June 1987), p. 269, deplores the postmodernist tendency to make "all contexts . . . alike."

45. Counterdiscourse is the term and theory of Terdiman, *Discourse/Counter-Discourse;* see esp. pp. 13–19, 54–59.

46. Both Martin Jay, *Marxism and Totality: The Adventures of a Concept from Lukács to Habermas* (Berkeley: University of California Press, 1984); and John E. Grumley, *History and Totality: Radical Historicism from Hegel to Foucault* (London: Routledge, 1989), end their books with Foucault.

47. Foucault, *The Archaeology of Knowledge*, pp. 9–10. Compare his comments in "Politics and the Study of Discourse" on misguided efforts to unify periods or history as a whole.

48. Foucault's shift from archaeology to genealogy is discussed in Dreyfus and Rabinow, *Michel Foucault;* but see his own essay "Truth and Power," in *Power/Knowledge*. See also Patricia O'Brien, "Michel Foucault's History of Culture," in *The New Cultural History*, ed. Lynn Hunt (Berkeley: University of California Press, 1989), pp. 25–46.

49. Jean-François Lyotard, *The Postmodern Condition: A Report on Knowledge*, trans. Geoff Bennington and Brian Massumi (Minneapolis: University of Minnesota Press, 1984), p. 82.

50. These lists are derived from Vincent B. Leitch, *Cultural Criticism, Literary Theory, Poststructuralism* (New York: Columbia University Press, 1992), pp. 5–6.

51. That Foucault himself totalized history is the charge of Marshall Berman, *All That Is Solid Melts into Air: The Experience of Modernity* (New York: Simon and Schuster, 1988), pp. 34–35; Leitch, *Cultural Criticism, Literary Theory, Poststructuralism*, raises the issue, pp. 7–8. This critique of self-contradiction was leveled against Foucault early, and he replied to his critics already in *The Archaeology of Knowledge*, pp. 16–17. Brook Thomas, *The New Historicism and Other Old-Fashioned Topics* (Princeton: Princeton University Press, 1991), pp. 48–49, charges New Historicists with totalizing in the name of antitotality. Steven Best and Douglas Kellner, *Postmodern Theory: Critical Interrogations* (London: Macmillan, 1992), pp. 171–173, distinguish between good and bad totalization. Does some antitotalization theory assume a "reality" prior to its textualization as discourse? To make the assertion, does it presume what it says it cannot know? Robert D'Amico, *Historicism and Knowledge* (New York: Routledge, 1989), chap. 5, discusses Foucault in relation to these two questions.

52. Eve Tavor Bannet, *Structuralism and the Logic of Dissent: Barthes, Derrida, Foucault, Lacan* (Urbana: University of Illinois Press, 1989), p. 4.

53. Ibid., p. 5.

54. Madan Sarup, *An Introductory Guide to Post-Structuralism and Postmodernism* (New York: Harvester Wheatsheaf, 1988), p. 166.

55. That Foucault merely substituted different unities of discourse for previous ones is the charge of Barrett, *The Politics of Truth*, p. 128; but see the defense of Jana Sawicki, "Feminism and the Power of Foucauldian Discourse," in *After Foucault: Humanistic Knowledge, Postmodern Challenges*, ed. Jonathan Arac (New Brunswick,

N.J.: Rutgers University Press, 1988), p. 169. Compare Best and Kellner, *Postmodern Theory*, p. 43. Thomas R. Flynn, "Michel Foucault and the Career of the Historical Event," in *At the Nexus of Philosophy and History*, ed. Bernard P. Dauenhauer (Athens: University of Georgia Press, 1987), pp. 178–200, clarifies some of the issues through his analysis of Foucault's multiple meanings of event.

56. Foucault defines what he means by archives in "Politics and the Study of Discourse," pp. 59–60; but see also *The Archaeology of Knowledge,* esp. pp. 126–131.

57. This paragraph attempts no more than to suggest a few of the problems raised by scholars about the texts of Foucault and others following his lead about power/knowledge. See, for example, among many, Dreyfus and Rabinow, *Michel Foucault;* Nancy Fraser, *Unruly Practices: Power, Discourse, and Gender in Contemporary Social Theory* (Minneapolis: University of Minnesota Press, 1989), chaps. 1–3; D'Amico, *Historicism and Truth*, pp. 90–95; and the essays gathered in Arac, *After Foucault;* David C. Hoy, ed., *Foucault: A Critical Reader* (Oxford: Basil Blackwell, 1986); *Michel Foucault, Philosopher: Essays,* trans. Timothy J. Armstrong (New York: Harvester Wheatsheaf, 1992). The essayists in Burchell, Gordon, and Miller, *The Foucault Effect,* try to answer some of these criticisms.

58. The quotations come from his own summary in Jonathan Arac, ed., *Postmodernism and Politics* (Minneapolis: University of Minnesota Press, 1986), p. 18; but see his "Ethnography as Narrative," in *The Anthropology of Experience,* ed. Victor W. Turner and Edmund Bruner (Urbana: University of Illinois Press, 1986), pp. 139–155.

59. For one version of this changing Great Story see Talal Asad, "Afterword: From the History of Colonial Anthropology to the Anthropology of Western Hegemony," in *Colonial Situations: Essays on the Contextualization of Ethnographic Knowledge,* ed. George Stocking, Jr. (Madison: University of Wisconsin Press, 1991), pp. 314–324. See the essays in Marc Manganaro, ed., *Modernist Anthropology: From Fieldwork to Text* (Princeton: Princeton University Press, 1990), for the old Great Story of anthropology translated into the new through the critique of classic ethnographies.

60. The word "postmodernism" and its various forms, such as "postmodernist" and "postmodernity," have became increasingly polysemous as they are applied ever more widely across the disciplinary boundaries of art, architecture, literary criticism, political science (and political economy), history, cinema, communications theory, music, philosophy, feminist theory, and theology, among others. While some scholars argue its merits as a concept and as a politics, others devote whole books to tracking down the multiple, often contradictory meanings. From the many, many references, the following offer some guidance to the many meanings and related issues: Allan Megill, "What Does the Term 'Postmodern' Mean?" *Annals of Scholarship*, 6, nos. 2–3 (1989), 129–151; Margaret A. Rose, *The Post-modern and the Post-industrial: A Critical Analysis* (Cambridge: Cambridge University Press, 1991); Andreas Huyssen, "Mapping the Postmodern," in *After the Great Divide: Modernism, Mass Culture, Postmodernism* (Bloomington: Indiana University Press, 1986), chap. 10; Arac, "Introduction," in *Postmodernism and Politics.* See also David Harvey, *The Condition of Postmodernity* (Oxford: Basil Blackwell, 1989); E. Ann Kaplan, ed., *Postmodernism and Its Discontents: Theories, Practices,* (London: Verso, 1988); Christopher Norris, *What's Wrong with Postmodernism: Critical Theory and the Ends of Philosophy* (Baltimore: Johns Hopkins University Press, 1990); Steven Connor, *Postmodern*

Culture: An Introduction to Theories of the Contemporary (Oxford: Basil Blackwell, 1989); Linda Hutcheon, *A Poetics of Postmodernism: History, Theory, and Fiction* (New York and London: Routledge, 1988), esp. pt. 1; idem, *The Politics of Postmodernism* (London: Routledge, 1989); Jim Collins, *Uncommon Cultures: Popular Culture and Post-Modernism* (New York: Routledge, 1989); Joe Doherty, Elspeth Graham, and Mo Malek, eds., *Postmodernism and the Social Sciences* (New York: St. Martin's Press, 1992); Seidman and Wagner, *Postmodernism and Social Theory;* Nicholson, *Feminism/Postmodernism;* Best and Kellner, *Postmodern Theory.* Hal Foster, ed., *The Anti-Aesthetic: Essays on Postmodern Culture* (Port Townsend, Wash.: Bay Press, 1983), was an important collection of essays in the debate on the topic.

61. Lyotard, *The Postmodernist Condition,* pp. xxiii, xxiv, 50.

62. If postmodernism is defined as the end of grand or metanarrative, following Lyotard, should we liken it to the earlier end of ideology debate in the United States, for which see Job Dittberner, *The End of Ideology and American Social Thought, 1930–1960* (Ann Arbor, Mich.: University Microfilms International Research Press, 1979)? Compare Julian Pefanis, *Heterology and the Postmodern: Bataille, Baudrillard, and Lyotard* (Durham, N.C.: Duke University Press, 1991).

63. Warren Montag, "What Is at Stake in the Debate on Postmodernism?" in Kaplan, *Postmodernism and Its Discontents,* p. 91. Compare the criticisms of Lyotard in Nancy Fraser and Linda J. Nicholson, "Social Criticism without Philosophy: An Encounter between Feminism and Postmodernism," in Nicholson, *Feminism/Postmodernism,* pp. 21–25; and Best and Kellner, *Postmodern Theory,* p. 146.

64. Ernst Behler, *Irony and the Discourse of Modernity* (Seattle: University of Washington Press, 1990), p. 16. For an even grander Habermasian metanarrative, see Brian J. Whitten, "Universal Pragmatics and the Formation of Western Civilization: A Critique of Habermas's Theory of Human Moral Evolution," *History and Theory,* 31, no. 3 (1992), 298–313.

65. That the Habermas–Lyotard debate calls upon the past and how various sides historicize it can be seen in Richard J. Bernstein, ed., *Habermas and Modernity* (Oxford: Basil Blackwell, 1985). Compare Best and Kellner, *Postmodern Theory,* pp. 246–254.

66. Jürgen Habermas, "Modernity—An Incomplete Project," in Foster, *The Anti-Aesthetic,* p. 9.

67. Ibid. Both Megill, "What Does the Term 'Postmodern' Mean?" and David J. Herman, "Modernism and Postmodernism: Towards an Analytic Distinction," *Poetics Today,* 12 (Spring 1991), 55–86, point out the significance of the Enlightenment as a beginning for the Postmodernist Great Story.

68. Habermas, "Modernity," pp. 9–10.

69. To adopt the typographic conventions of Harvey, *The Condition of Postmodernity,* p. 113.

70. Whether irony is the archetypal discourse of modernism or of postmodernity (or even of premodernity) is treated in Behler, *Irony and the Discourse of Modernity.* On the other hand, Timothy Reiss, *The Discourse of Modernism* (Ithaca: Cornell University Press, 1982), argues that the dominant discourse of modernism is "analytico-referential." Not only do the two authors differ over the dominant form of

modern discourse; they also date modernity differently. In the end they both constitute and contextualize their facts through different Great Stories.

71. See Elspeth Graham and Joe Doherty on the paradoxes of periodization, grand narrative, and politics in their concluding essay, "Postmodern Horizons," in Doherty, Graham, and Malek, *Postmodernism and the Social Sciences*, pp. 196–220. Best and Kellner, *Postmodern Theory*, pp. 13–16; and Pauline Rosenau, *Post-Modernism and the Social Sciences: Insights, Inroads, and Intrusions* (Princeton: Princeton University Press, 1992), chap. 8, contend that conflicting postmodernists promote both left and right politics, are both cultural conservatives and avant-gardists.

72. Quoted in Harvey, *The Condition of Postmodernity*, p. 9.

73. In this version postmodernism and poststructuralism share goals—so much so that Sarup, *Post-Structuralism and Postmodernism*, p. 131, finds it "difficult to make a clear distinction between them." Best and Kellner, *Postmodern Theory*, chap. 1, esp. pp. 25–26, maintain that poststructuralism has been absorbed into postmodernism. See Jane Flax, "The End of Innocence," in *Feminists Theorize the Political*, ed. Judith Butler and Joan Wallach Scott (New York: Routledge, 1992), pp. 445–463, for a brief but powerful statement on the implications of poststructuralism for postmodernism. Compare Flax, *Thinking Fragments*. Whether the relationship between structuralism and poststructuralism should be depicted as rupture or continuity poses another emplotment problem.

74. On the politics of postmodernism and the concern for a foundation validating left politics, see esp. Best and Kellner, *Postmodern Theory*, but also Andrew Ross, ed., *Universal Abandon? The Politics of Postmodernism* (Minneapolis: University of Minnesota Press, 1988); John Fekete, ed., *Life after Postmodernism: Essays on Value and Culture* (New York: St. Martin's Press, 1987); Fred Pfeil, *Another Tale to Tell: Politics and Narrative in Postmodern Culture* (London: Verso, 1990); Thomas Docherty, *After Theory: Postmodernism/Postmarxism* (London: Routledge, 1990); and Ben Agger, *The Decline of Discourse: Reading, Writing, and Resistance in Postmodern Capitalism* (New York: Falmer Press, 1990), among many also addressing this matter.

75. As defined by Robert Young, *White Mythologies: Writing History and the West* (London: Routledge, 1990), pp. 19–20.

76. Compare F. R. Ankersmit, "Historiography and Postmodernism," *History and Theory*, 28, no. 2 (1989), 137–153; and Linda Hutcheon, "The Postmodern Problematizing of History," in *English Studies in Canada*, 14 (Dec. 1988), 365–382, reprinted in Hutcheon, *A Poetics of Postmodernism*, chap. 6, on the implications of postmodernism for historicization. See also Derek Attridge, Geoff Bennington, and Robert Young, eds., *Post-Structuralism and the Question of History* (Cambridge: Cambridge University Press, 1987).

77. See, for example, O'Brien, "Michel Foucault's History of Culture." That Foucault can be variously interpreted as he is assimilated into professional history seems illustrated by Laura Engelstein, "Combined Underdevelopment: Discipline and the Law in Late Imperial and Soviet Russia," *American Historical Review*, 98 (April 1993), 338–353, and the comments by Rudy Koshar and Jan Goldstein with reply by Engelstein, ibid., pp. 354–381.

78. Sande Cohen, *Historical Culture: On the Recoding of an Academic Discipline* (Berkeley: University of California Press, 1986), can be read as a polemic against the totalization of historical narrative from this viewpoint.

79. Hence the plea of Harvey J. Kaye, *The Powers of the Past: Reflections on the Crisis and the Promise of History* (New York: Harvester Wheatsheaf, 1991), for the return of "grand governing narratives" as politically desirable, even necessary. Similarly, Fraser and Nicholson, "Social Criticism without Philosophy," pp. 34–35, express the need for large historical narratives and social macrostructures in feminist theory and history. Best and Kellner, *Postmodern Theory,* echo this plea (p. 209) and differentiate between a good and bad "Big Story" (pp. 172–174); compare pp. 301–302. According to Steven Best, "Jameson, Totality, and the Poststructuralist Critique," in *Postmodernism/Jameson/Critique,* ed. Douglas Kellner (Washington, D.C.: Maisonneuve Press, 1989), pp. 333–368, good big stories empower social transformation while bad big stories disable it.

80. To borrow from the title of Steven Seidman, "Postmodern Social Theory as Narrative with a Moral Intent," in Seidman and Wagner, *Postmodernism and Social Theory,* chap. 2. Compare Jörn Rüsen's typology of historical narration, "Historical Narration: Foundation, Types, Reason," *History and Theory,* 26, no. 4 (1987), 87–97, which stresses the orienting function of memory in the formation of present identity.

81. As Edward Said argues in "The Problem of Textuality: Two Exemplary Positions," *Critical Inquiry,* 4 (Summer 1978), 680–681.

82. Compare Wayne Booth, "Freedom of Interpretation: Bakhtin and the Challenge of Feminist Criticism," *Critical Inquiry,* 9 (Sept. 1982), 46. Everything that I have argued in this paragraph applies also to teaching history.

83. Williams in *Marxism and Literature* and Jameson in *The Political Unconscious* wrestle with the problems of reconciling modes of understanding as representations with a belief in referentiality. E. P. Thompson never seemed to understand fully all that was at issue in these matters. Compare, for example, Perry Anderson, *Arguments within English Marxism* (London: Verso Editions and NLB, 1980), chap. 1 and passim; and Gregor McLennan, *Marxism and the Methodologies of History* (London: Verso Editions and NLB, 1981), pt. 1.

84. Ermarth, *Sequel to History,* pp. 55, 20, and 151.

85. The point of Cohen, *Historical Culture.*

86. As Susan Bordo (quoted by Linda Nicholson in her introduction to *Feminism/Postmodernism,* p. 9) proclaims: "reality itself may be relentlessly plural and heterogeneous, but human understanding and *interest* cannot be."

87. "Master interpretive code" is the term of Fredric Jameson, "Marxism and Historicism," *New Literary History,* 11 (Autumn 1979), 46.

88. Historians frequently use the metaphors of road and path to discuss the paradigmatic alternatives confronting the profession. Novick, *That Noble Dream,* pp. 625–628, employs "middle-of-the-road" in addition to "centrist" to designate how most historians would like to mediate the conflicting options.

89. See particularly Kloppenberg, "Deconstruction and Hermeneutic Strategies for Intellectual History," for one such effort. Compare the fears of many of the essayists in John Higham and Paul Conkin, eds., *New Directions in American Intellectual History* (Baltimore: Johns Hopkins University Press, 1979), about the reduction of intellectual history to social history with the efforts of the essayists in Dominick LaCapra and Steven L. Kaplan, eds., *Modern European Intellectual History: Reappraisals and New Perspectives* (Ithaca: Cornell University Press, 1982), to cope with

the new currents from the continent as examples of such boundary maintenance in one historical subspecialty.

90. For example, Gabrielle M. Spiegel, "History, Historicism, and the Social Logic of the Text in the Middle Ages," *Speculum,* 65 (Jan. 1990), 75, argues that historians, unlike literary theorists, cannot "evade the issue of causality—of *why* and '*how* a given form of literary work appeared *as* it did, *where* it did, and when it did.'" The embedded quotation is from Hayden White.

91. Early expressions of this position are Fredric Jameson, "Postmodernism and Consumer Society," in Foster, *The Anti-Aesthetic;* and idem, "Postmodernism, or the Cultural Logic of Late Capitalism," *New Left Review,* no. 146 (July–Aug. 1984), 52–92. For Jameson's later reflections see idem, *Postmodernism, or the Cultural Logic of Late Capitalism* (Durham, N.C.: Duke University Press, 1991), and the essays discussing his theory in Kellner, *Postmodernism/Jameson/Critique.*

92. Cited in note 21 above.

93. Bryan D. Palmer, *The Descent into Discourse: The Reification of Language and the Writing of Social History* (Philadelphia: Temple University Press, 1990), p. 198; but see his entire argument, pp. 198–206; p. 198, n. 5, contains the blunt statement that poststructuralism is the ideology of postmodernism.

94. To use the words of Mascia-Lees, Sharpe, and Cohen, "The Postmodernist Turn in Anthropology," p. 15.

95. Hutcheon, *The Politics of Postmodernism,* p. 25. Stratton, *Writing Sites,* pp. 23–26, offers another brief history of the connection between stages of capitalism and kinds of representation.

96. Jameson, *The Political Unconscious,* pp. 100–102. Frank Lentricchia, "Foucault's Legacy—A New Historicism?" in *The New Historicism,* ed. H. Aram Veeser (New York: Routledge, 1989), p. 231, concludes: "for without causal explanations, there is no historicism, old or new."

97. Is this not the problem that so-called structuralist and culturalist Marxisms tried to resolve? Raymond Williams, *Marxism and Literature,* thus wrestles with the problem; for example, on p. 83, he writes: "A Marxism without some concept of determination is in effect worthless. A Marxism with many of the concepts of determination it now has is quite radically disabled."

98. Compare the criticism of Richard Freadman and Seamus Miller, *Re-Thinking Theory: A Critique of Contemporary Literary Theory and an Alternative Account* (Cambridge: Cambridge University Press, 1992), pp. 173–175, of the strong version of discourse/power theory. For example, Terdiman, *Discourse/Counter-Discourse,* p. 57, asks how hegemonic discourse can be located and characterized if it is ubiquitous. Since such discourse is process and not a "thing," he goes on to argue, "no 'empirical proof' of the existence of a dominant discourse is possible," because its "massive seemingly ineradicable power" results in its "transparency." Only the contestation of it proves its existence and its efficacy in a society. Such an argument can lead all too easily to the conclusion that presumably, like a conspiracy, the less proof there is, the more complete the discursive hegemony, hence the more nearly total the power.

99. The complaint of Philippe Carrard, *Poetics of the New History: French Historical Discourse from Braudel to Chartier* (Baltimore: Johns Hopkins University

Press, 1992), pp. 206–207, 209–210, 214–216. The essays in Burchell, Gordon, and Miller, *The Foucault Effect,* seek to clarify many of these issues in relation to Foucault.

100. This is my modification of a definition by Peter C. Sederberg, *Politics of Meaning: Power and Explanation in the Construction of Social Reality* (Tucson: University of Arizona Press, 1984), p. 9: "politics . . . [is] the deliberate effort to control shared meaning"; but see chaps. 1–3 in general.

101. For the latter question as customary to history, see, for example, Spiegel, "History, Historicism, and the Social Logic of the Text," p. 75; Myra Jehlen and Belle Chevigny, "Patrolling the Borders," *Radical Historical Review,* 43 (Winter 1989), 35, 39.

102. Alford and Friedland, *Powers of Theory,* p. 411, liken the contending theories of the state and their assumptions about power to disputes about what constitutes proper plays in a game, rules of the game, and the very game itself.

103. Hence the methodological conflict in literature over the theory of literature versus current literary theory and the historicization of critical practices and schools: Gerald Graff, *Professing Literature: An Institutional History* (Chicago: University of Chicago Press, 1987); Vincent B. Leitch, *American Literary Criticism from the Thirties to the Eighties* (New York: Columbia University Press, 1988); Russell Reising, *The Unusable Past: Theory and the Study of American Literature* (New York and London: Methuen, 1986). Does the popularity of Novick, *That Noble Dream,* indicate that it serves the same purposes in and for the historical profession in the United States?

104. Whether the radicalness of the use of the medium necessarily results in a radical message is less clear. To convey an explicit radical political message effectively, historians, like others, should probably employ traditional forms of textualization, because a radical form of the medium tends to distract the audience from the intended message.

105. Thomas Bender, "Wholes and Parts: The Need for Synthesis in American History," *Journal of American History,* 73 (June 1986), 120–136.

106. Nell Irvin Painter, "Bias and Synthesis in History," ibid., 74 (June 1987), 109–112.

107. In addition to Painter, Richard Wightman Fox, "Public Culture and the Problem of Synthesis," ibid., pp. 113–116; Roy Rosenzweig, "What Is the Matter with History?" ibid., pp. 117–122.

108. *Bringing the State Back In* is the title of an anthology edited by Peter S. Evans, Dietrich Rueschemeyer, and Theda Skocpol (Cambridge: Cambridge University Press, 1985).

109. Jean-Christophe Agnew, *Worlds Apart: The Market and the Theater in Anglo-American Thought, 1550–1750* (Cambridge: Cambridge University Press, 1986); Walter Benn Michaels, *The Gold Standard and the Logic of Naturalism: American Literature at the Turn of the Century* (Berkeley: University of California Press, 1987). The latter is the second volume in a series titled "The New Historicism: Studies in Cultural Poetics."

110. Is that because the synchronicity practiced by so many New Historicists allows their texts to escape the dilemmas of historicizing diachrony? Brook Thomas treats Michaels' book as an exemplar of New Historicist approaches in general in *The New Historicism and Other Old-Fashioned Topics* (Princeton: Princeton University Press, 1991), chap. 5, and offers extended criticism.

111. Agnew, *Worlds Apart,* p. xiii.

112. Michaels, *The Gold Standard*, p. 27.
113. Ibid., pp. 169–170.

9. Reflexive (Con)Textualization

1. Louis A. Montrose, "Professing the Renaissance: The Poetics and Politics of Culture," in *The New Historicism,* ed. H. Aram Veeser (London: Routledge, 1989), p. 20.

2. Hilary Lawson, *Reflexivity: The Post-Modern Dilemma* (London: Hutchinson, 1985), discusses those modern philosophers most responsible for the crisis of contemporary truths and values through reflexivity. Malcolm Ashmore, *The Reflexive Thesis: Wrighting Sociology of Scientific Knowledge* (Chicago: University of Chicago, 1989), illustrates the difficulties of textualizing reflexivity as he discusses it in its original disciplinary field. Robert Siegle, *The Politics of Reflexivity: Narrative and the Constitutive Poetics of Culture* (Baltimore: Johns Hopkins University Press, 1986), defines and applies reflexivity to the history of novels and literary criticism.

3. The headings and the quotations are from James Clifford, "Introduction," in *Writing Culture: The Poetics and Politics of Ethnography,* ed. James Clifford and George E. Marcus (Berkeley: University of California Press, 1986), p. 6.

4. This and the series that follow do not pretend to be either definitive in the number of their elements or comprehensive in what is covered under each element. Each series merely suggests a minimum of what seems necessary for reflexive contextualization.

5. On postmodernism and metafictional novels in general, see Linda Hutcheon, *A Poetics of Postmodernism: History, Theory, and Fiction* (New York and London: Routledge, 1988); Brian McHale, *Postmodernist Fiction* (New York: Methuen, 1987); and Allen Thiher, *Words in Reflection: Modern Language Theory and Postmodern Fiction* (Chicago: University of Chicago Press, 1984). That late modernist novels also innovated in form is the argument of David Hayman, *Re-Forming the Novel: Toward a Mechanics of Modernist Fiction* (Ithaca: Cornell University Press, 1987).

6. Compare, for example, the editorial introductions by Robert Brent Toplin in *Journal of American History,* 73 (Dec. 1986), 819–821; and by Robert Rosenstone in *American Historical Review,* 94 (Oct. 1989), 1031–33, inaugurating the film review sections in those journals, as well as subsequent reviews for differences about what kinds of films to review and how to review them as historical representations. From these two sections one could construct a spectrum of films ranging from documentary histories to historical fiction to fictional history, just like the range mentioned above in Chapter 3. See also Lonnie Bunch and Spencer Crew, "Exhibits and Interpretive Programs: Critical Elements of a Good Review," *Perspectives,* 29 (Dec. 1991), 12, 14, for museum presentations.

7. Such as those efforts already in existence for classrooms that combine traditional text with contrasting interpretations, documents, pictures, artifacts, oral interviews, film excerpts, gaming simulation, and other methods through the aid of computers and CD-ROM media.

8. Both Hayden White and Richard Rorty have been accused of ethical relativism in their approaches to history and philosophy. For White see, for example, Saul Friedlander, ed., *Probing the Limits of Representation: Nazism and the "Final Solu-*

tion" (Cambridge, Mass.: Harvard University Press, 1992). Jack W. Meiland and Michael Krausz, eds., *Relativism: Cognitive and Moral* (Notre Dame, Ind.: University of Notre Dame Press, 1982), contains essays on these two kinds of relativism.

9. Joan W. Scott, "The Campaign against Political Correctness: What's Really at Stake," *Radical History Review*, 54 (Fall 1992), 77.

10. Jane Flax, *Thinking Fragments: Psychoanalysis, Feminism, and Postmodernism in the Contemporary West* (Berkeley: University of California Press, 1990), p. 233.

11. For various literary theories see, among others, Raman Selden, *A Reader's Guide to Contemporary Literary Theory: A Comparative Introduction,* 2d ed. (Lexington: University Press of Kentucky, 1989); G. Douglas Atkins and Laura Morrow, eds., *Contemporary Literary Theory* (Amherst: University of Massachusetts Press, 1989); Ann Jefferson and David Robey, eds., *Modern Literary Theory: A Comparative Introduction,* 2d ed. (London: B. T. Batsford, 1986); Joseph Natoli, ed., *Tracing Literary Theory* (Urbana: University of Illinois Press, 1987); Ralph Cohen, ed., *The Future of Literary Theory* (New York: Routledge, 1989); Joseph Natoli, ed., *Literary Theory's Future(s)* (Urbana: University of Illinois Press, 1989); Peter Collier and Helga Geyer-Ryan, eds., *Literary Theory Today* (Cambridge: Polity Press, 1990); David Carroll, ed., *The States of "Theory": History, Art, and Critical Discourse* (New York: Columbia University Press, 1990); and many of the essays in Stephen Greenblatt and Giles Gunn, eds., *Redrawing the Boundaries: The Transformation of English and American Literary Studies* (New York: Modern Language Association of America, 1992). The assumptions underlying contemporary literary theory are seen quite clearly in those who criticize it, for example, Richard Freadman and Seamus Miller, *Re-Thinking Theory: A Critique of Contemporary Literary Theory and an Alternative Account* (Cambridge: Cambridge University Press, 1992); Eve Tavor Bannet, *Postcultural Theory: Critical Theory and the Marxist Paradigm* (New York: Paragon House, 1993); and Christopher Norris, *Contest of Faculties: Philosophy and Theory after Deconstruction* (London: Methuen, 1985).

12. For introductions to various sociological theories see Anthony Giddens and H. Jonathan Turner, eds., *Social Theory Today* (Stanford: Stanford University Press, 1987); Tom Bottomore and Robert Nisbet, eds., *A History of Sociological Analysis* (New York: Basic Books, 1978); Philip Abrams, *Historical Sociology* (Ithaca: Cornell University Press, 1982); Theda Skocpol, ed., *Vision and Method in Historical Sociology* (Cambridge: Cambridge University Press, 1984).

13. See in general the essays in Quentin Skinner, ed., *The Return of Grand Theory in the Human Sciences* (Cambridge: Cambridge University Press, 1985).

14. These problems prove particularly vexing in the social sciences, as the essayists point out in Steven Seidman and David G. Wagner, eds., *Postmodernism and Social Theory: The Debate over General Theory* (Oxford: Basil Blackwell, 1992). Pauline Marie Rosenau, *Post-Modernism and the Social Sciences: Insights, Inroads, and Intrusions* (Princeton: Princeton University Press, 1992), surveys the problems from a modernist perspective. Peter Burke, *History and Social Theory* (Cambridge: Polity Press, 1992), provides a good example of a historian trying to combine an earlier modernist approach to social theory with a more recent postmodernist critique of that kind of theory.

15. Compare the complaint of Steven Best and Douglas Kellner, *Postmodern Theory: Critical Interrogations* (London: Macmillan, 1992), pp. 259–261, that liter-

ary theory does not map or chart society and operates in too eclectic a fashion. Is this criticism based on too unqualified an objectivist realism?

16. For these and other questions see, for example, Geoff Eley, "Is All the World a Text? From Social History to the History of Society Twenty Years Later," in *The Historic Turn in the Social Sciences,* ed. Terrence McDonald (Ann Arbor: University of Michigan Press, forthcoming); and Bannet, *Postcultural Theory,* pp. 5–13.

17. Guidebooks to such models in the social sciences can be reread as taxonomies of such models in history, for example, Christopher Lloyd, *Explanation in Social History* (Oxford: Basil Blackwell, 1986).

18. Raymie E. McKerrow, "Critical Rhetoric and the Possibility of the Subject," in *The Critical Turn: Rhetoric and Philosophy in Postmodern Discourse,* ed. Ian Angus and Lenore Langsdorf (Carbondale: Southern Illinois Press, 1993), pp. 51–67, summarizes recent concerns about these issues. Compare Richard L. Lanigan, "The Algebra of History: Merleau-Ponty and Foucault on the Rhetoric of the Person," ibid., pp. 140–174.

19. I have borrowed the phrasing of this notion from Dennis Wrong, "The Oversocialized Conception of Man in Modern Sociology," *American Sociological Review,* 26 (April 1961), 183–193. Compare "plastic" and "autonomous" in Martin Hollis, *Models of Man: Philosophical Thoughts on Social Action* (Cambridge: Cambridge University Press, 1977); and the arguments over human agency versus structural explanation in interpreting social behavior, for which see, for example, Anthony Appiah, "Tolerable Falsehoods: Agency and the Interests of Theory," in *Consequences of Theory,* ed. Jonathan Arac and Barbara Johnson (Baltimore: Johns Hopkins University Press, 1991), pp. 63–90. Bannet, *Postcultural Theory,* chaps. 1–2, examines the problems of an oversocialized model in recent theories.

20. In addition to McKerrow, "Critical Rhetoric and the Possibility of the Subjective," the role of the self in postmodernist theory is raised in Flax, *Thinking Fragments.*

21. A major theme of Freadman and Miller, *Re-Thinking Theory.*

22. To use the categories of Robert R. Alford and Roger Friedland in *Powers of Theory: Capitalism, the State, and Democracy* (Cambridge: Cambridge University Press, 1985).

23. Patrick Gardiner, ed., *Theories of History* (Glencoe, Ill.: Free Press, 1959) and *The Philosophy of History* (Oxford: Oxford University Press, 1974), allow sampling of these older debates through anthology, while Paul Ricoeur, *Time and Narrative,* vol. 1, trans. Kathleen McLaughlin Blamey and David Pellauer (Chicago: University of Chicago Press, 1984), pt. 2, provides an overview and analysis. Murray Murphy, *Our Knowledge of the Historical Past* (Indianapolis: Bobbs-Merrill, 1973), is a good example of the application of analytic philosophy to historical discourse.

24. Robert W. Fogel presents the rationale for this approach in Robert W. Fogel and G. R. Elton, *Which Road to the Past? Two Views of History* (New Haven: Yale University Press, 1983), pp. 5–70. A good example of what such modeling and methodology entailed is Peter D. McClelland, *Causal Explanation and Model Building in History, Economics, and Economic History* (Ithaca: Cornell University Press, 1975). Compare David Harvey, *Explanation in Geography* (New York: St. Martin's Press, 1969).

25. Compare, for example, Lloyd, *Explanation in Social History;* or Alan Garfinkel, *Forms of Explanation: Rethinking the Questions in Social Theory* (New

Haven: Yale University Press, 1981); with Morton White, *Foundations of Historical Knowledge* (New York: Harper and Row, 1965); or Louis Gottschalk, *Understanding History: A Primer of Historical Methods,* 2d ed. (New York: Alfred A. Knopf, 1969), chap. 11; and even the more recent C. Behan McCullagh, *Justifying Historical Descriptions* (Cambridge: Cambridge University Press, 1984).

26. McHale, *Postmodernist Fiction,* esp. pt. 1.

27. Linda Alcoff and Elizabeth Potter, eds., *Feminist Epistemologies* (London: Routledge, 1993), provides a recent overview of the field from a critical perspective; but see also Lorraine Code, *What Can She Know? Feminist Theory and the Construction of Knowledge* (Ithaca: Cornell University Press, 1991). Allan Megill, ed., "Rethinking Objectivity," *Annals of Scholarship: An International Quarterly in the Humanities and Social Sciences,* 8, nos. 3–4 (1991), and 9, nos. 1–2 (1992), offers recent views in that area. Derek Layder, *The Realist Image in Social Science* (London: Macmillan, 1990), points up the issues as he argues for a revised view of realism in light of discourse and other theories. See also Steve Fuller, *Social Epistemology* (Bloomington: Indiana University Press, 1988). Also relevant in their way are Pierre Bourdieu's notion of "habitus," for which see *Outline of a Theory of Practice,* trans. Richard Nice (Cambridge: Cambridge University Press, 1977); and Anthony Gidden's concept of "structuration," for which see *The Constitution of Society: Outline of the Theory of Structuration* (Berkeley: University of California Press, 1984).

28. On the latter problem see, among many, the essays in Richard Rorty, J. B. Schneewind, and Quentin Skinner, eds., *Philosophy in History: Essays on the Historiography of Philosophy* (Cambridge: Cambridge University Press, 1984); and Bernard P. Dauenhauer, ed., *At the Nexus of Philosophy and History* (Athens: University of Georgia Press, 1987), pt. 1. Compare David Perkins, *Is Literary History Possible?* (Baltimore: Johns Hopkins University Press, 1992), for a similar argument in that field.

29. R. S. Khare, "The Other's Double—The Anthropologist's Bracketed Self: Notes on Cultural Representation and Privileged Discourse," *New Literary Review,* 23 (Winter 1992), 1–23.

30. Richard H. Brown, *A Poetics for Sociology: Toward a Logic of Discovery for the Human Sciences* (Cambridge: Cambridge University Press, 1977), pp. 145–153, discusses language as a root metaphor in modeling society in the social sciences. His other root metaphors are organicism, mechanism, drama, and games. As Raymond Tallis, *Not Saussure: A Critique of Post-Saussurean Literary Theory* (London: Macmillan, 1988), questions the appropriation of linguistics by literary theorists, he highlights what is at issue in this category.

31. F. R. Ankersmit in *Narrative Logic: A Semantic Analysis of the Historian's Language* (The Hague: Martinus Nijhoff, 1983), pp. 66–78; but see also idem, "The Use of Language in the Writing of History," in *Working with Language: A Multidisciplinary Consideration of Language Use in Work Contexts* (Berlin: Mouton de Gruyter, 1986), pp. 71–78.

32. Hayden White, *The Content of the Form: Narrative Discourse and Historical Representation* (Baltimore: Johns Hopkins University Press, 1987), pp. 189.

33. A clear message of Raymond Williams, *Keywords: A Vocabulary of Culture and Society,* rev. ed. (New York: Oxford University Press, 1985). Compare the essays

in Penelope J. Corfield, ed., *Language, History and Class* (Oxford: Basil Blackwell, 1991). Corfield's own essay "Historians and Language" provides a good introduction to its subject.

34. An interesting effort to cope with these problems in social and political theory is the glossary in Alford and Friedland, *Powers of Theory*, pp. 444–451, showing that the same concepts are expressed by different words or phrases depending upon whether they are part of pluralist, managerial, or class perspectives on society, capitalism, the state, democracy, and "knowledge." For the purposes of my argument here, the last category is the most pertinent. Their whole book is an attempt at resolving conflicting presuppositional frameworks in what is today a highly contested area of scholarship. Their resolution, however, used theories from the various conflicting problematics as answers to questions they posed according to the common overall framework they had developed.

35. Since social science historians emphasized their models and theories through explicit discussions in the text, they were more reflexive according to that criterion than traditional historians.

36. Greg Dening, *Islands and Beaches: Discourse on a Silent Land, Marquesas, 1774–1880* (Honolulu: University of Hawaii, 1980).

37. Susan Gearhart, *The Open Boundary of History and Fiction: A Critical Approach to the French Enlightenment* (Princeton: Princeton University Press, 1984).

38. For example, among many, Best and Kellner, *Postmodern Theory*.

39. Elizabeth Deeds Ermarth, *Sequel to History: Postmodernism and the Crisis of Time* (Princeton: Princeton University Press, 1992), p. 99, uses the term "guerrilla tactic."

40. David G. Wagner uses the term "orienting strategies" in "Daring Modesty: On Metatheory, Observation, and Theory Growth," in Seidman and Wagner, *Postmodernism and Social Theory*, pp. 209–219; but see the whole book for essays wrestling with the status of theory problem. Compare any of the books on literary theory listed in note 10 above for quite a different approach to what theory is and how one goes about applying it.

41. I leave the gendering as in the original: Carl Becker, "Every Man His Own Historian," *American Historical Review,* 37 (Jan. 1932), 221–236.

42. Stephen Bann, *The Clothing of Clio: A Study of Representation of History in Nineteenth-Century Britain and France* (Cambridge: Cambridge University Press, 1984); Linda Orr, *Jules Michelet: Nature, History, and Language* (Ithaca: Cornell University Press, 1976); Ann Rigney, *The Rhetoric of Historical Representation: Three Narrative Theories of the French Revolution* (Cambridge: Cambridge University Press, 1990).

43. Linda Hutcheon, *The Politics of Postmodernism* (London: Routledge, 1989), p. 58.

44. Roy Porter, "History of the Body," in *New Perspectives on Historical Writing,* ed. Peter Burke (University Park: Pennsylvania State University Press, 1991), pp. 206–232.

45. Compare the stricter approach to conceptual history taken in the multivolume project edited by Otto Bruner, Werner Conze, and Reinhart Koselleck, *Geschichtliche Grundbegriffe: Historische Lexicon zur politisch-socialen Sprache im Deutschland,* 7 vols. to date (Stuttgart: E. Klett, 1972–), for an overview of which see Keith Tribe,

"The *Geschichtliche Grundbegriffe* Project: From History of Ideas to Conceptual History," *Comparative Studies in Society and History,* 31 (Jan. 1989), 180–184. One of the editors, Reinhart Koselleck, explains the connection between *"Begriffes-geschichte* and Social History" in *Futures Past: On the Semantics of Historical Time,* trans. Keith Tribe (Cambridge, Mass.: MIT Press, 1985), pp. 73–91.

46. Particularly as represented by *The Order of Things: An Archaeology of Human Sciences* (New York: Pantheon, 1970), as the product and by *The Archaeology of Knowledge,* including "The Discourse on Language" in an appendix, trans. Alan Sheridan (New York: Harper Colophon, 1972), as the pronouncement.

47. Peter De Bolla, "Disfiguring History," *Diacritics,* 16 (Winter 1986), 55–57.

48. Joan W. Scott, "The Evidence of Experience," *Critical Inquiry,* 17 (Summer 1991), 790–797; quotation on p. 796.

49. Compare the dilemma of representationalism with what Sande Cohen, in *Historical Culture: On the Recoding of an Academic Discipline* (Berkeley: University of California Press, 1986), p. 100, calls the "semiotic absolute": "The conceptual result is that no instance of historical narration can say the way it tells what is shown as it tries to show: this silence of every historical narrative is a semiotic absolute."

50. The first words of his preface, Fredric Jameson, *The Political Unconscious: Narrative as Socially Symbolic Act* (Ithaca: Cornell University Press, 1981), p. 9.

51. On Jameson's dilemmas see, among others, William C. Dowling, *Jameson, Althusser, Marx: An Introduction to the Political Unconscious* (Ithaca: Cornell University Press, 1984); Cornel West, "Ethics and Action in Fredric Jameson's Marxist Hermeneutics," in *Postmodernism and Politics,* ed. Jonathan Arac (Minneapolis: University of Minnesota Press, 1986), pp. 123–144; and Ellen Rooney, *Seductive Reasoning: Pluralism as the Problematic of Contemporary Theory* (Ithaca: Cornell University Press, 1989). Compare Douglas Kellner, ed., *Postmodernism/Jameson/Critique* (Washington, D.C.: Maisonneuve Press, 1989).

52. Such as Gerald Graff, *Professing Literature: An Institutional History* (Chicago: University of Chicago Press, 1987); Vincent B. Leitch, *American Literary Criticism from the Thirties to the Eighties* (New York: Columbia University Press, 1988); and Russell Reising, *The Unusable Past: Theory and the Study of American Literature* (New York and London: Methuen, 1986), for literature in the United States; Peter Novick, *That Noble Dream: The "Objectivity Quest" and the American Historical Profession* (Cambridge: Cambridge University Press, 1988), for the historical profession.

53. Sacvan Bercovitch, ed., *Reconstructing American Literary History* (Cambridge: Cambridge University Press, 1986), p. viii.

54. Mieke Bal, "First Person, Second Person, Same Person: Narrative as Epistemology," *New Literary History,* 24 (Spring 1993), 293–320, offers this scheme for specifying the nature of the narrative site. One of her exemplars of the proper approach is an art history.

55. According to Thomas R. Flynn, "Michel Foucault and the Career of the Historical Event," in Dauenhauer, *At the Nexus of Philosophy and History,* p. 200, n. 22, Paul Veyne employed the image of the kaleidoscope to describe Foucault's mode of textualizing. Foucault, of course, used the notion of Bentham's Panopticon to describe the development of a new incarceral architecture of discipline and, by extension, the surveillant nature of modern society.

56. "Narratives and Social Identities," *Social Science History,* 16 (Fall 1992), 479–537, and (Winter 1992), 591–692.

57. This is a theme of Stephen Yeo in a survey of oral history, "Whose Story? An Argument from within Current Historical Practice in Britain," *Journal of Contemporary History,* 21 (April 1986), 295–320. Compare Gwyn Prins, "Oral History," in Burke, *New Perspectives on Historical Writing,* pp. 114–139.

58. Fernand Braudel, *The Mediterranean and the Mediterranean World in the Age of Philip II,* trans. Siân Reynolds (New York: Harper and Row, 1972), vol. 1, pp. 20–21.

59. See also Fernand Braudel, "History and the Social Sciences: The *Longue Durée,*" in idem, *On History,* trans. Sarah Matthews (Chicago: University of Chicago Press, 1980), pp. 25–54.

60. For example, ibid., pp. 48–49.

61. As he acknowledged in *The Archaeology of Knowledge,* pp. 3–4.

62. Linda Nicholson, *Gender and History: The Limits of Social Theory in the Age of the Family* (New York: Columbia University Press, 1986), presents a self-acknowledged feminist (but normal) history of changing political and economic theory about the public/private spheres in Western society since 1500. Denise Riley, *"Am I That Name?" Feminism and the Category of "Women" in History* (Minneapolis: University of Minnesota Press, 1988), also uses a traditional approach to the past in explicating her topic.

63. Julia Kristeva, "Women's Time," reprinted in *The Kristeva Reader,* ed. Toril Moi (New York: Columbia University Press, 1986), pp. 188–189; but see also the editor's introduction to the essay.

64. Ermarth, *Sequel to History,* esp. pt. 3.

65. Flynn, "Foucault and the Career of the Historical Event," discusses the several kinds of events employed by Foucault, including what he terms the "series event."

66. Thomas L. Slaughter, "The Historian's Quest for Early American Culture(s), c. 1750–1825," *American Studies International,* 24 (April 1986), 29–59, analyzes nineteen books according to whether they assume static or dynamic, homogeneous or heterogeneous models of American society during the half-century of the Revolutionary and early national periods and what political implications such choices held for how the texts presented matters.

67. Emile Benveniste, *Problems in General Linguistics,* trans. Mary Elizabeth Meek (Coral Gables, Fla.: University of Miami Press, 1971), chap. 19, discusses verbal tense and historical narration.

68. In addition to Foucault's own writings on this matter, Hubert L. Dreyfus and Paul Rabinow, *Michel Foucault: Beyond Structuralism and Hermeneutics* (Chicago: University of Chicago Press, 1982), cover Foucault's treatment of subject and object practices throughout their book, but particularly in chaps. 7–8; but see again Flynn, "Foucault and the Career of the Historical Event."

69. Should one read in this light the efforts of Marshall Sahlins in *Historical Metaphors and Mythical Realities: Structure in the Early History of the Sandwich Islands Kingdom* (Ann Arbor: University of Michigan Press, 1981) and *Islands of History* (Chicago: University of Chicago Press, 1985) to reconstruct event and structure in terms of each other?

70. Linda Hutcheon, "Metafictional implications for Novelistic Reference," in *On Referring in Literature,* ed. Anna Whiteside and Michael Issacharoff (Bloomington: Indiana University Press, 1987), p. 2.

71. For examples of combining oral and documentary history, folk and professional, personal and other histories in different ways, see Timothy H. Breen, *Imagining the Past: East Hampton Histories* (Reading, Mass.: Addison-Wesley, 1989); Ronald Fraser, *In Search of a Past: The Manor House, Amnersfield, 1933–1945* (London: Verso, 1984); Martin Duberman, *Black Mountain: An Exploration in Community* (New York: E. P. Dutton, 1972).

72. Particularly pertinent to this complex subject is Hutcheon, *A Poetics of Postmodernism*, esp. chap. 6, "The Postmodern Problematizing of History," which first appeared in *English Studies in Canada*, 14 (Dec. 1988), 365–399. Cohen, *Historical Culture*, maintains that traditional forms of narrativization necessarily limit or contain political diversity and conflict.

73. Greg Dening, *Mr. Bligh's Bad Language: Passion, Power and Theatre on the Bounty* (Cambridge: Cambridge University Press, 1992). Given the complexity of Dening's organization and representation, I can do no more than suggest what in my opinion he attempts.

74. Compare, however, Philippe Carrard's judgment on what the *Annalistes* have achieved in hybrid style, genres, and polyphony of voices; *Poetics of the New History: French Historical Discourse from Braudel to Chartier* (Baltimore: Johns Hopkins University Press, 1992), pp. 221–225.

75. Burke discusses some new ways of writing history in the introduction and chap. 11 of *New Perspectives on Historical Writing*. How far does the new cultural history expand the nature of historical representation as form, interesting as the results may be? See, for example, Lynn Hunt, ed., *The New Cultural History* (Berkeley: University of California Press, 1989), esp. the introduction; and Roger Chartier, *Cultural History: Between Practices and Representation*, trans. Lydia G. Cochrane (Cambridge: Polity Press, 1988).

76. Robert Rosenstone, "Experiments in Writing the Past: Is Anybody Interested?" *Perspectives*, 30 (Dec. 1992), 10, 12, 20. Compare the interesting commentary of Stephan Yeo on the innovations of oral history in "Whose Story?" Yeo mentions, among other innovators of form, Fraser on Amnersfield Manor House.

77. Robert Rosenstone, *Mirror in the Shrine: American Encounters with Meiji Japan* (Cambridge, Mass.: Harvard University Press, 1988).

78. After pointing out the dilemma, Stanley Fish argues that it is a false one in "Commentary: The Young and the Restless," in Veeser, *The New Historicism*, pp. 303–316. I am less sanguine than Fish, as this book indicates. Brook Thomas, *The New Historicism and Other Old-Fashioned Topics* (Princeton: Princeton University Press, 1991), questions its newness and its methodology, as does Carolyn Porter, "Are We Being Historical Yet?" in *The States of "Theory": History, Art, and Cultural Discourse*, ed. David Carroll (New York: Columbia University Press, 1990), chap. 1.

79. If we use the authors represented in Emiko Ohnuki-Tierney, ed., *Culture through Time: Anthropological Approaches* (Stanford: Stanford University Press, 1990), interesting as some of their efforts may be to reconcile synchronic symbolic anthropology with a diachronic historical analysis or combine the varying macro and micro structures of different societies in interaction.

80. Numerous examples include Richard Price, *Alabi's World*; Dening, *Mr. Bligh's Bad Language*; Stephen A. Tyler, *The Unspeakable: Discourse, Dialogue, and Rhetoric in the Postmodern World* (Madison: University of Wisconsin Press, 1987);

and James A. Boon, *Affinities and Extremes: Crisscrossing the Bittersweet Ethnology of East Indies History, Hindu-Balinese Culture, and Indo-European Allure* (Chicago: University of Chicago Press, 1990).

81. Will new reflexive and dialogic textualizations of history also eventuate in such typographic and other innovations as Tyler, *The Unspeakable;* the complicated textual organization of Malcolm Ashmore, *The Reflexive Thesis: Wrighting Sociology of Scientific Knowledge* (Chicago: University of Chicago Press, 1989); and Boon, *Affinities and Extremes,* as they attempt to reflect on their own reflexivity?

82. Simon Schama, *Citizens: A Chronicle of the French Revolution* (New York: Alfred A. Knopf, 1989).

83. Simon Schama, *Dead Certainties (Unwarranted Speculations)* (New York: Alfred A. Knopf, 1992).

84. Cushing Strout, "Border Crossings: History, Fiction, and *Dead Certainties,*" *History and Theory,* 31, no. 2 (1992), 156. This review is interesting not only for what its says about Schama's book but also for what it says about normal historical practice.

85. Perhaps few books offer a greater challenge to historical juxtaposition and the construction of context than music and popular culture critic Greil Marcus' *Lipstick Traces: A Secret History of the Twentieth Century* (Cambridge, Mass.: Harvard University Press, 1989), which connects surrealism, the Paris Commune, and even radical Anabaptists of the 1530s to punk rock and post–Second World War counter-cultural tradition. His fragmented text, with its many juxtaposed quotations, descriptions of persons and events, and personal reminiscences, enhances the message through the use of the medium.

86. Dominick LaCapra, *History and Criticism* (Ithaca: Cornell University Press, 1985), offers one example of a newer approach to criticism within the profession, as does Carrard, *Poetics of the New History,* from without. Compare the provocative readings of Cohen, *Historical Culture,* as a model for criticism in as well as of the profession.

87. The word "new" is always difficult for historians to use, and never more so than when it is applied to historical discourses themselves. Too many previous calls for such a new history have been issued, each claiming to transform discourse and professional practice. The lesson of such a history is that new histories quickly become old, assimilated, superseded, or more manifesto than contribution. On new history as trope in historical discourse see, for example, Ernst Breisach, "Two New Histories: An Exploratory Comparison," in Dauenhauer, *At the Nexus of Philosophy and History,* pp. 138–156, which compares the New History of James Harvey Robinson and the *Annales* school.

Acknowledgments

As the abundance of notes makes clear, I owe a great deal to many scholars. Indeed, I perhaps owe the most to those who shaped my ideas so early that they are not even cited here.

In some ways the starting point for this book was the conclusion of *A Behavioral Approach to Historical Analysis* (New York: Free Press, 1969), which ended with a query about how best to present history in light of modernist fictional techniques. While I pondered the implications of new forms of historical (re)presentation, the English translations of Michel Foucault's *The Order of Things* and *The Archaeology of Knowledge* appeared and, not long afterward, Hayden White's *Metahistory*. Both authors stimulated structuralist and formalist thinking about both the writing and the reading of history. My own initial thinking about those issues culminated in a long paper, "The Irony of Metahistory," which was presented in the 1970s to sessions at the Organization of American Historians, conferences at the Hobart and William Smith Colleges and the University of Wyoming, and a colloquium of the Harvard American Civilization program. The comments of Thomas Haskell and Mary Young were particularly helpful at this stage.

Other projects intervened, and when I returned to the earlier one, in 1980, poststructuralist theory had reached America. Richard Vann and Dominick LaCapra kindly commented on a revised outline of the book. David Hollinger, then my colleague in the Department of History at the University of Michigan, encouraged me to summarize my thinking in another long article, versions of which were read at a conference on comparative history at Northwestern University, the new humanities centers at the Universities of Maryland and Utah, and a department of history colloquium at the University of California at Los Angeles, where Eric Monkkonon and Joyce Appleby acted as gracious hosts and discerning critics. Allan Megill was especially generous in his detailed analysis of the paper, which became the basis of "The Challenge of Poetics to (Normal) Historical Practice," published in *Poetics Today*, 9, no. 2 (1988), 435–452, and subsequently reprinted in Paul Hernadi, ed., *The Rhetoric of Interpretation and the Interpretation of Rhetoric* (Durham, N.C.: Duke University Press, 1989), pp. 183–200. I am grateful to Paul Hernadi for the invitation to participate in the lecture series sponsored by the Humanities Center at the University of California at Santa Barbara, which led to the special issue of *Poetics Today* and to the book, and for his many helpful comments on the article at each stage. I thank the Porter Institute for Poetics and Semiotics of Tel Aviv University and Duke University Press for permission to include various parts of that article in sections of Chapters 2 and 3 of this book.

The first draft of much of this volume was written during the academic year 1987–88 while I was a Martha Sutton Weeks Fellow at the Stanford University Humanities Center; there both Director W. Bliss Carnochan and Associate Director Morton Sosna were friends and valuable readers. Part of that draft was published as "A New Context for American Studies" in *American Quarterly*, 41 (Dec. 1989), 588–613; I thank *American Quarterly* and its editor, Gary Kulik, for permission to reprint revised portions in several sections of Chapters 1 and 8 of this text. My contribution to the summer institute on Narrative and the Human Sciences, sponsored by the Project on the Rhetoric of Inquiry at the University of Iowa, is now revised in part of Chapter 4. I thank the participants and particularly Linda Kerber and Bruce Gronbeck for their hospitality and insights. A similar paper was presented at the History of Social Sciences Workshop at the University of Chicago, where George W. Stocking was helpful.

Subsequent revision as a result of further reading in feminist and postmodernist theory enlarged both the text and the vision of the book to its present form. That undertaking was made possible by salaried leaves from the University of Michigan at Ann Arbor and the University of California at Santa Cruz, particularly with the help of Deans Peter Steiner and Gary Lease. As I completed the first revision, cultural studies, New Historicism, and feminist and postmodernist theory all challenged one another, more often as soliloquy than as dialogue. Part of my response to this challenge was an essay titled "A Point of View on Viewpoint in Historical Practice," first presented to the Cultural Studies colloquium at the University of California at Santa Cruz and soon to be published in *A New Philosophy of History*, edited by Frank R. Ankersmit and Hans Kellner. I thank both the editors for their comments and Reaktion Books for permission to republish these words as some sections of Chapter 7. Finally, I am grateful for permission from W. W. Norton to quote at length from *The Legacy of Conquest: The Unbroken Past of the American West*, copyright © 1987 by Patricia Nelson Limerick.

Several individuals tried to overcome my particular political and philosophical prejudices. Joan Scott and Martin Burke read the whole manuscript from quite different political and philosophical perspectives to my enormous benefit, although I continue to steer a different course than either would wish. Jonathan Beecher, Genevieve Berkhofer, Aida Donald, Michael Geyer, Gail Hershatter, and Hayden White made the book more complete and better argued by their own queries and arguments. The differences among their reactions to the manuscript provided me with firsthand applications of reader-response theory. Members of a graduate seminar on historical methodology at the University of California at Santa Cruz gave an early draft of the manuscript a "test run" to my enormous benefit. My editor, Ann Hawthorne, helped all subsequent readers by compelling me to say just what I meant as precisely as possible. Because of the differences among my friendly critics, I alone am ultimately responsible for what is argued in these pages.

Index